VIZ GRAPHIC NOVEL
◆◆◆◆◆◆◆◆◆◆◆◆◆◆◆

NO NEED FOR TENCHI!™
SWORD PLAY

STORY AND ART BY
HITOSHI OKUDA

CONTENTS

This volume contains NO NEED FOR TENCHI! PART TWO #1 through #7 in their entirety.

**STORY AND ART BY
HITOSHI OKUDA**

**ENGLISH ADAPTATION BY
FRED BURKE**

Translation/Shuko Shikata
Touch-Up Art & Lettering/Wayne Truman
Cover Design/Hidemi Sahara
Editor/Annette Roman

Managing Editor/Hyoe Narita
Editor-in-Chief/Satoru Fujii
Publisher/Seiji Horibuchi

Printed in Canada

Published by Viz Communications, Inc.
P.O. Box 77010 • San Francisco, CA 94107

10 9 8 7 6 5 4 3 2 1
First printing, December 1997

Vizit us at our World Wide Web site at www.viz.com and our Internet magazine, j-pop.com, at www.j-pop.com!

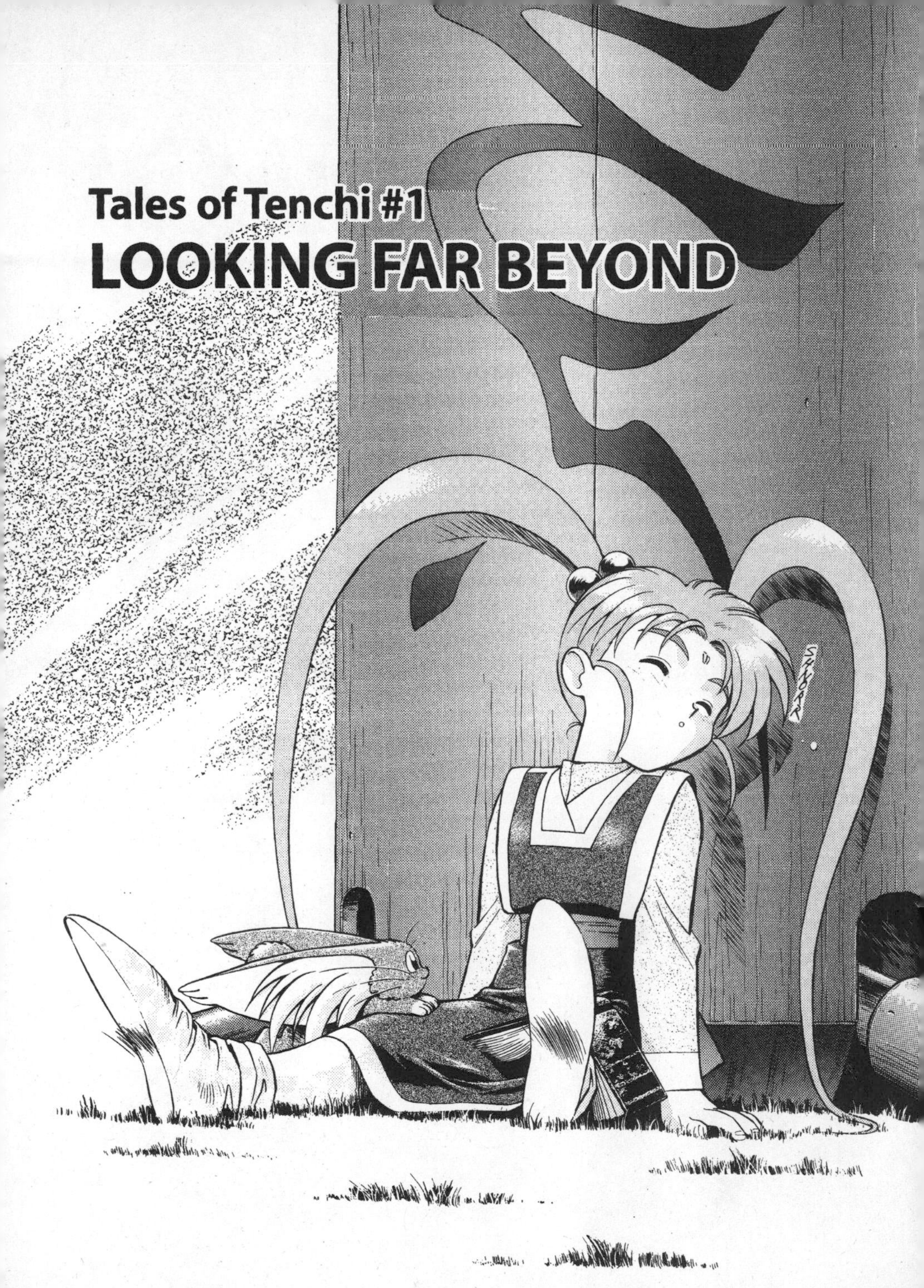
Tales of Tenchi #1
LOOKING FAR BEYOND
SHNORR

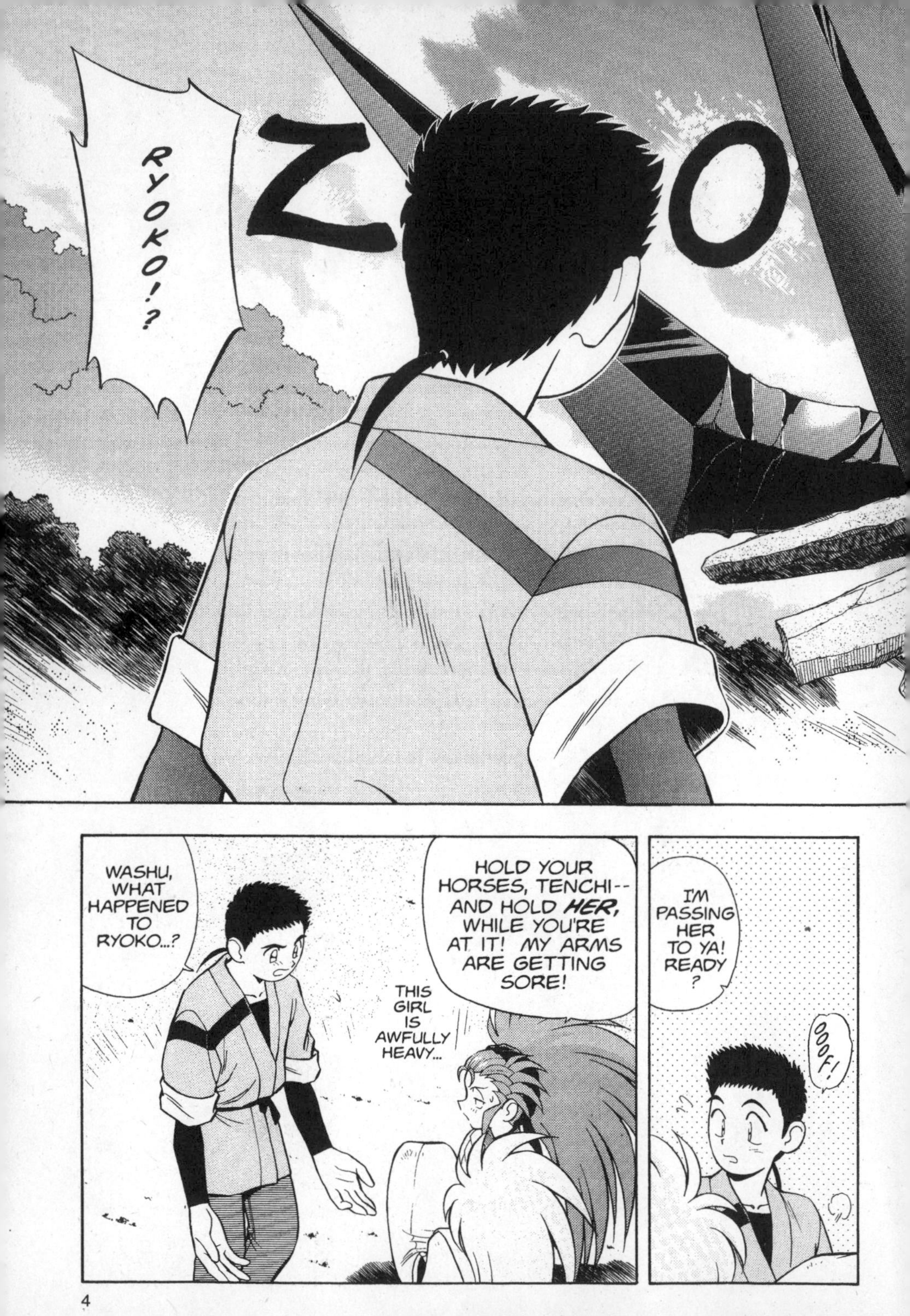
RYOKO!?
ZO
WASHU, WHAT HAPPENED TO RYOKO...?
HOLD YOUR HORSES, TENCHI-- AND HOLD *HER,* WHILE YOU'RE AT IT! MY ARMS ARE GETTING SORE!
THIS GIRL IS AWFULLY HEAVY...
I'M PASSING HER TO YA! READY?
OOOF!

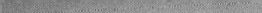

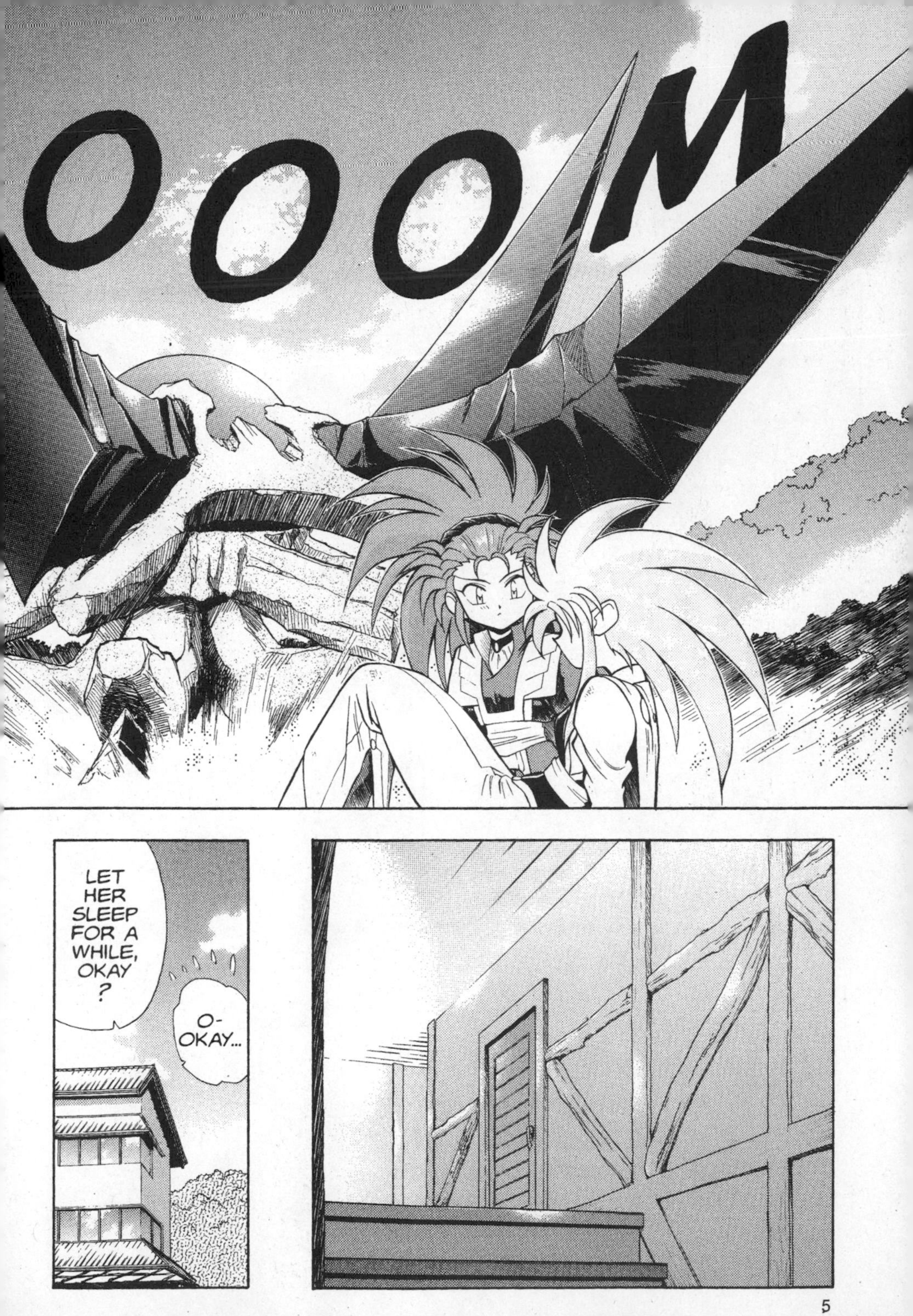
OOOM
LET HER SLEEP FOR A WHILE, OKAY?
O-OKAY...

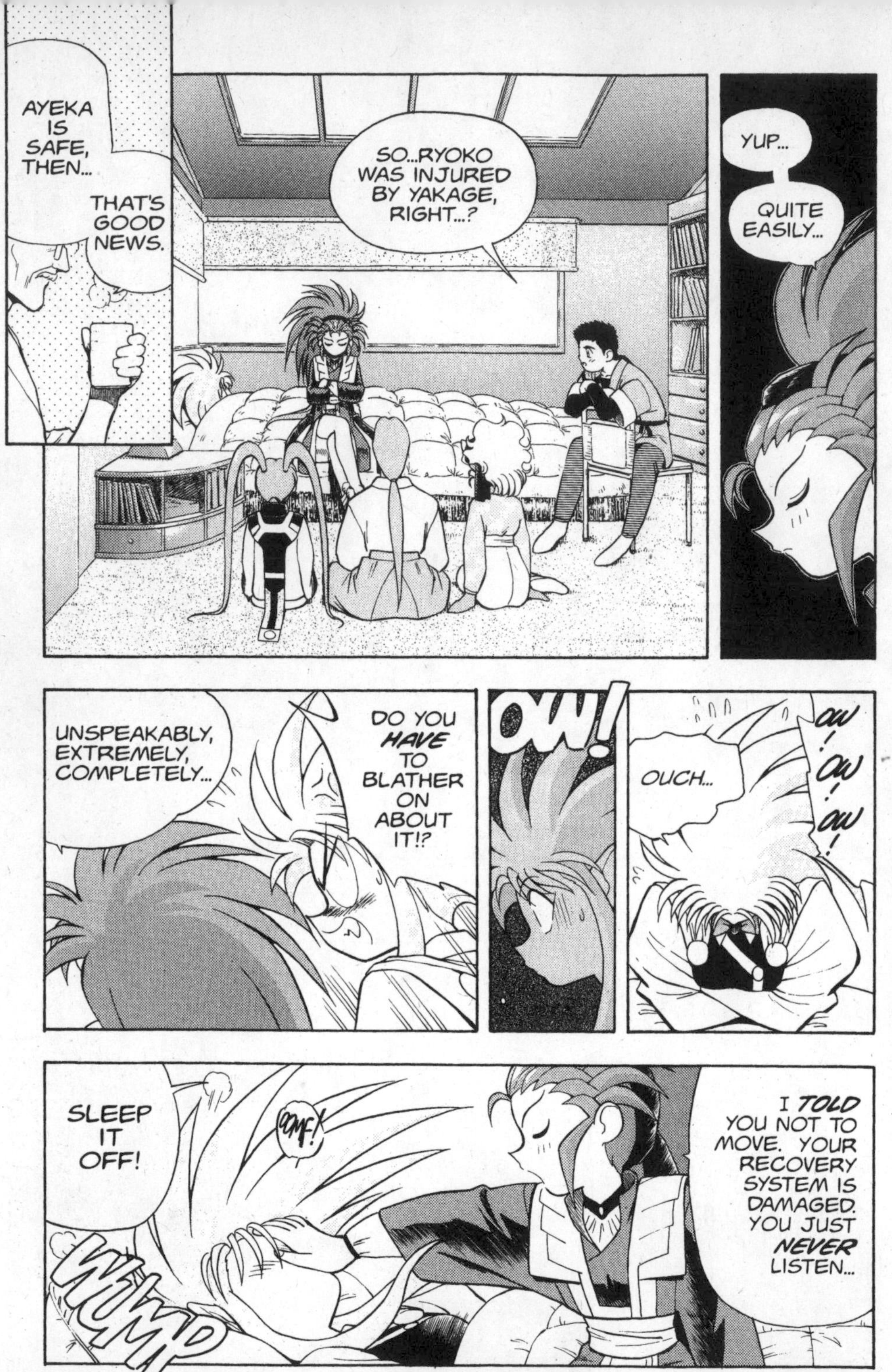
AYEKA IS SAFE, THEN...
THAT'S GOOD NEWS.
SO...RYOKO WAS INJURED BY YAKAGE, RIGHT...?
YUP...
QUITE EASILY...
UNSPEAKABLY, EXTREMELY, COMPLETELY...
DO YOU HAVE TO BLATHER ON ABOUT IT!?
OW!
OUCH...
OW! OW! OW!
SLEEP IT OFF!
OOMF!
WUMP
I TOLD YOU NOT TO MOVE. YOUR RECOVERY SYSTEM IS DAMAGED. YOU JUST NEVER LISTEN...

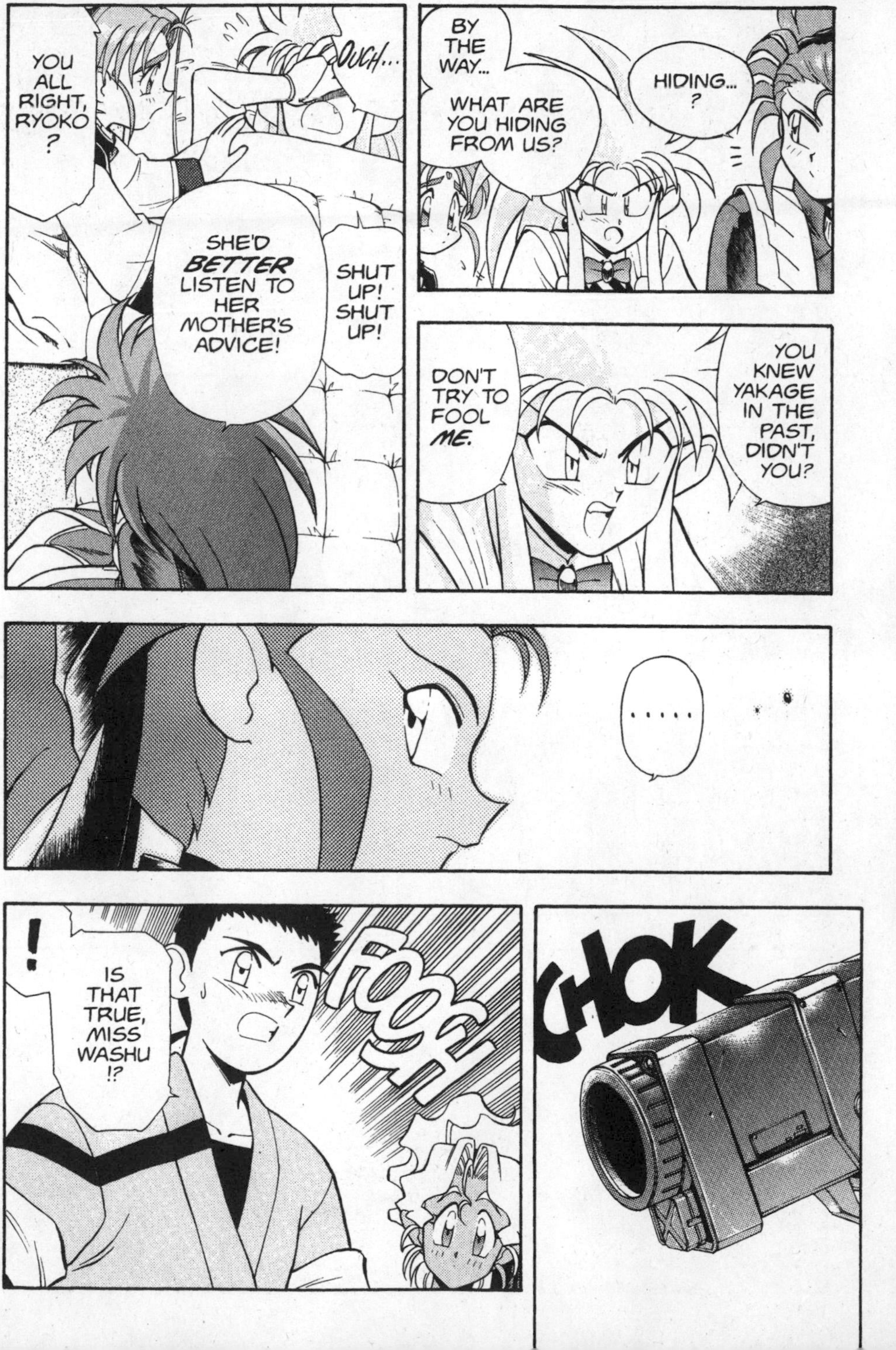
YOU ALL RIGHT, RYOKO?
OUCH...
SHE'D **BETTER** LISTEN TO HER MOTHER'S ADVICE!
SHUT UP! SHUT UP!
BY THE WAY...
WHAT ARE YOU HIDING FROM US?
HIDING...?
DON'T TRY TO FOOL **ME.**
YOU KNEW YAKAGE IN THE PAST, DIDN'T YOU?
.....
!
IS THAT TRUE, MISS WASHU!?
FOOSH
CHOK

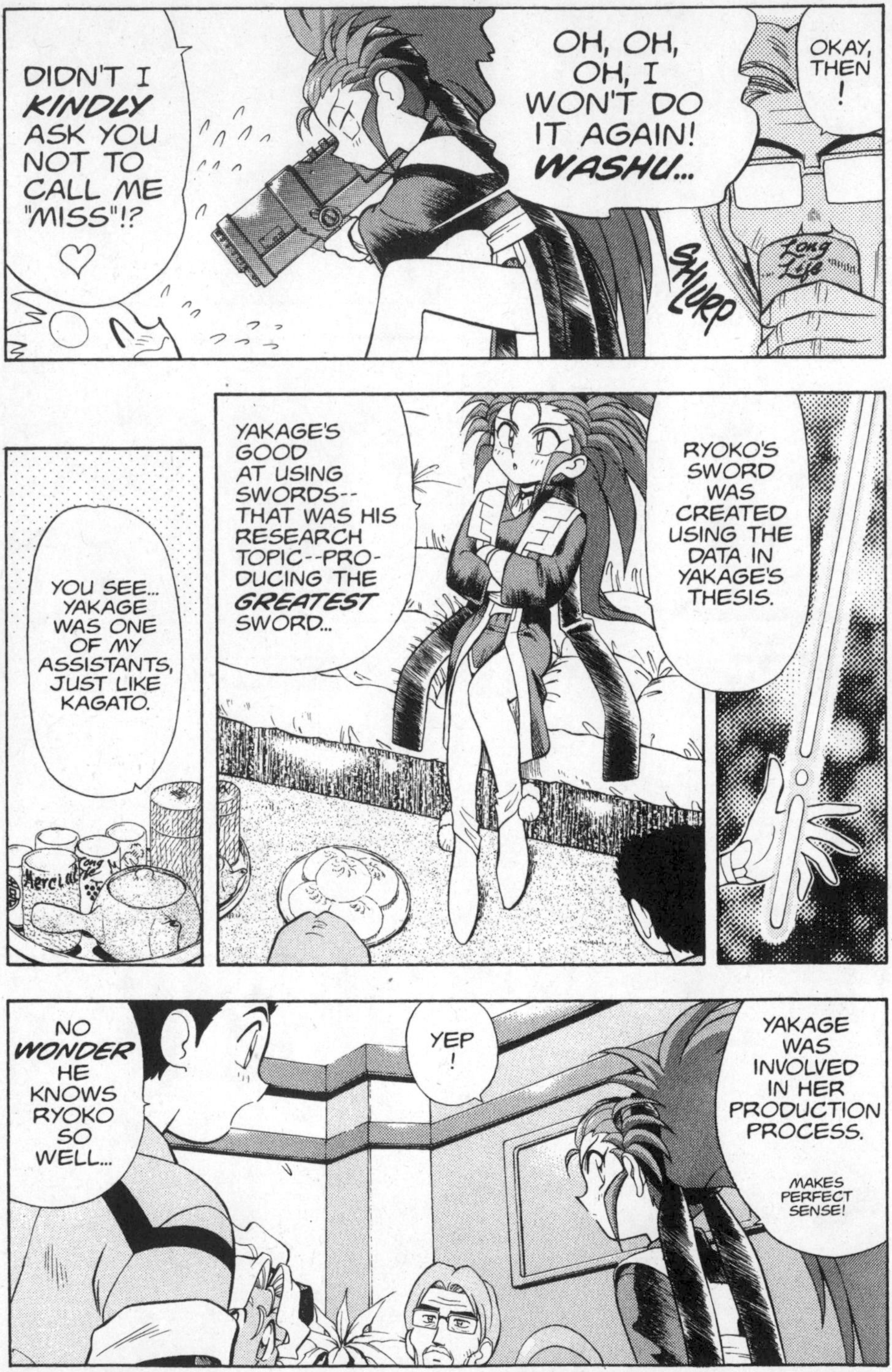
DIDN'T I KINDLY ASK YOU NOT TO CALL ME "MISS"!? ♡
OH, OH, OH, I WON'T DO IT AGAIN! WASHU...
OKAY, THEN!
Long Life
SHLURP
YOU SEE... YAKAGE WAS ONE OF MY ASSISTANTS, JUST LIKE KAGATO.
YAKAGE'S GOOD AT USING SWORDS--THAT WAS HIS RESEARCH TOPIC--PRODUCING THE GREATEST SWORD...
RYOKO'S SWORD WAS CREATED USING THE DATA IN YAKAGE'S THESIS.
NO WONDER HE KNOWS RYOKO SO WELL...
YEP!
YAKAGE WAS INVOLVED IN HER PRODUCTION PROCESS.
MAKES PERFECT SENSE!

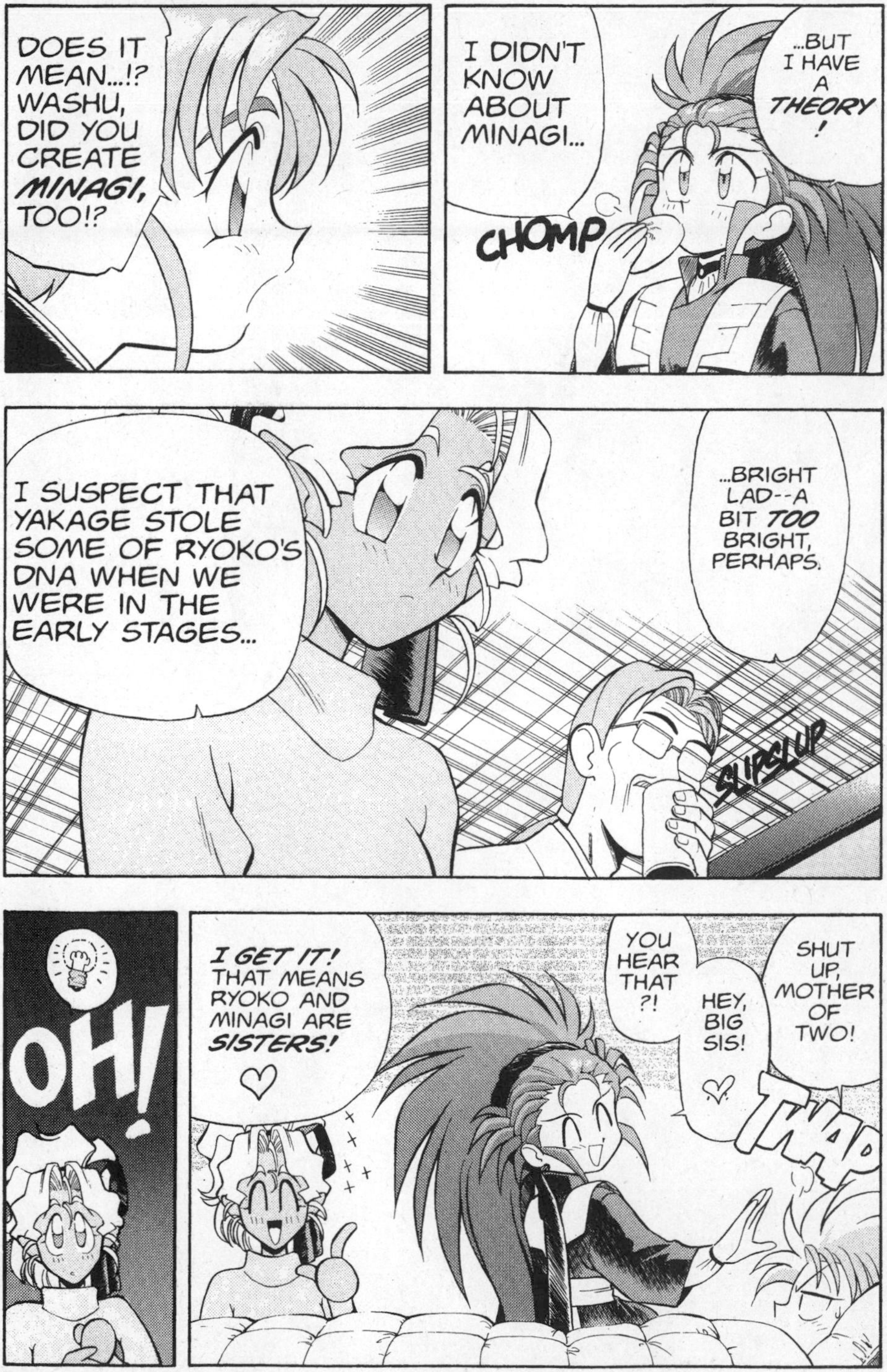
DOES IT MEAN...!? WASHU, DID YOU CREATE MINAGI, TOO!?
I DIDN'T KNOW ABOUT MINAGI...
...BUT I HAVE A THEORY!
CHOMP
I SUSPECT THAT YAKAGE STOLE SOME OF RYOKO'S DNA WHEN WE WERE IN THE EARLY STAGES...
...BRIGHT LAD--A BIT TOO BRIGHT, PERHAPS.
SLIPSLUP
OH!
I GET IT! THAT MEANS RYOKO AND MINAGI ARE SISTERS!
YOU HEAR THAT ?!
HEY, BIG SIS!
SHUT UP, MOTHER OF TWO!
THWAP

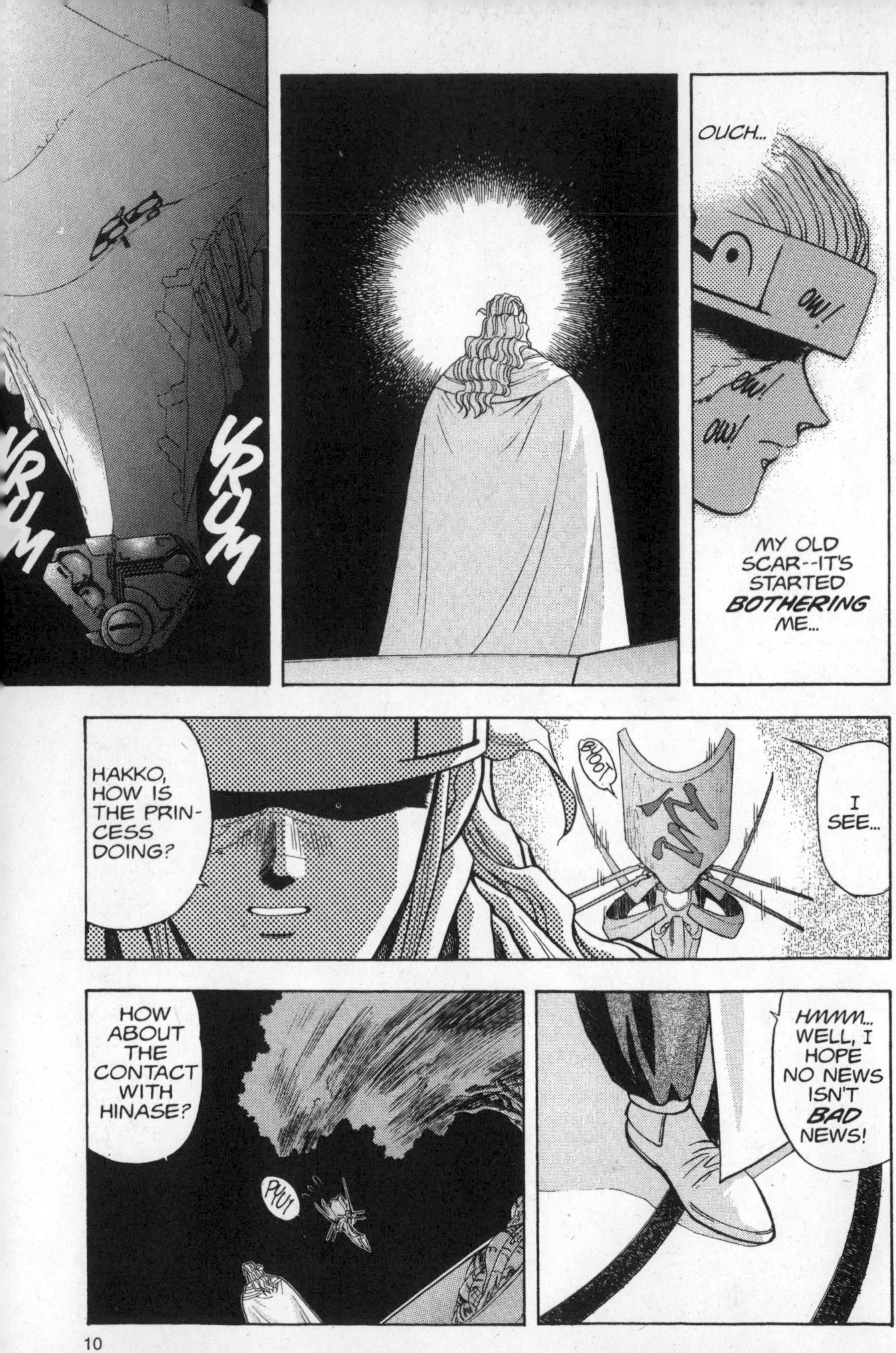
VRUM
VRUM
OUCH...
OW!
OW!
OW!
MY OLD SCAR--IT'S STARTED *BOTHERING* ME...
HAKKO, HOW IS THE PRIN-CESS DOING?
BHOOT
I SEE...
HOW ABOUT THE CONTACT WITH HINASE?
PYU!
HMMM... WELL, I HOPE NO NEWS ISN'T *BAD* NEWS!

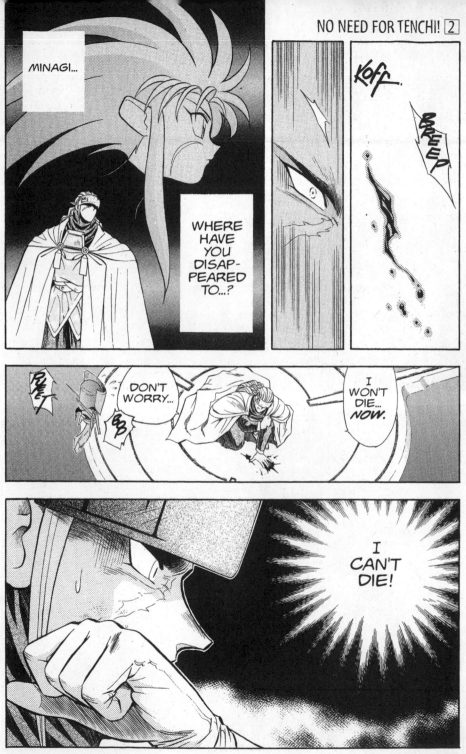

MINAGI...

WHERE HAVE YOU DISAP- PEARED TO...?

KOFF.

BREEP

DON'T WORRY...

I WON'T DIE... *NOW.*

I CAN'T DIE!

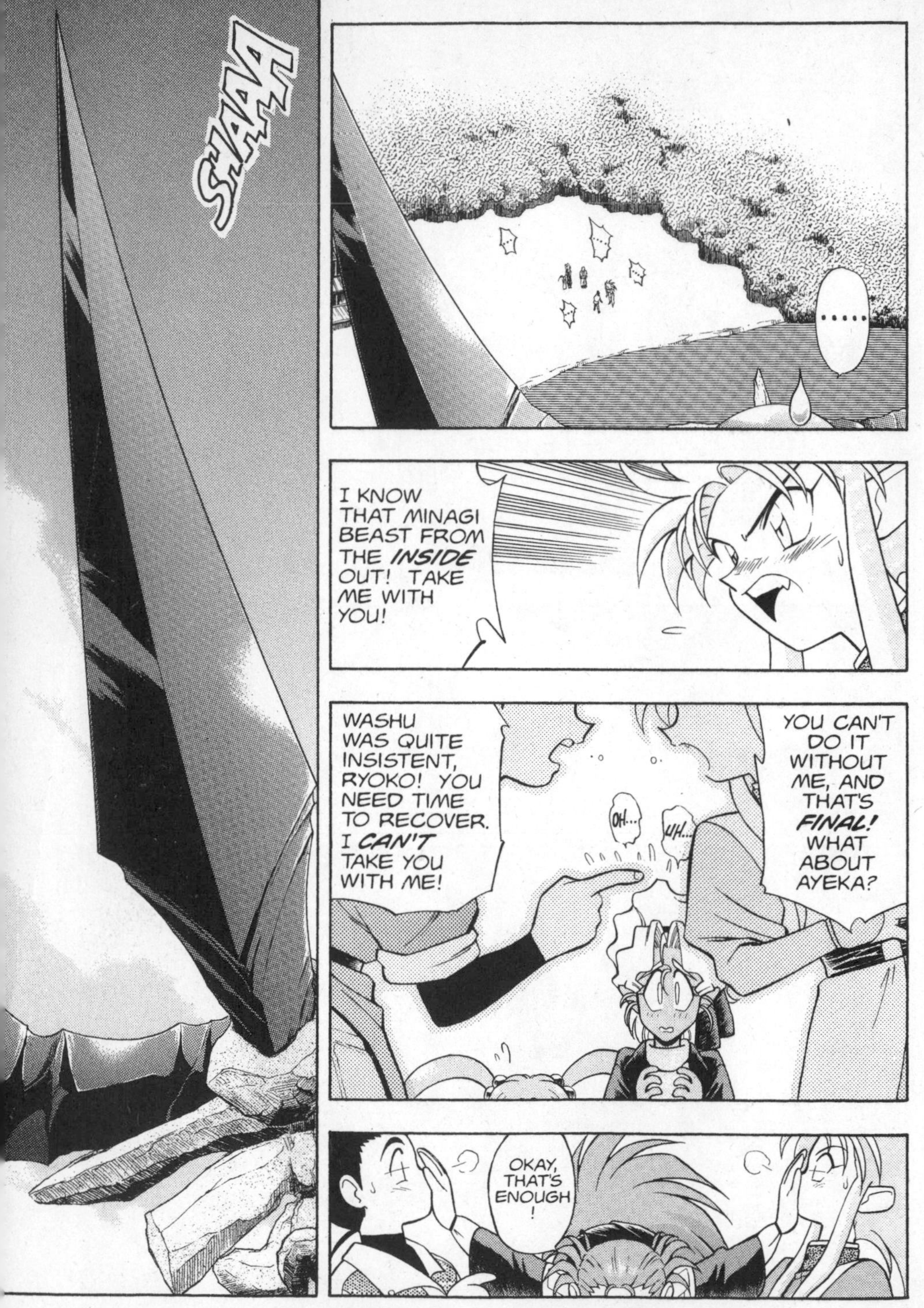
SHAAA
......
I KNOW THAT MINAGI BEAST FROM THE *INSIDE* OUT! TAKE ME WITH YOU!
WASHU WAS QUITE INSISTENT, RYOKO! YOU NEED TIME TO RECOVER. I *CAN'T* TAKE YOU WITH ME!
OH...
UH...
YOU CAN'T DO IT WITHOUT ME, AND THAT'S *FINAL!* WHAT ABOUT AYEKA?
OKAY, THAT'S ENOUGH!

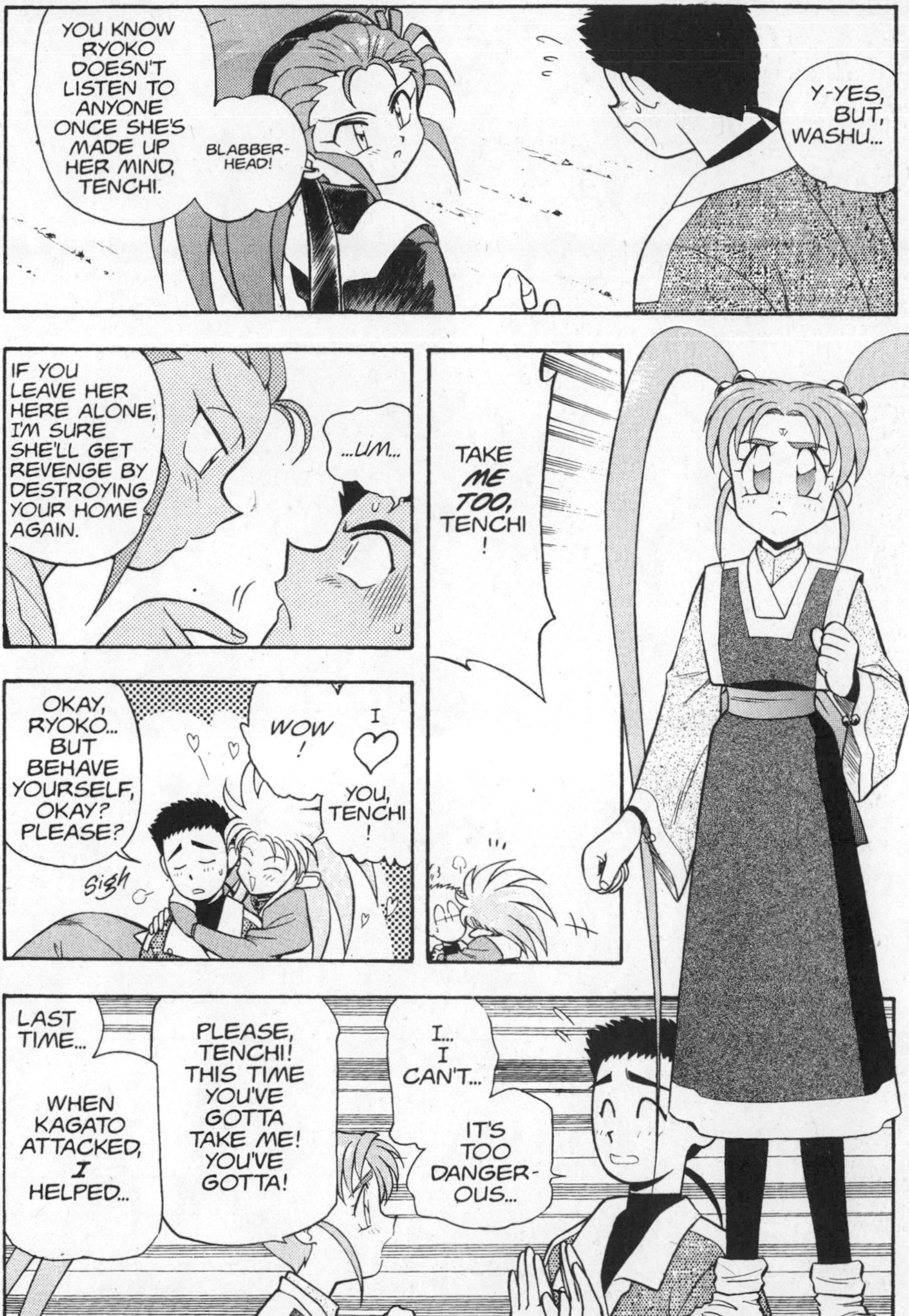
YOU KNOW RYOKO DOESN'T LISTEN TO ANYONE ONCE SHE'S MADE UP HER MIND, TENCHI.
BLABBER-HEAD!
Y-YES, BUT, WASHU...
IF YOU LEAVE HER HERE ALONE, I'M SURE SHE'LL GET REVENGE BY DESTROYING YOUR HOME AGAIN.
...UM...
OKAY, RYOKO... BUT BEHAVE YOURSELF, OKAY? PLEASE?
WOW!
I ♥ YOU, TENCHI!
Sigh
TAKE *ME TOO*, TENCHI!
LAST TIME...
WHEN KAGATO ATTACKED, *I* HELPED...
PLEASE, TENCHI! THIS TIME YOU'VE GOTTA TAKE ME! YOU'VE GOTTA!
I... I CAN'T...
IT'S TOO DANGER-OUS...

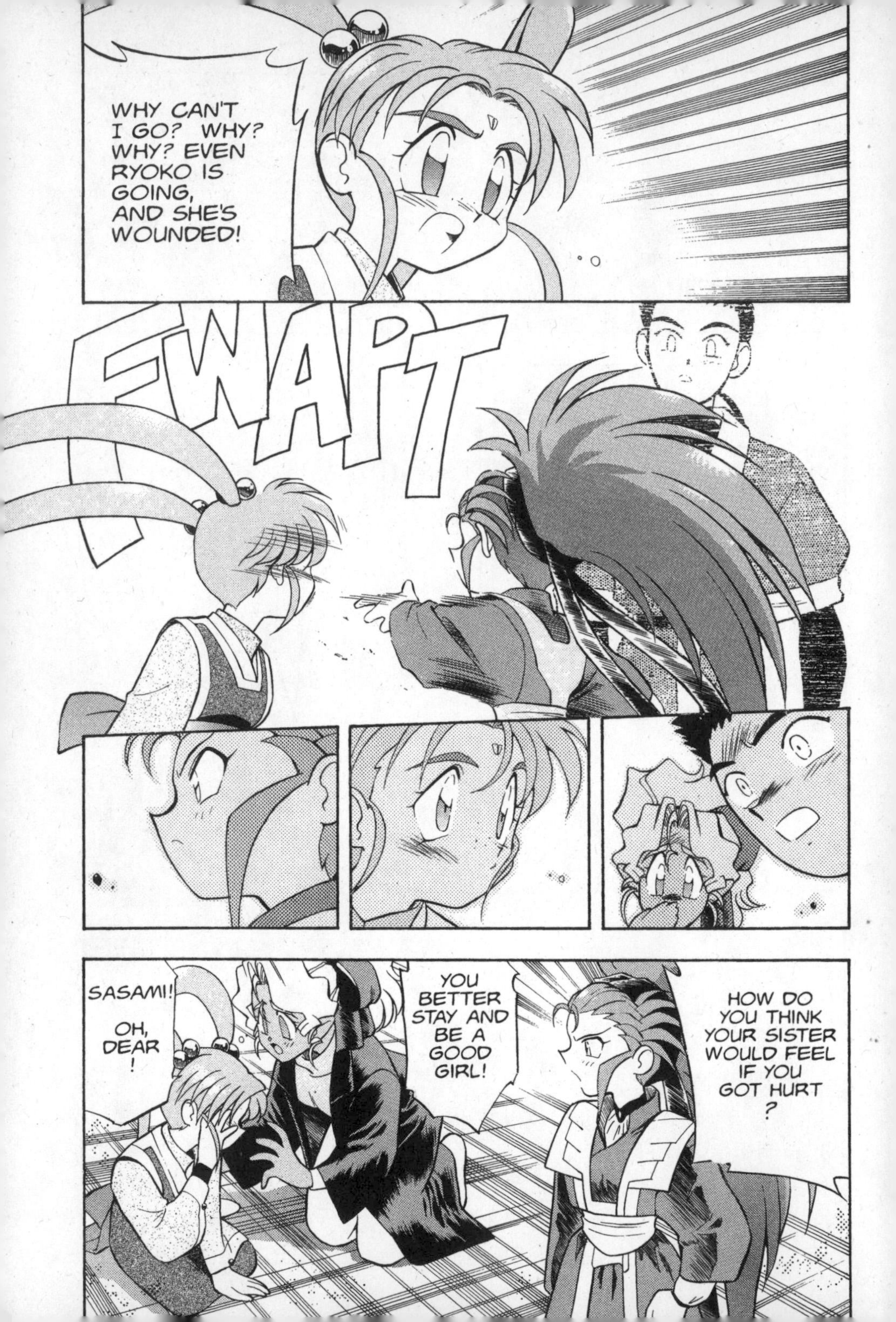
WHY CAN'T I GO? WHY? WHY? EVEN RYOKO IS GOING, AND SHE'S WOUNDED!
FWAPT
SASAMI!
OH, DEAR!
YOU BETTER STAY AND BE A GOOD GIRL!
HOW DO YOU THINK YOUR SISTER WOULD FEEL IF YOU GOT HURT?

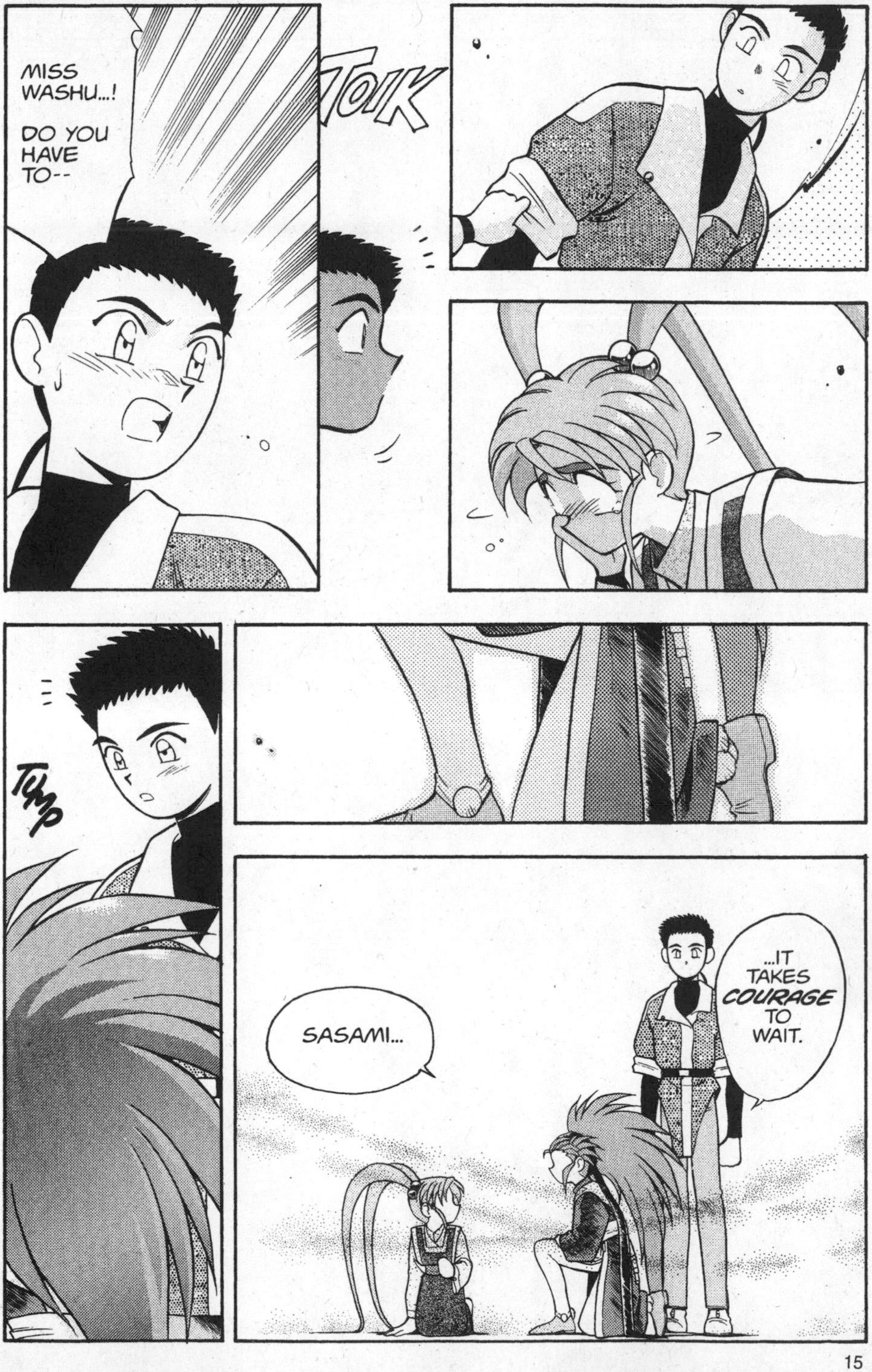
MISS WASHU...!
DO YOU HAVE TO--
TOIK
TUMP
SASAMI...
...IT TAKES COURAGE TO WAIT.

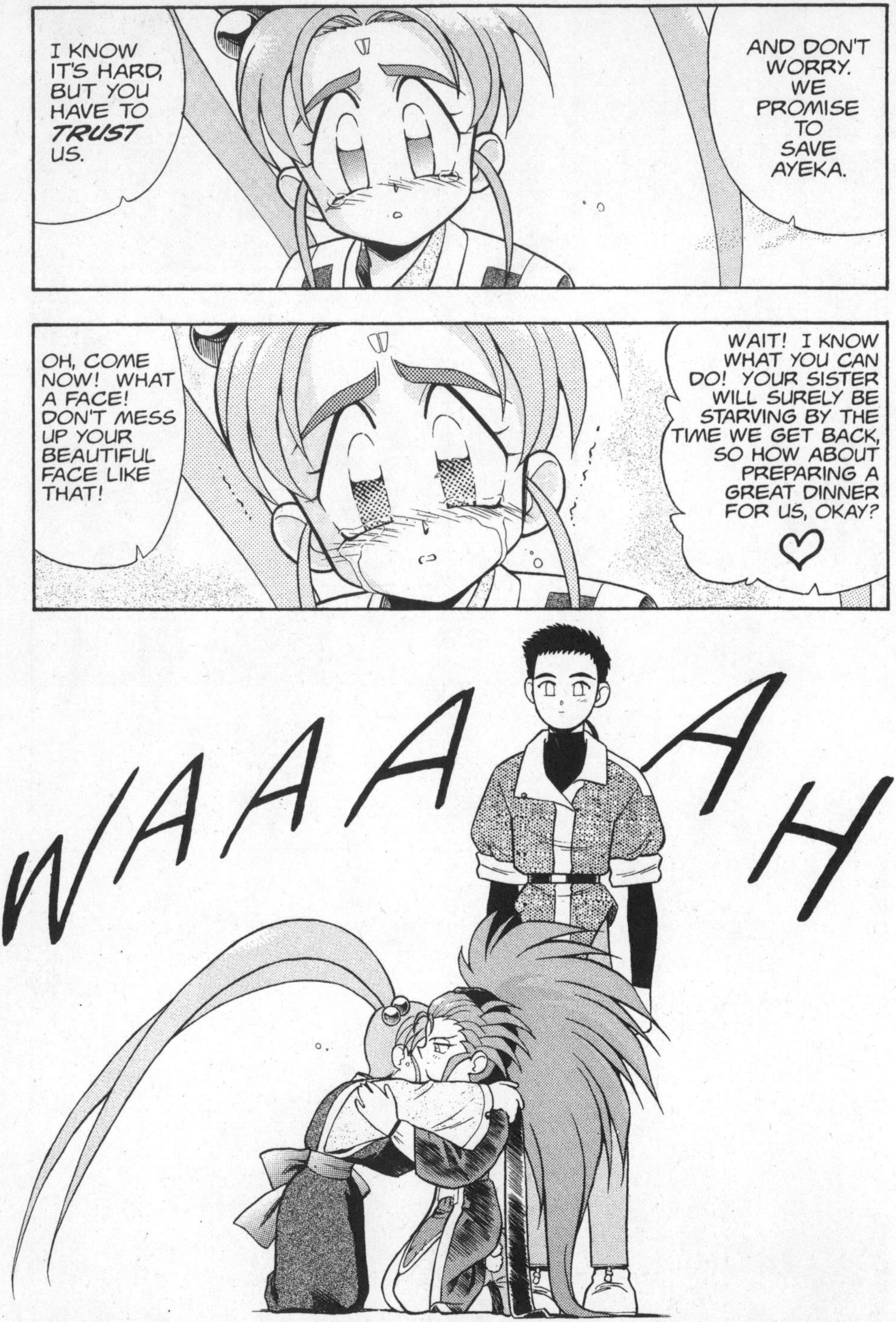
I KNOW IT'S HARD, BUT YOU HAVE TO TRUST US.
AND DON'T WORRY. WE PROMISE TO SAVE AYEKA.
OH, COME NOW! WHAT A FACE! DON'T MESS UP YOUR BEAUTIFUL FACE LIKE THAT!
WAIT! I KNOW WHAT YOU CAN DO! YOUR SISTER WILL SURELY BE STARVING BY THE TIME WE GET BACK, SO HOW ABOUT PREPARING A GREAT DINNER FOR US, OKAY? ♡
WAAAAH

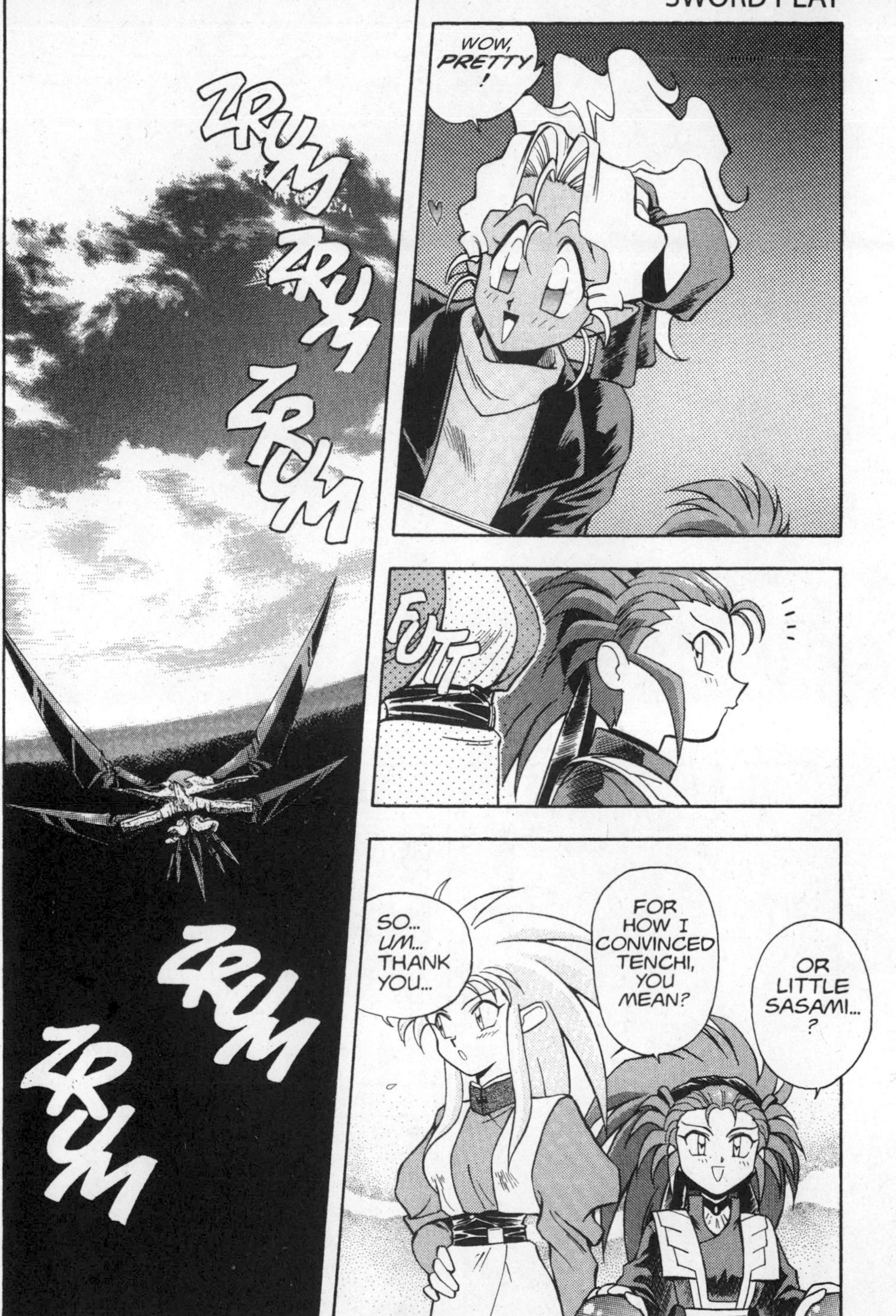
ZRUM
ZRUM
ZRUM
ZRUM
ZRUM
ZRUM
WOW, PRETTY!
FUTT
SO... UM... THANK YOU...
FOR HOW I CONVINCED TENCHI, YOU MEAN?
OR LITTLE SASAMI...?

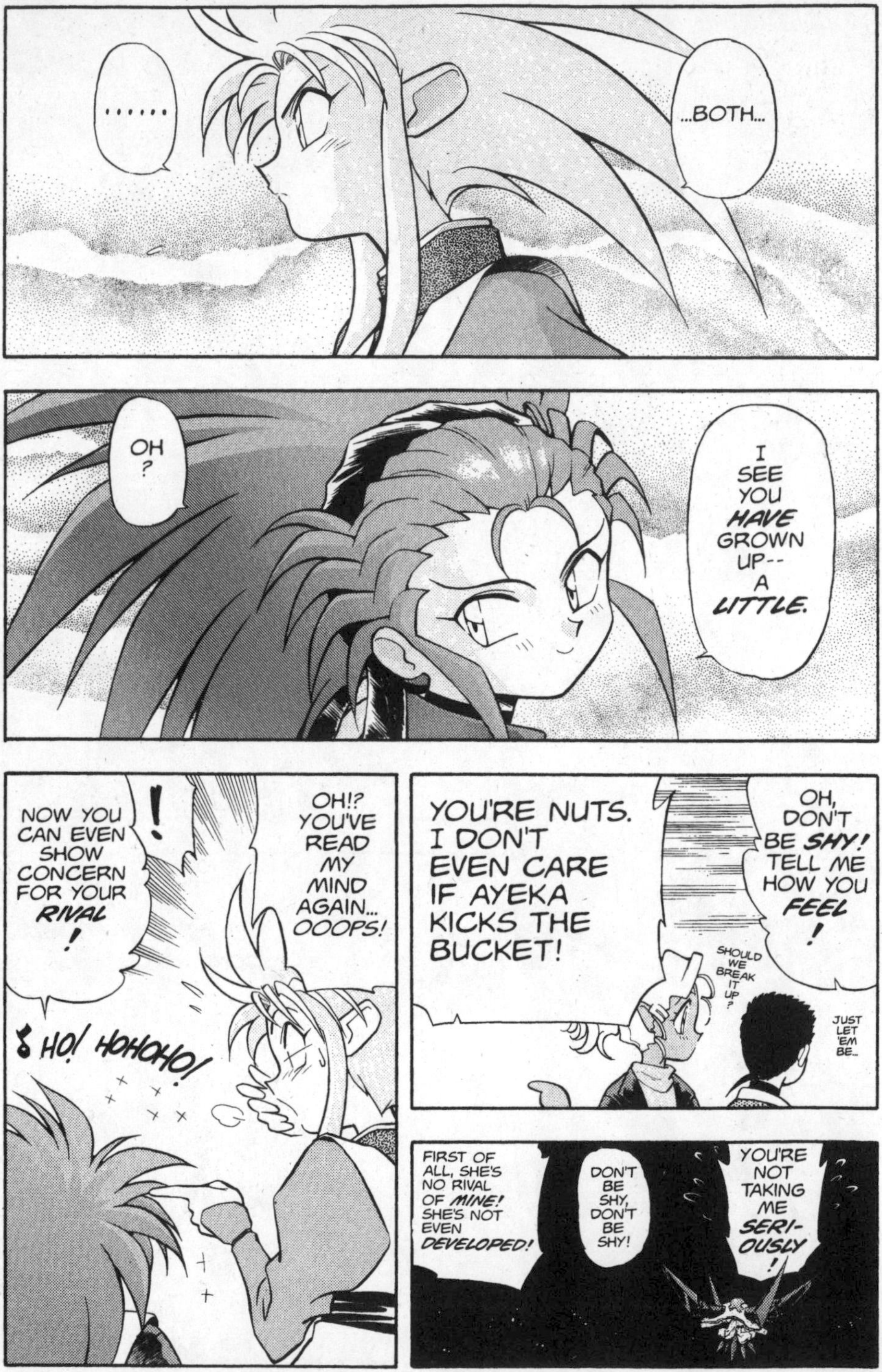
......
...BOTH...
OH?
I SEE YOU HAVE GROWN UP-- A LITTLE.
NOW YOU CAN EVEN SHOW CONCERN FOR YOUR RIVAL!
!
OH!? YOU'VE READ MY MIND AGAIN... OOOPS!
HO! HOHOHO!
YOU'RE NUTS. I DON'T EVEN CARE IF AYEKA KICKS THE BUCKET!
OH, DON'T BE SHY! TELL ME HOW YOU FEEL!
SHOULD WE BREAK IT UP?
JUST LET 'EM BE...
FIRST OF ALL, SHE'S NO RIVAL OF MINE! SHE'S NOT EVEN DEVELOPED!
DON'T BE SHY, DON'T BE SHY!
YOU'RE NOT TAKING ME SERIOUSLY!

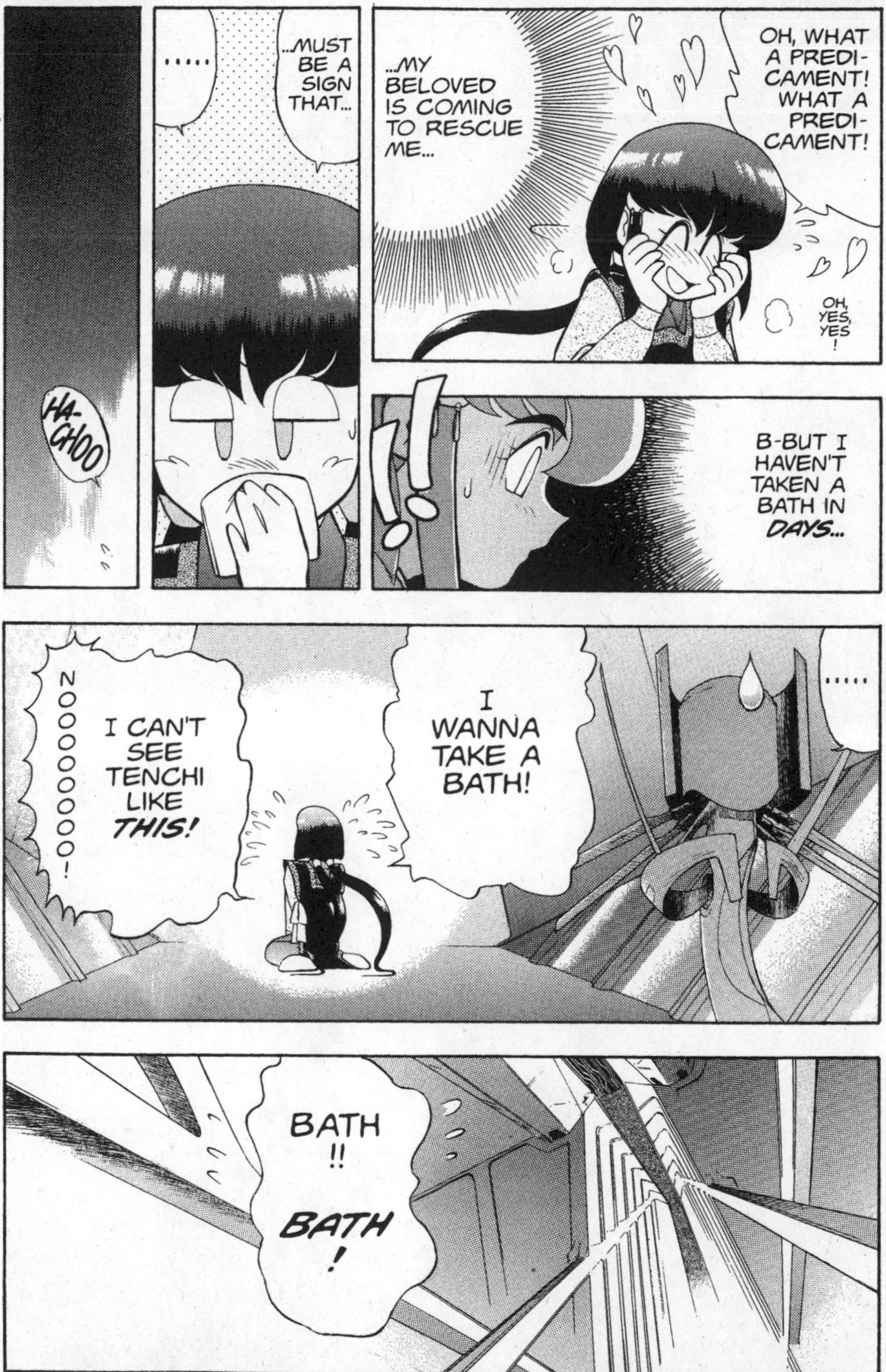
HA-CHOO
.....
...MUST BE A SIGN THAT...
...MY BELOVED IS COMING TO RESCUE ME...
OH, WHAT A PREDI-CAMENT! WHAT A PREDI-CAMENT!
OH, YES, YES!
B-BUT I HAVEN'T TAKEN A BATH IN *DAYS...*
NOOOOOOOOOO!
I CAN'T SEE TENCHI LIKE *THIS!*
I WANNA TAKE A BATH!
.....
BATH!!
BATH!

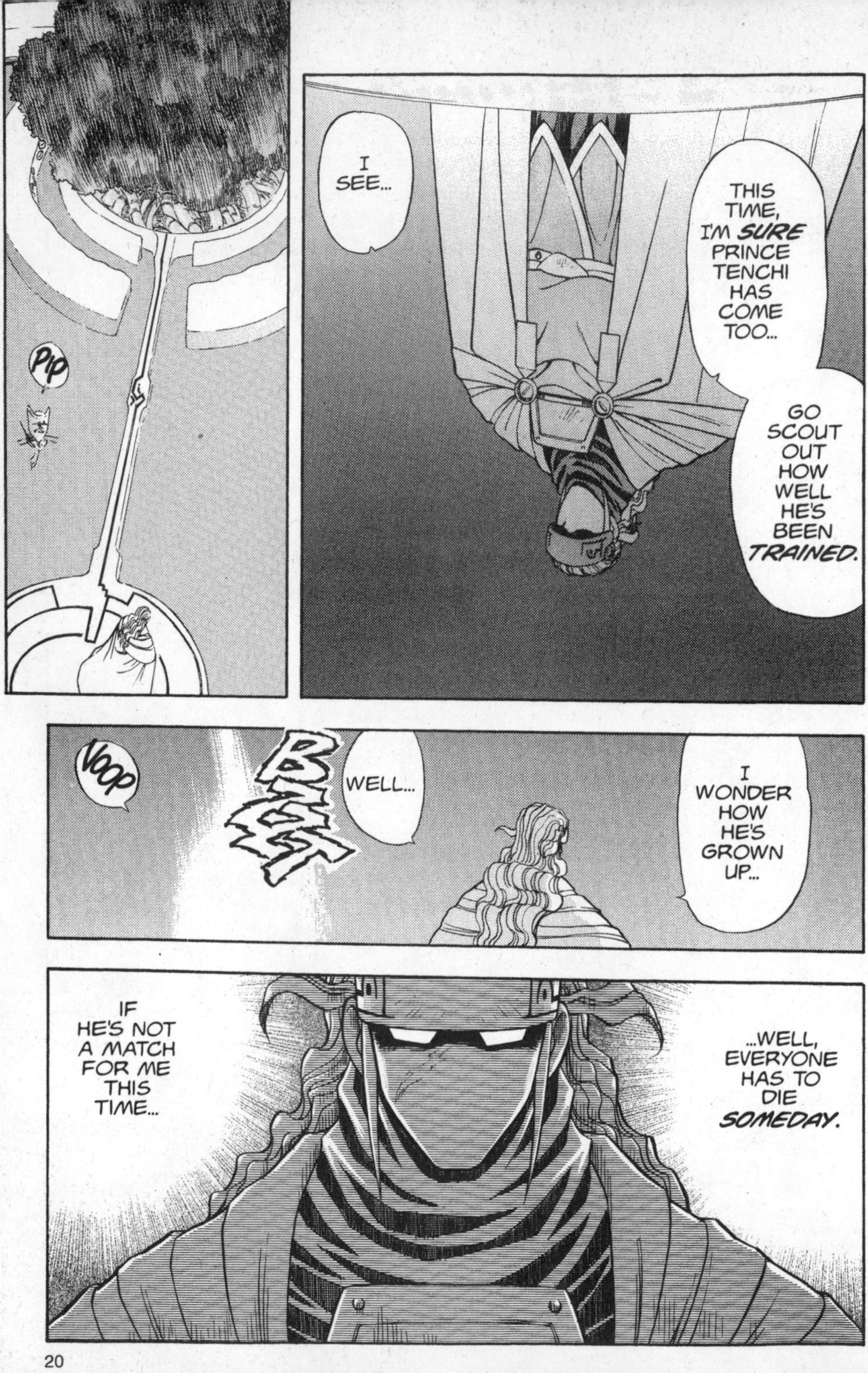
PIP
I SEE...
THIS TIME, I'M SURE PRINCE TENCHI HAS COME TOO...
GO SCOUT OUT HOW WELL HE'S BEEN TRAINED.
VOOP
BAMF
WELL...
I WONDER HOW HE'S GROWN UP...
IF HE'S NOT A MATCH FOR ME THIS TIME...
...WELL, EVERYONE HAS TO DIE SOMEDAY.

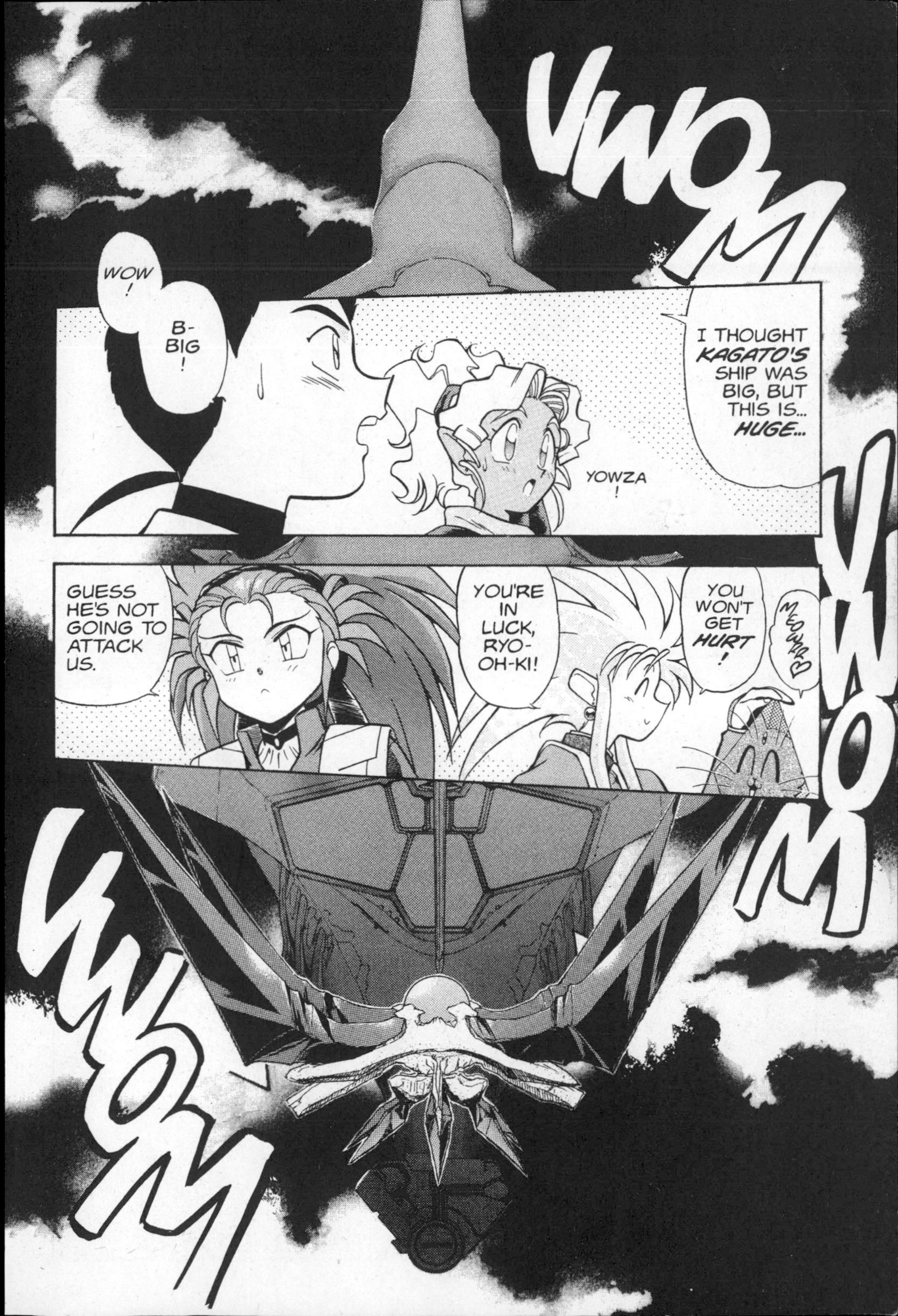
VWOM
WOW!
B-BIG!
I THOUGHT KAGATO'S SHIP WAS BIG, BUT THIS IS... HUGE...
YOWZA!
GUESS HE'S NOT GOING TO ATTACK US.
YOU'RE IN LUCK, RYO-OH-KI!
YOU WON'T GET HURT!
VWOM
VWOM

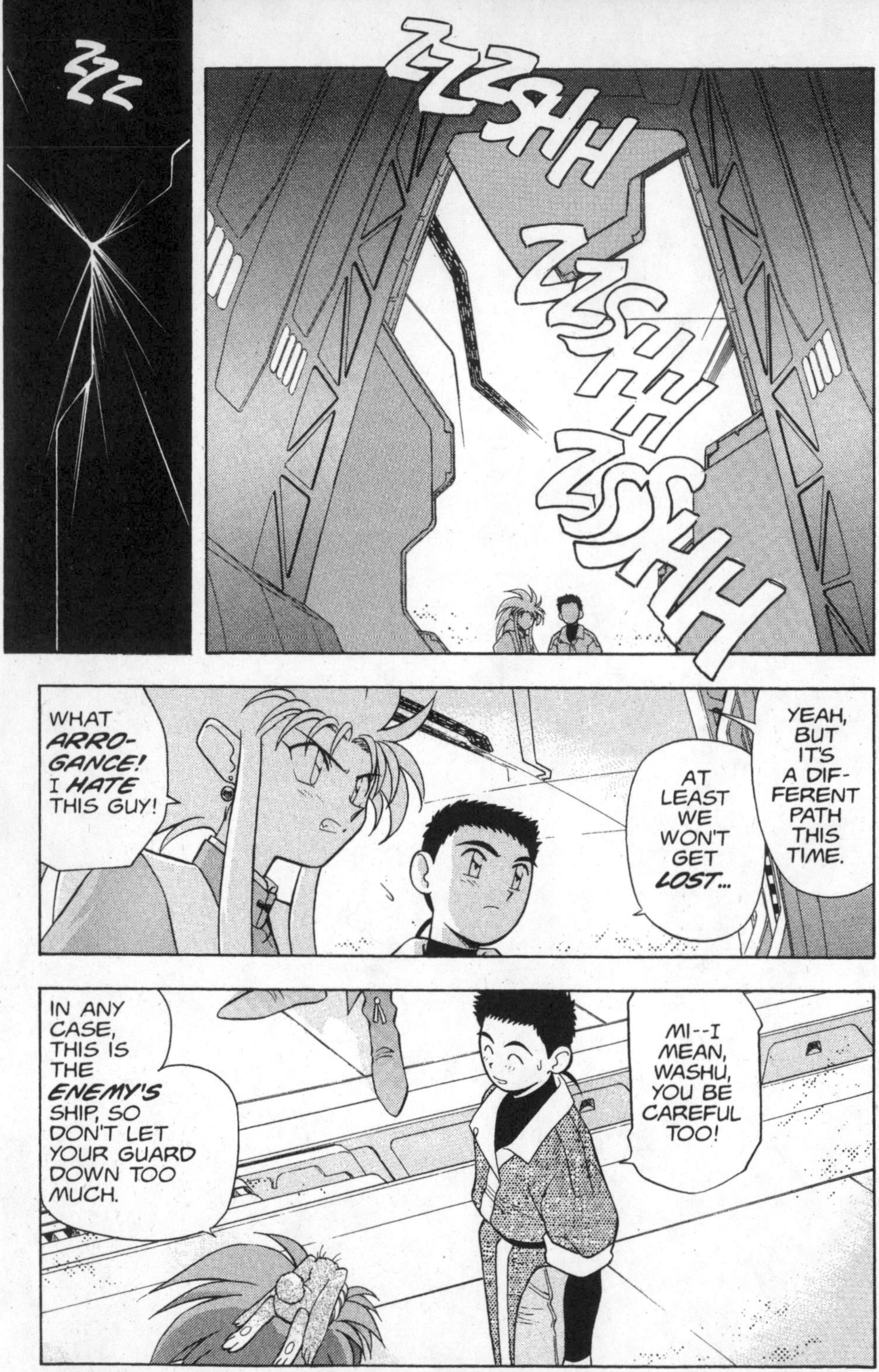
ZZZ
ZZZSHH
ZZSHHH
ZSHH
WHAT ARRO-GANCE! I HATE THIS GUY!
AT LEAST WE WON'T GET LOST...
YEAH, BUT IT'S A DIF-FERENT PATH THIS TIME.
IN ANY CASE, THIS IS THE ENEMY'S SHIP, SO DON'T LET YOUR GUARD DOWN TOO MUCH.
MI--I MEAN, WASHU, YOU BE CAREFUL TOO!

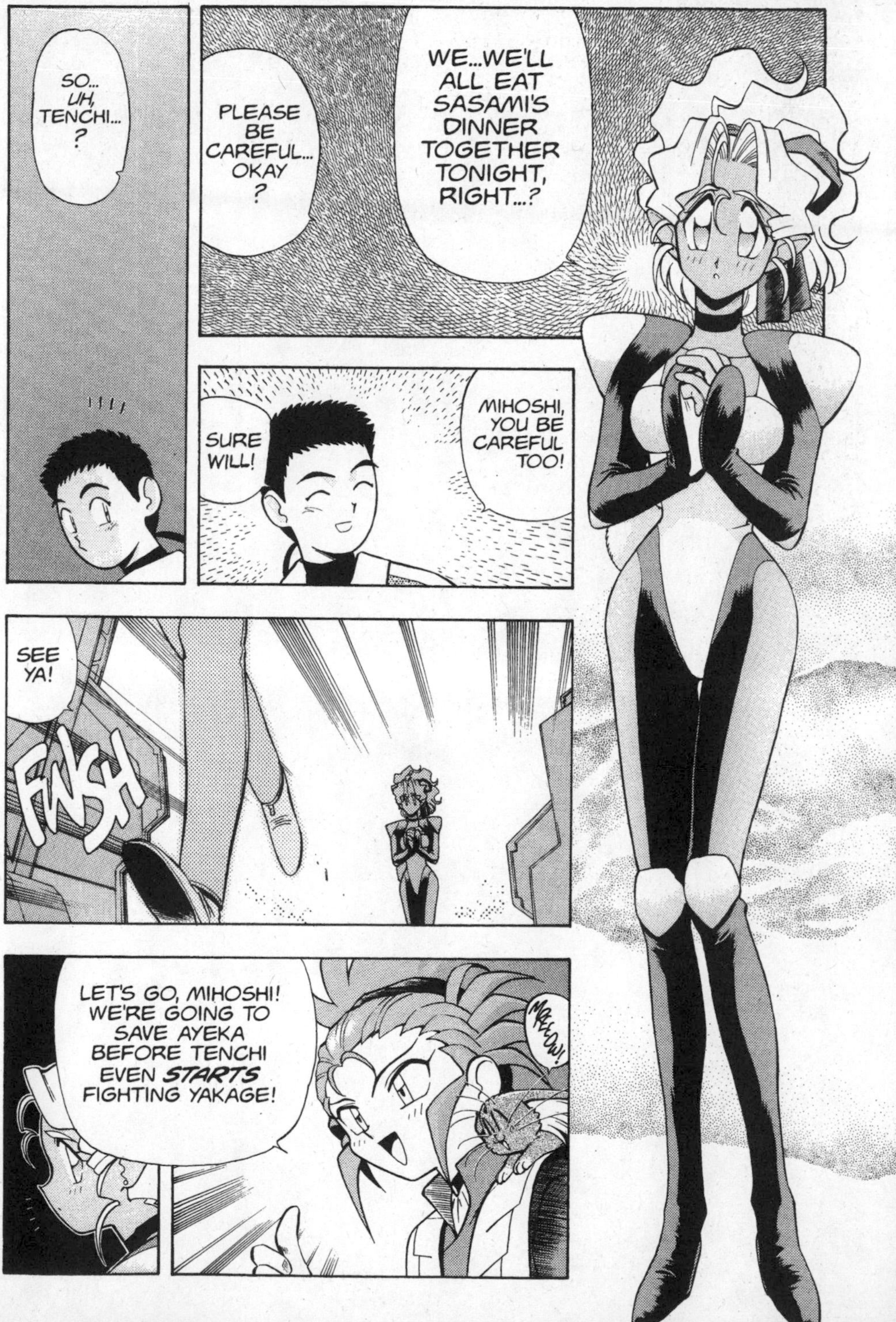
SO... UH, TENCHI... ?
PLEASE BE CAREFUL... OKAY ?
WE...WE'LL ALL EAT SASAMI'S DINNER TOGETHER TONIGHT, RIGHT...?
SURE WILL!
MIHOSHI, YOU BE CAREFUL TOO!
SEE YA!
FWSH
LET'S GO, MIHOSHI! WE'RE GOING TO SAVE AYEKA BEFORE TENCHI EVEN ***STARTS*** FIGHTING YAKAGE!
MREEOW!

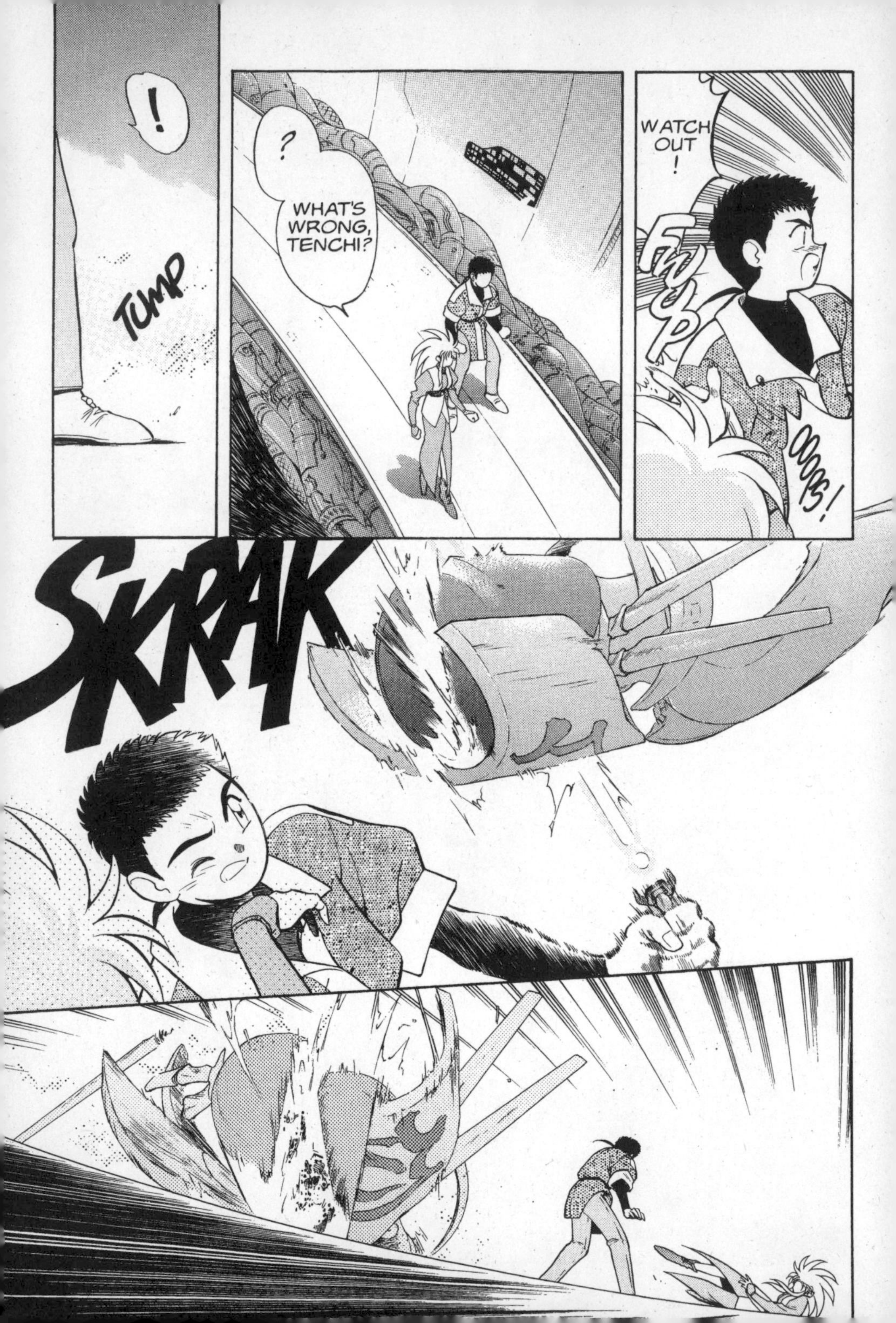
!
TUMP
?
WHAT'S WRONG, TENCHI?
WATCH OUT!
FWUP
OOOPS!
SKRAK

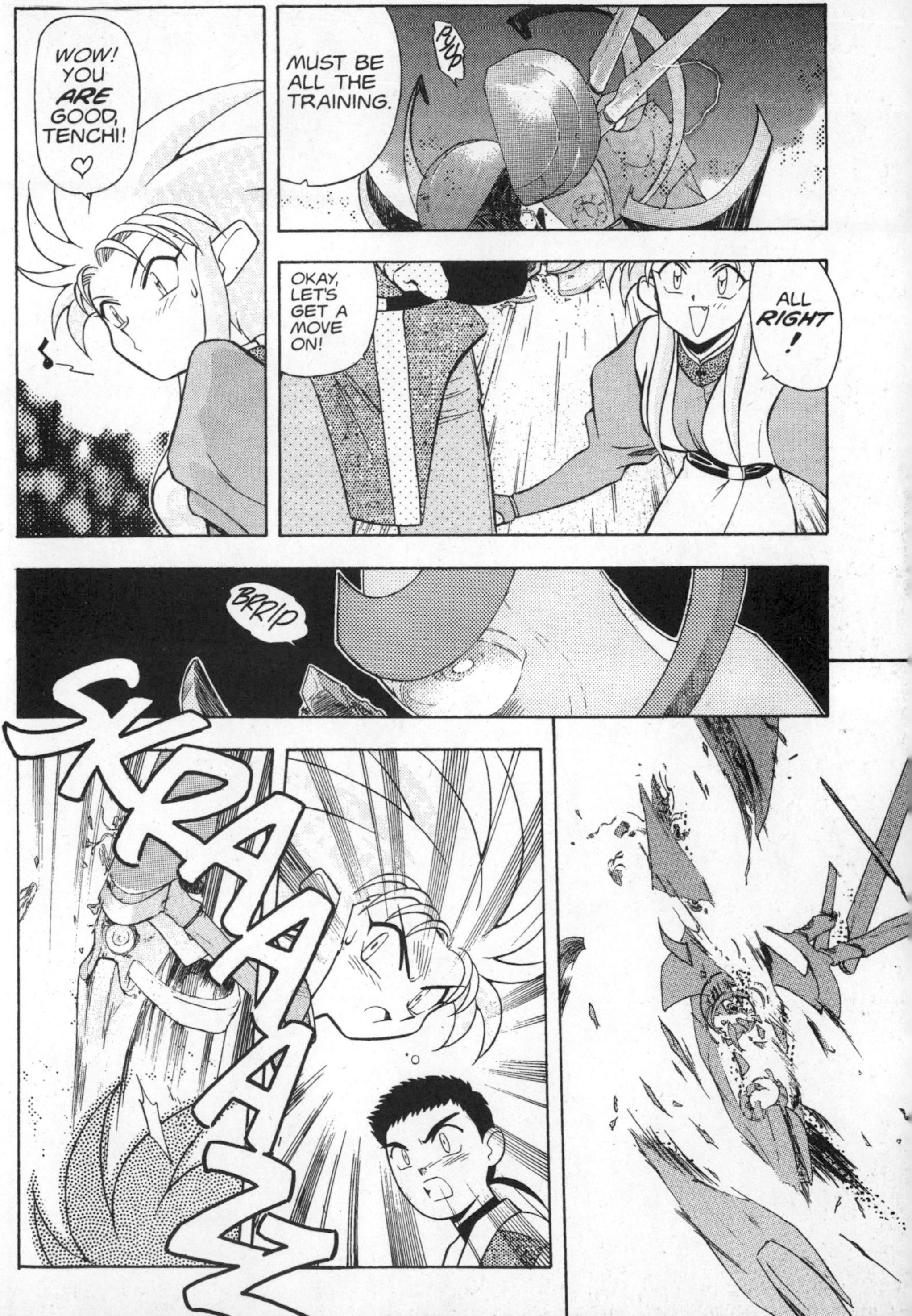
WOW! YOU ARE GOOD, TENCHI! ♡
PYUP
MUST BE ALL THE TRAINING.
OKAY, LET'S GET A MOVE ON!
ALL RIGHT!
BRRIP
SKRAAAAAM

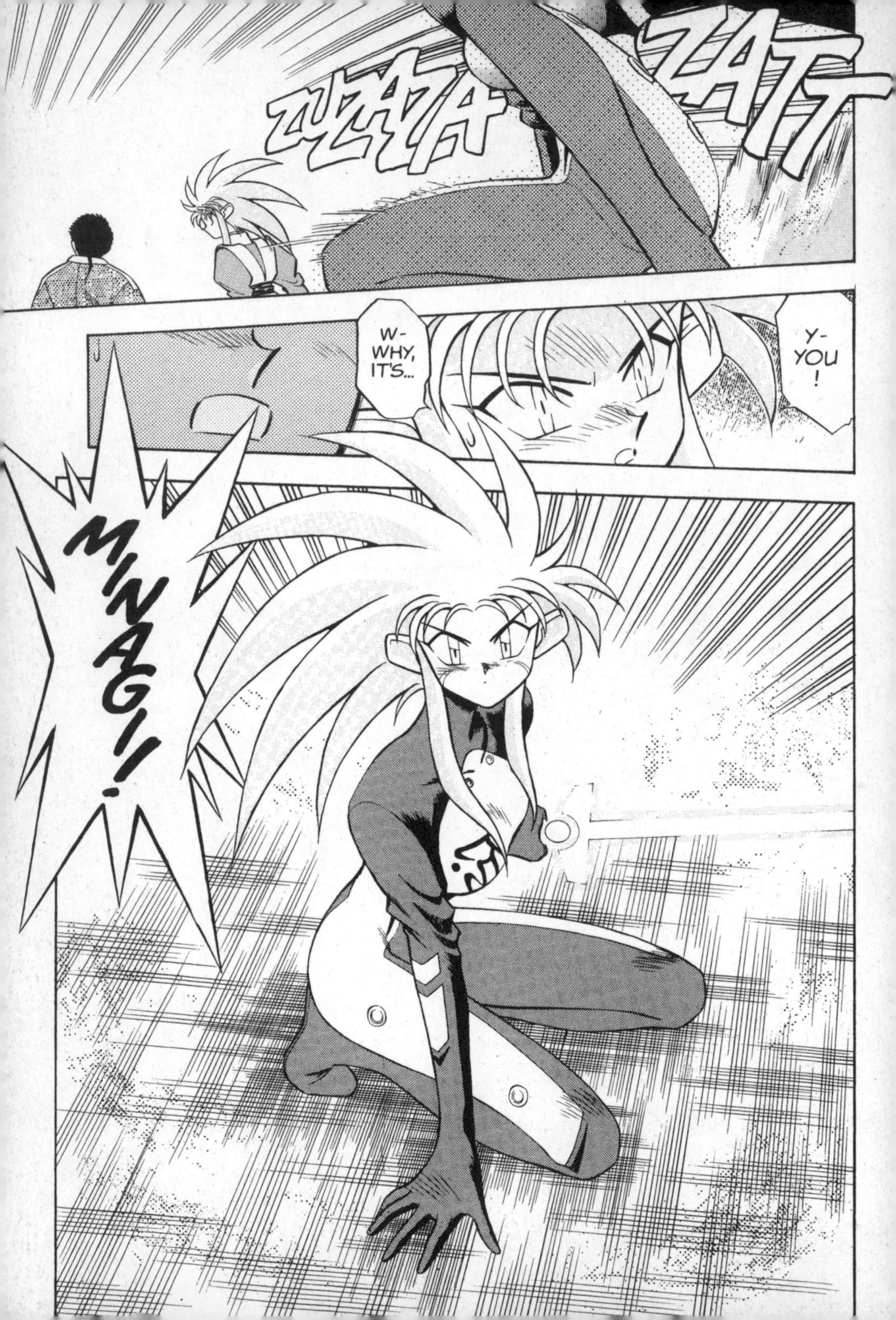
ZUZZAAA
ZATT
W-WHY, IT'S...
Y-YOU!
MINAGI!!

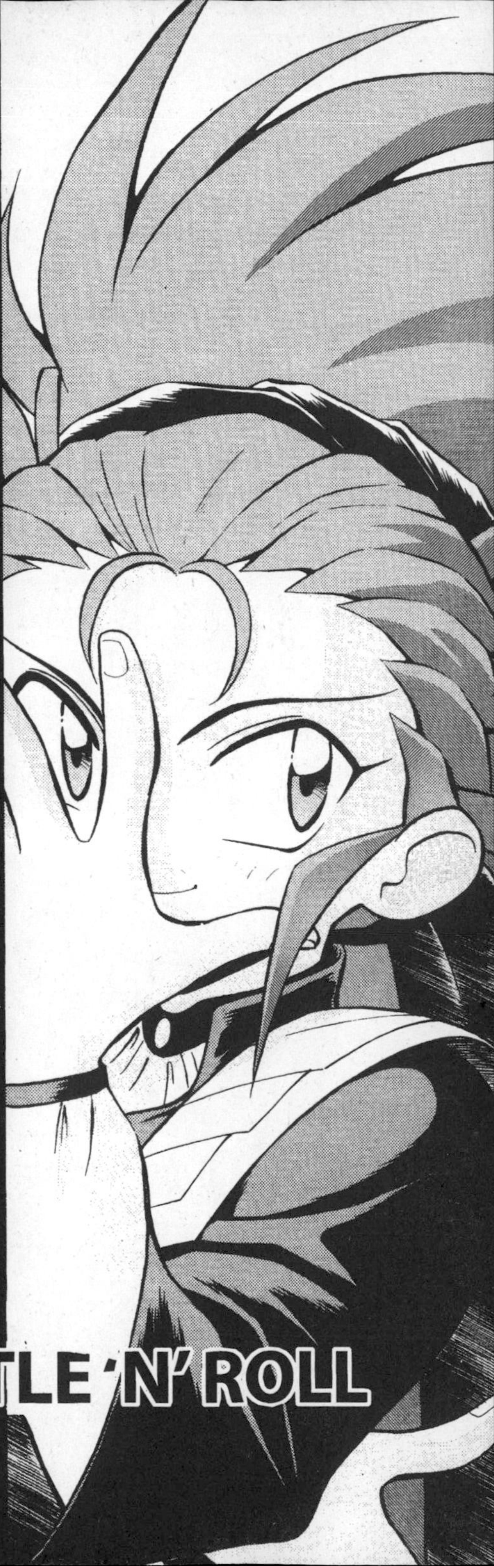

Tales of Tenchi #2

SHAKE, RATTLE 'N' ROLL

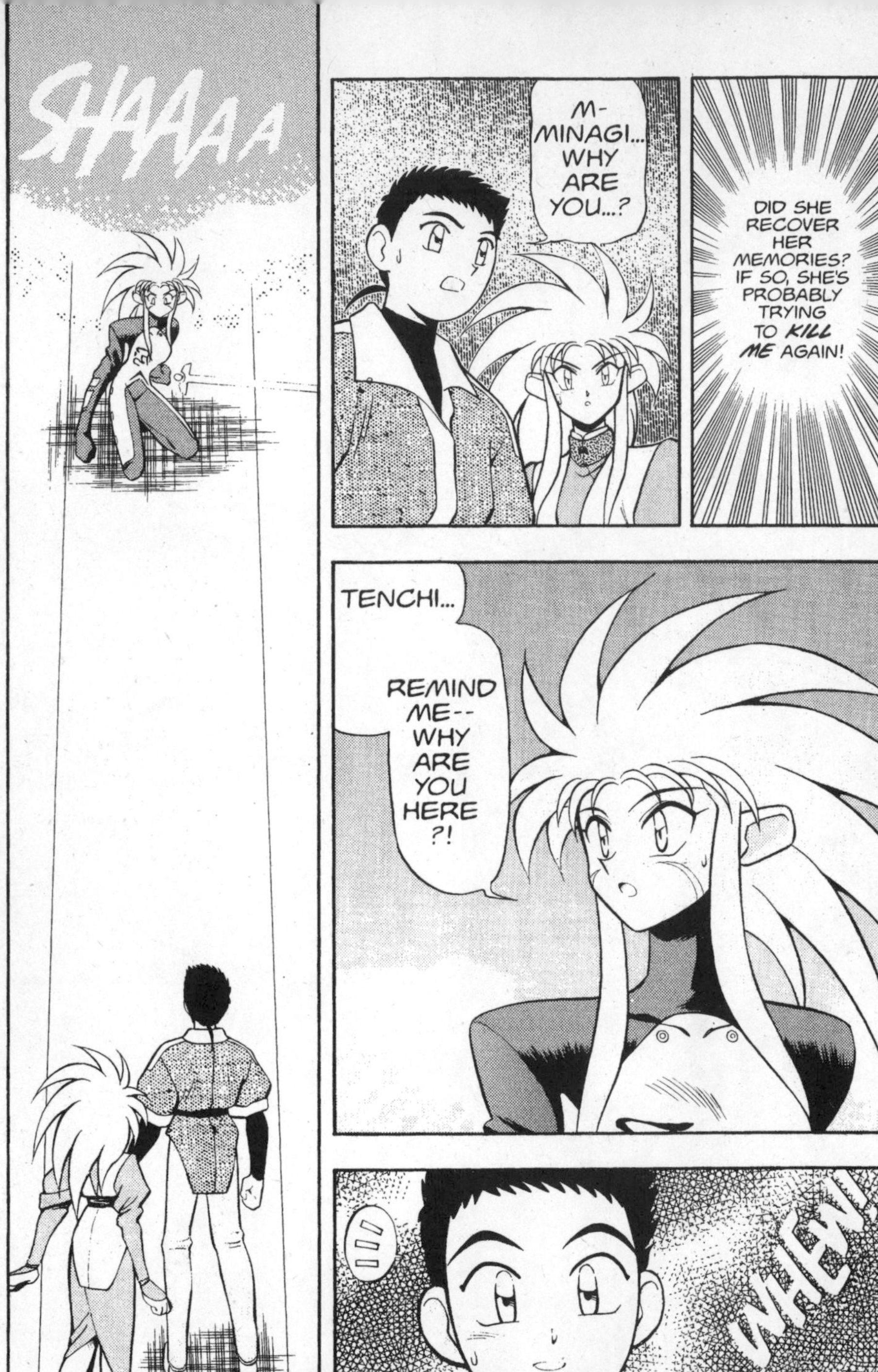
SHAAAA
M-MINAGI... WHY ARE YOU...?
DID SHE RECOVER HER MEMORIES? IF SO, SHE'S PROBABLY TRYING TO KILL ME AGAIN!
TENCHI...
REMIND ME-- WHY ARE YOU HERE?!
WHEW!

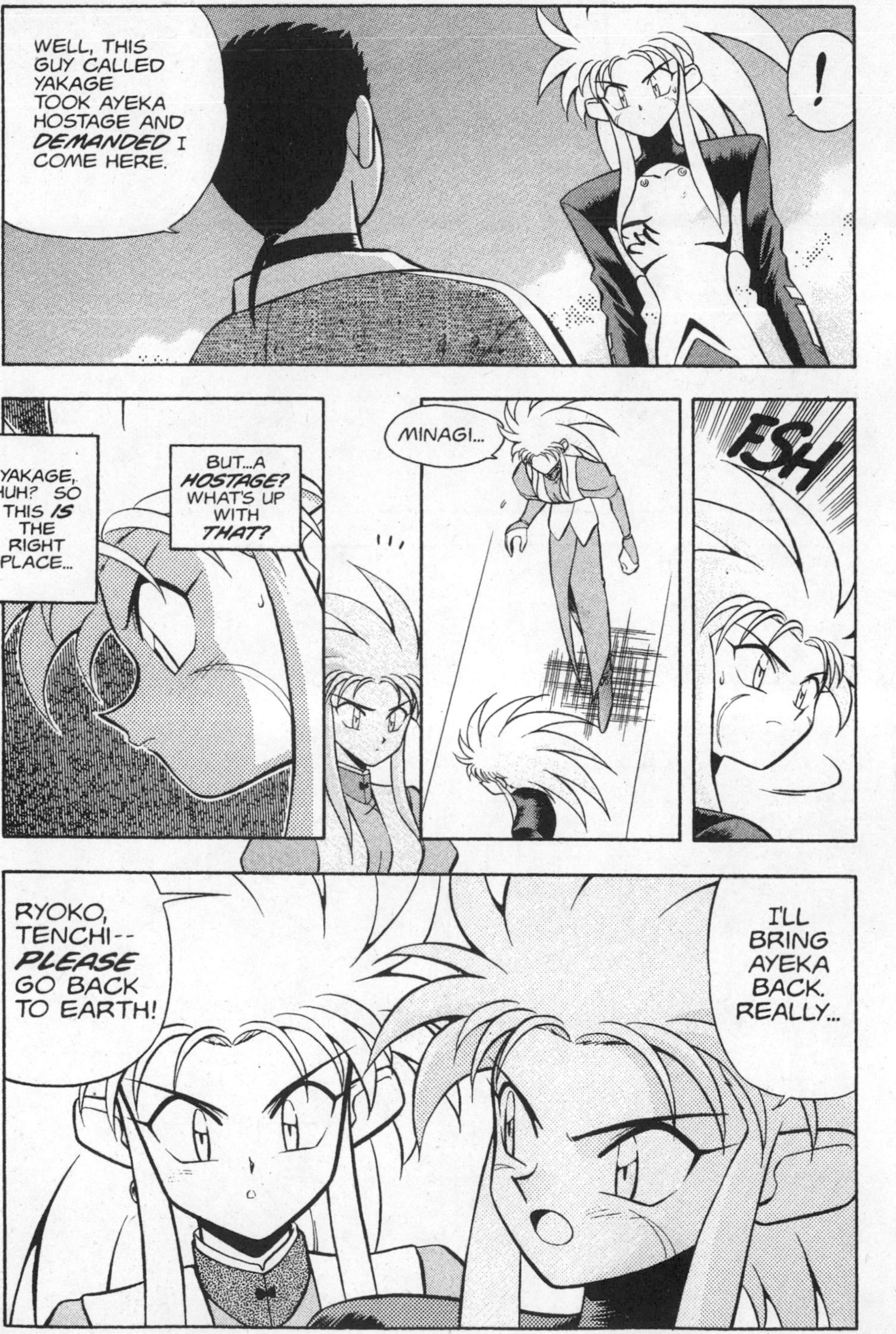
WELL, THIS GUY CALLED YAKAGE TOOK AYEKA HOSTAGE AND *DEMANDED* I COME HERE.
!
YAKAGE, HUH? SO THIS *IS* THE RIGHT PLACE...
BUT...A *HOSTAGE?* WHAT'S UP WITH *THAT?*
MINAGI...
FSH
RYOKO, TENCHI-- *PLEASE* GO BACK TO EARTH!
I'LL BRING AYEKA BACK. REALLY...

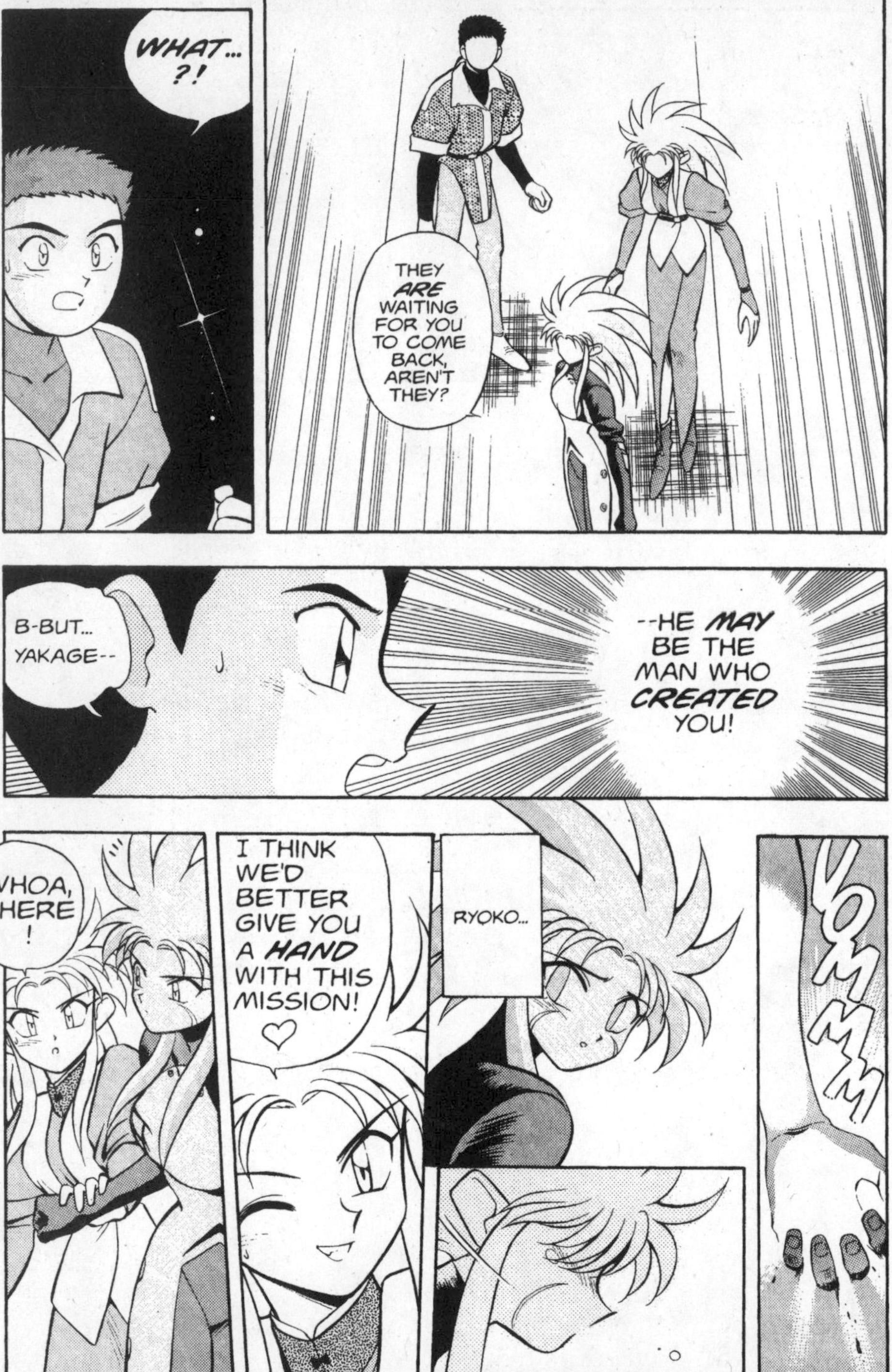

WHAT... ?!
THEY ARE WAITING FOR YOU TO COME BACK, AREN'T THEY?
B-BUT... YAKAGE--
--HE MAY BE THE MAN WHO CREATED YOU!
WHOA, THERE !
I THINK WE'D BETTER GIVE YOU A HAND WITH THIS MISSION! ♡
RYOKO...
VOMMM

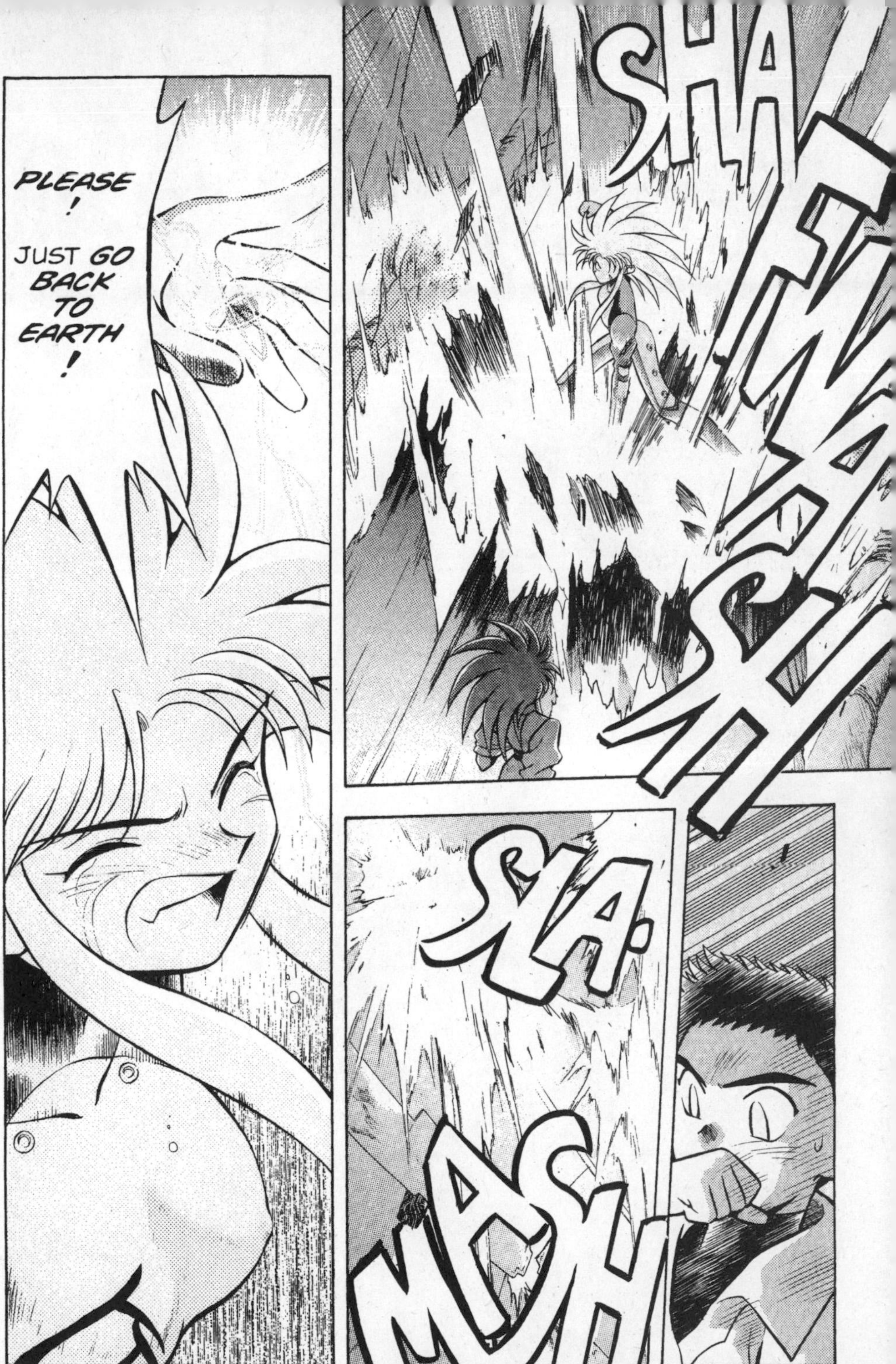
PLEASE!
JUST GO BACK TO EARTH!
SHA
SHA
SLA
SH
MASH

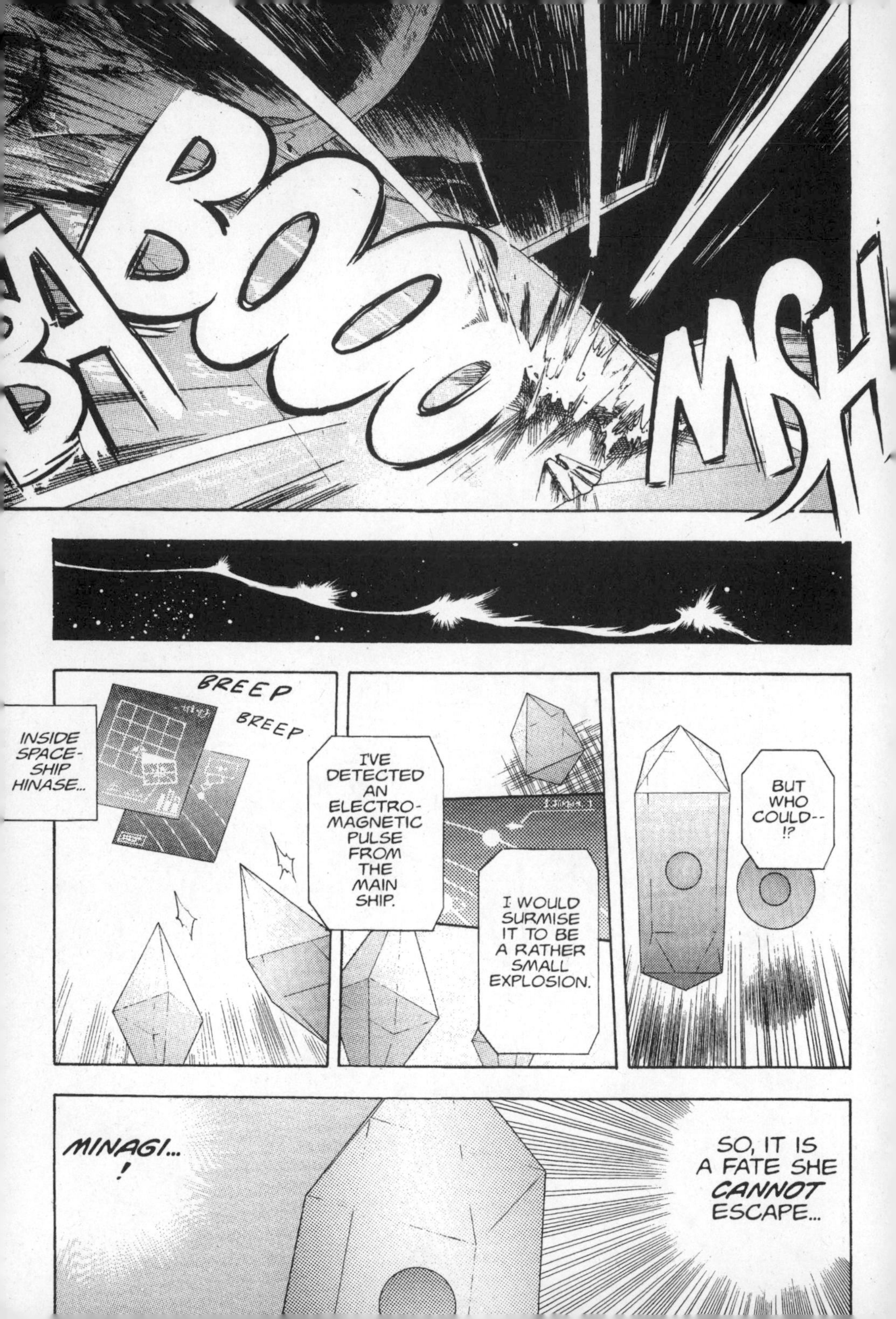
BREEP
BREEP
INSIDE SPACE-SHIP HINASE...
I'VE DETECTED AN ELECTRO-MAGNETIC PULSE FROM THE MAIN SHIP.
I WOULD SURMISE IT TO BE A RATHER SMALL EXPLOSION.
BUT WHO COULD--!?
MINAGI... !
SO, IT IS A FATE SHE CANNOT ESCAPE...

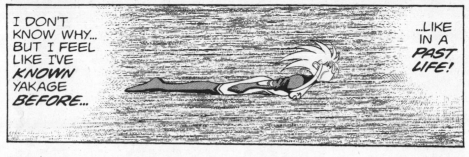

I DON'T KNOW WHY... BUT I FEEL LIKE I'VE *KNOWN* YAKAGE *BEFORE*...

...LIKE IN A *PAST LIFE!*

SO IT WAS *IMPOSSIBLE* TO STOP MINAGI...?

SO SORRY... SO SORRY!

IT'S ALL MY FAULT...

BUT THE YAKAGE *I KNOW* WOULDN'T TAKE A *HOSTAGE!*

NO, IT'S NOT *YOUR* FAULT...

...IT'S HER BLOOD...

YES! IT'S YAKAGE'S *BLOOD* CALLING MINAGI!

HE SHOULD BE *ASHAMED* OF HIMSELF!

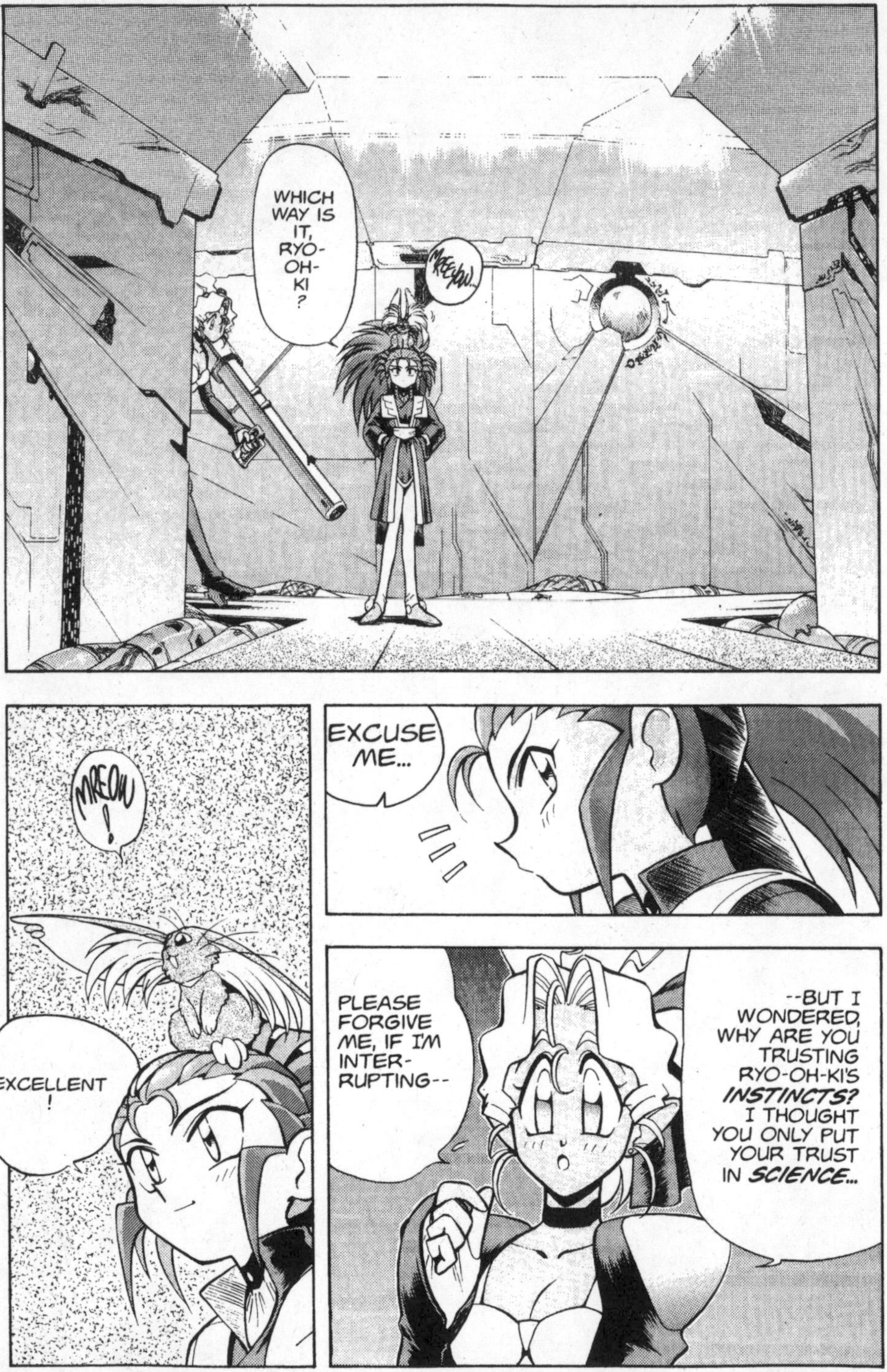
WHICH WAY IS IT, RYO-OH-KI?
MREEYOW...
MREOW!
EXCELLENT!
EXCUSE ME...
PLEASE FORGIVE ME, IF I'M INTERRUPTING--
--BUT I WONDERED, WHY ARE YOU TRUSTING RYO-OH-KI'S *INSTINCTS?* I THOUGHT YOU ONLY PUT YOUR TRUST IN *SCIENCE*...

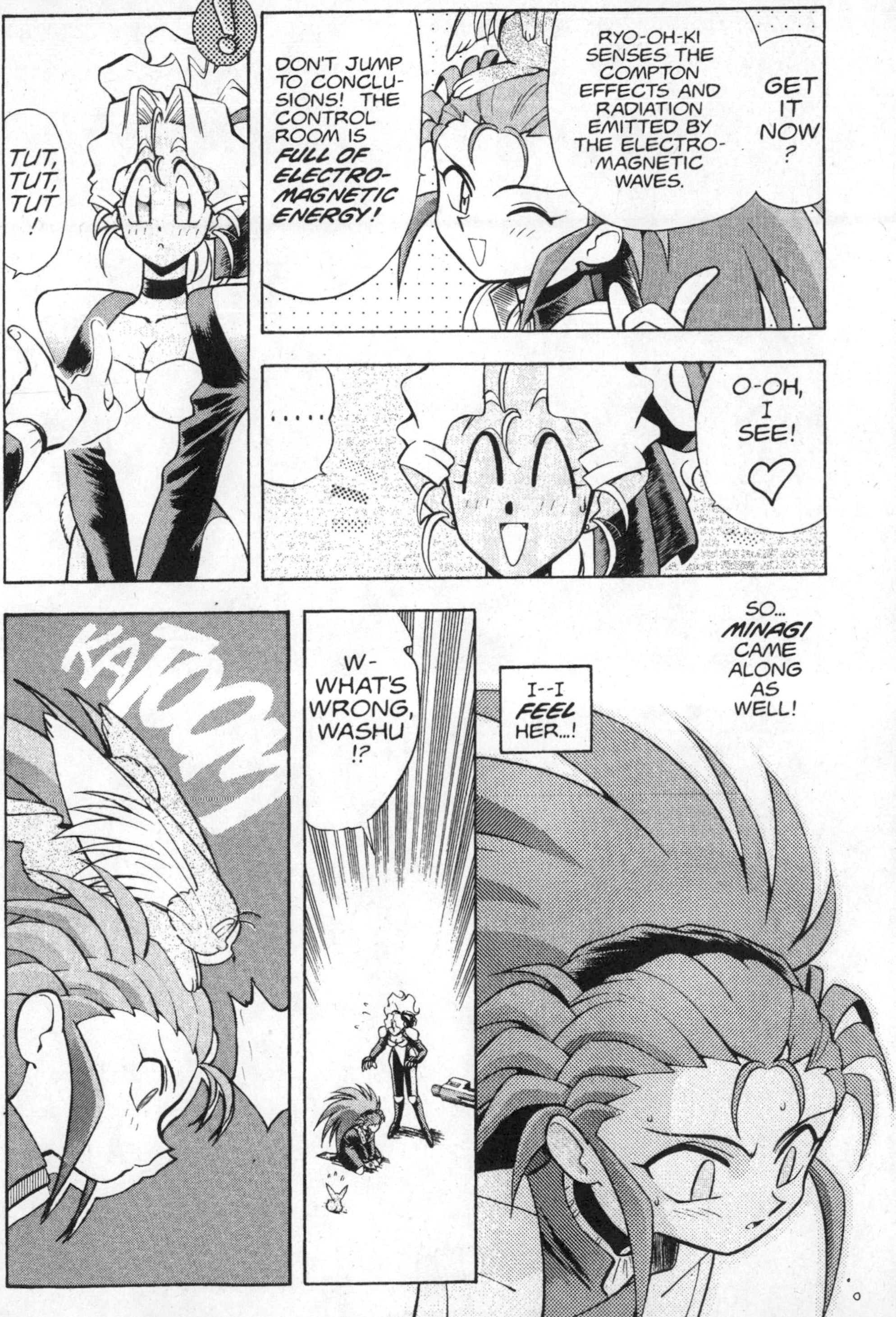
!
TUT, TUT, TUT!
DON'T JUMP TO CONCLUSIONS! THE CONTROL ROOM IS FULL OF ELECTRO-MAGNETIC ENERGY!
RYO-OH-KI SENSES THE COMPTON EFFECTS AND RADIATION EMITTED BY THE ELECTRO-MAGNETIC WAVES.
GET IT NOW?
.....
O-OH, I SEE! ♡
KATOOM
W-WHAT'S WRONG, WASHU!?
I--I FEEL HER...!
SO... MINAGI CAME ALONG AS WELL!

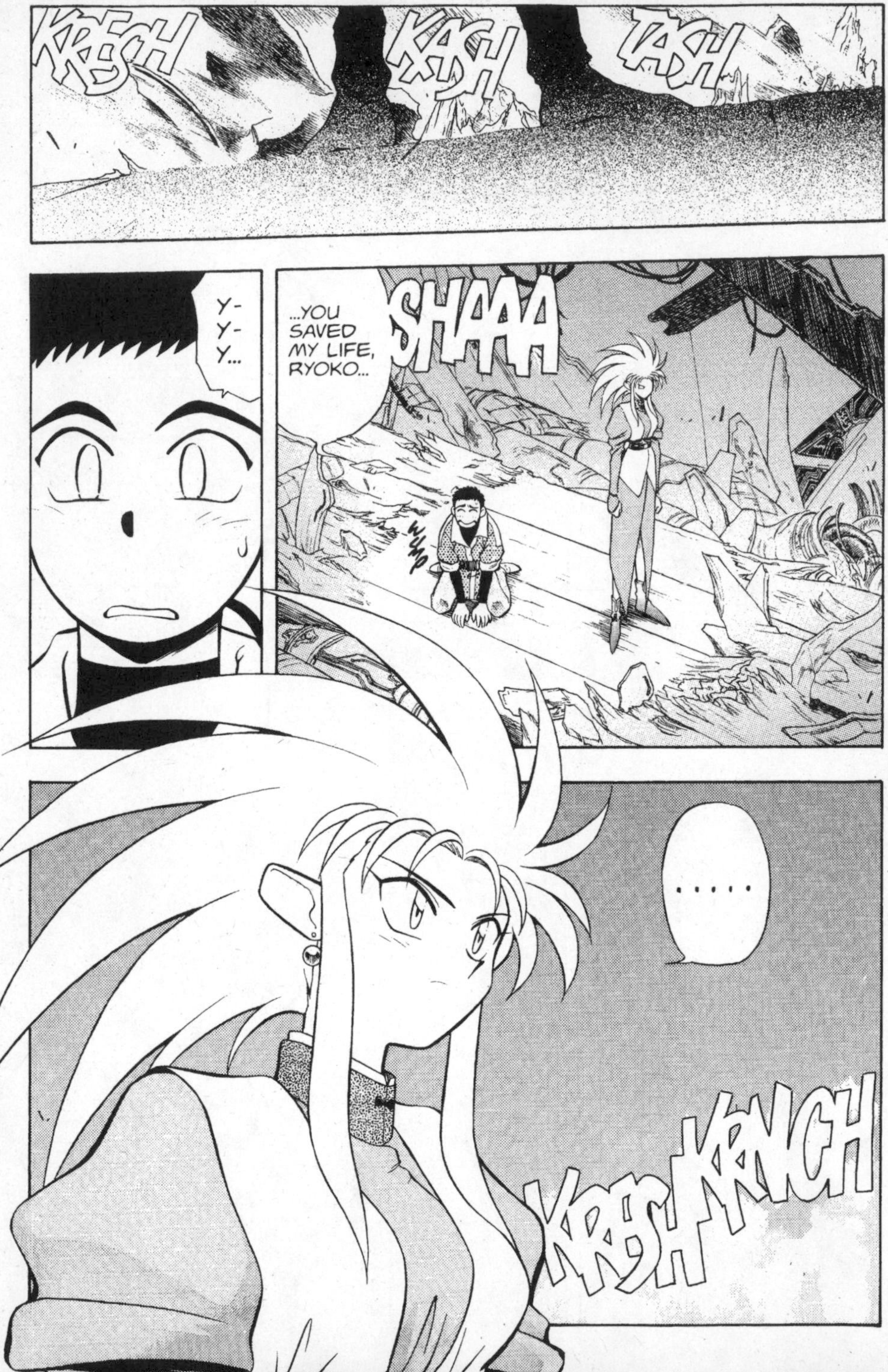
KRESH
KASH
TASH
Y-Y-Y...
...YOU SAVED MY LIFE, RYOKO...
SHAAA
WUMP
......
KRESH
KRNCH

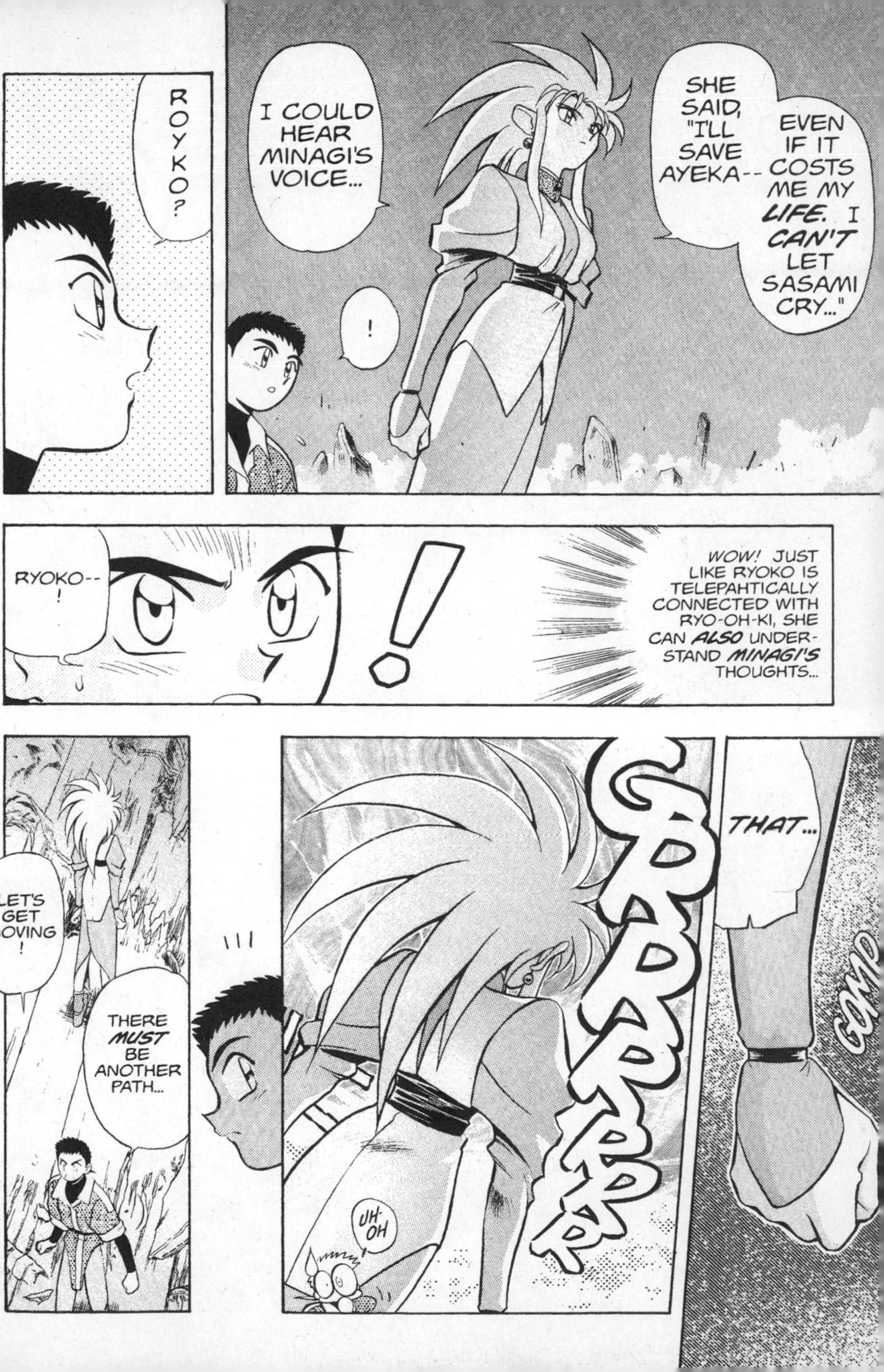
ROYKO?
I COULD HEAR MINAGI'S VOICE...
!
SHE SAID, "I'LL SAVE AYEKA-- EVEN IF IT COSTS ME MY LIFE. I CAN'T LET SASAMI CRY..."
RYOKO-- !
WOW! JUST LIKE RYOKO IS TELEPAHTICALLY CONNECTED WITH RYO-OH-KI, SHE CAN ALSO UNDERSTAND MINAGI'S THOUGHTS...
THAT...
UH-OH
LET'S GET MOVING !
THERE MUST BE ANOTHER PATH...

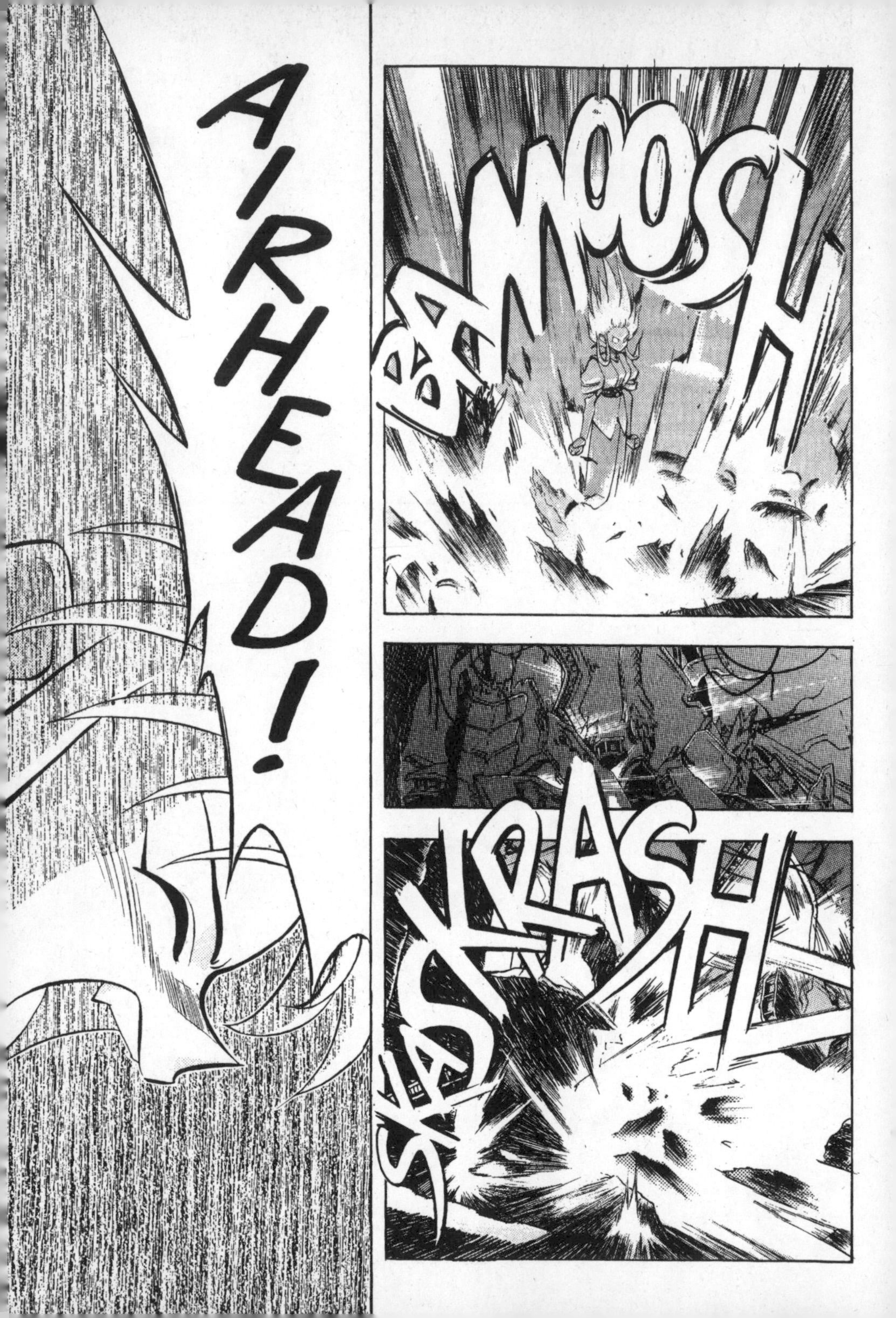
AIRHEAD!
BWOOSH
KRASH
SMASH

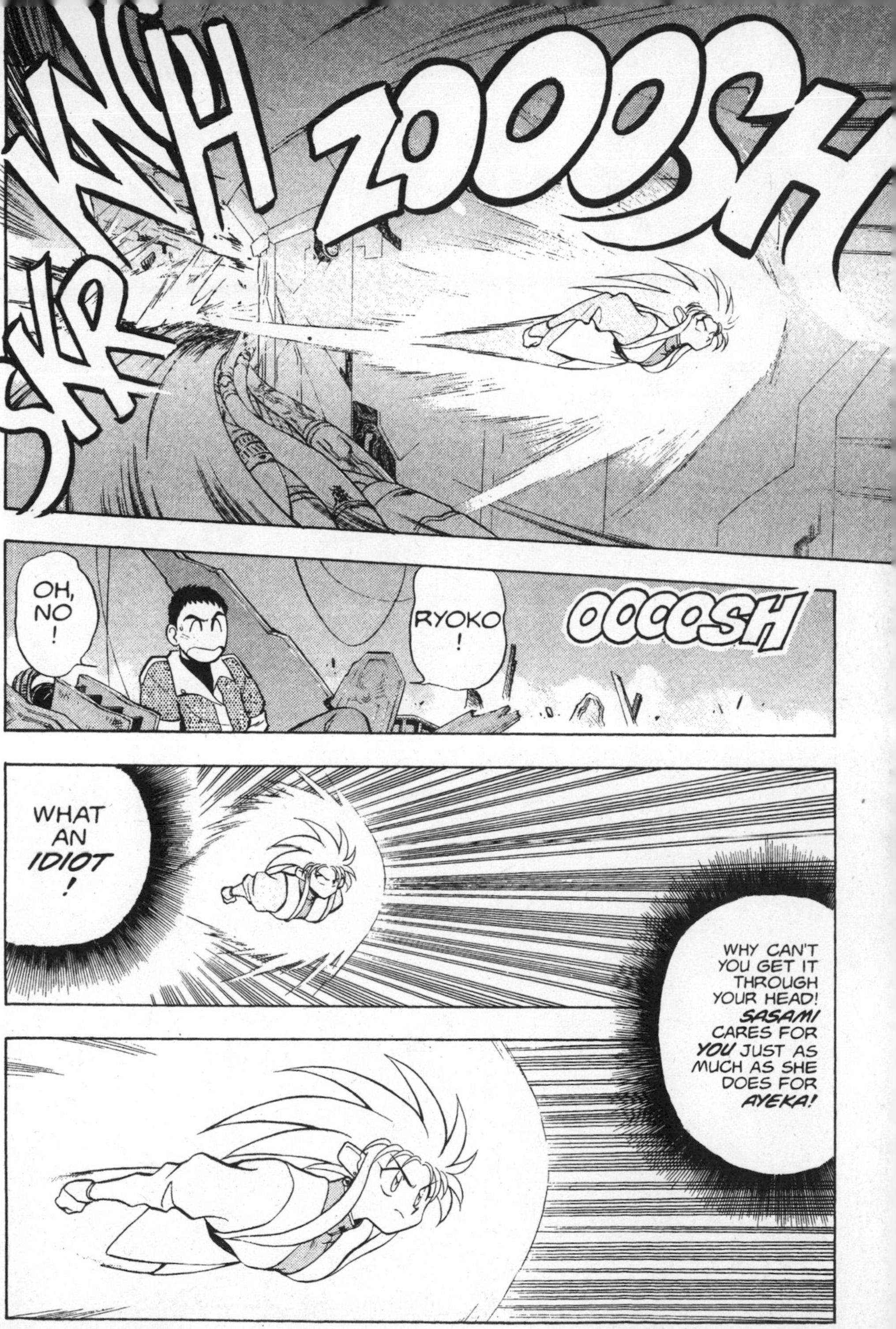
SKRNCH
ZOOOSH
OH, NO!
RYOKO!
OOCOSH
WHAT AN IDIOT!
WHY CAN'T YOU GET IT THROUGH YOUR HEAD! SASAMI CARES FOR YOU JUST AS MUCH AS SHE DOES FOR AYEKA!

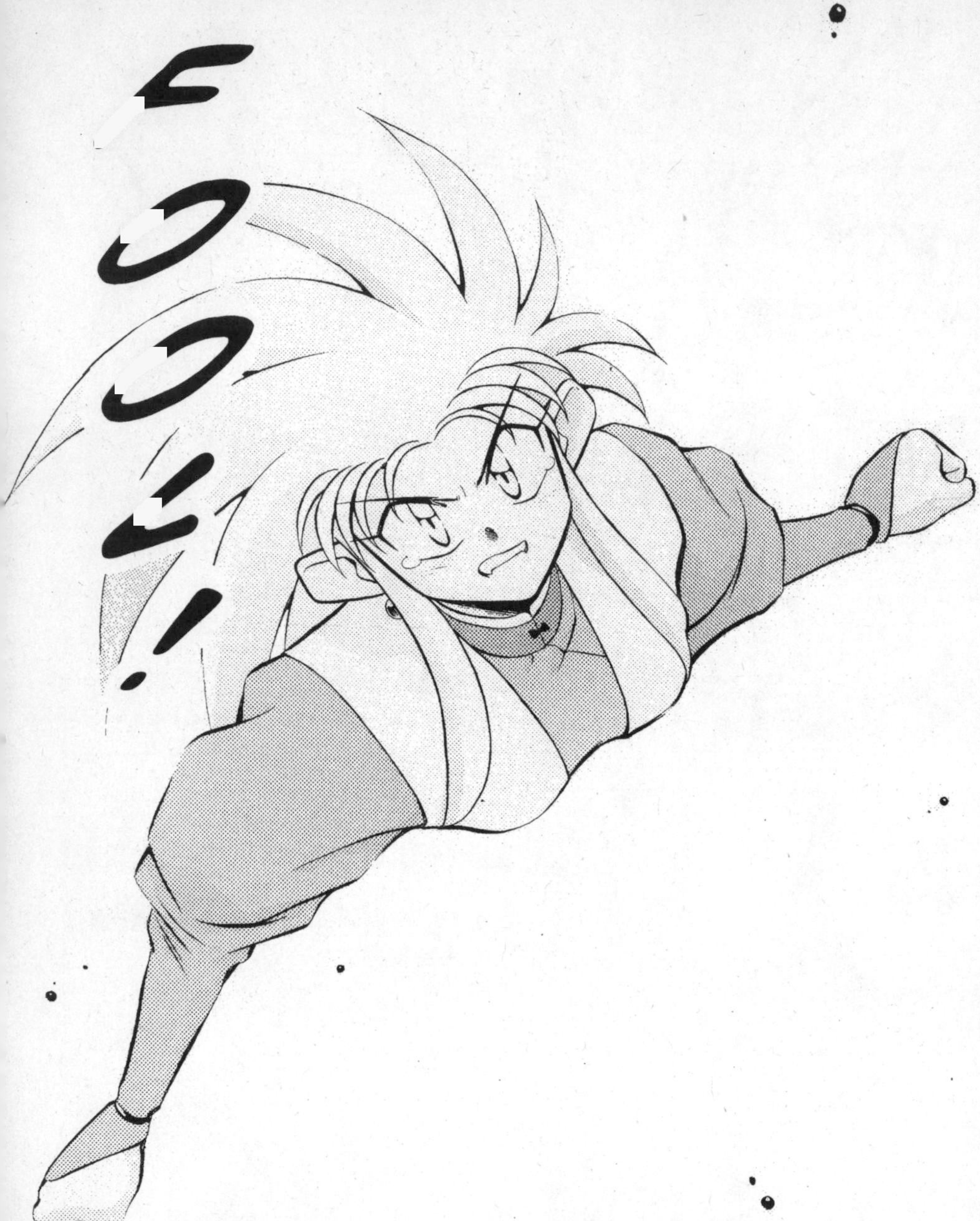

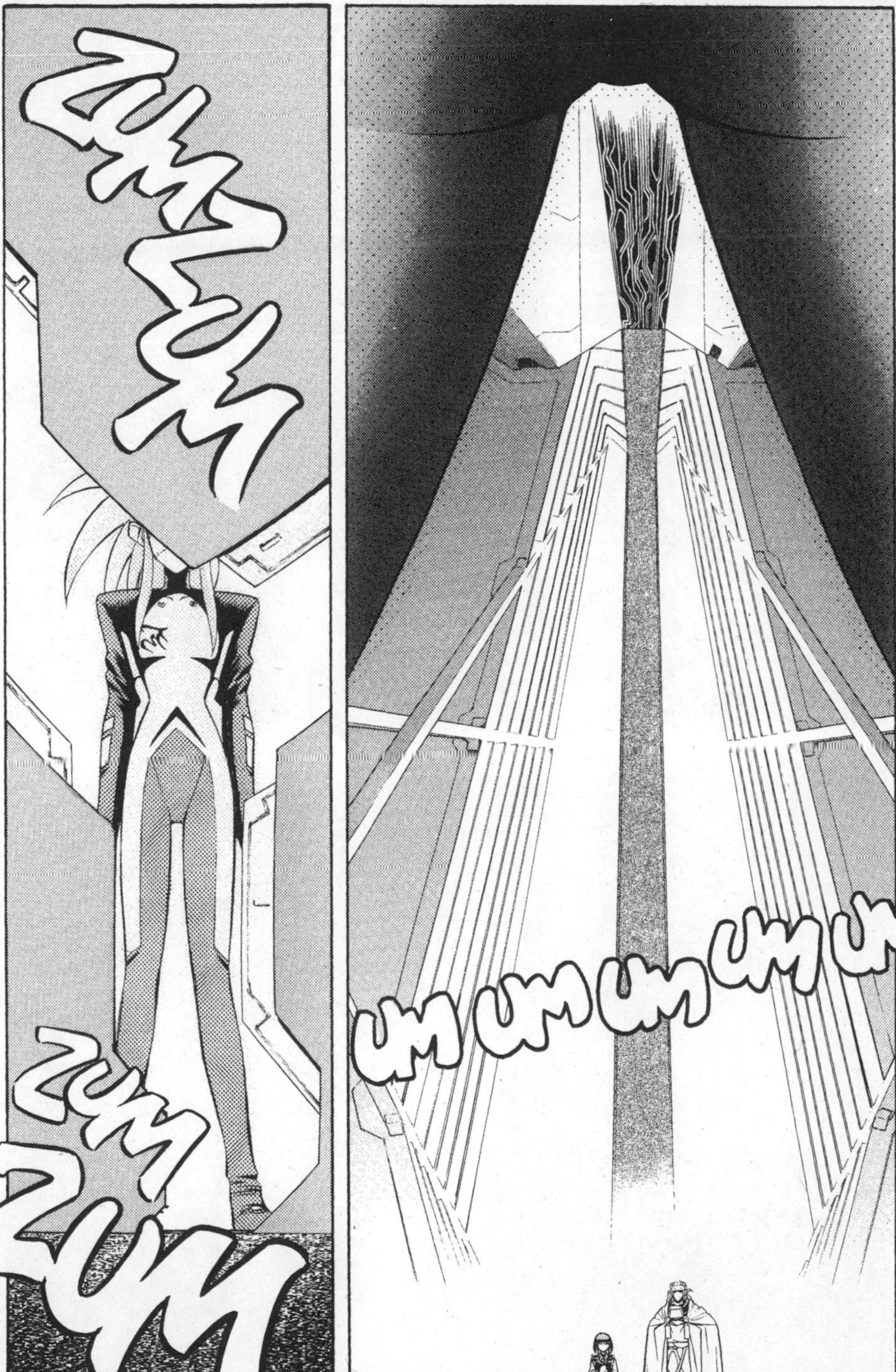
ZUM ZUM
ZUM
ZUM
UM UM UM UM UM

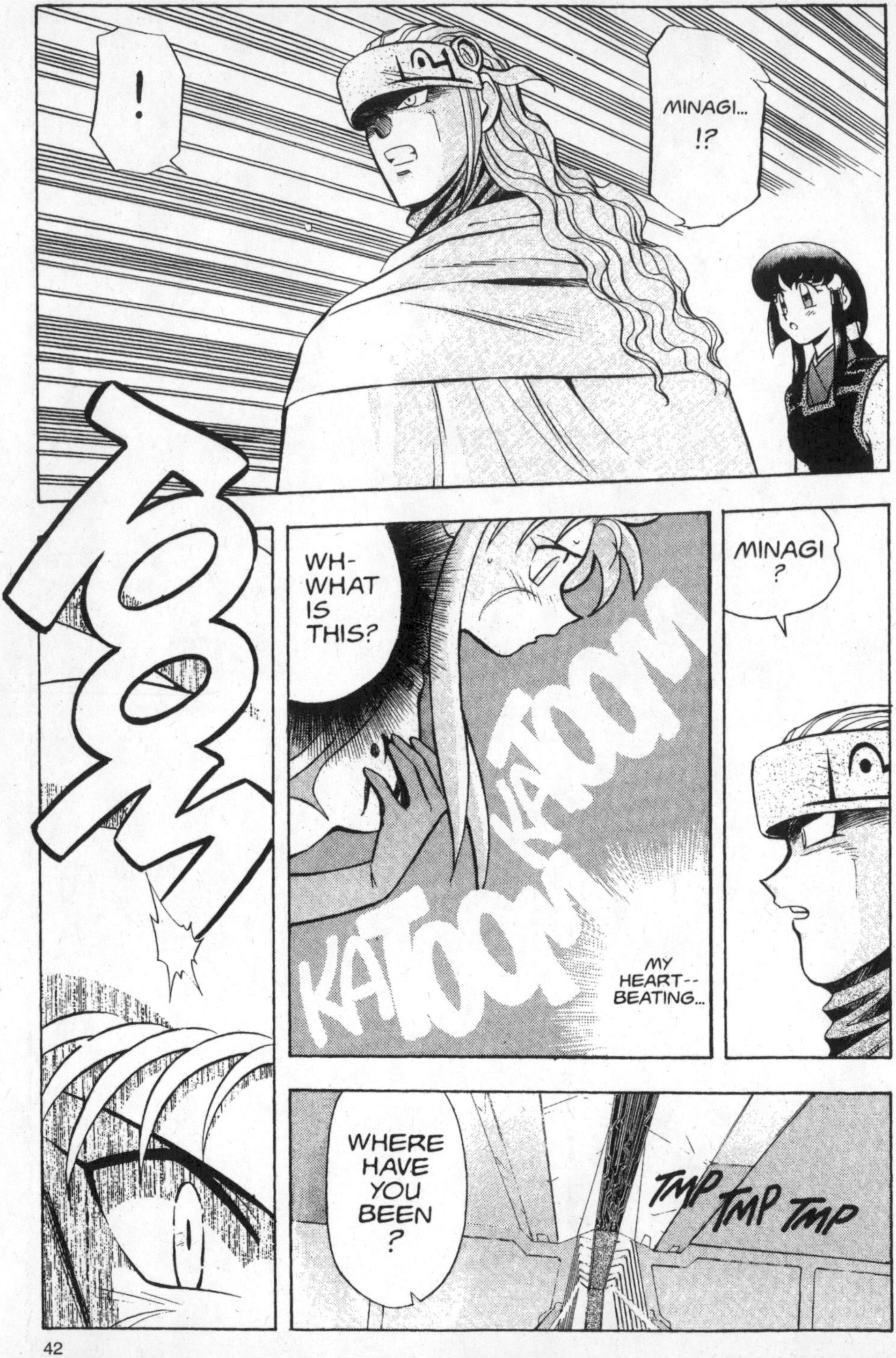
!
MINAGI... !?
TOOM
WH- WHAT IS THIS?
KATOOM KATOOM
MY HEART-- BEATING...
MINAGI ?
WHERE HAVE YOU BEEN ?
TMP TMP TMP

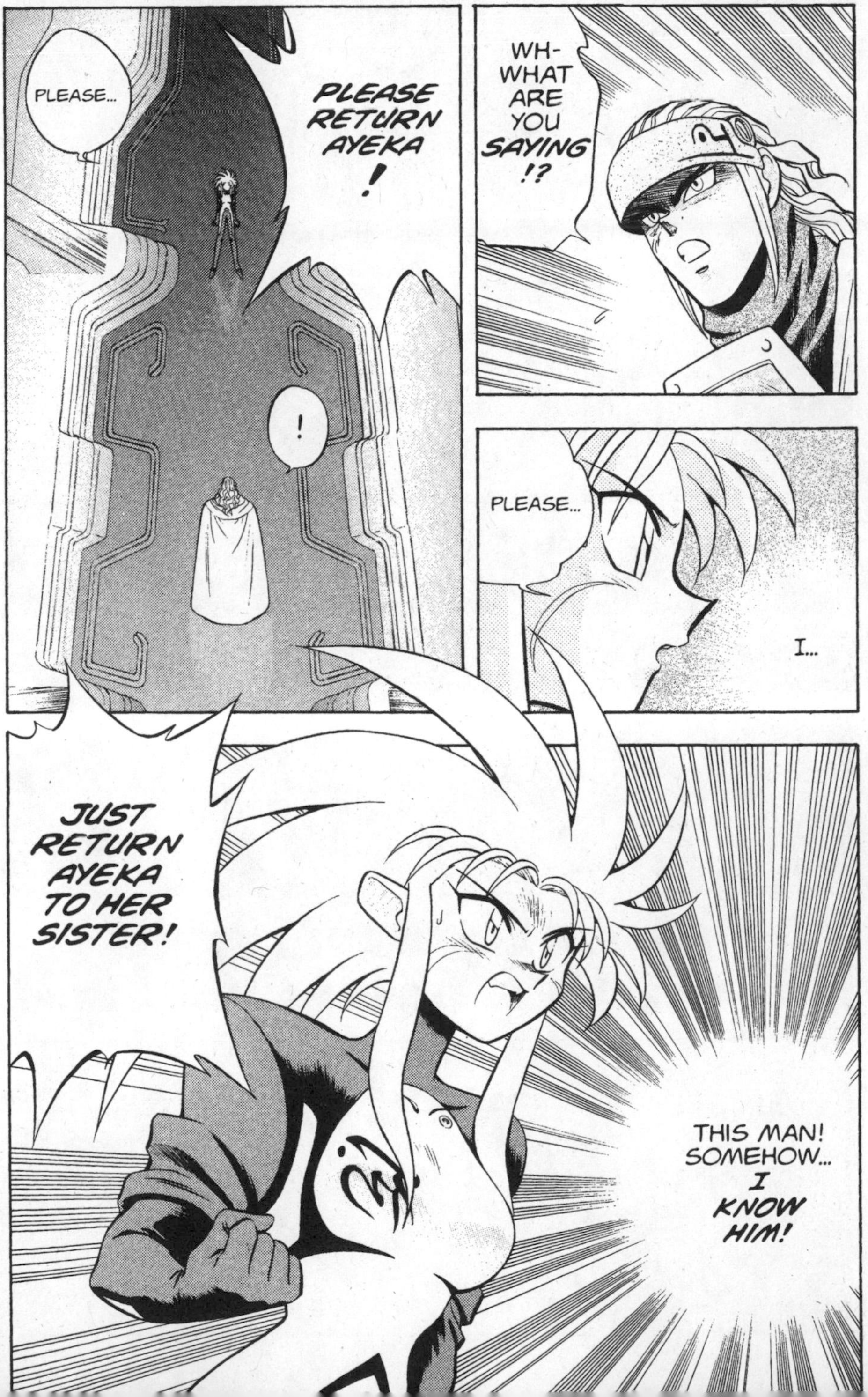
PLEASE...
PLEASE RETURN AYEKA!
!
WH-WHAT ARE YOU SAYING!?
PLEASE...
I...
JUST RETURN AYEKA TO HER SISTER!
THIS MAN! SOMEHOW... I KNOW HIM!

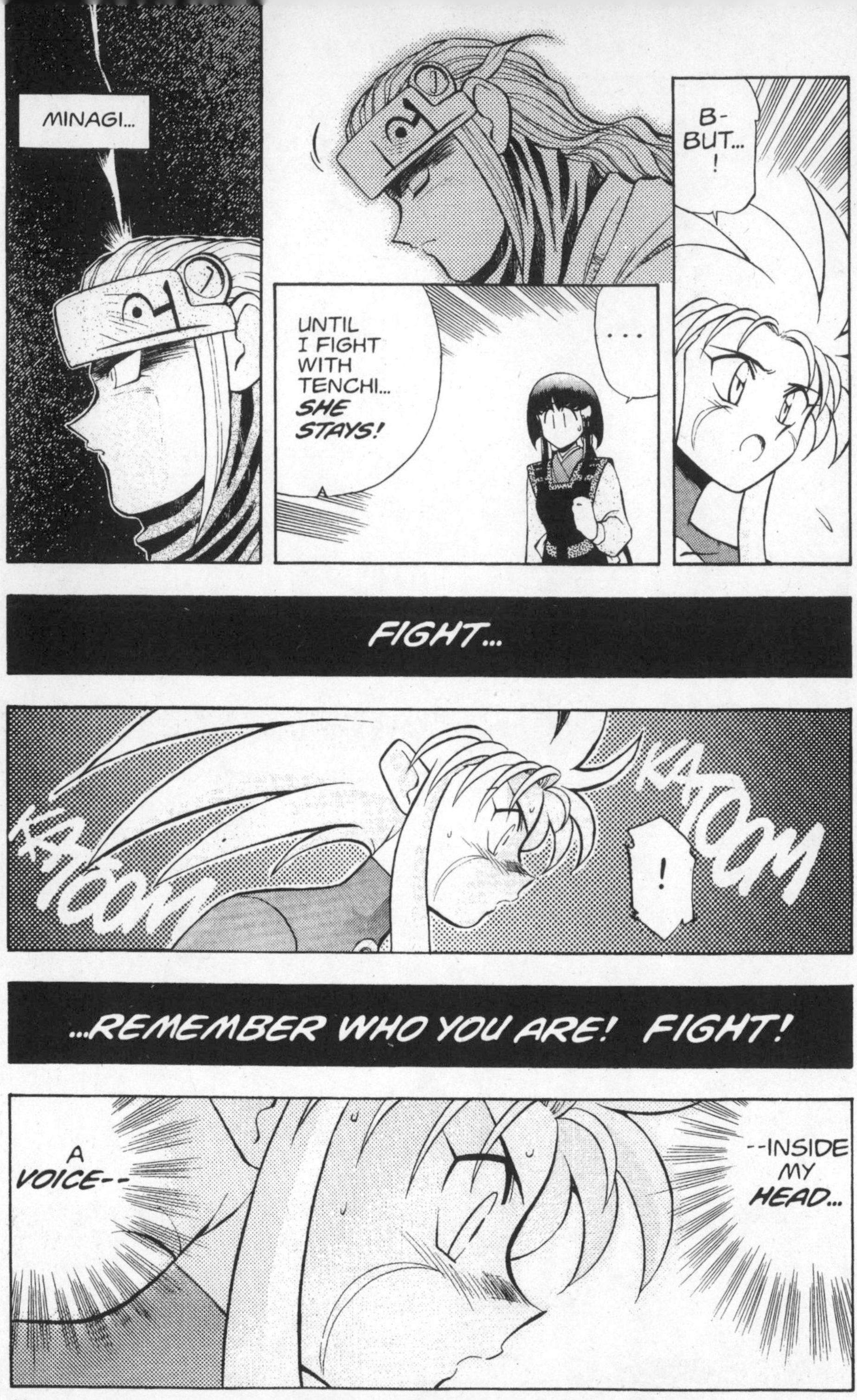

MINAGI...
UNTIL I FIGHT WITH TENCHI... SHE STAYS!
. . .
B- BUT... !
FIGHT...
KATOOM
KATOOM
!
...REMEMBER WHO YOU ARE! FIGHT!
A VOICE--
--INSIDE MY HEAD...

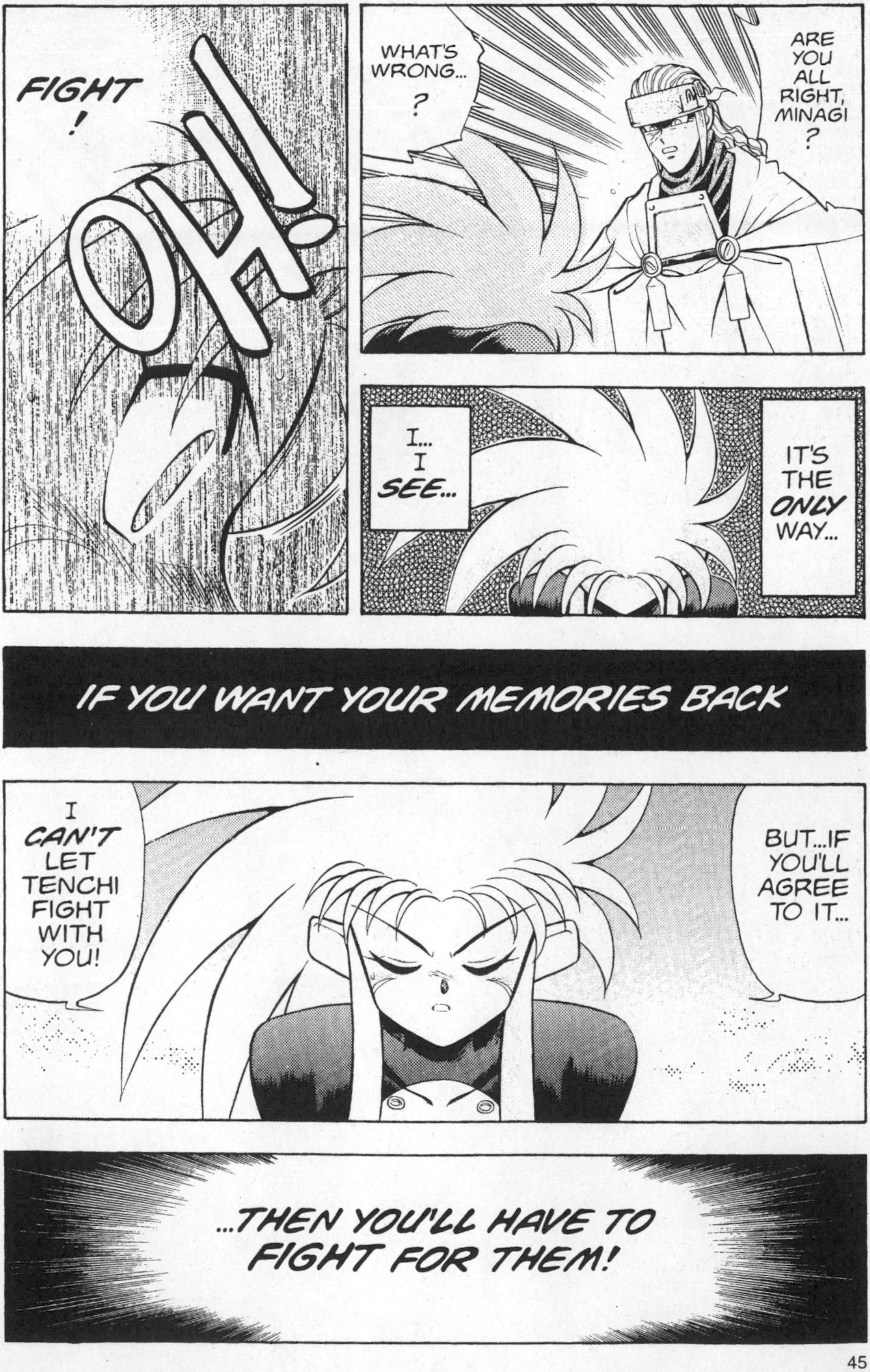
FIGHT!
OH!
WHAT'S WRONG...?
ARE YOU ALL RIGHT, MINAGI?
I... I SEE...
IT'S THE ONLY WAY...
IF YOU WANT YOUR MEMORIES BACK
I CAN'T LET TENCHI FIGHT WITH YOU!
BUT...IF YOU'LL AGREE TO IT...
...THEN YOU'LL HAVE TO FIGHT FOR THEM!

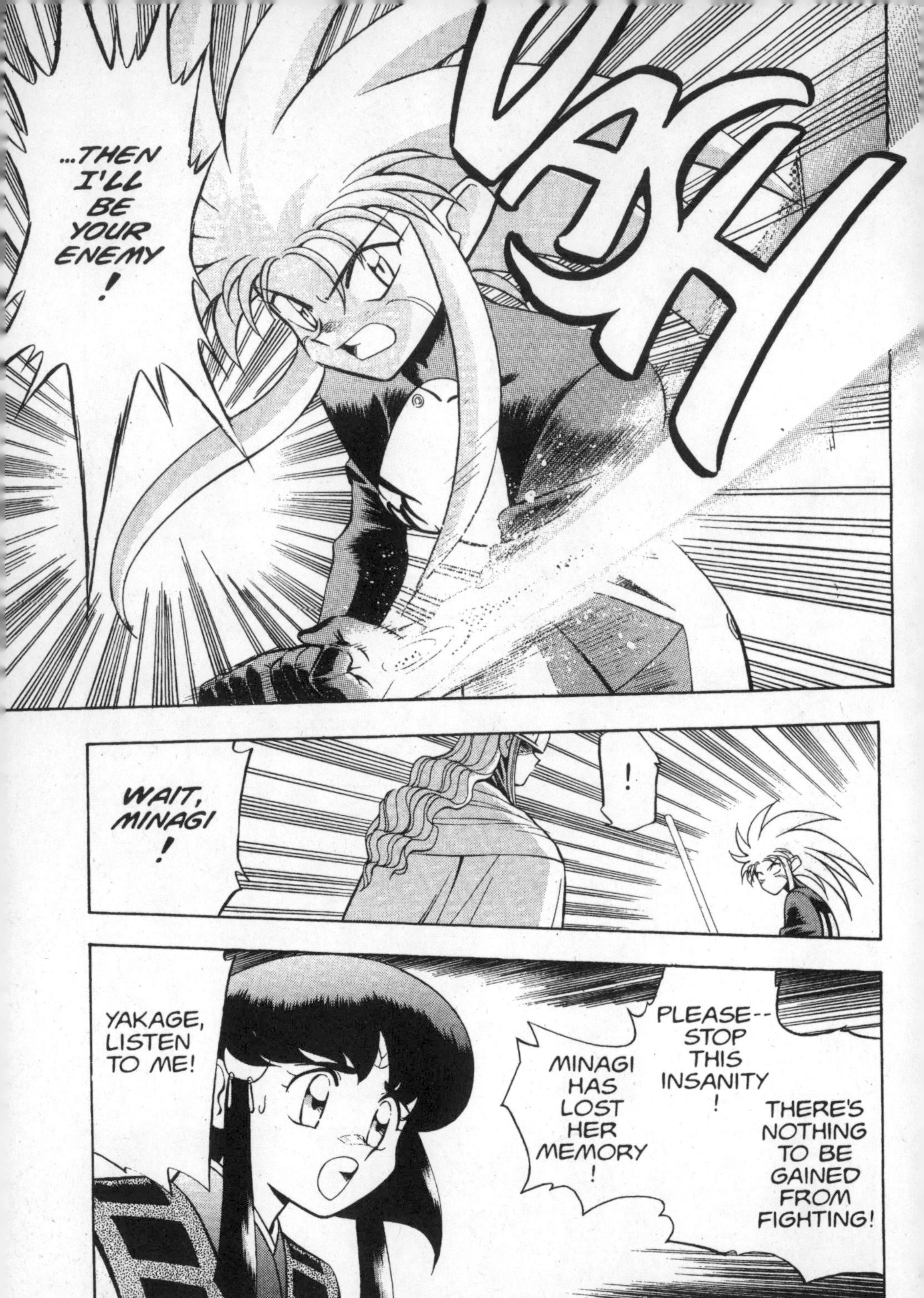
...THEN I'LL BE YOUR ENEMY!
YAAH!
WAIT, MINAGI!
!
YAKAGE, LISTEN TO ME!
MINAGI HAS LOST HER MEMORY!
PLEASE-- STOP THIS INSANITY!
THERE'S NOTHING TO BE GAINED FROM FIGHTING!

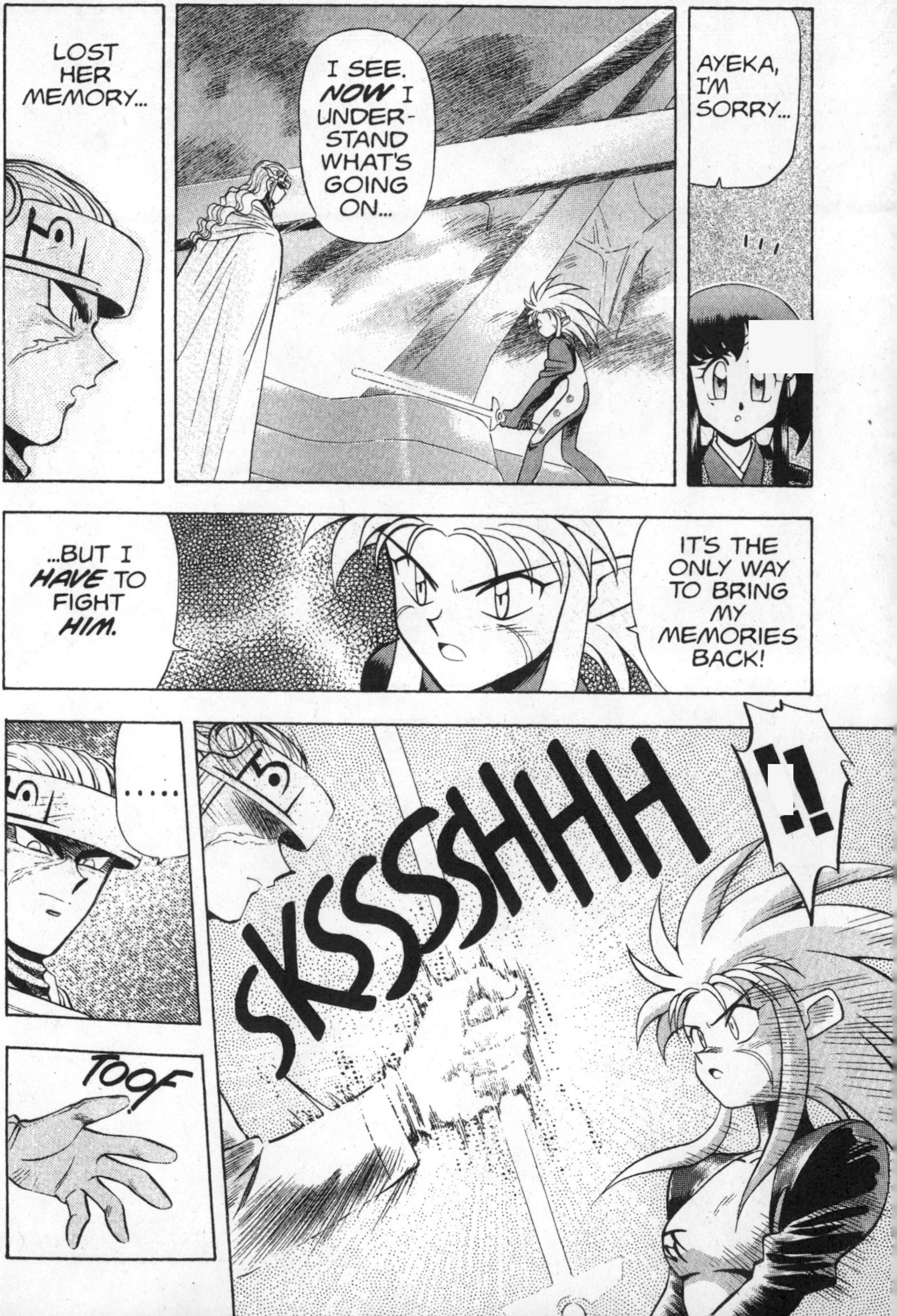
LOST HER MEMORY...
I SEE. NOW I UNDERSTAND WHAT'S GOING ON...
AYEKA, I'M SORRY...
...BUT I HAVE TO FIGHT HIM.
IT'S THE ONLY WAY TO BRING MY MEMORIES BACK!
.....
SKSSSHHH
!!
TOOF

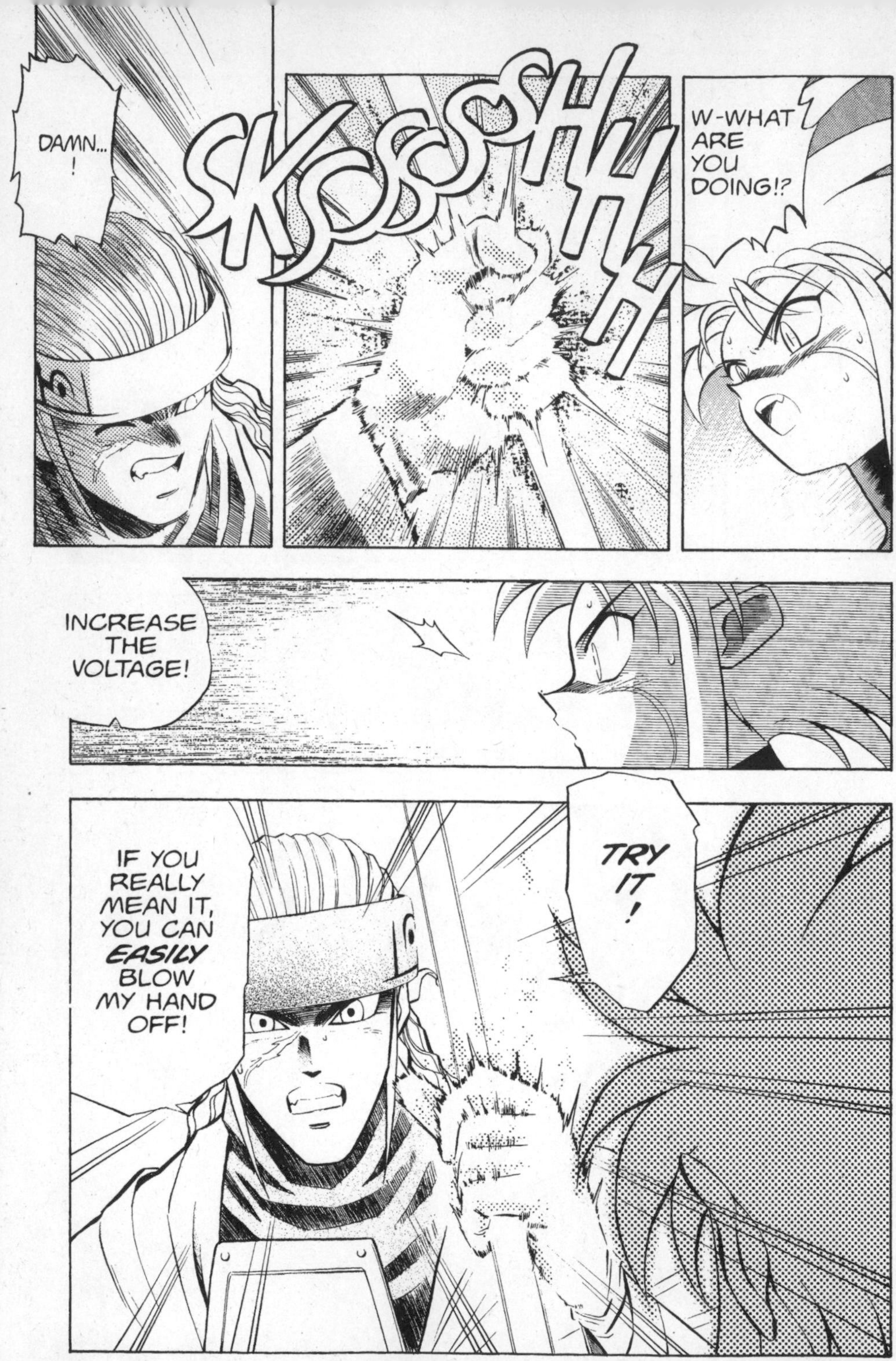
DAMN... !
SKSSSHH
W-WHAT ARE YOU DOING!?
INCREASE THE VOLTAGE!
IF YOU REALLY MEAN IT, YOU CAN EASILY BLOW MY HAND OFF!
TRY IT!

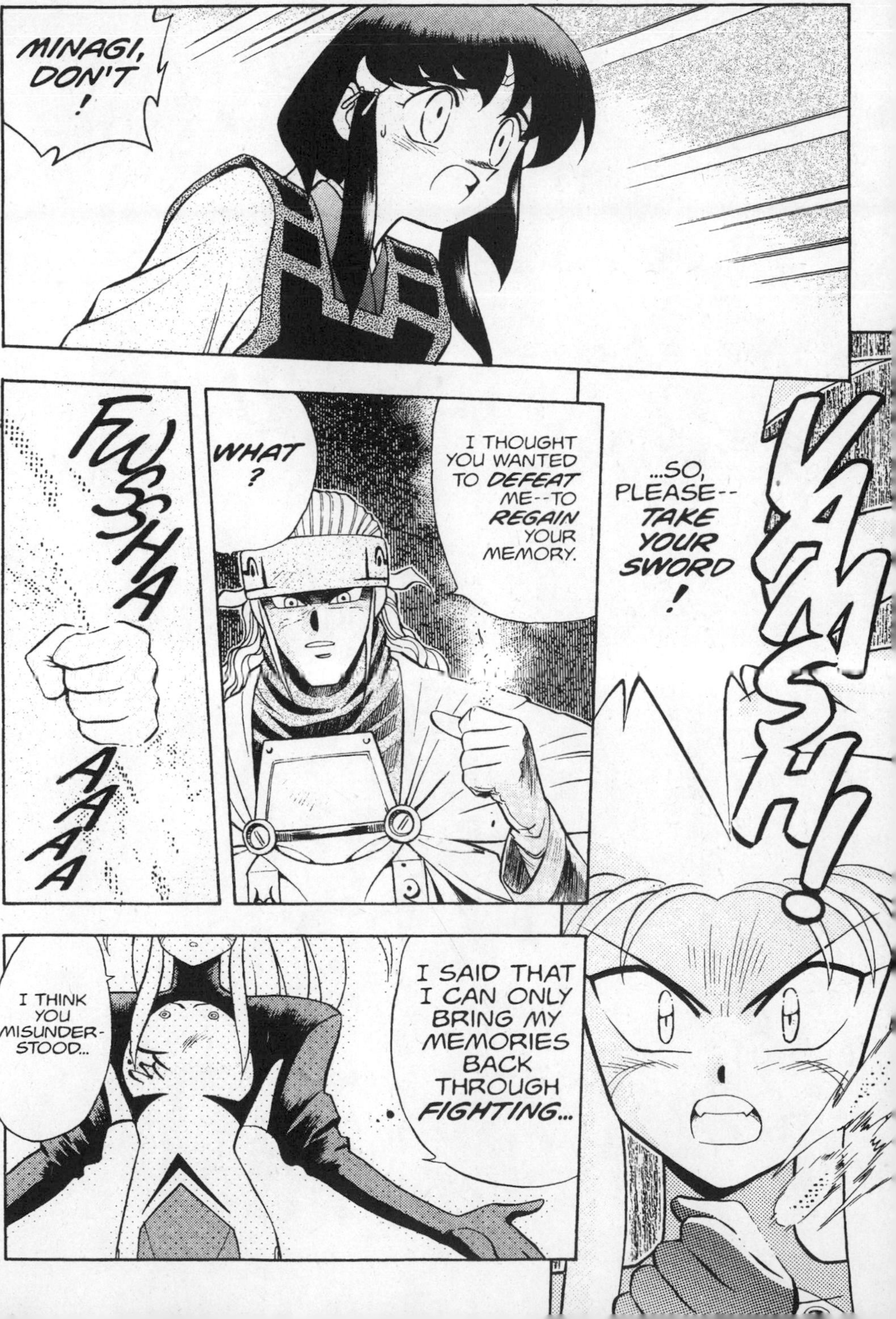
MINAGI, DON'T!
FUSSHAAAAA
WHAT?
I THOUGHT YOU WANTED TO DEFEAT ME--TO REGAIN YOUR MEMORY.
...SO, PLEASE--TAKE YOUR SWORD!
YAMSH!
I THINK YOU MISUNDERSTOOD...
I SAID THAT I CAN ONLY BRING MY MEMORIES BACK THROUGH FIGHTING...

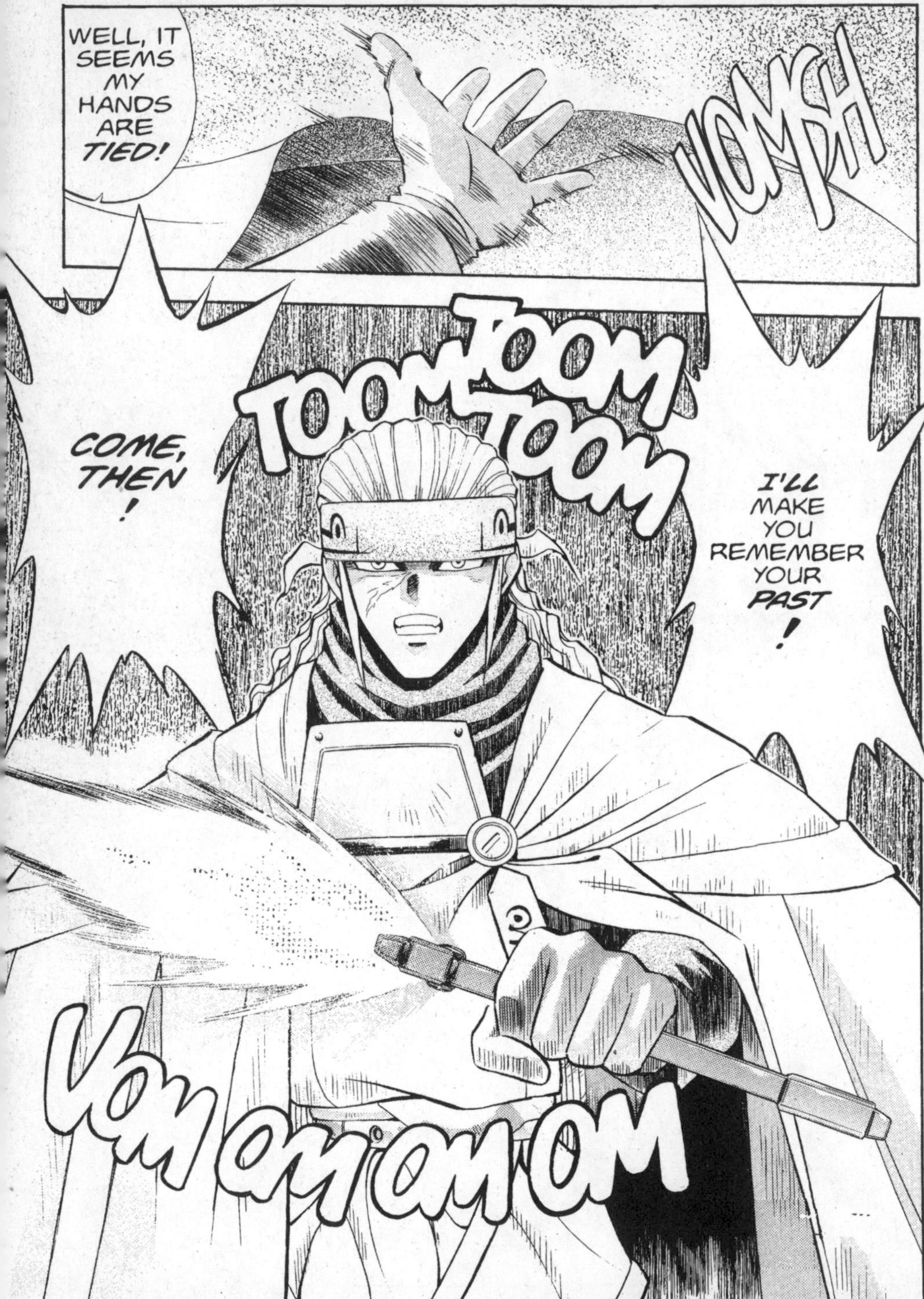
WELL, IT SEEMS MY HANDS ARE TIED!
VOMSH
TOOM TOOM TOOM TOOM
COME, THEN!
I'LL MAKE YOU REMEMBER YOUR PAST!
VOM OM OM OM OM

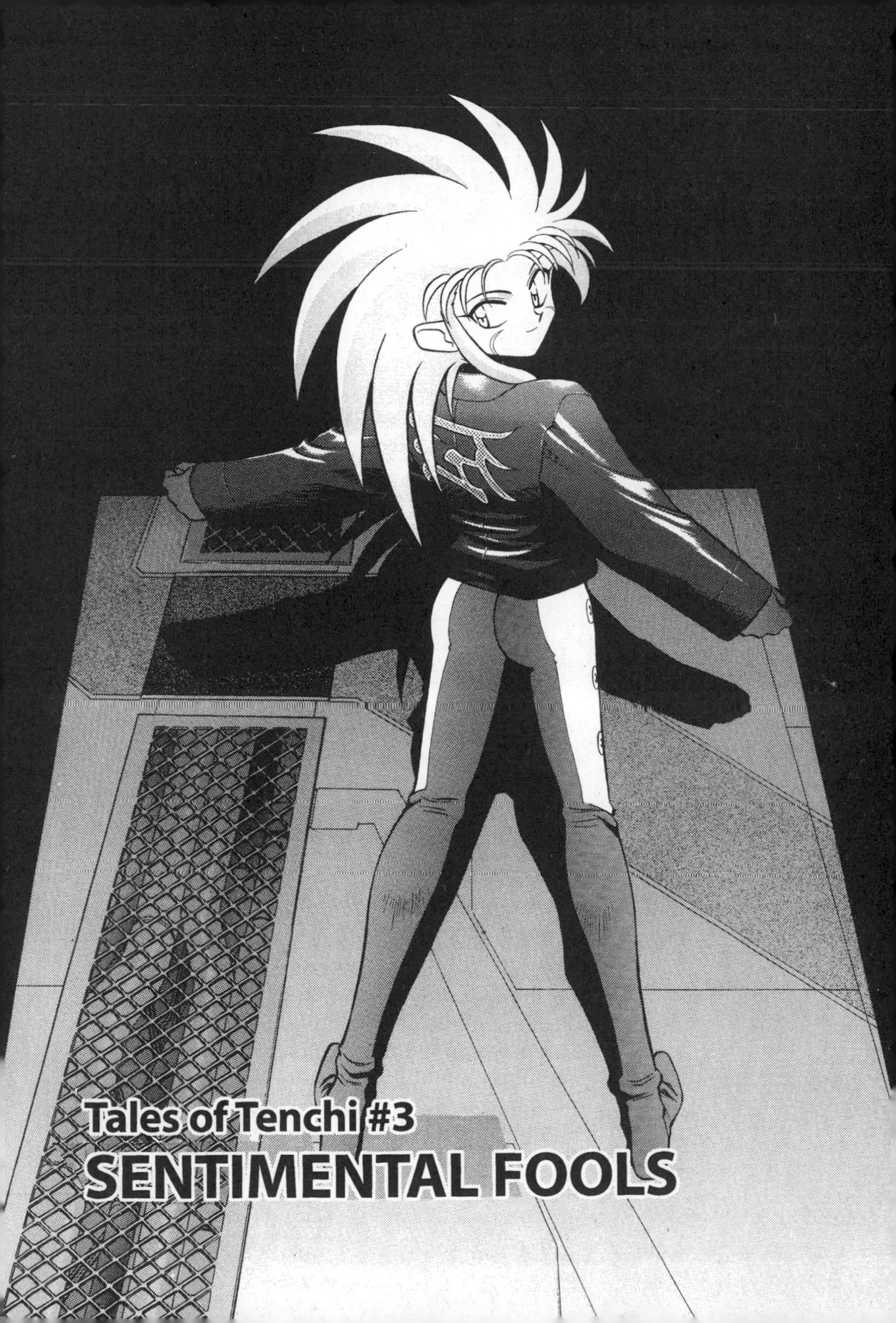
Tales of Tenchi #3
SENTIMENTAL FOOLS

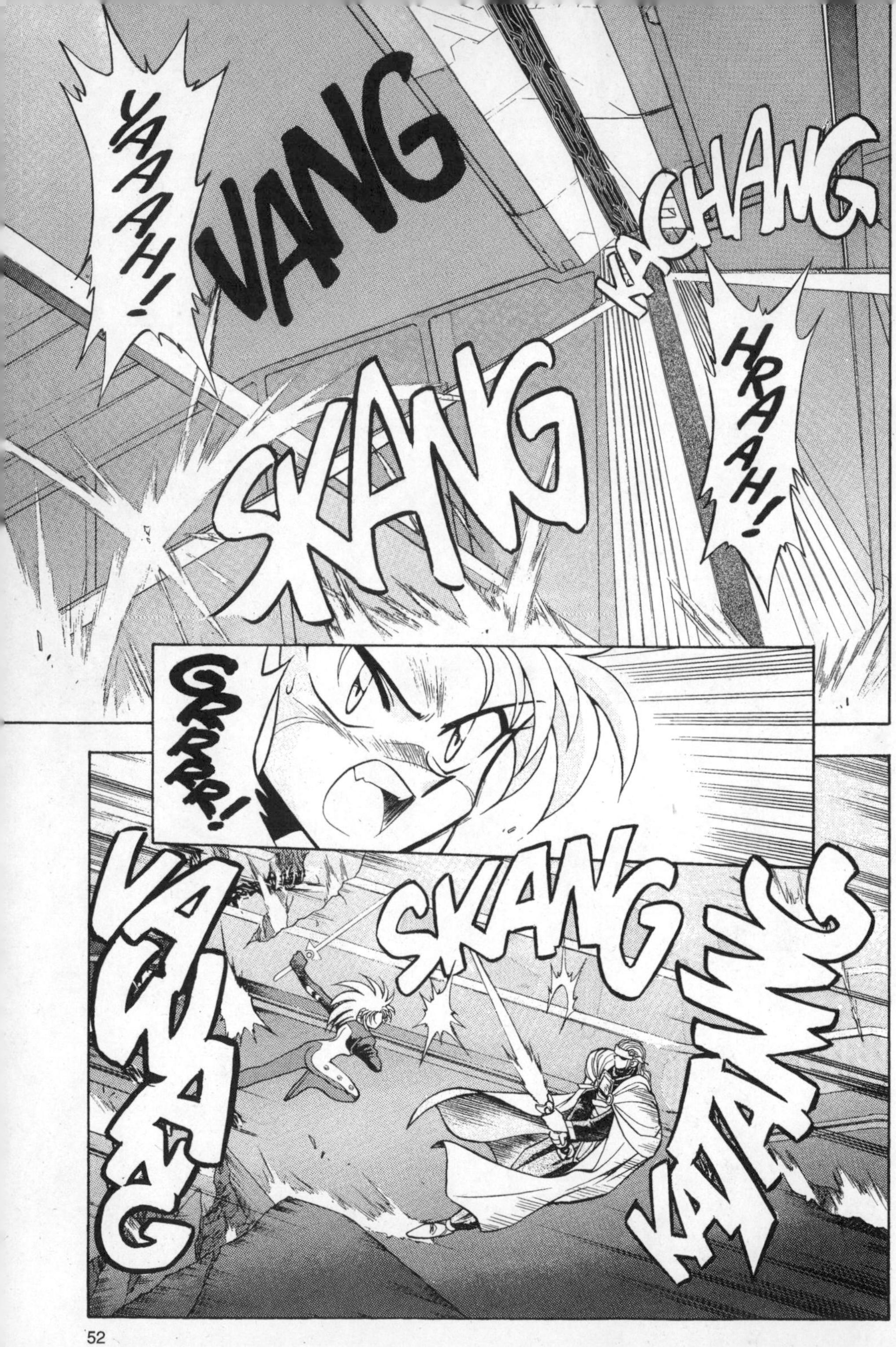
YAAAH!
VANG
KACHANG
SKANG
HRAAAH!
GRRRR!
VAVARAG
SKANG
KAVANG

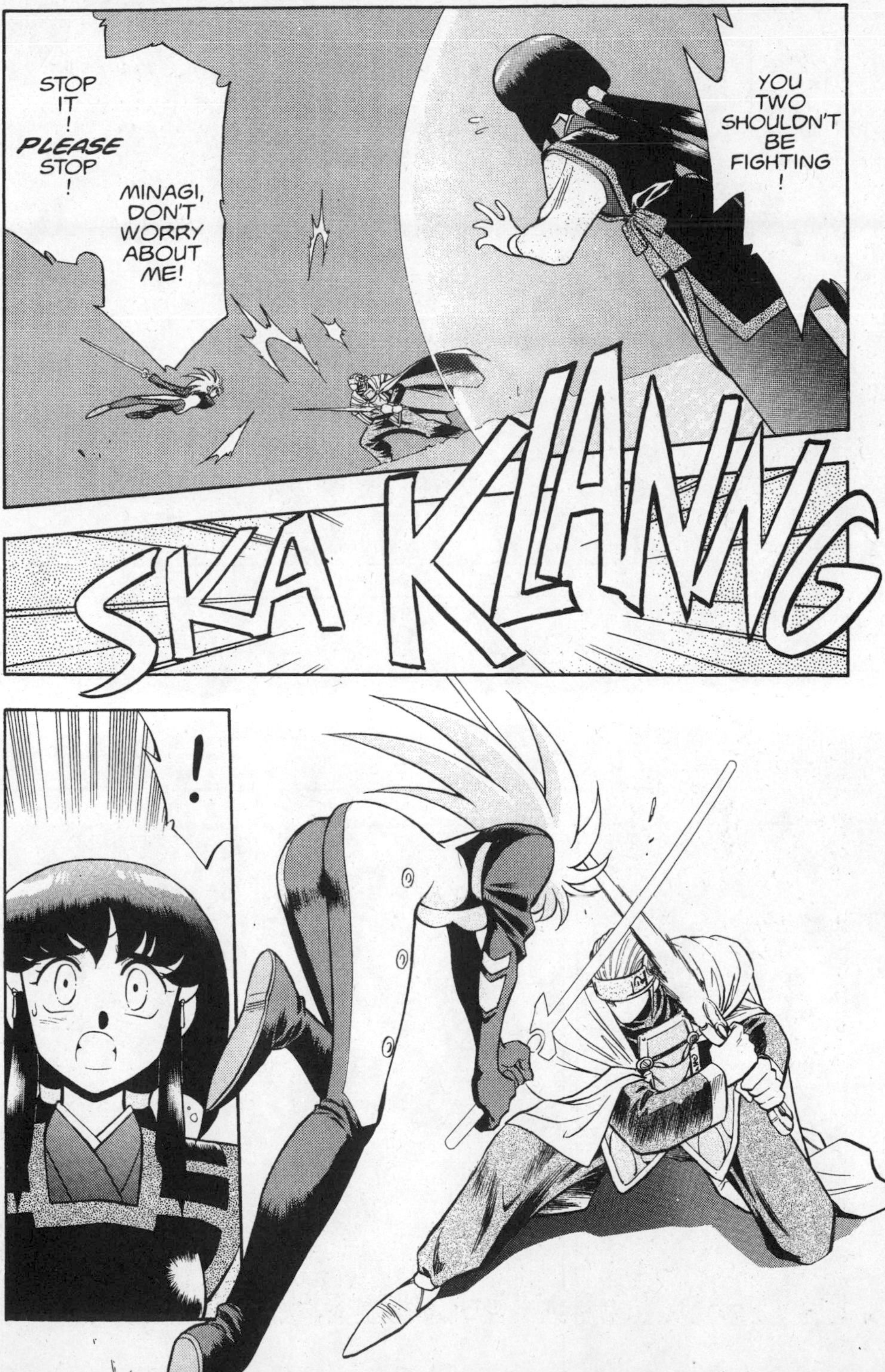
STOP IT! PLEASE STOP!
MINAGI, DON'T WORRY ABOUT ME!
YOU TWO SHOULDN'T BE FIGHTING!
SKA KLLANNG
!

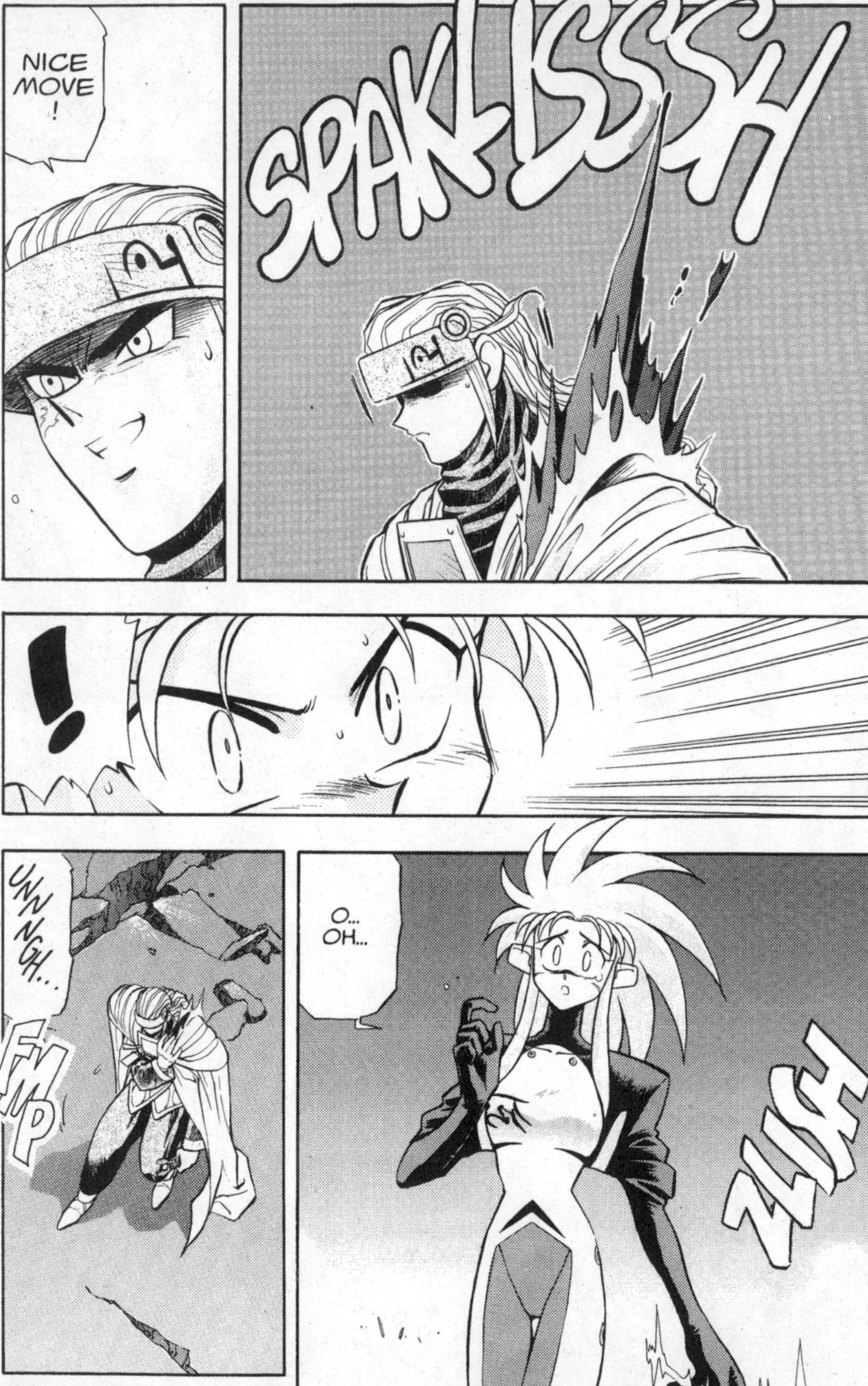
NICE MOVE !
SPAKLISSSH
!
UNNNGH...
FMP
O... OH...
ZLISH

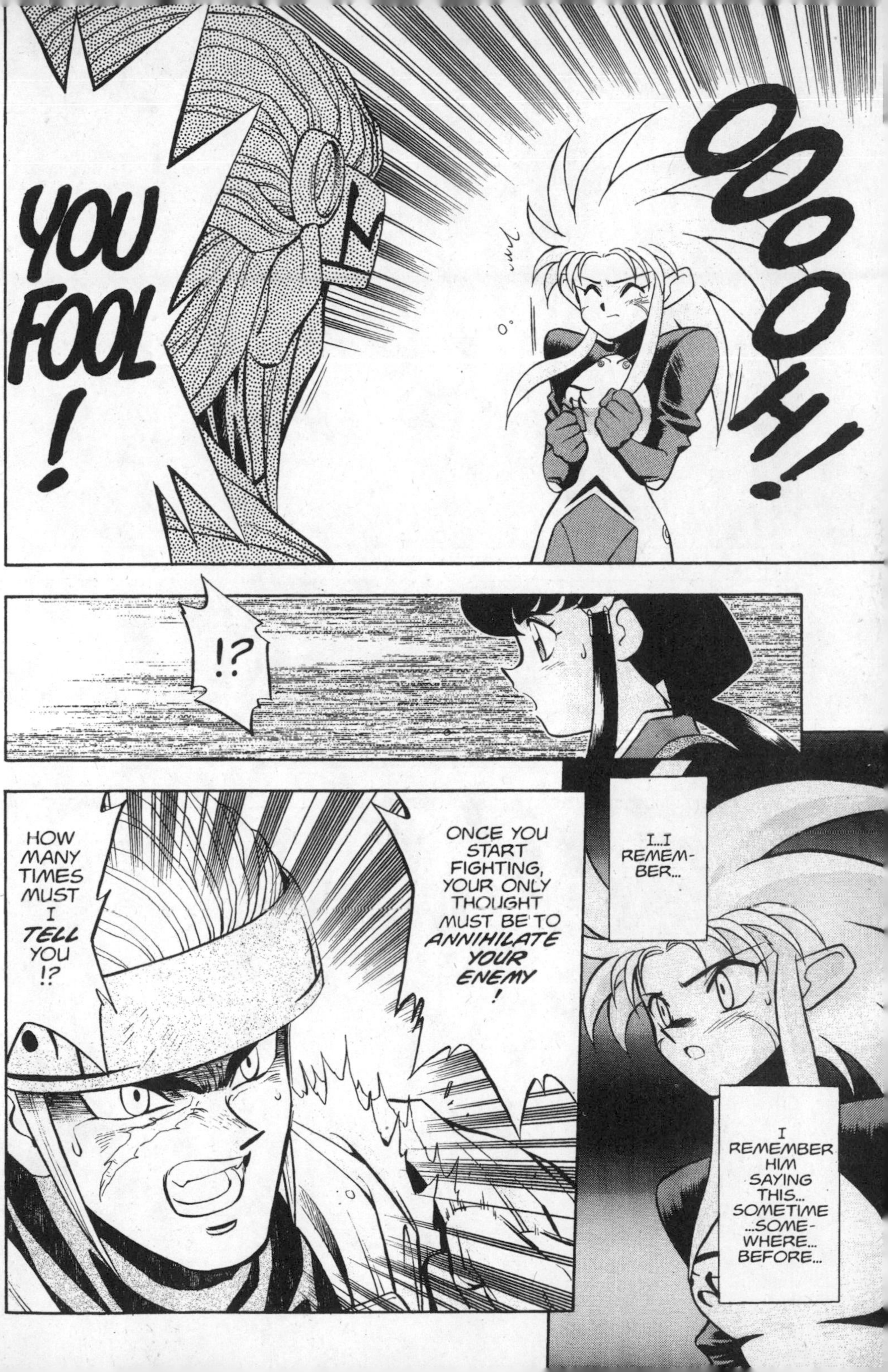
YOU FOOL!
OOOOOH!!
!?
HOW MANY TIMES MUST I TELL YOU!?
ONCE YOU START FIGHTING, YOUR ONLY THOUGHT MUST BE TO ANNIHILATE YOUR ENEMY!
I...I REMEMBER...
I REMEMBER HIM SAYING THIS... SOMETIME ...SOMEWHERE... BEFORE...

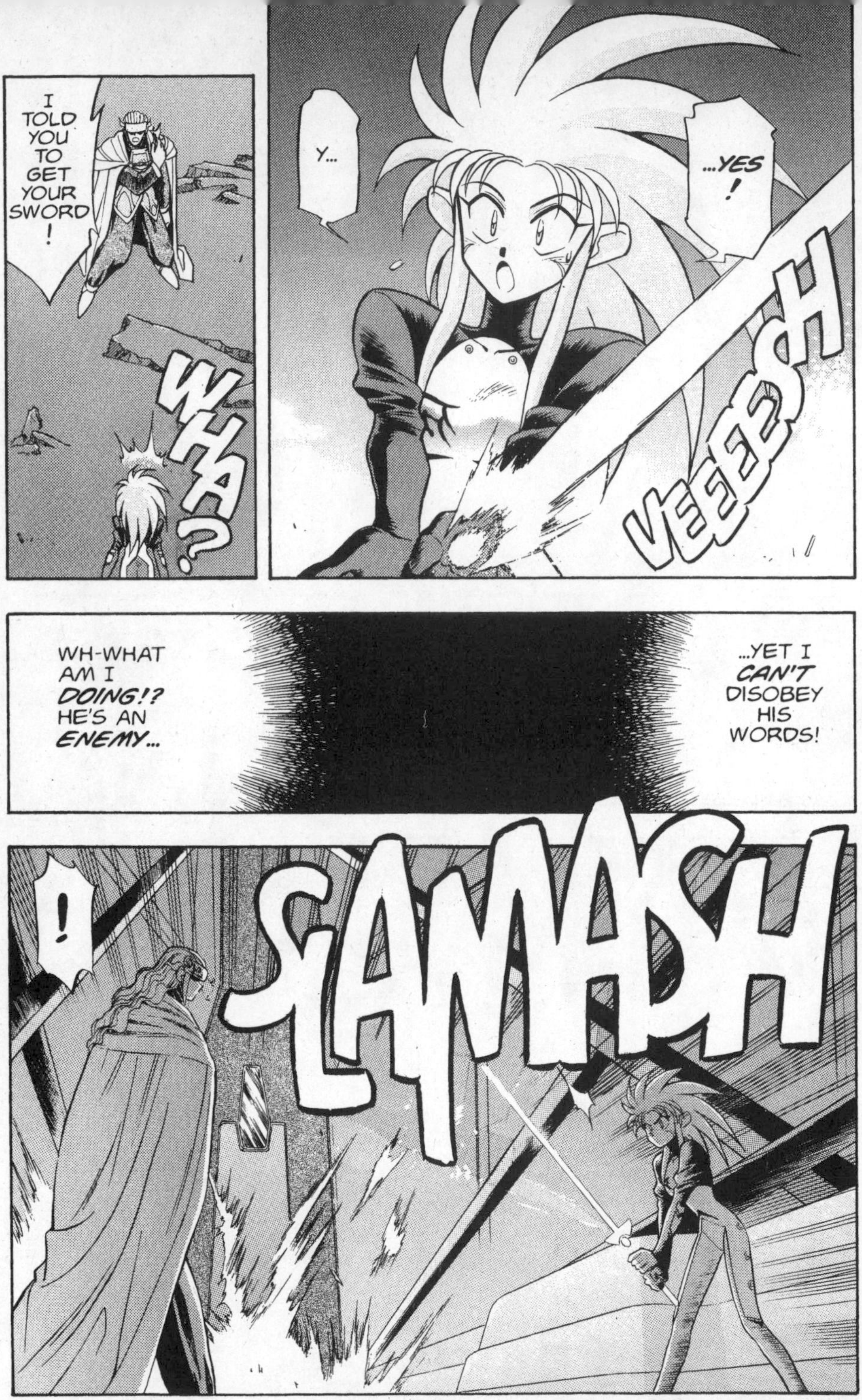

I TOLD YOU TO GET YOUR SWORD!
WHA?
Y...
...YES!
VEEESH
WH-WHAT AM I DOING!? HE'S AN ENEMY...
...YET I CAN'T DISOBEY HIS WORDS!
!
SMASH

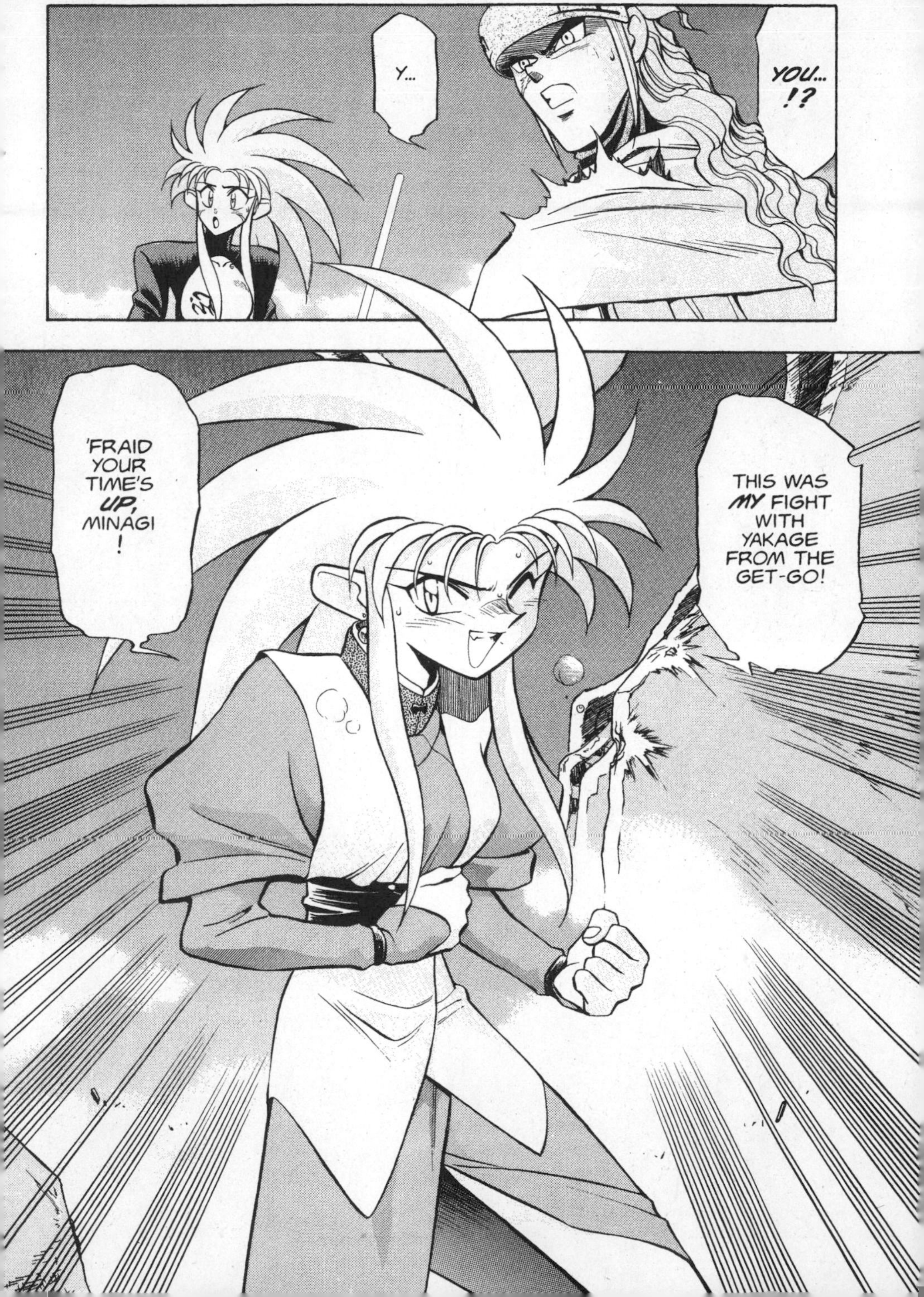
Y...
YOU... !?
'FRAID YOUR TIME'S UP, MINAGI !
THIS WAS MY FIGHT WITH YAKAGE FROM THE GET-GO!

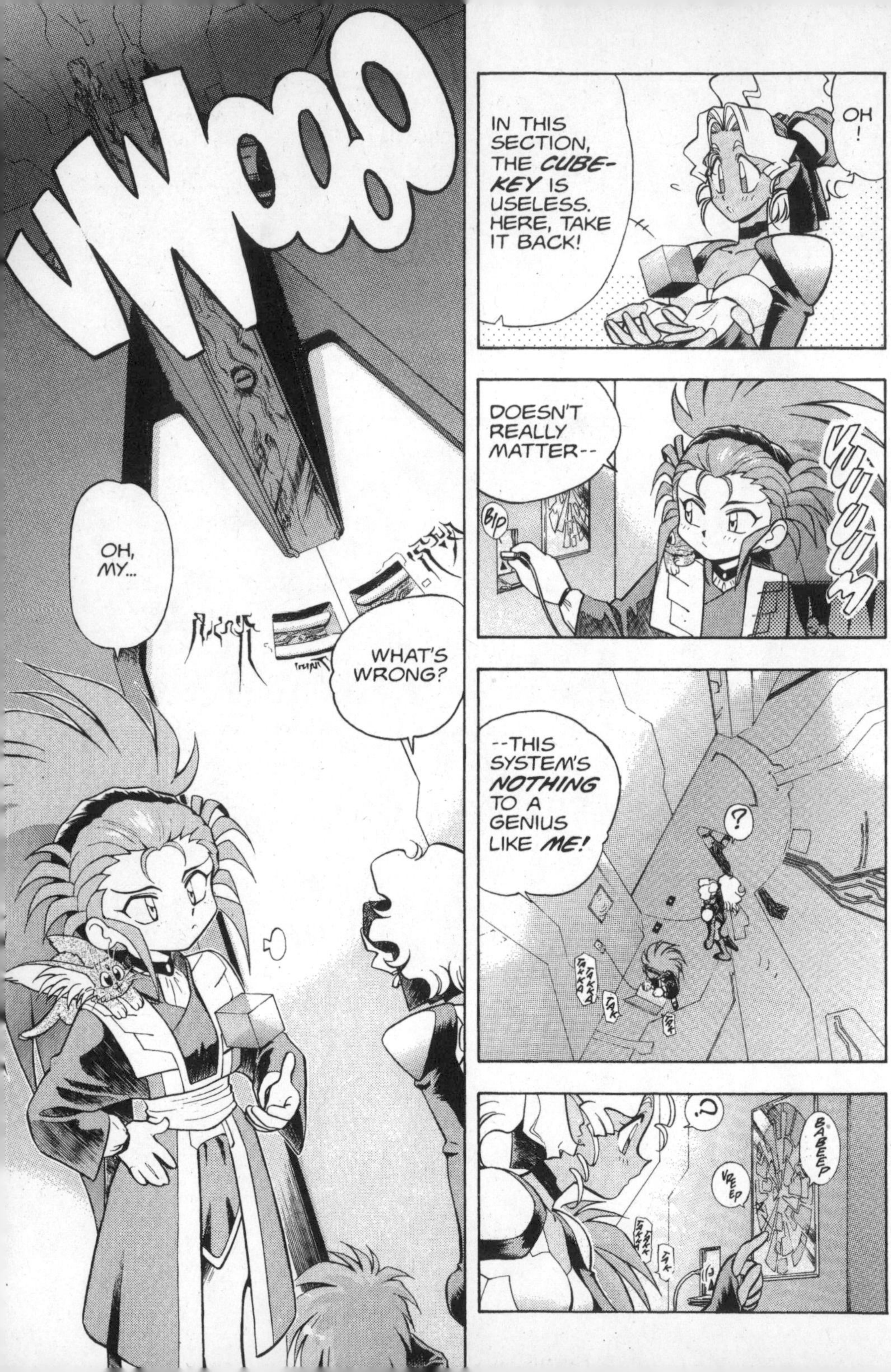
VWOOO
OH, MY...
WHAT'S WRONG?
IN THIS SECTION, THE *CUBE-KEY* IS USELESS. HERE, TAKE IT BACK!
OH!
DOESN'T REALLY MATTER--
BIP
VUUUUUM
--THIS SYSTEM'S *NOTHING* TO A GENIUS LIKE *ME!*
?
?
BABEEP
VREEP

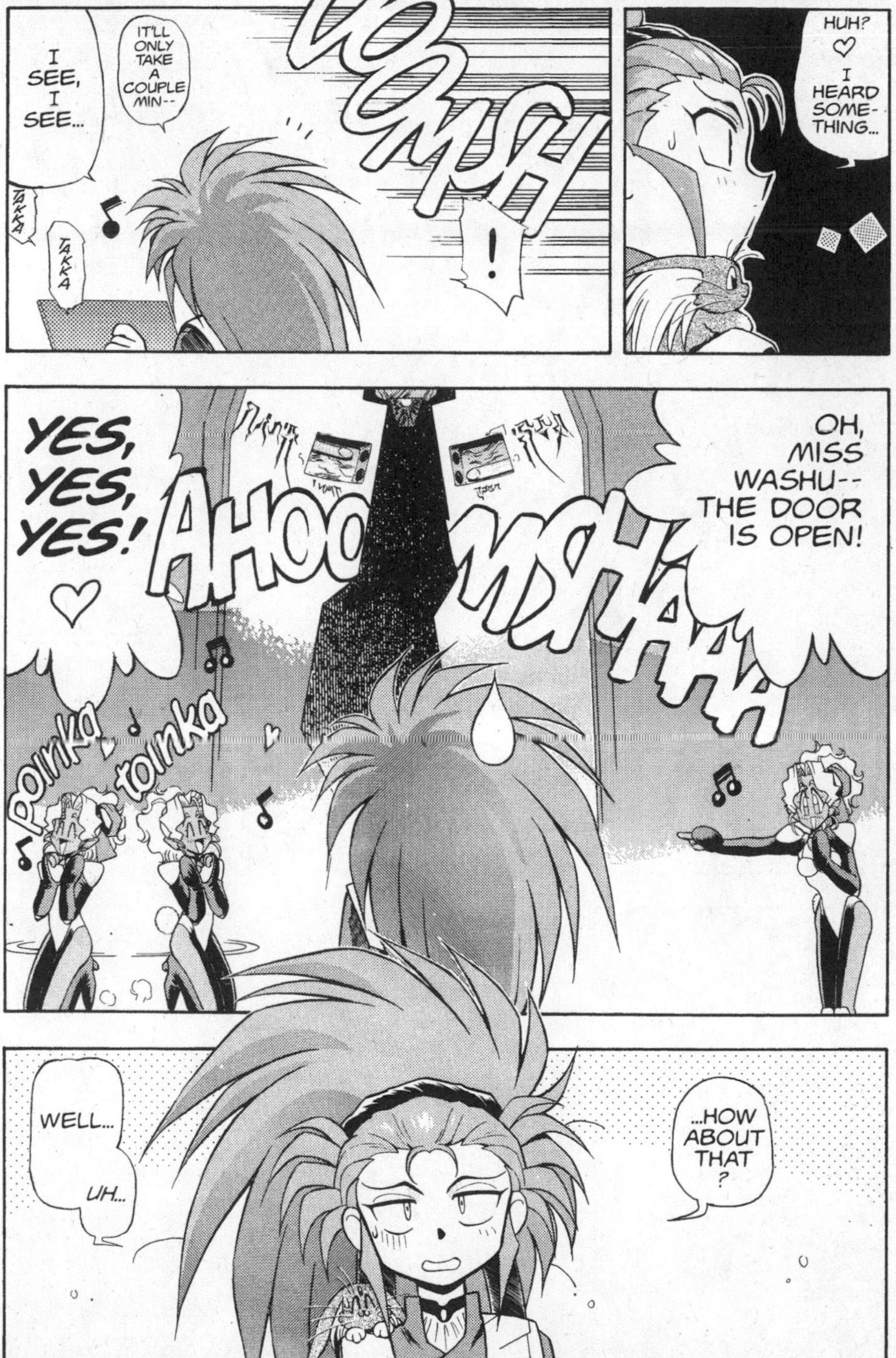
I SEE, I SEE...
IT'LL ONLY TAKE A COUPLE MIN--
TAKKA
TAKKA
!
HUH? ♡ I HEARD SOMETHING...
YES, YES, YES! ♡
OH, MISS WASHU-- THE DOOR IS OPEN!
WELL...
UH...
...HOW ABOUT THAT ?

HAAH!

VAMOOOSH

DAMN...

OWOW
OW
OW
OW

...I'M STILL FEELING THE DAMAGE FROM *LAST TIME!*

RYOKO! PLEASE LET ME FIGHT!

JUST A BIT MORE... AND I'LL BE ABLE TO REMEM-BER...

...I'LL REMEMBER WHO I AM!

YAAH!

SHACHIK

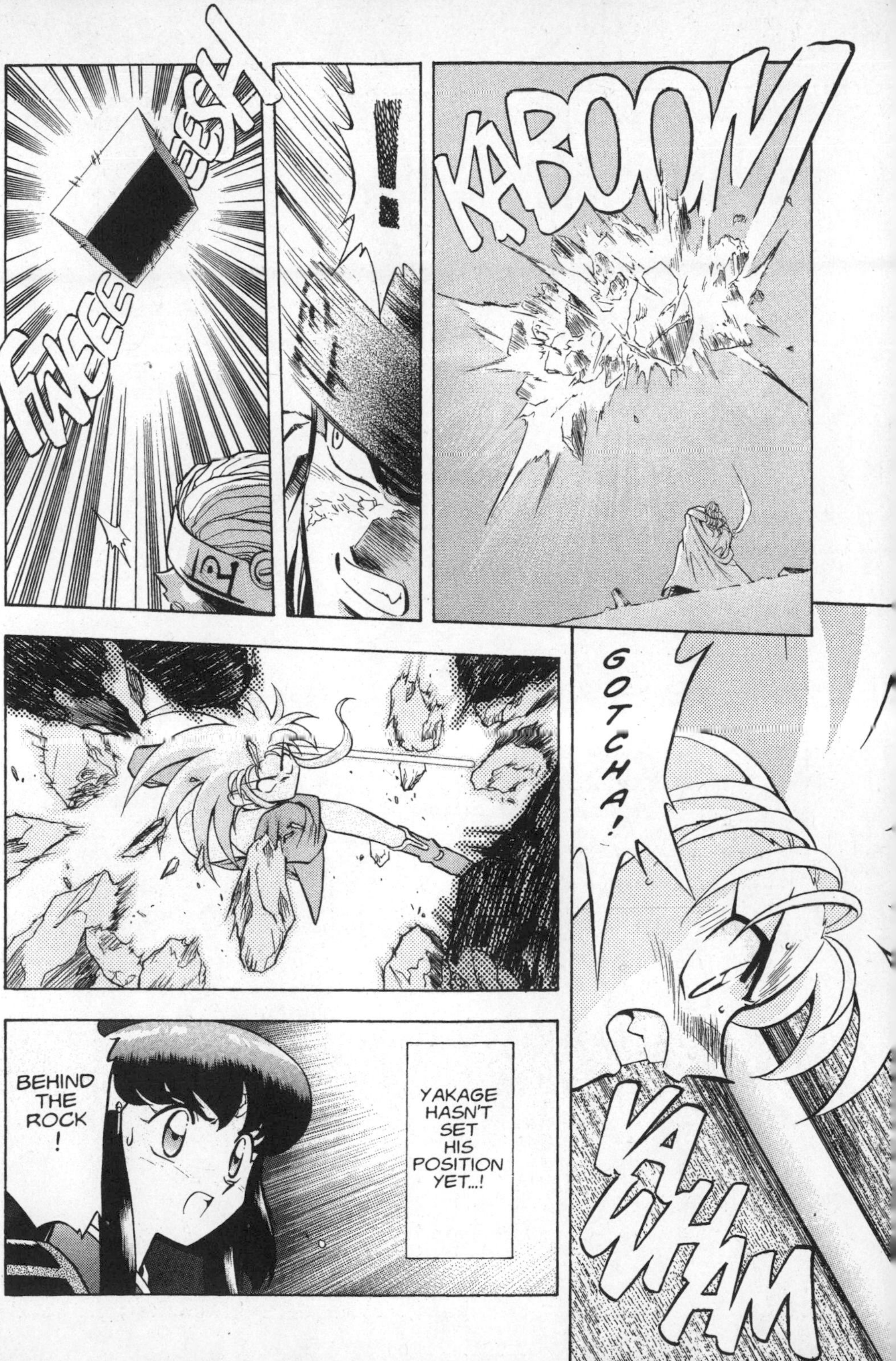
FWEEEESH
!
KABOOM
BEHIND THE ROCK!
YAKAGE HASN'T SET HIS POSITION YET...!
GOTCHA!
VAWHAM

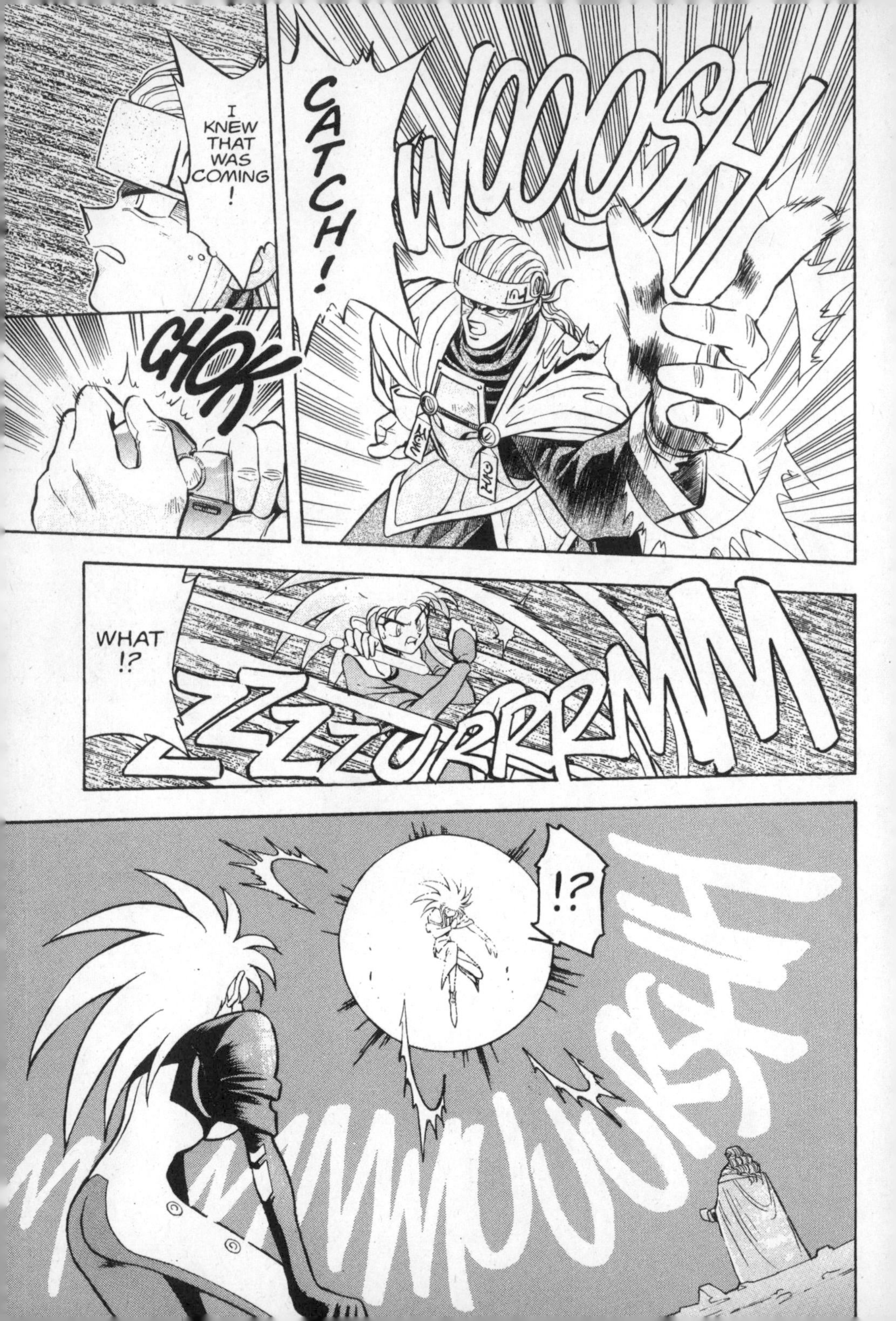

I KNEW THAT WAS COMING!
CHOK
CATCH!
WOOOSH
WHAT!?
ZZZZURRRMMM
!?
MMMMWUUOOSH

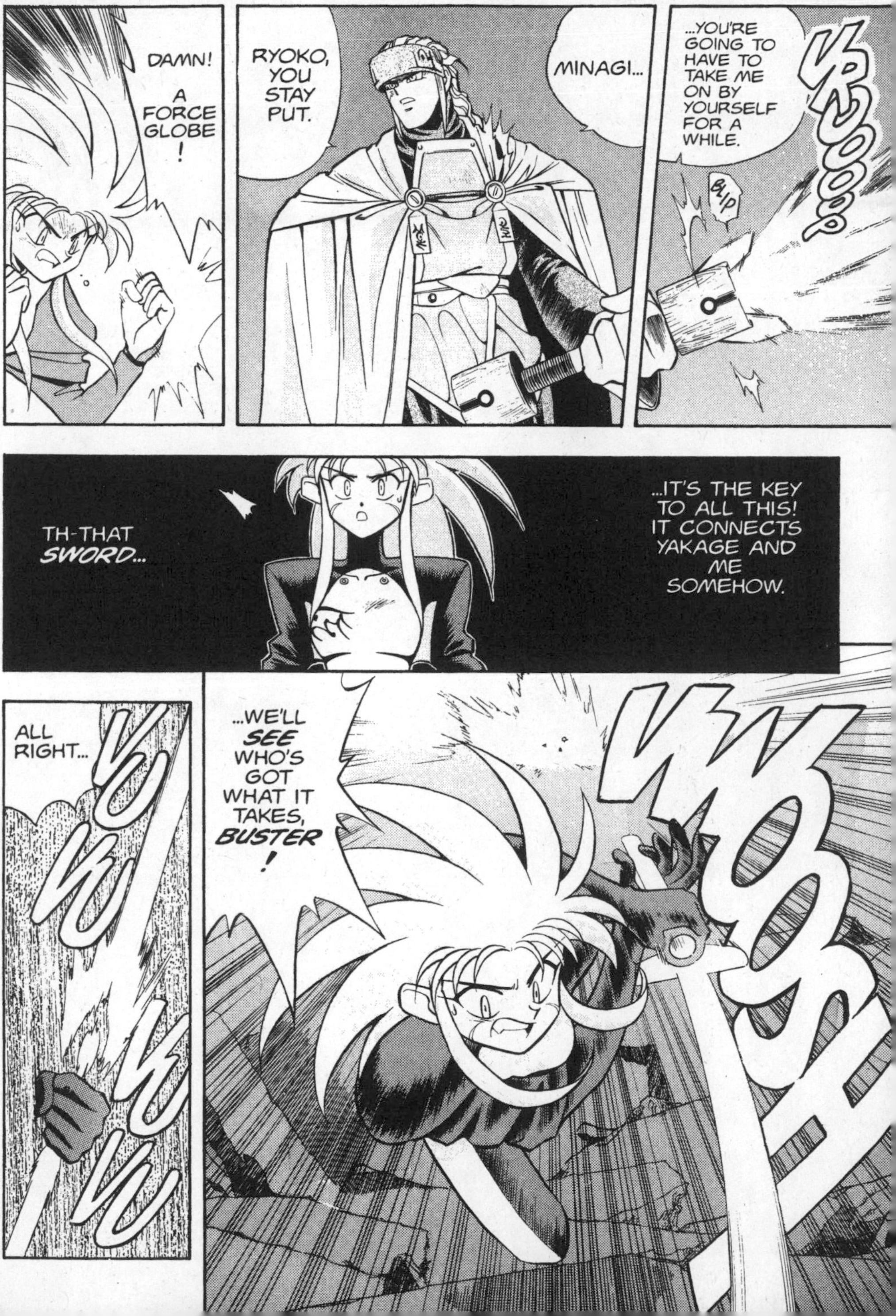
DAMN!
A FORCE GLOBE!
RYOKO, YOU STAY PUT.
MINAGI...
...YOU'RE GOING TO HAVE TO TAKE ME ON BY YOURSELF FOR A WHILE.
BLIP
TH-THAT SWORD...
...IT'S THE KEY TO ALL THIS! IT CONNECTS YAKAGE AND ME SOMEHOW.
ALL RIGHT...
...WE'LL SEE WHO'S GOT WHAT IT TAKES, BUSTER!
WOOSH

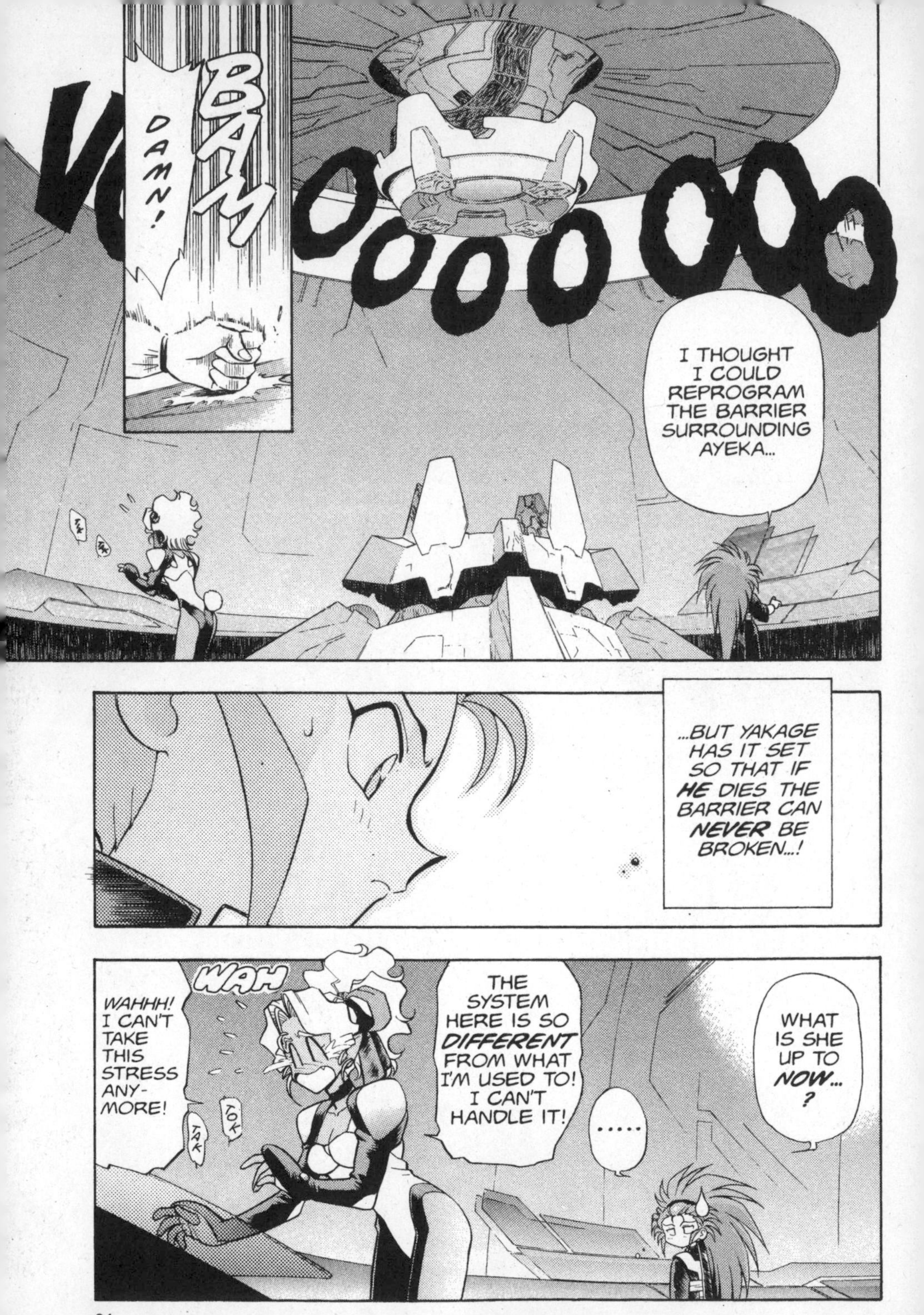
BAM
DAMN!
VOOOOOOOOO
I THOUGHT I COULD REPROGRAM THE BARRIER SURROUNDING AYEKA...
...BUT YAKAGE HAS IT SET SO THAT IF *HE* DIES THE BARRIER CAN *NEVER* BE BROKEN...!
WAH
WAHHH! I CAN'T TAKE THIS STRESS ANY-MORE!
TOK
TAK
THE SYSTEM HERE IS SO *DIFFERENT* FROM WHAT I'M USED TO! I CAN'T HANDLE IT!
......
WHAT IS SHE UP TO *NOW*...?

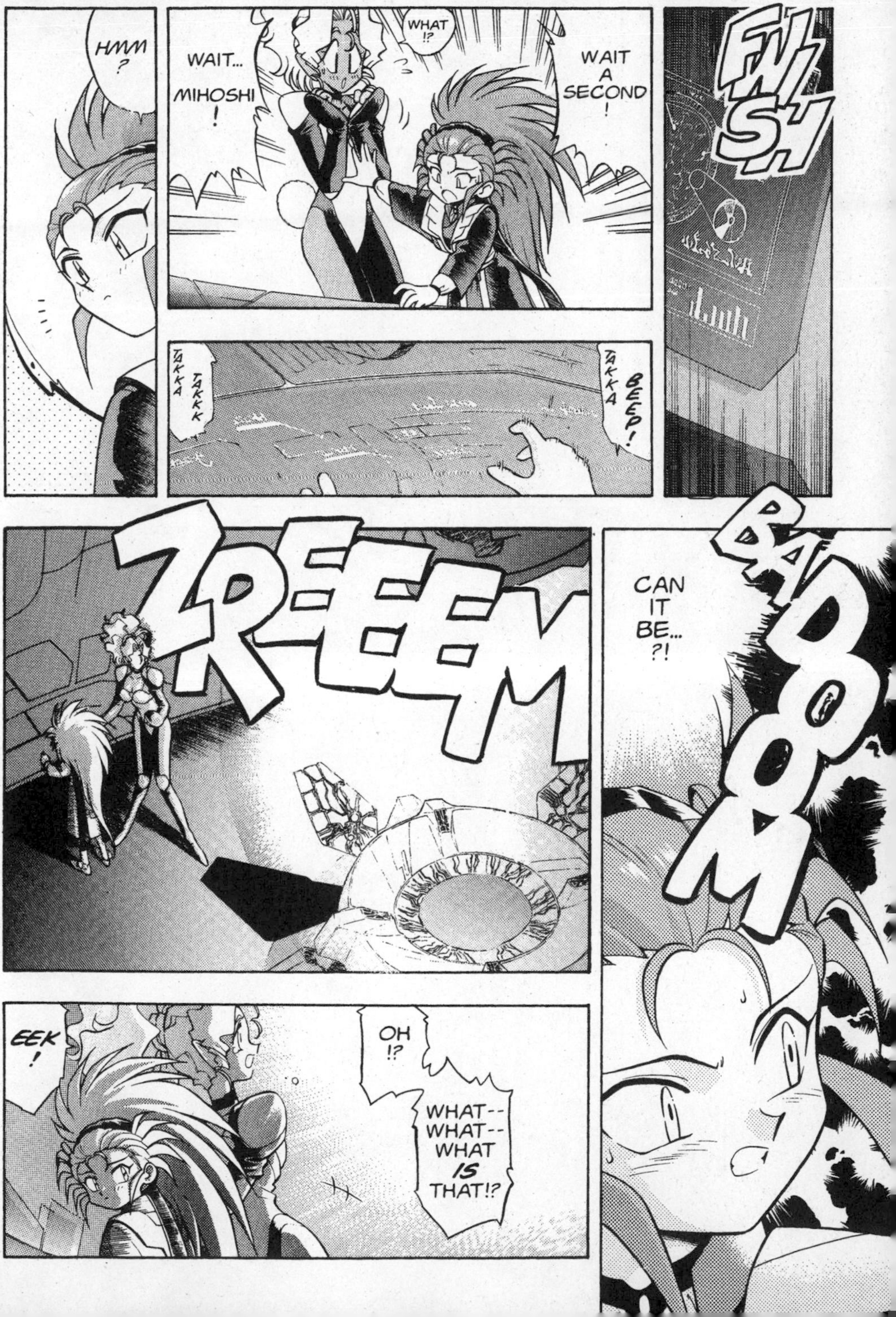
HMM ?
WAIT... MIHOSHI !
WHAT !?
WAIT A SECOND !
FWISH
TAKKA TAKKK
TAKKA BEEP!
ZREEEEM
CAN IT BE... ?!
BADOOM
EEK !
OH !?
WHAT-- WHAT-- WHAT IS THAT!?

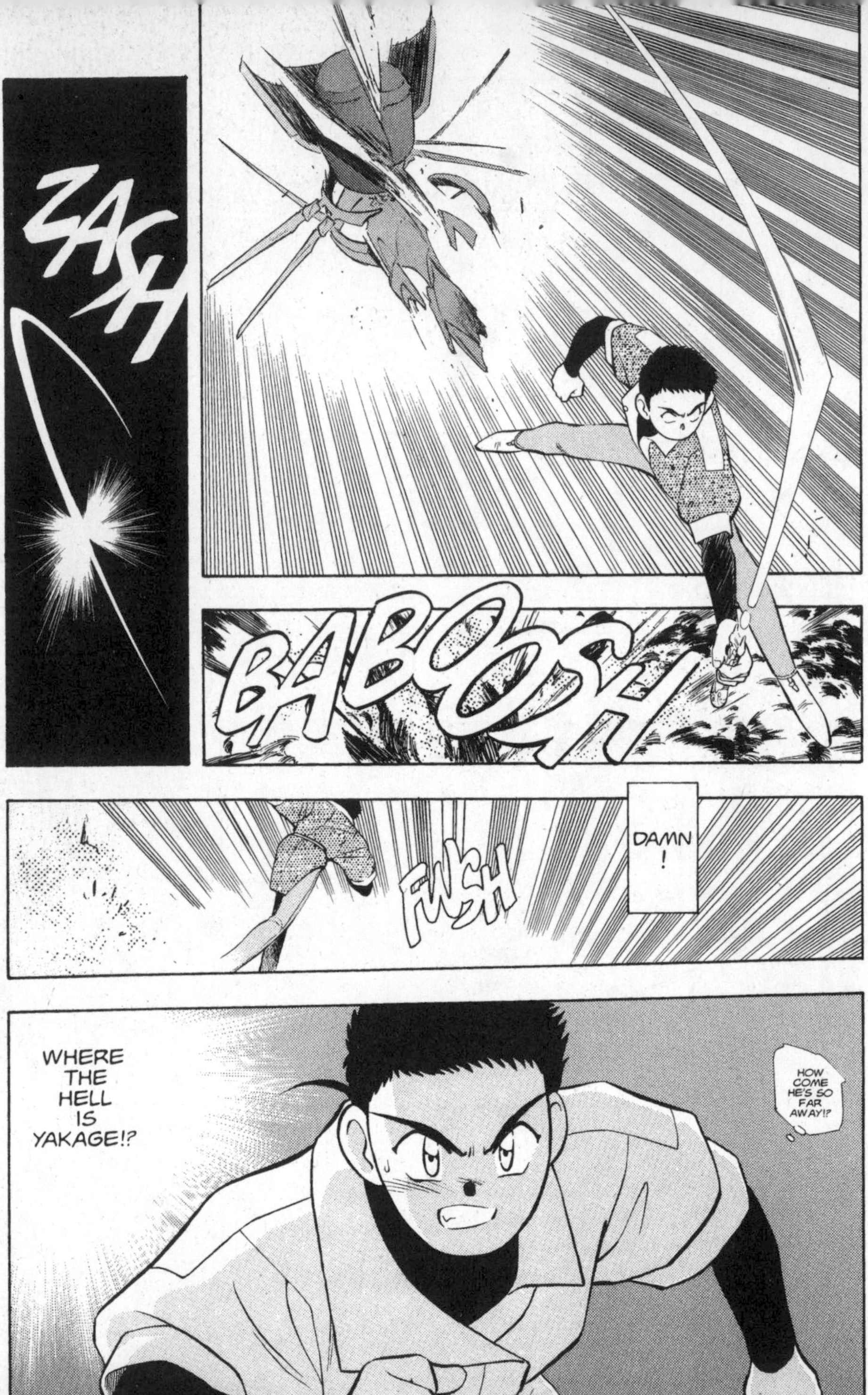
ZASH
BABOOSH
FWSH
DAMN!
WHERE THE HELL IS YAKAGE!?
HOW COME HE'S SO FAR AWAY!?

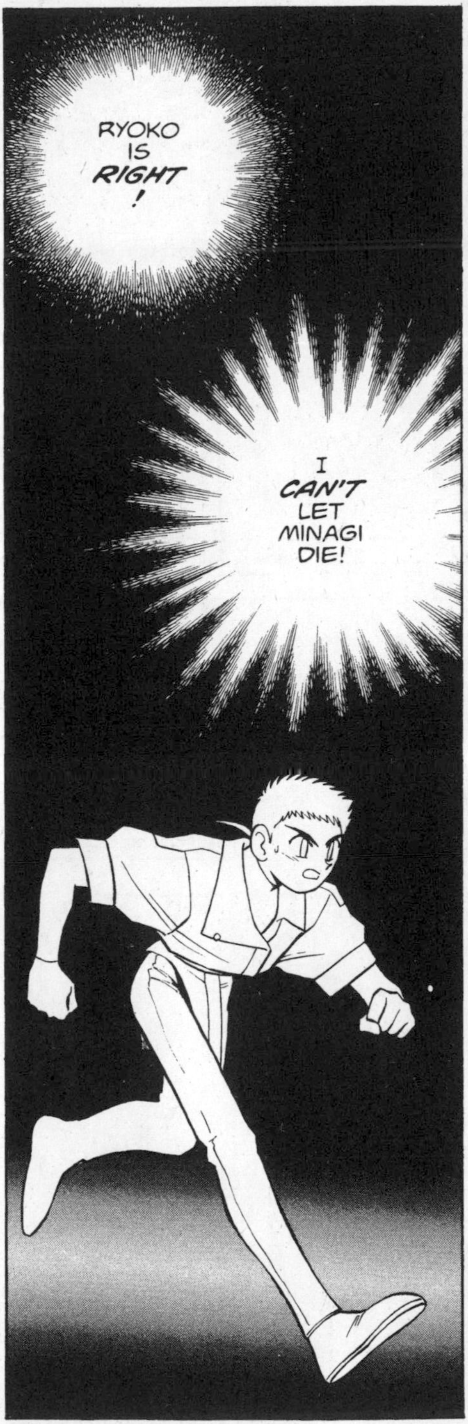
RYOKO IS *RIGHT*!
I *CAN'T* LET MINAGI DIE!
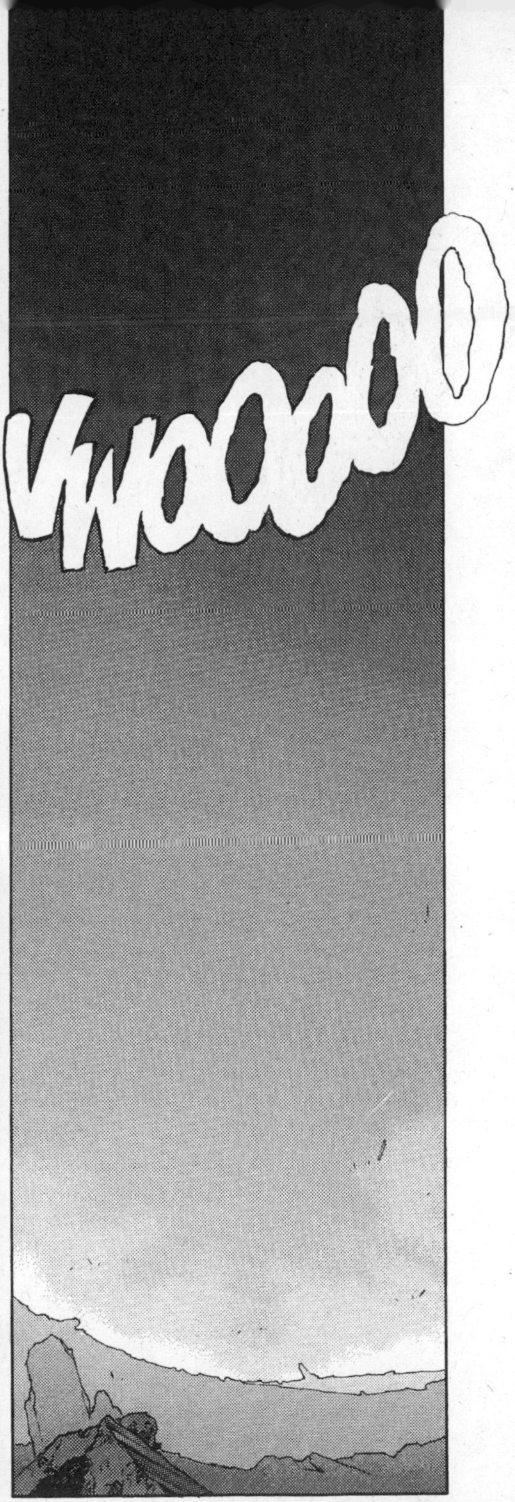
VWOOOOO

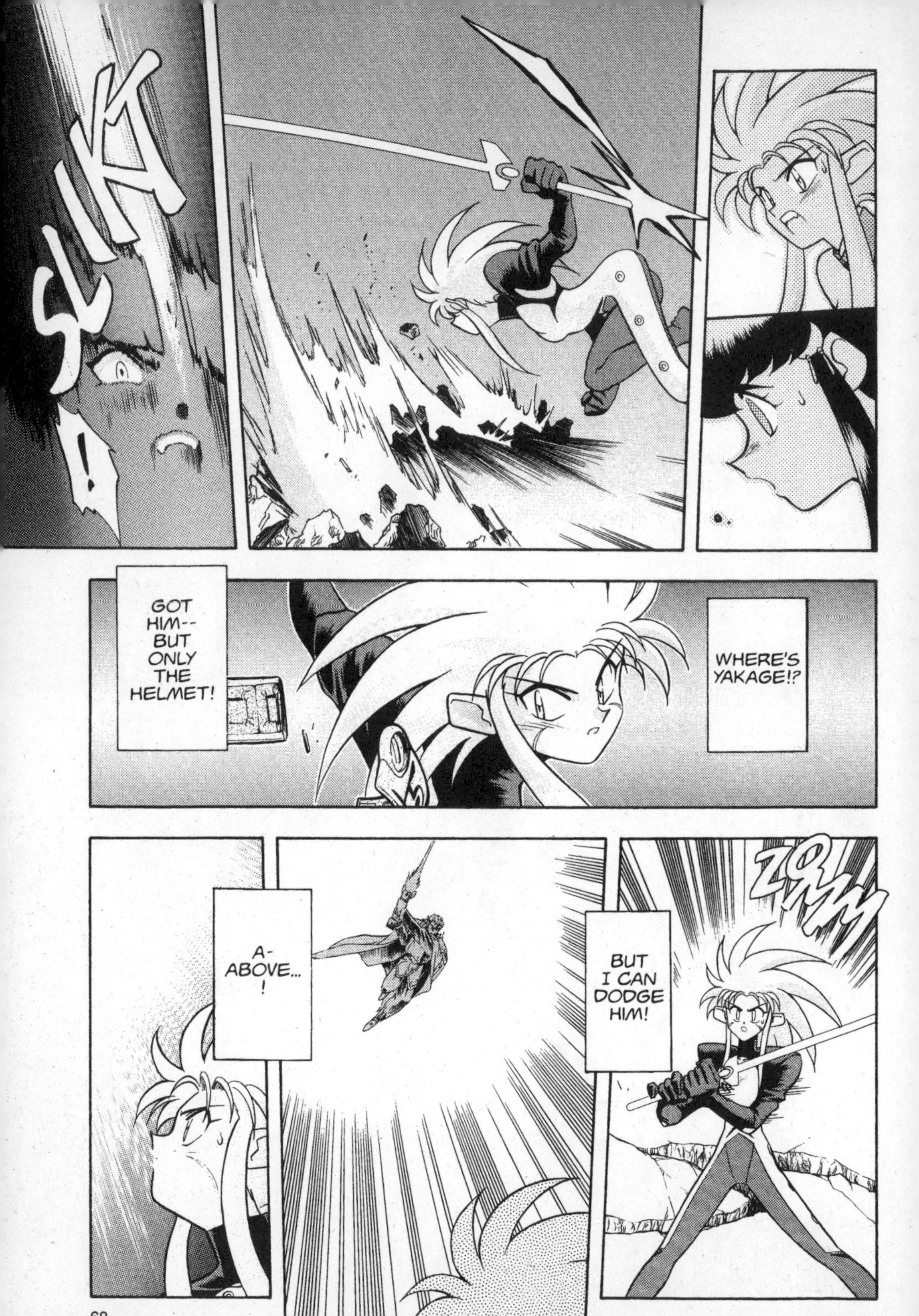
SLIKT
!
GOT HIM-- BUT ONLY THE HELMET!
WHERE'S YAKAGE!?
A- ABOVE... !
ZOOM
BUT I CAN DODGE HIM!
!

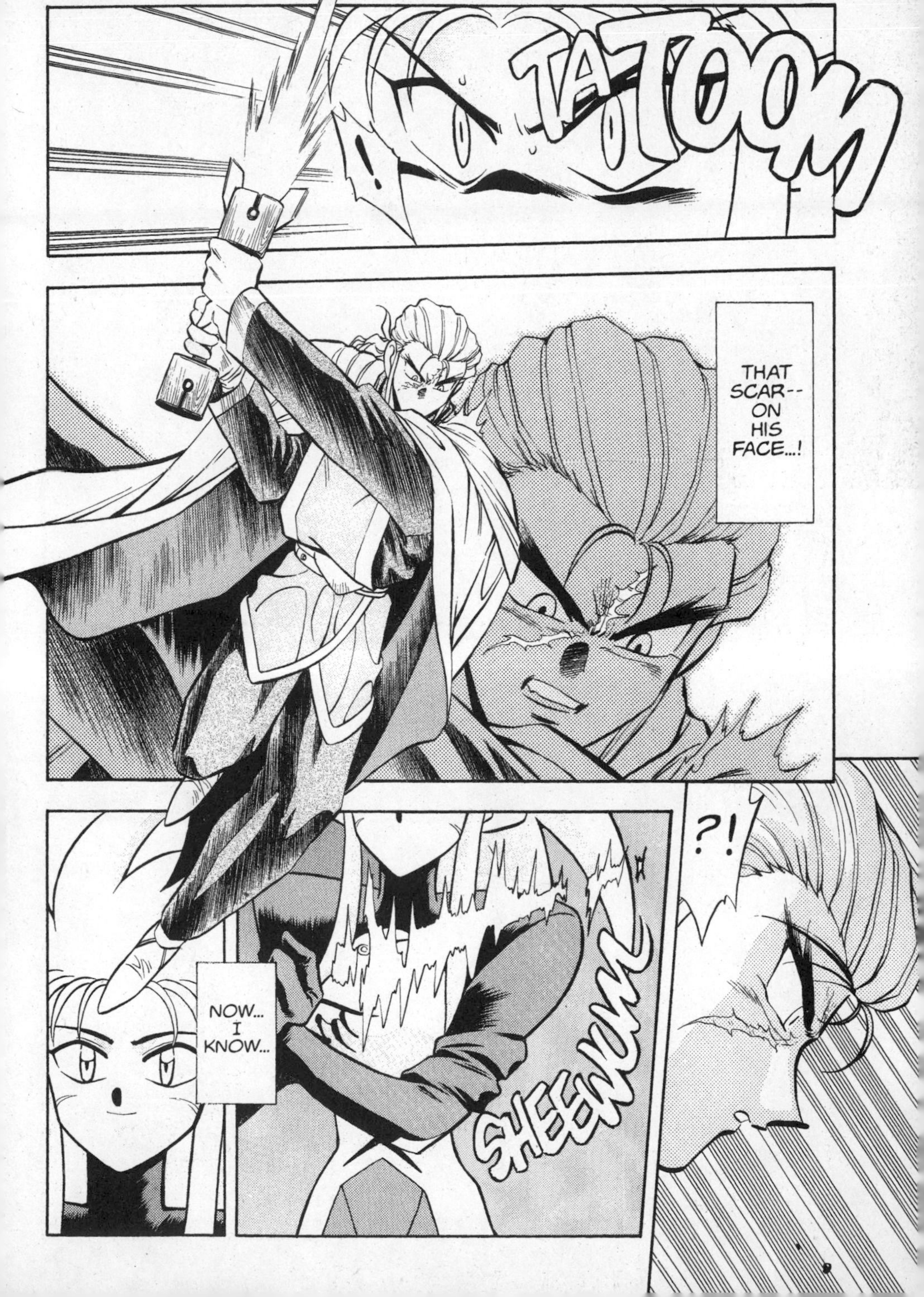
TATOOM
THAT SCAR-- ON HIS FACE...!
NOW... I KNOW...
?!
SHEEWWW

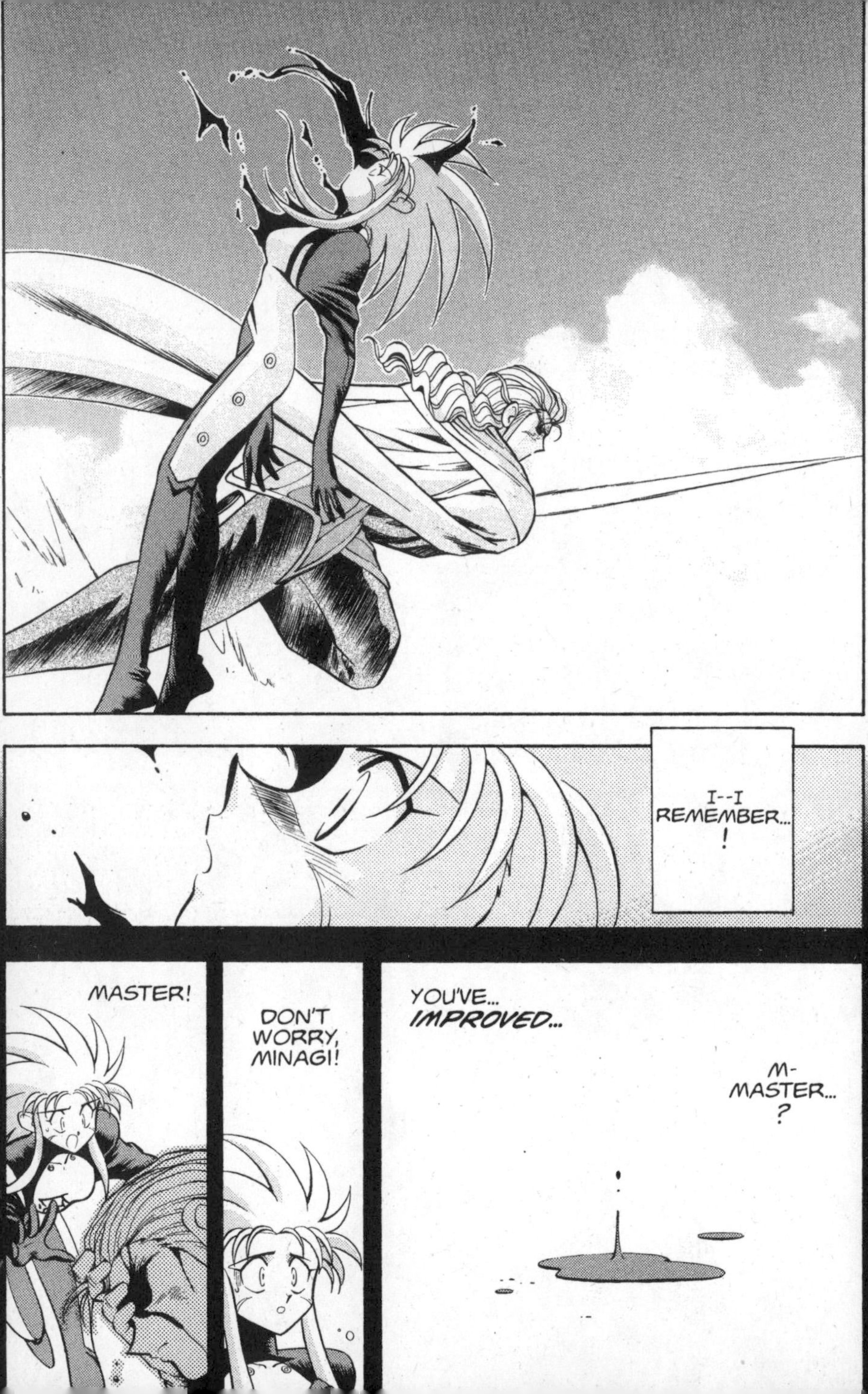
I--I REMEMBER...!
MASTER!
DON'T WORRY, MINAGI!
YOU'VE... *IMPROVED*...
M-MASTER...?

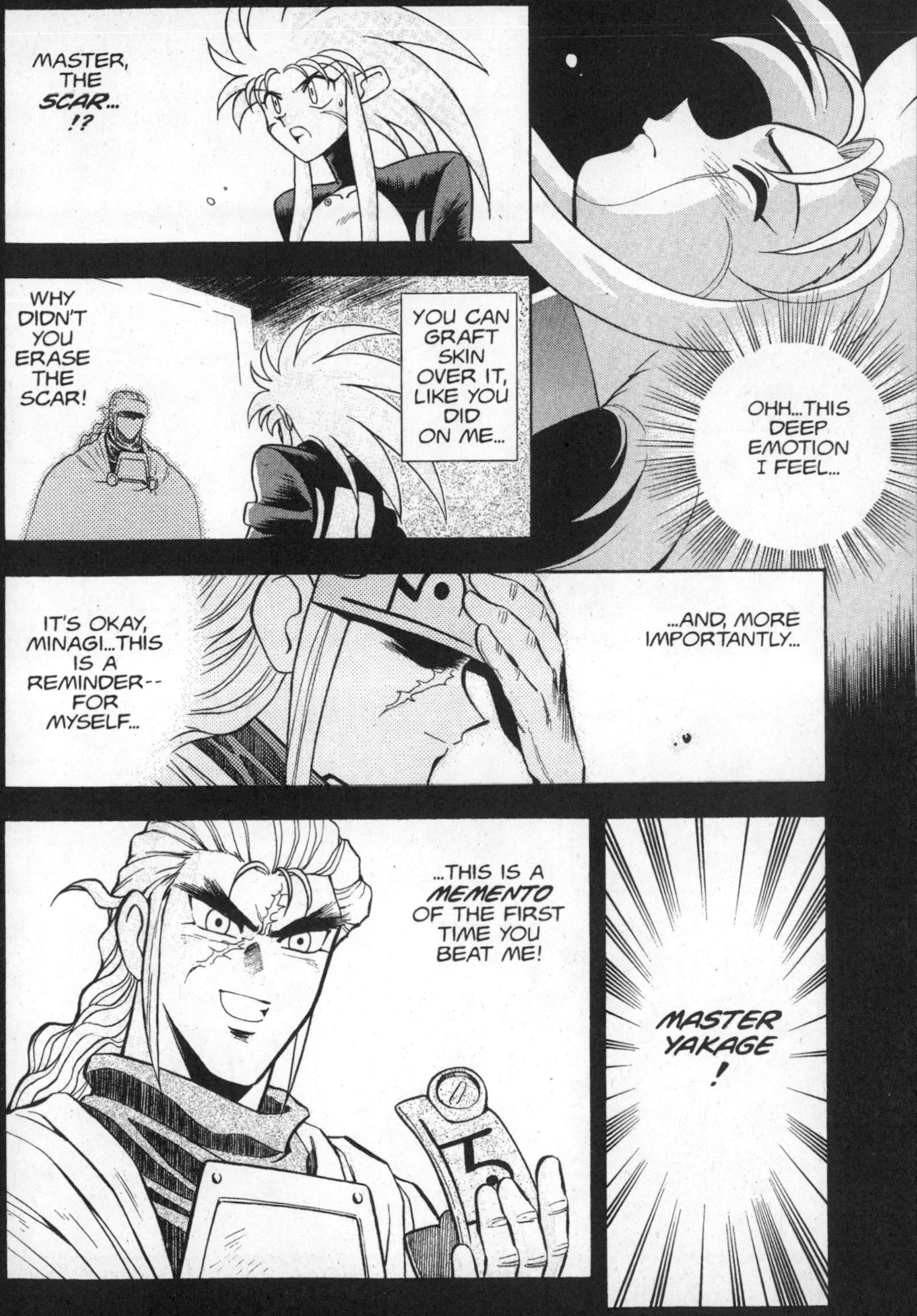
MASTER, THE *SCAR*... !?
WHY DIDN'T YOU ERASE THE SCAR!
YOU CAN GRAFT SKIN OVER IT, LIKE YOU DID ON ME...
OHH...THIS DEEP EMOTION I FEEL...
IT'S OKAY, MINAGI...THIS IS A REMINDER--FOR *MYSELF*...
...AND, MORE IMPORTANTLY...
...THIS IS A *MEMENTO* OF THE FIRST TIME YOU BEAT ME!
MASTER YAKAGE !

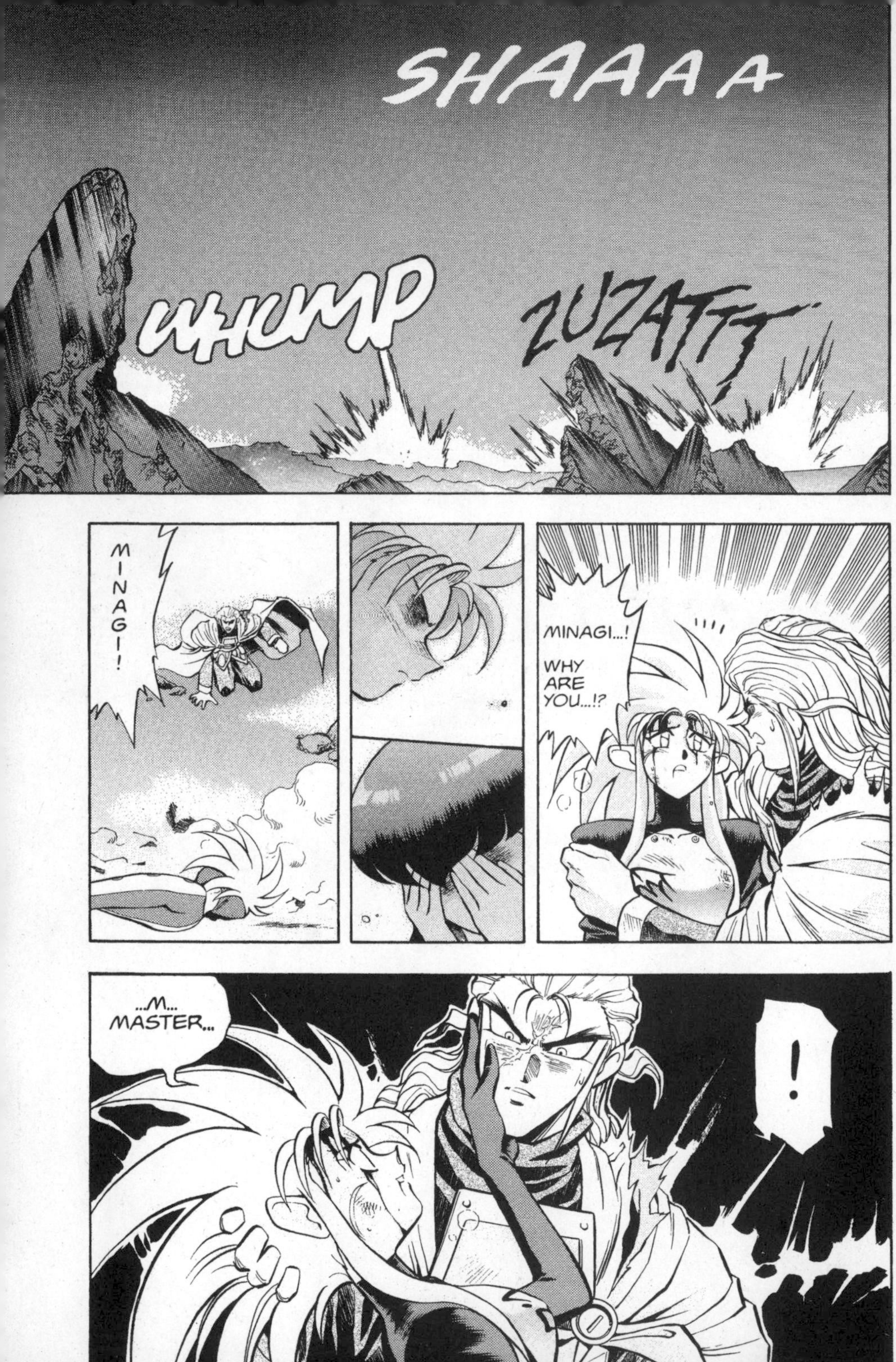
SHAAAAA
WHUMP
ZUZATTT
MINAGI!
MINAGI...!
WHY ARE YOU...!?
...M... MASTER...
!

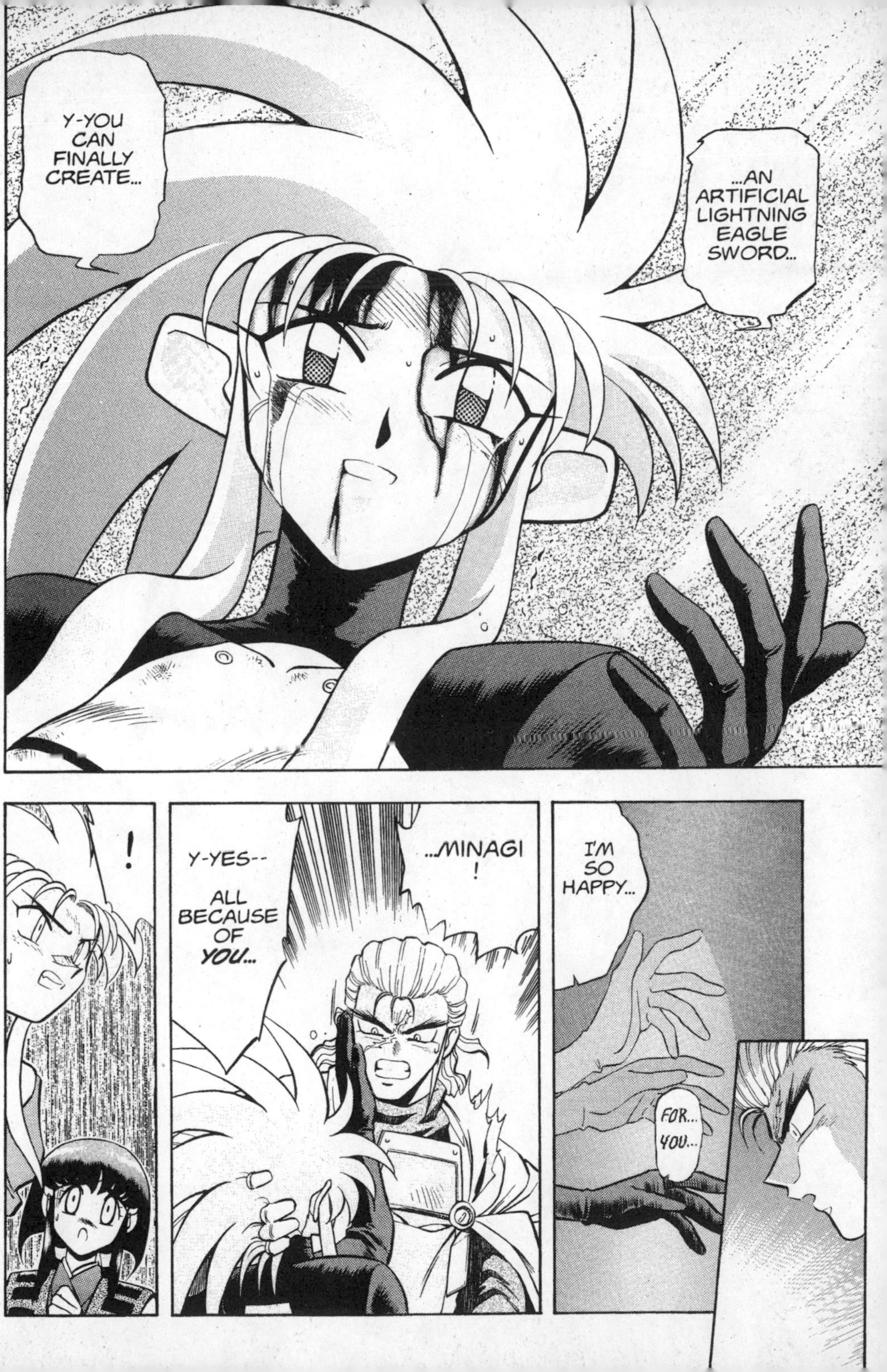
Y-YOU CAN FINALLY CREATE...
...AN ARTIFICIAL LIGHTNING EAGLE SWORD...
!
Y-YES--
ALL BECAUSE OF *YOU*...
...MINAGI !
I'M SO HAPPY...
FOR... YOU...

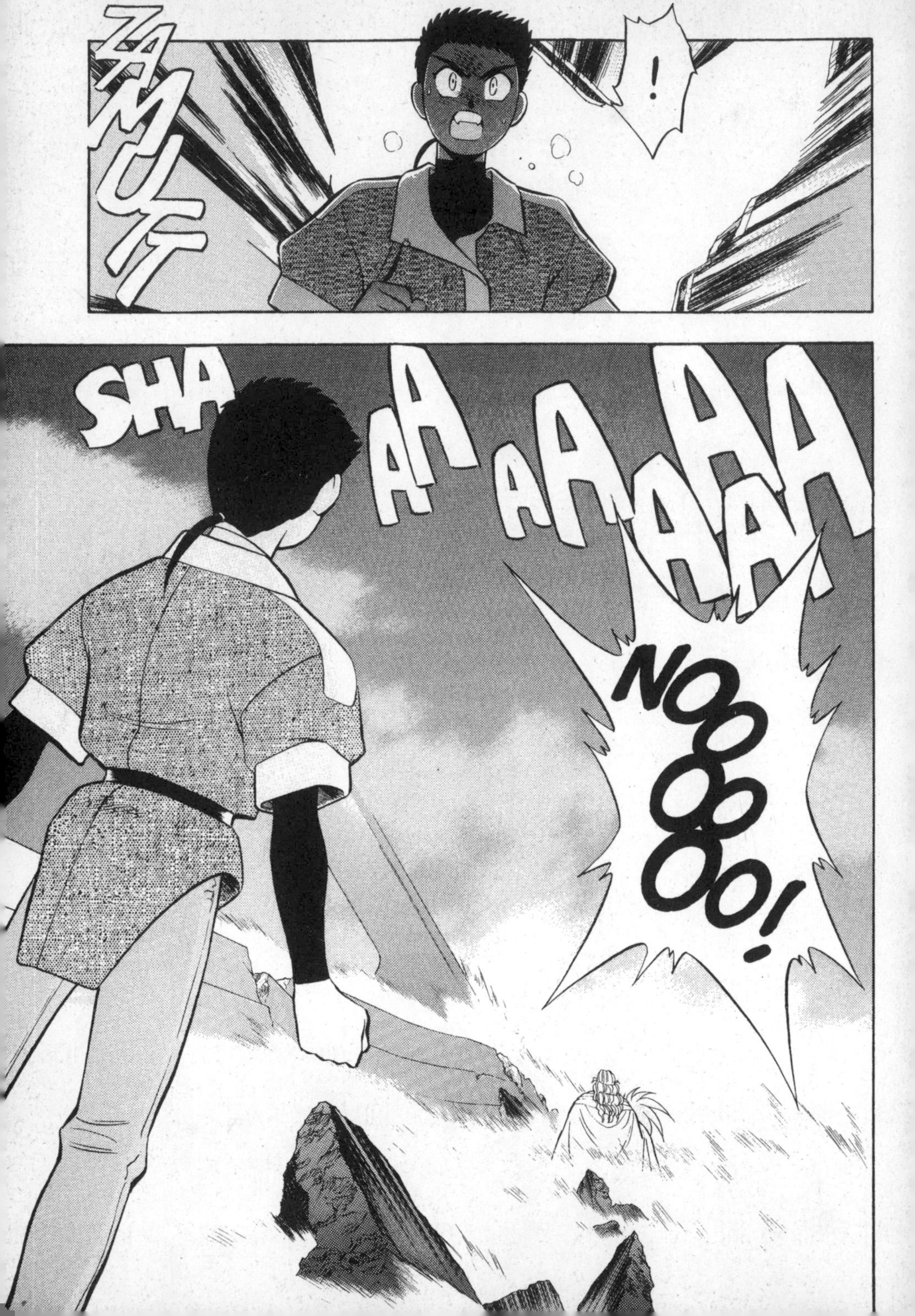
ZAMUFT
!
SHAAAAAAAAA
NOOOOOOO!

Tales of Tenchi #4

HOME OF THE BRAVE

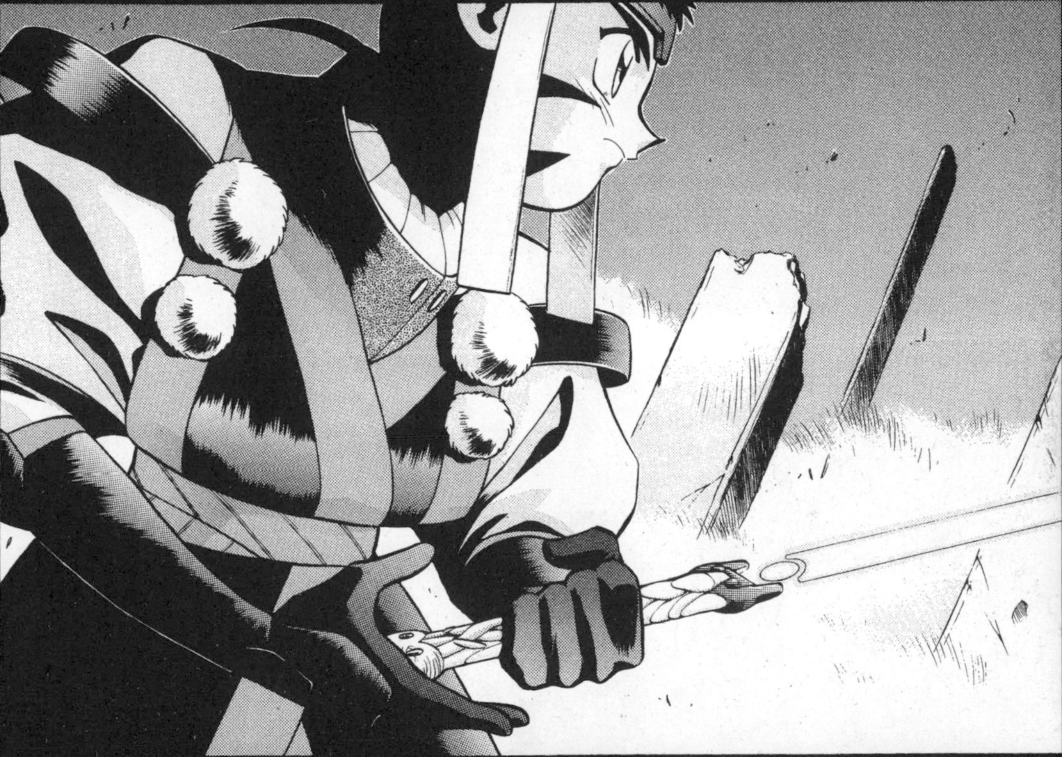

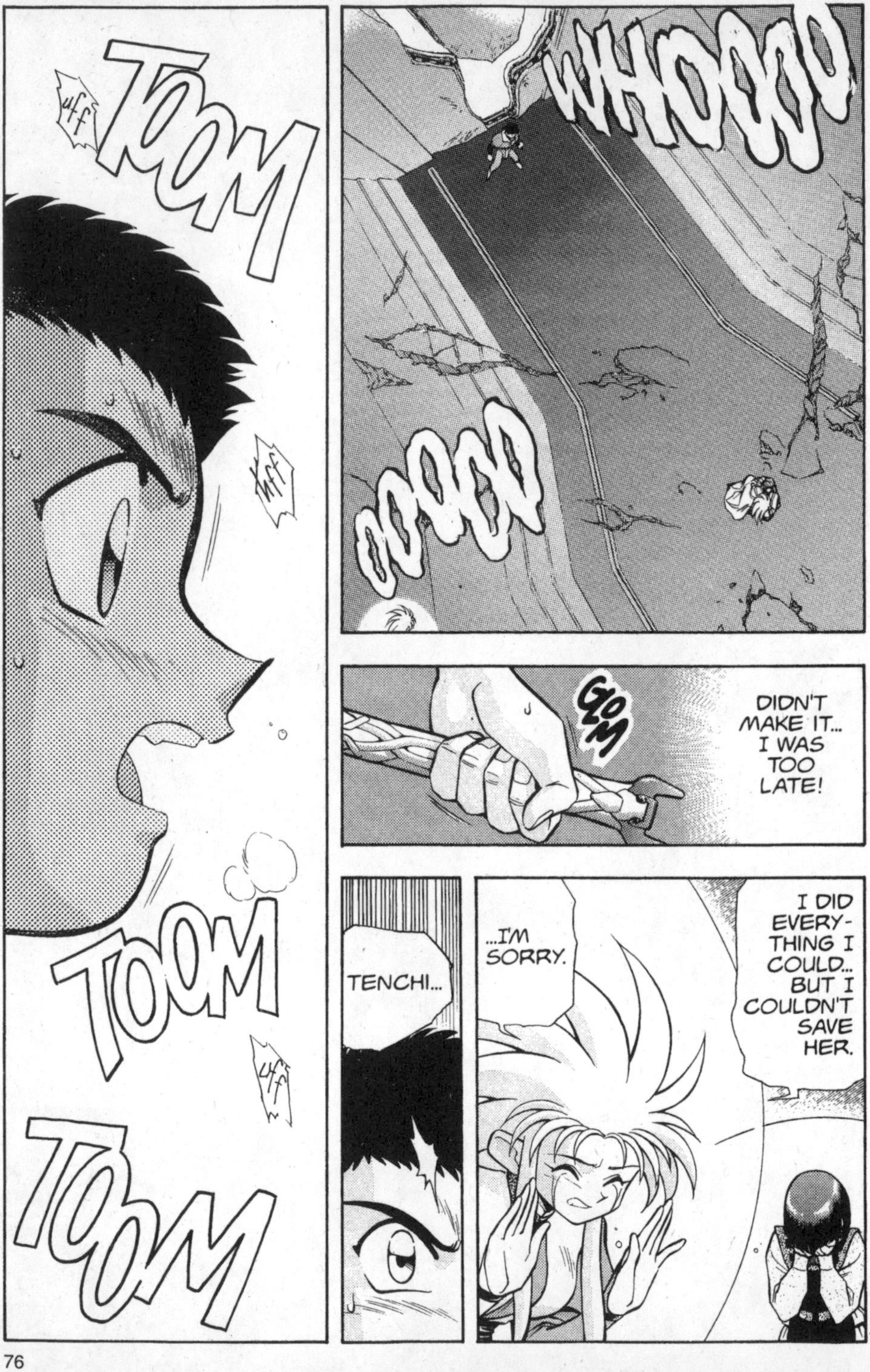
uff
TOOM
TOOM
uff
TOOM
WHOOOOOOOOO
GOM
DIDN'T MAKE IT... I WAS TOO LATE!
TENCHI...
...I'M SORRY.
I DID EVERY-THING I COULD... BUT I COULDN'T SAVE HER.

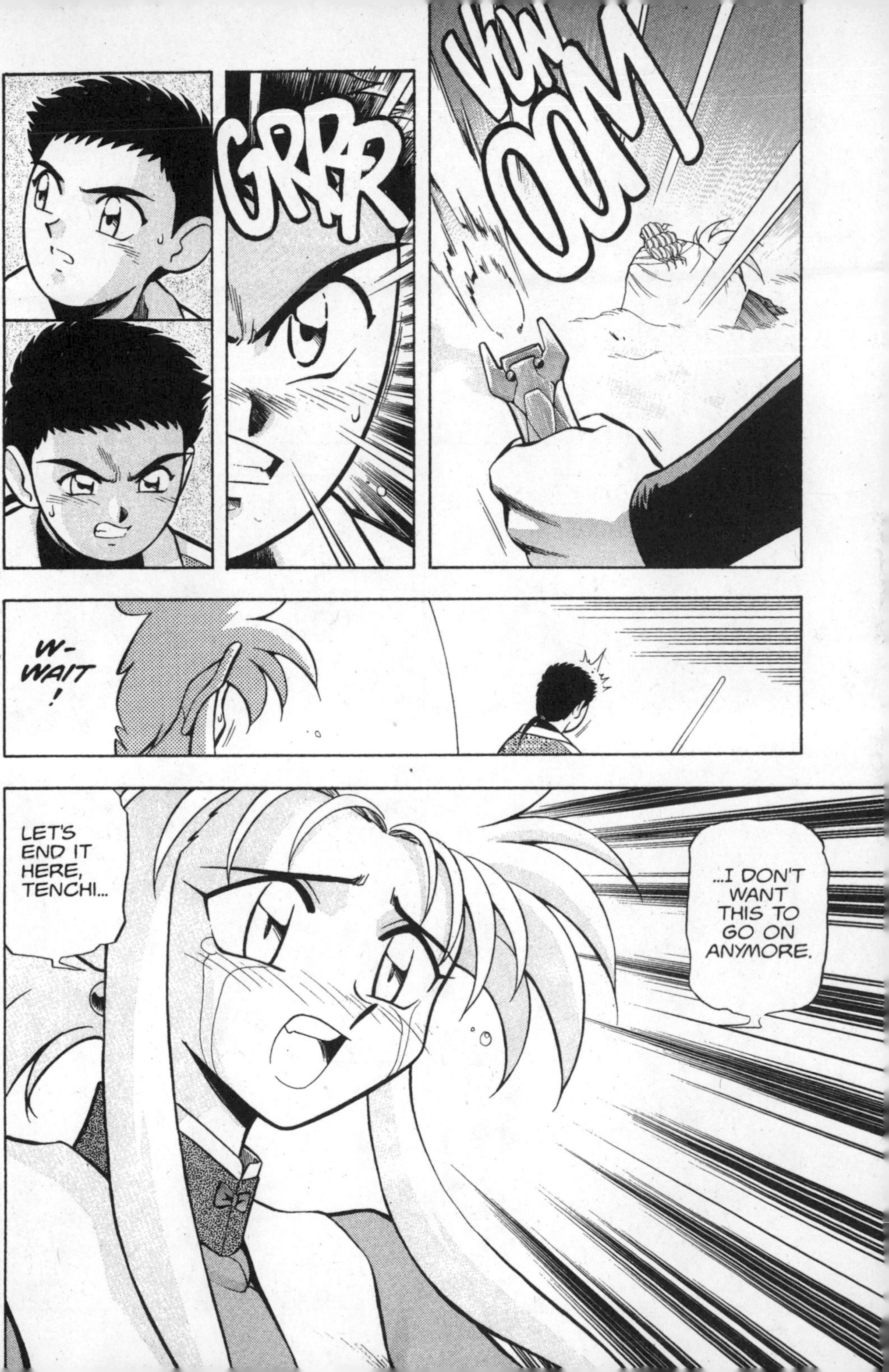
GRRR
VOOM
W-WAIT!
LET'S END IT HERE, TENCHI...
...I DON'T WANT THIS TO GO ON ANYMORE.

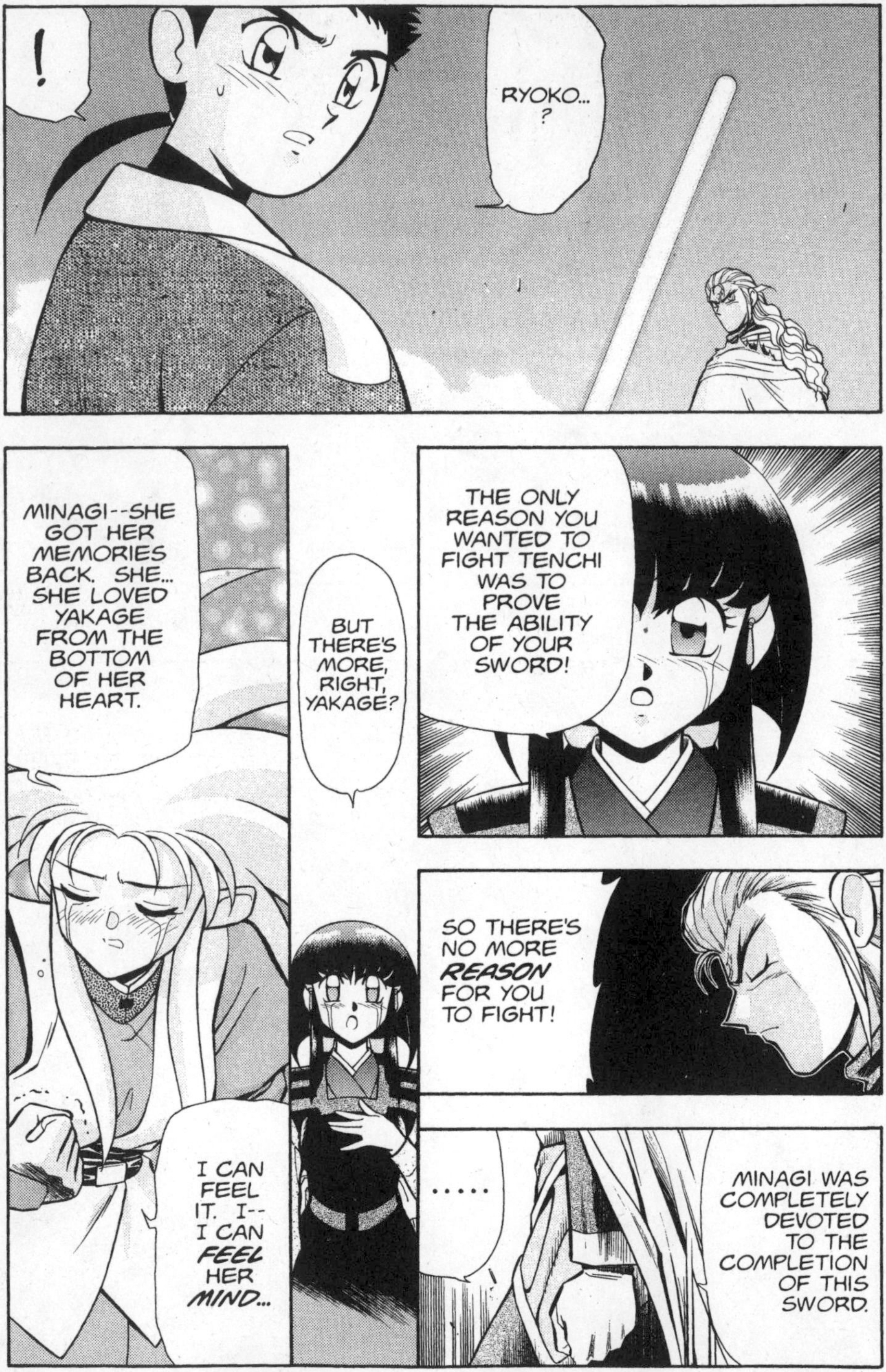
!
RYOKO... ?
MINAGI--SHE GOT HER MEMORIES BACK. SHE... SHE LOVED YAKAGE FROM THE BOTTOM OF HER HEART.
I CAN FEEL IT. I-- I CAN *FEEL* HER *MIND*...
THE ONLY REASON YOU WANTED TO FIGHT TENCHI WAS TO PROVE THE ABILITY OF YOUR SWORD!
BUT THERE'S MORE, RIGHT, YAKAGE?
SO THERE'S NO MORE *REASON* FOR YOU TO FIGHT!
.....
MINAGI WAS COMPLETELY DEVOTED TO THE COMPLETION OF THIS SWORD.

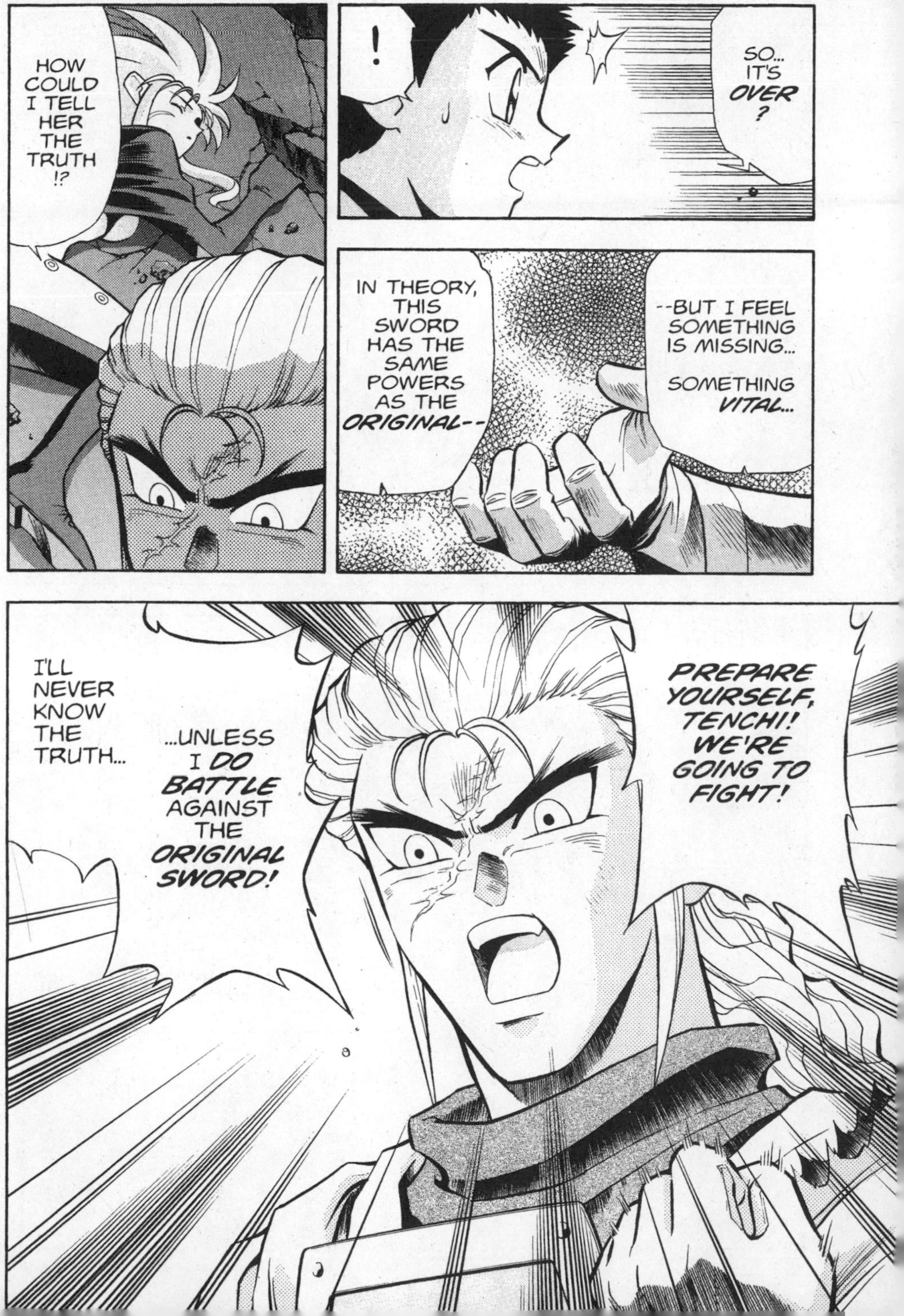
HOW COULD I TELL HER THE TRUTH !?
!
SO... IT'S OVER ?
IN THEORY, THIS SWORD HAS THE SAME POWERS AS THE ORIGINAL--
--BUT I FEEL SOMETHING IS MISSING...
SOMETHING VITAL...
I'LL NEVER KNOW THE TRUTH...
...UNLESS I DO BATTLE AGAINST THE ORIGINAL SWORD!
PREPARE YOURSELF, TENCHI! WE'RE GOING TO FIGHT!

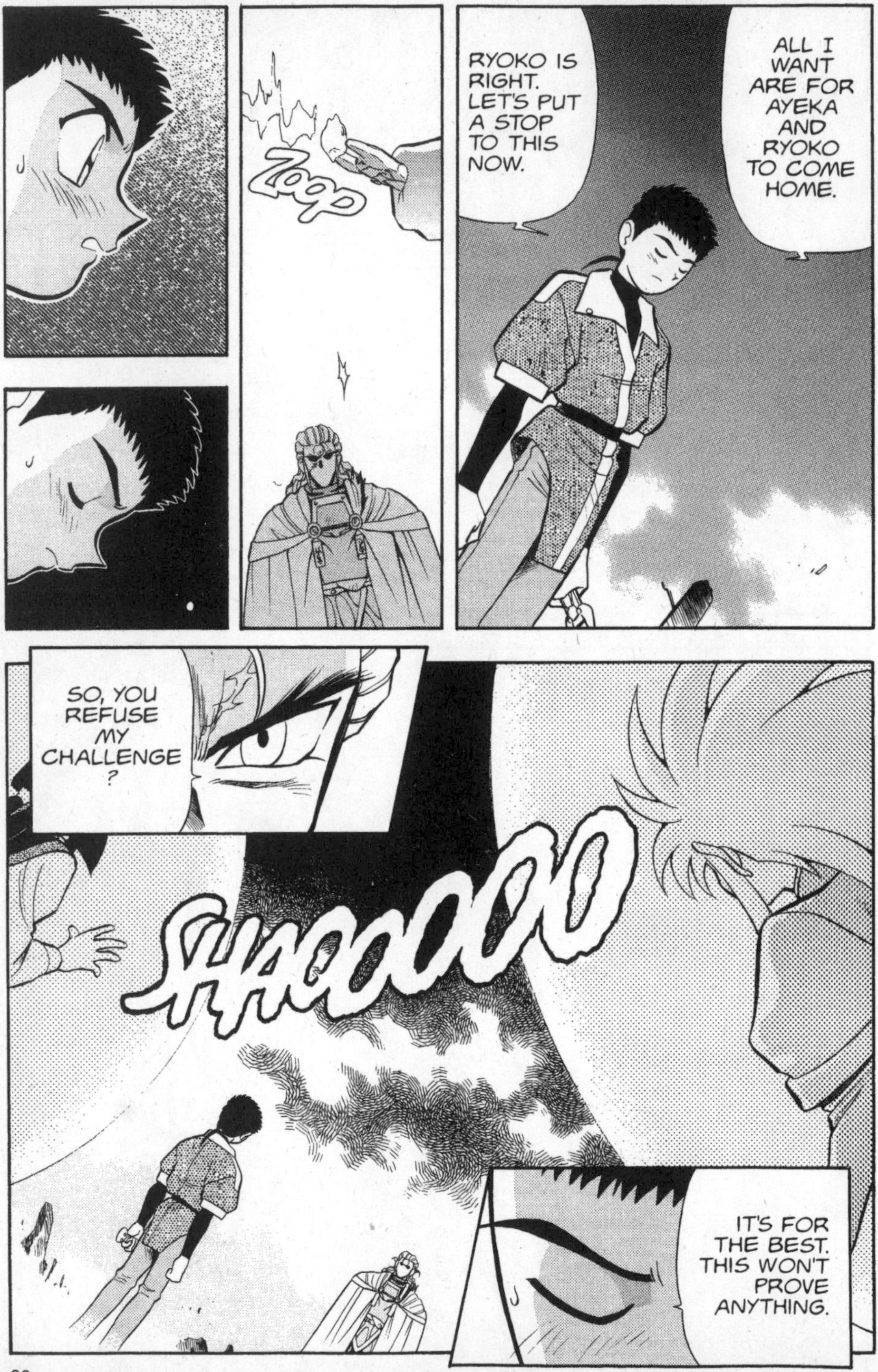
ZOOP
RYOKO IS RIGHT. LET'S PUT A STOP TO THIS NOW.
ALL I WANT ARE FOR AYEKA AND RYOKO TO COME HOME.
SO, YOU REFUSE MY CHALLENGE ?
SHAOOOOO
IT'S FOR THE BEST. THIS WON'T PROVE ANYTHING.

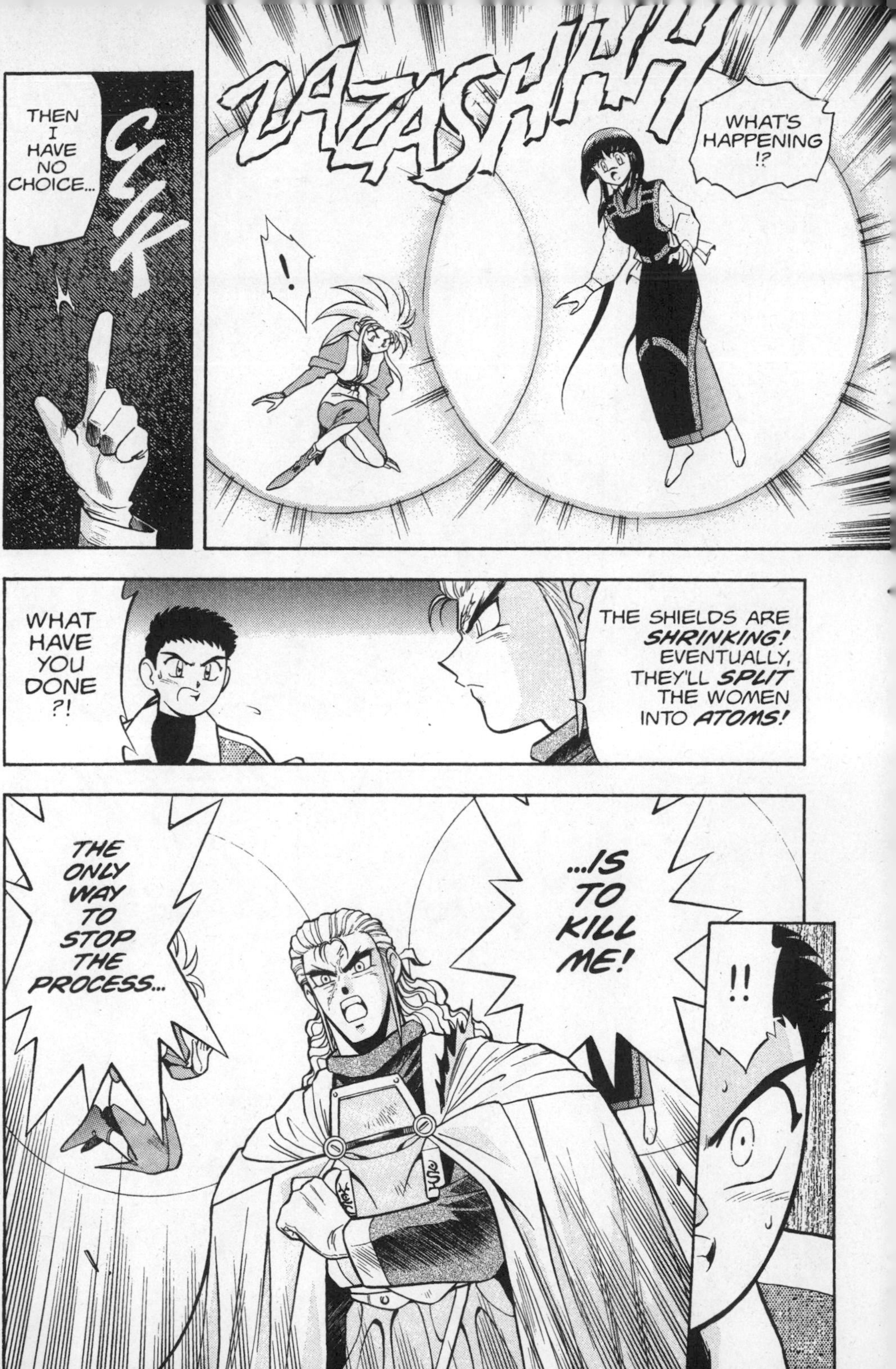
THEN I HAVE NO CHOICE...
CLIK
ZAZASHHH
!
WHAT'S HAPPENING !?
WHAT HAVE YOU DONE ?!
THE SHIELDS ARE SHRINKING! EVENTUALLY, THEY'LL SPLIT THE WOMEN INTO ATOMS!
THE ONLY WAY TO STOP THE PROCESS...
...IS TO KILL ME!
!!

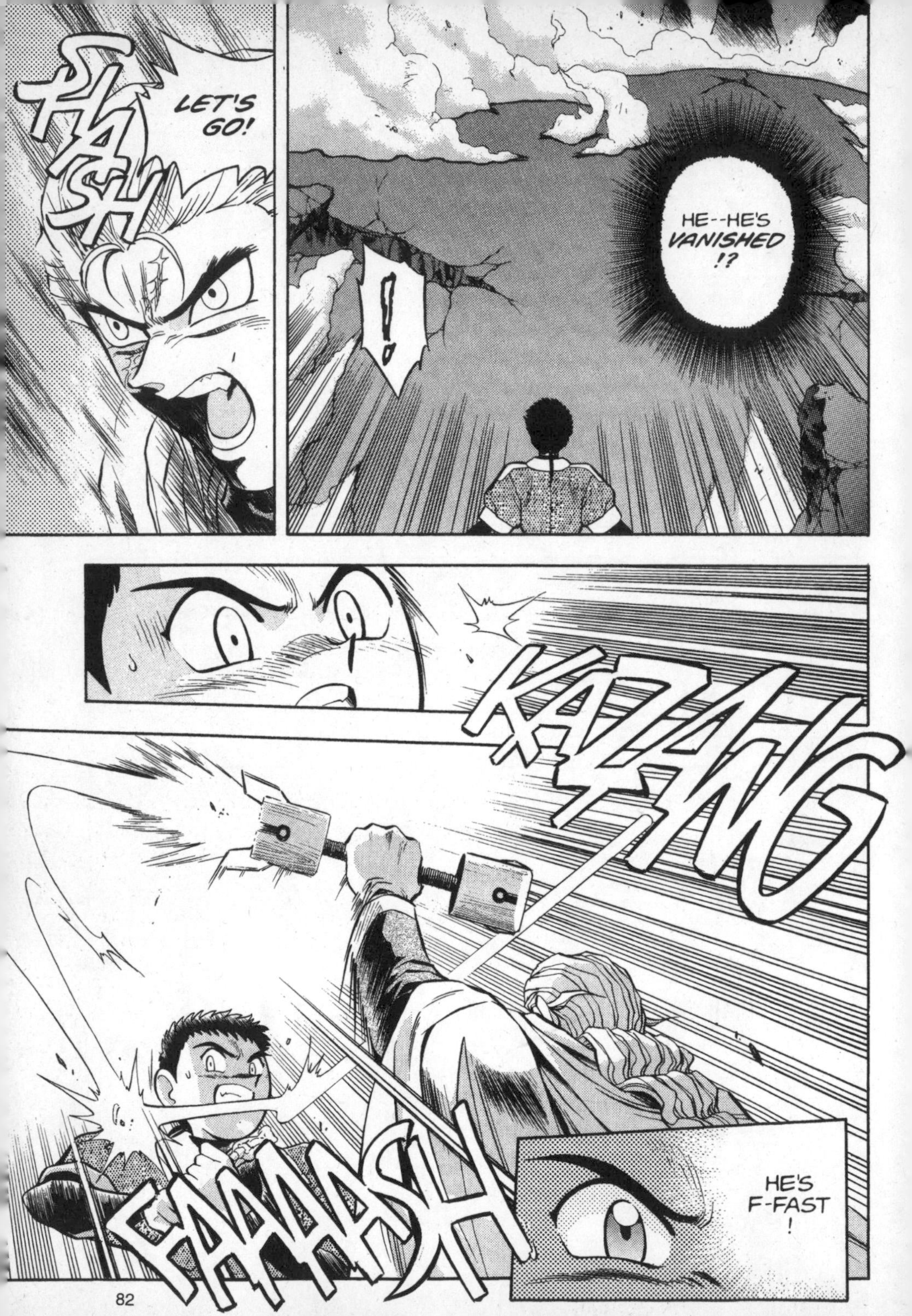
SHASH
LET'S GO!
HE--HE'S VANISHED !?
!
KAZANG
FAAASH
HE'S F-FAST !

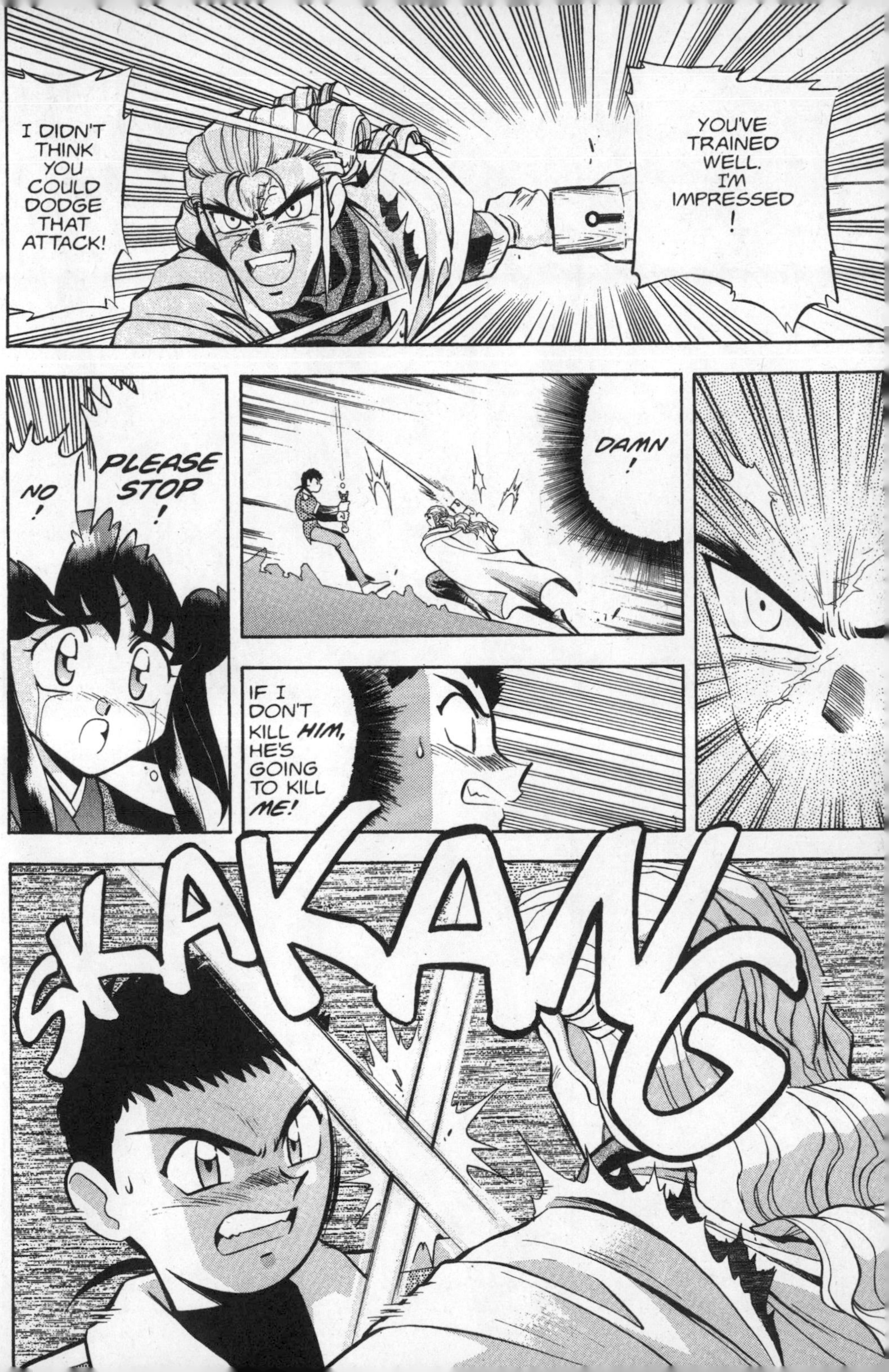
I DIDN'T THINK YOU COULD DODGE THAT ATTACK!
YOU'VE TRAINED WELL. I'M IMPRESSED!
NO!
PLEASE STOP!
DAMN!
IF I DON'T KILL HIM, HE'S GOING TO KILL ME!
SKAANG

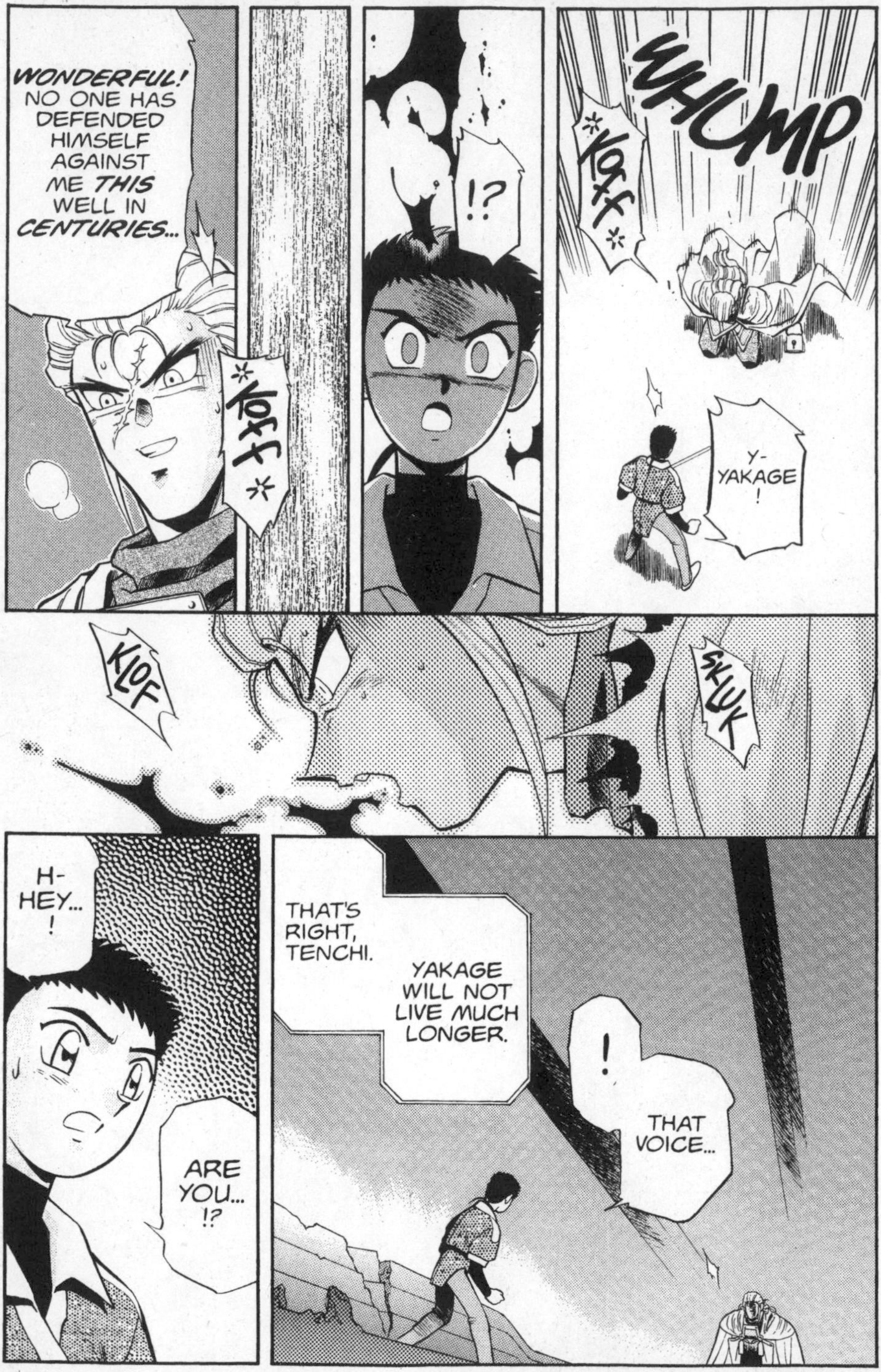
WONDERFUL! NO ONE HAS DEFENDED HIMSELF AGAINST ME THIS WELL IN CENTURIES...
KOFF
!?
WHUMP
KOFF
Y-YAKAGE!
KLOF
SKLUK
H-HEY...!
ARE YOU...!?
THAT'S RIGHT, TENCHI.
YAKAGE WILL NOT LIVE MUCH LONGER.
!
THAT VOICE...

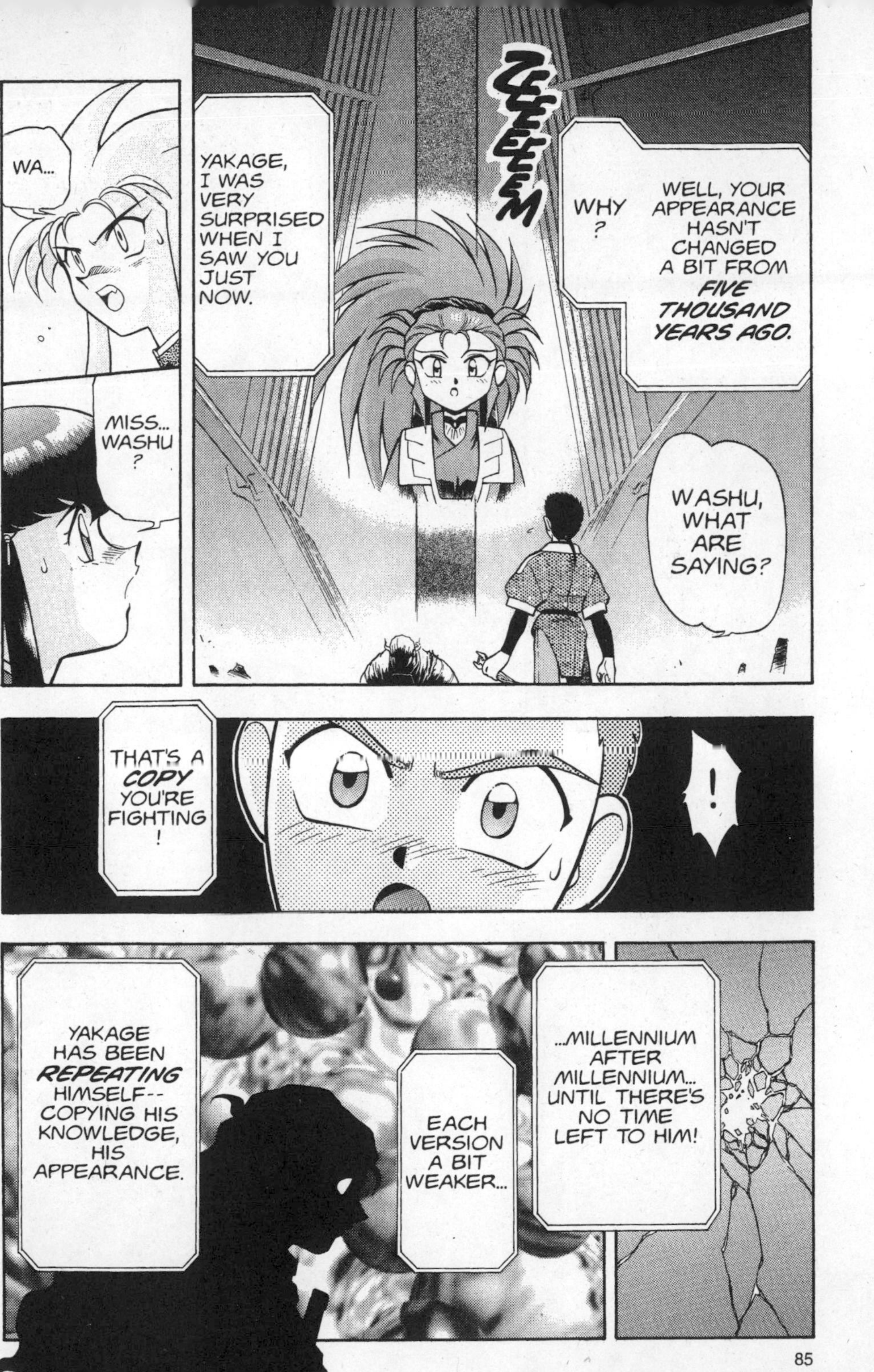
WA...
YAKAGE, I WAS VERY SURPRISED WHEN I SAW YOU JUST NOW.
ZEEEEEEM
WHY?
WELL, YOUR APPEARANCE HASN'T CHANGED A BIT FROM FIVE THOUSAND YEARS AGO.
MISS... WASHU?
WASHU, WHAT ARE SAYING?
THAT'S A COPY YOU'RE FIGHTING!
!
YAKAGE HAS BEEN REPEATING HIMSELF--COPYING HIS KNOWLEDGE, HIS APPEARANCE.
EACH VERSION A BIT WEAKER...
...MILLENNIUM AFTER MILLENNIUM... UNTIL THERE'S NO TIME LEFT TO HIM!

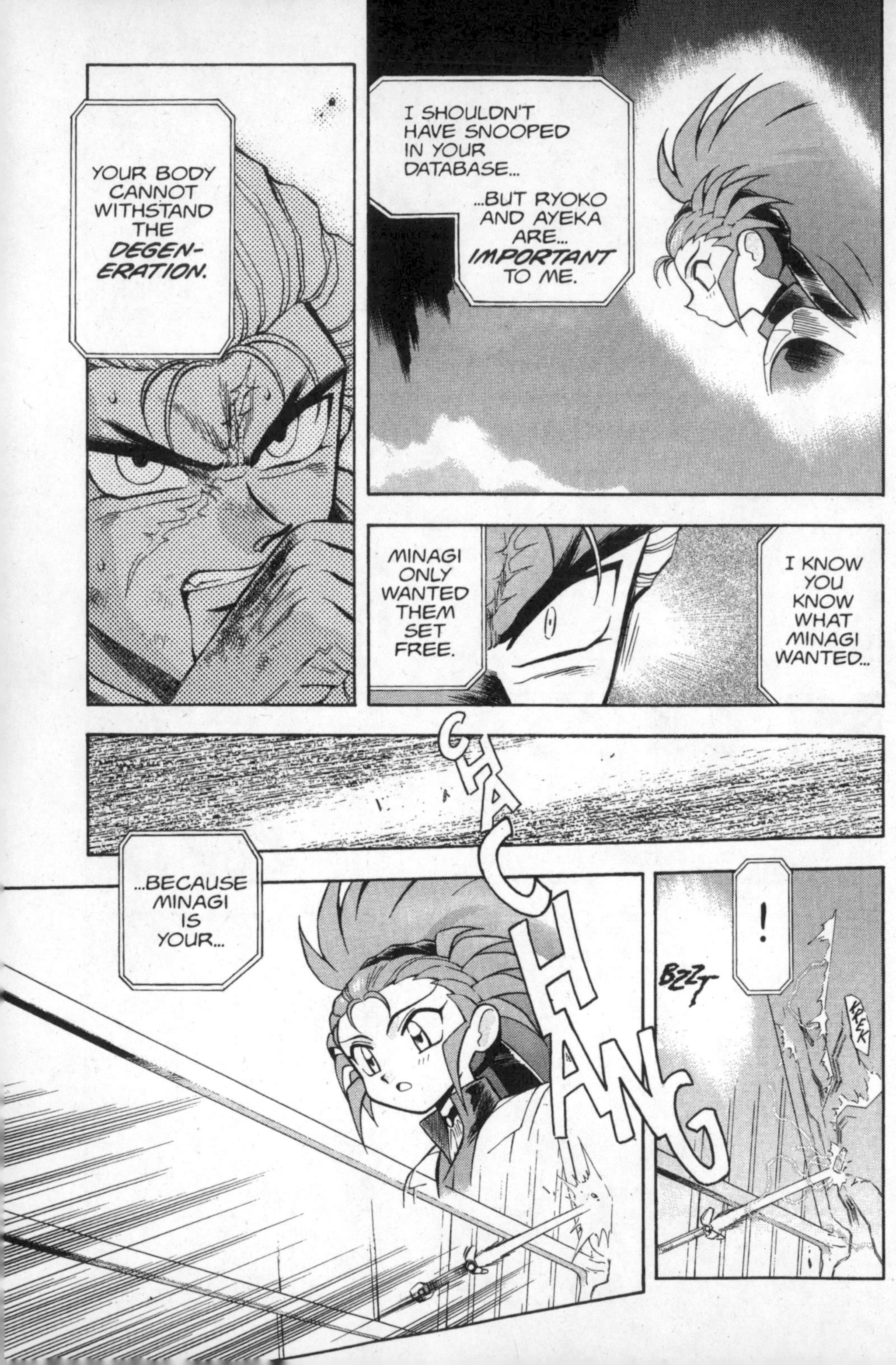
YOUR BODY CANNOT WITHSTAND THE *DEGEN-ERATION.*
I SHOULDN'T HAVE SNOOPED IN YOUR DATABASE...
...BUT RYOKO AND AYEKA ARE... *IMPORTANT* TO ME.
MINAGI ONLY WANTED THEM SET FREE.
I KNOW YOU KNOW WHAT MINAGI WANTED...
...BECAUSE MINAGI IS YOUR...
CHACHANG
!
BZZT
KREK

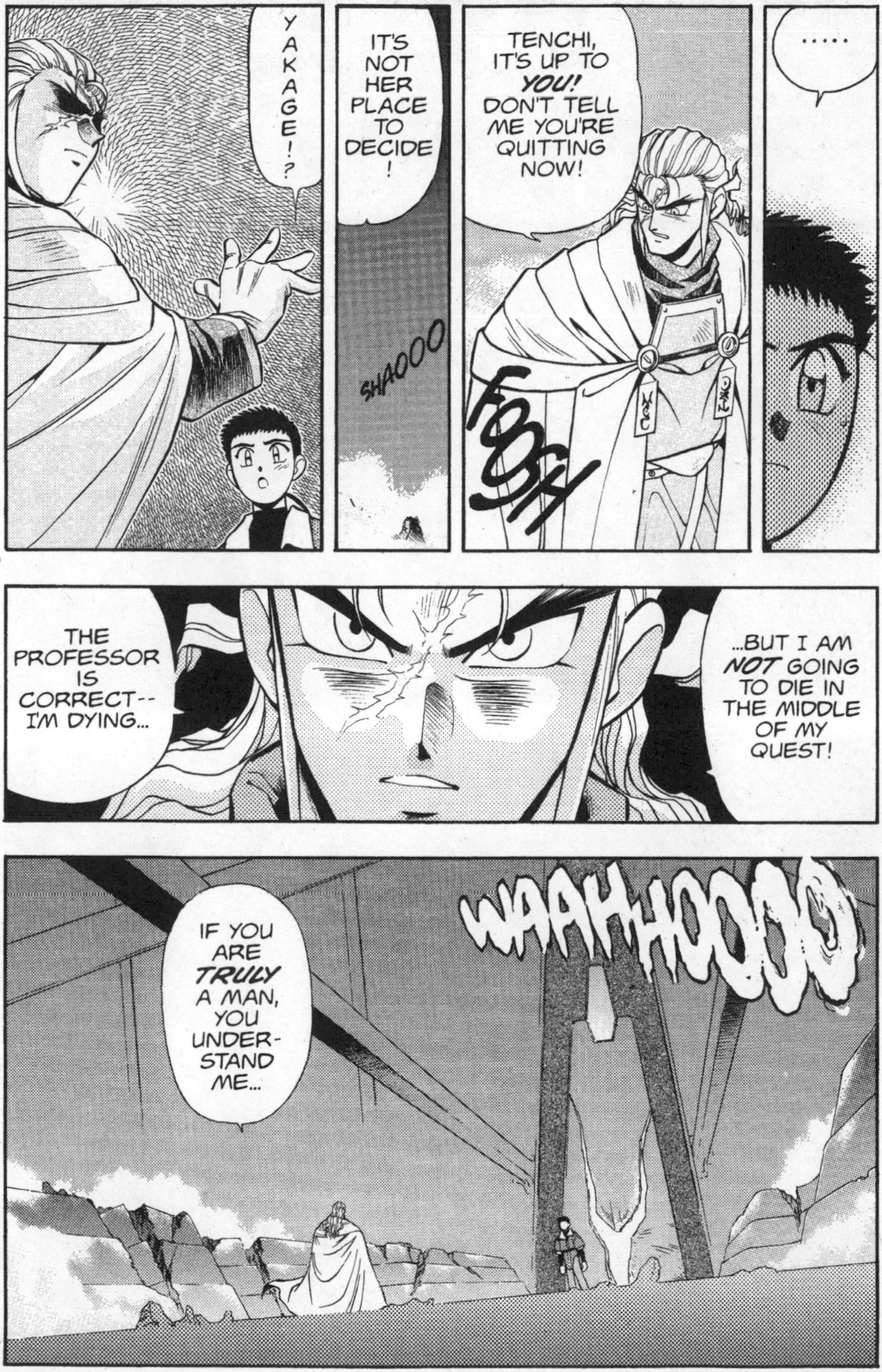
YAKAGE!?
IT'S NOT HER PLACE TO DECIDE!
SHAOOO
TENCHI, IT'S UP TO YOU! DON'T TELL ME YOU'RE QUITTING NOW!
FOOSH
.....
THE PROFESSOR IS CORRECT-- I'M DYING...
...BUT I AM NOT GOING TO DIE IN THE MIDDLE OF MY QUEST!
IF YOU ARE TRULY A MAN, YOU UNDER-STAND ME...
WAAHOOOO

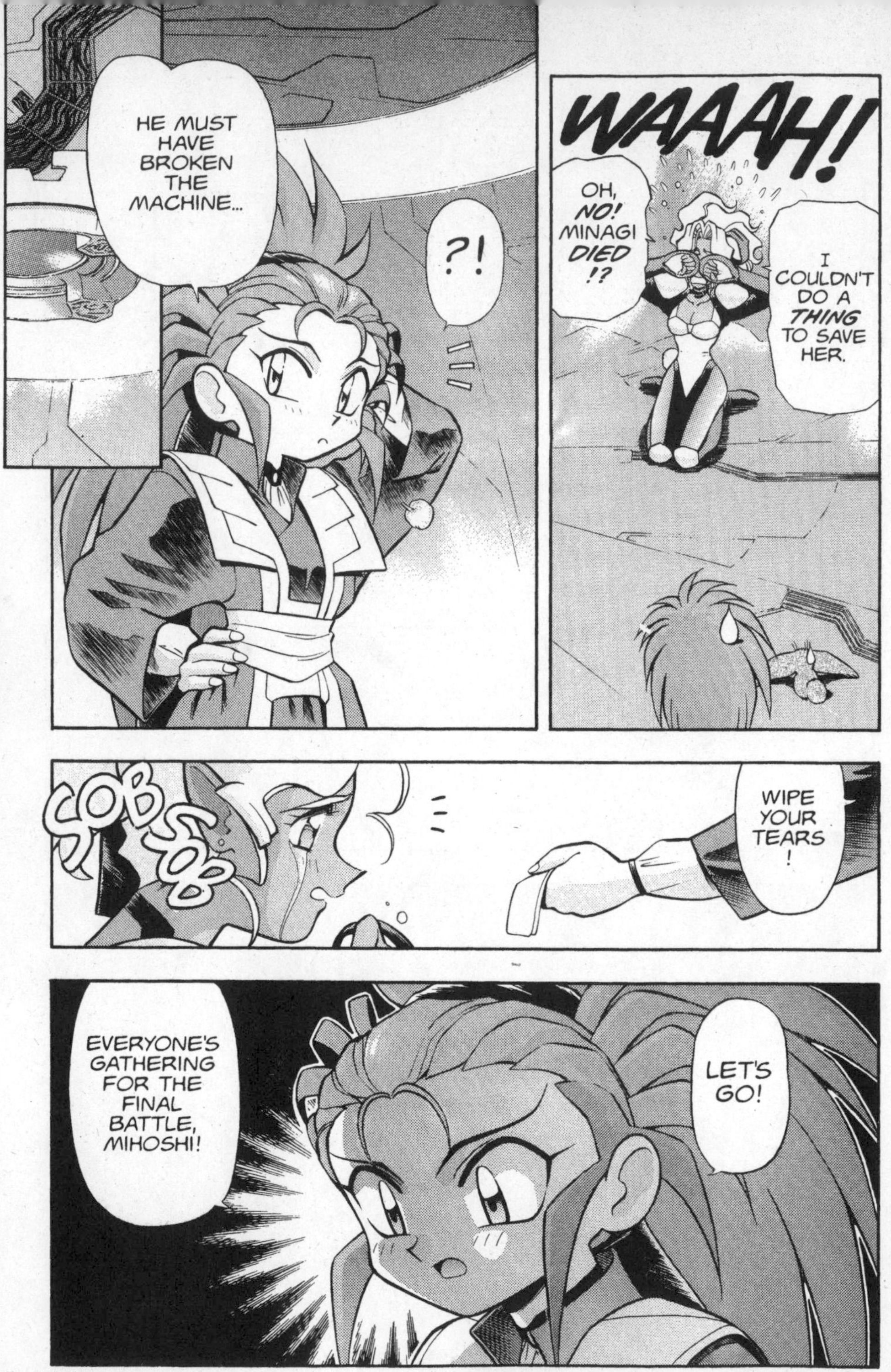

HE MUST HAVE BROKEN THE MACHINE...
?!
WAAAH!
OH, NO! MINAGI DIED!?
I COULDN'T DO A THING TO SAVE HER.
SOB SOB
WIPE YOUR TEARS!
EVERYONE'S GATHERING FOR THE FINAL BATTLE, MIHOSHI!
LET'S GO!

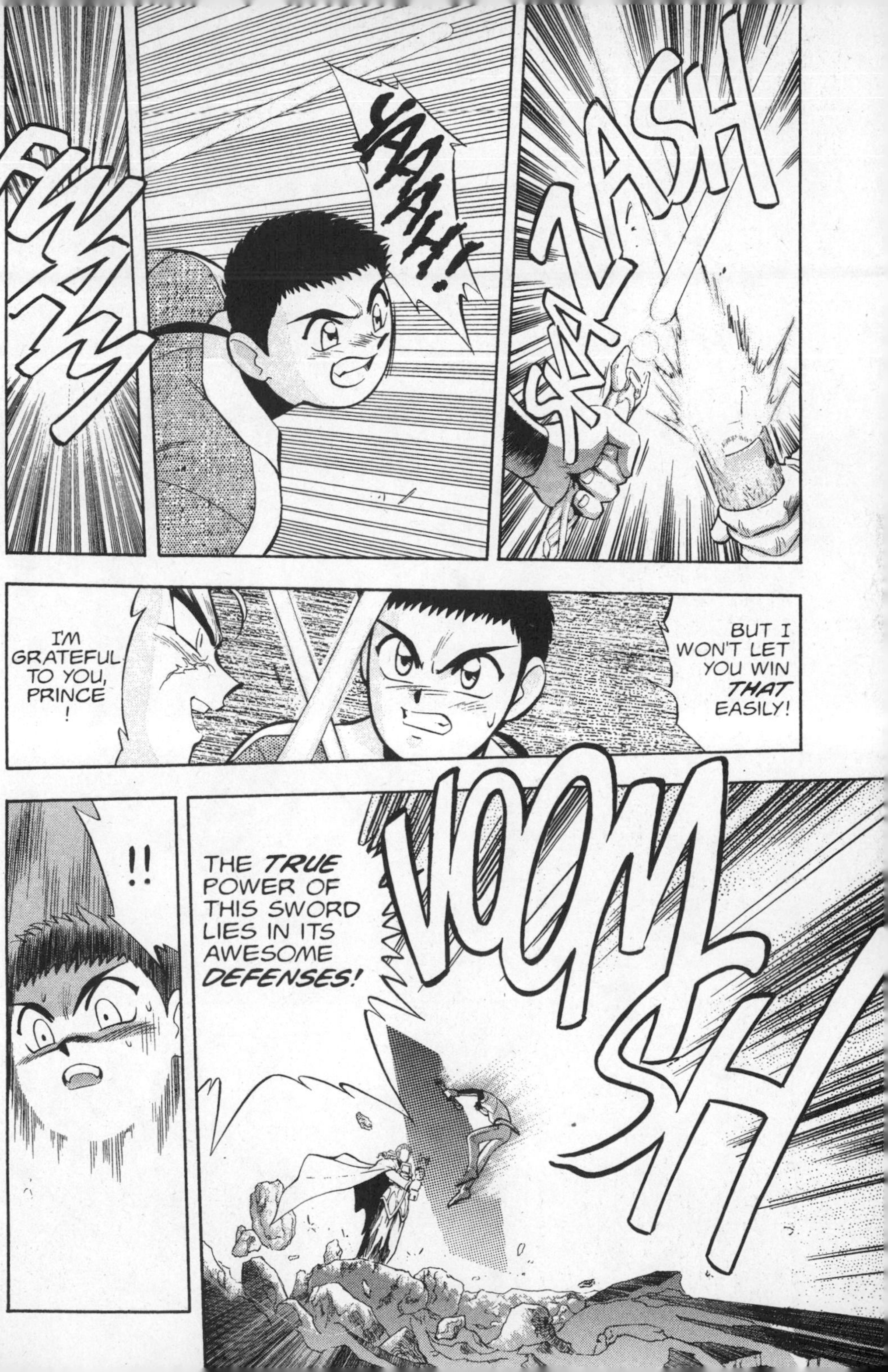
FWAM
YAAAH!!
SKA
ZASH
I'M GRATEFUL TO YOU, PRINCE!
BUT I WON'T LET YOU WIN *THAT* EASILY!
!!
THE *TRUE* POWER OF THIS SWORD LIES IN ITS AWESOME *DEFENSES!*
VOOM
SH

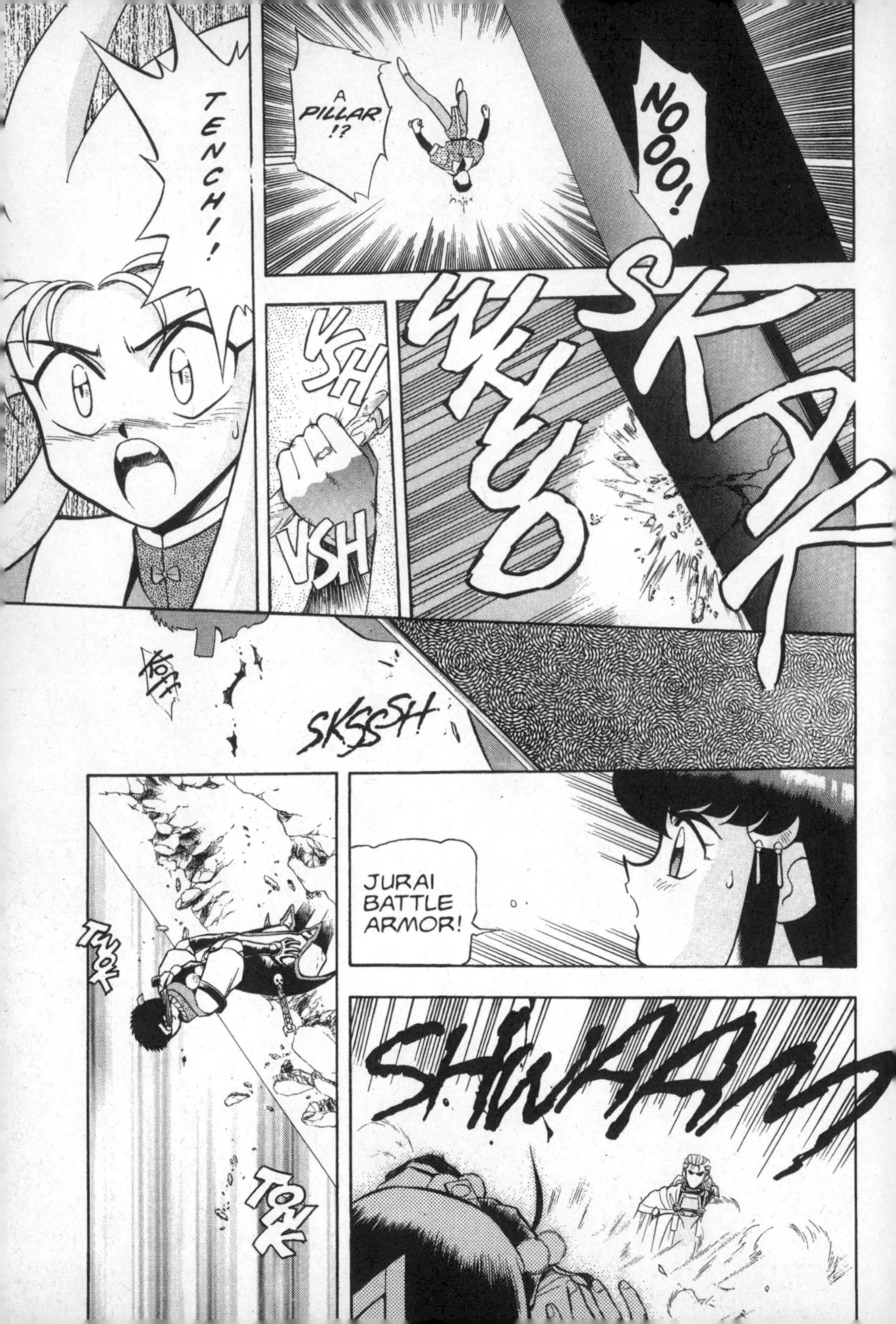
TENCHI!
A PILLAR!?
NOOOO!
SKAY
WHUD
VSH
VSH
KOFF
SKSSSH!
TNOK
TONK
JURAI BATTLE ARMOR!
SHWAAAM

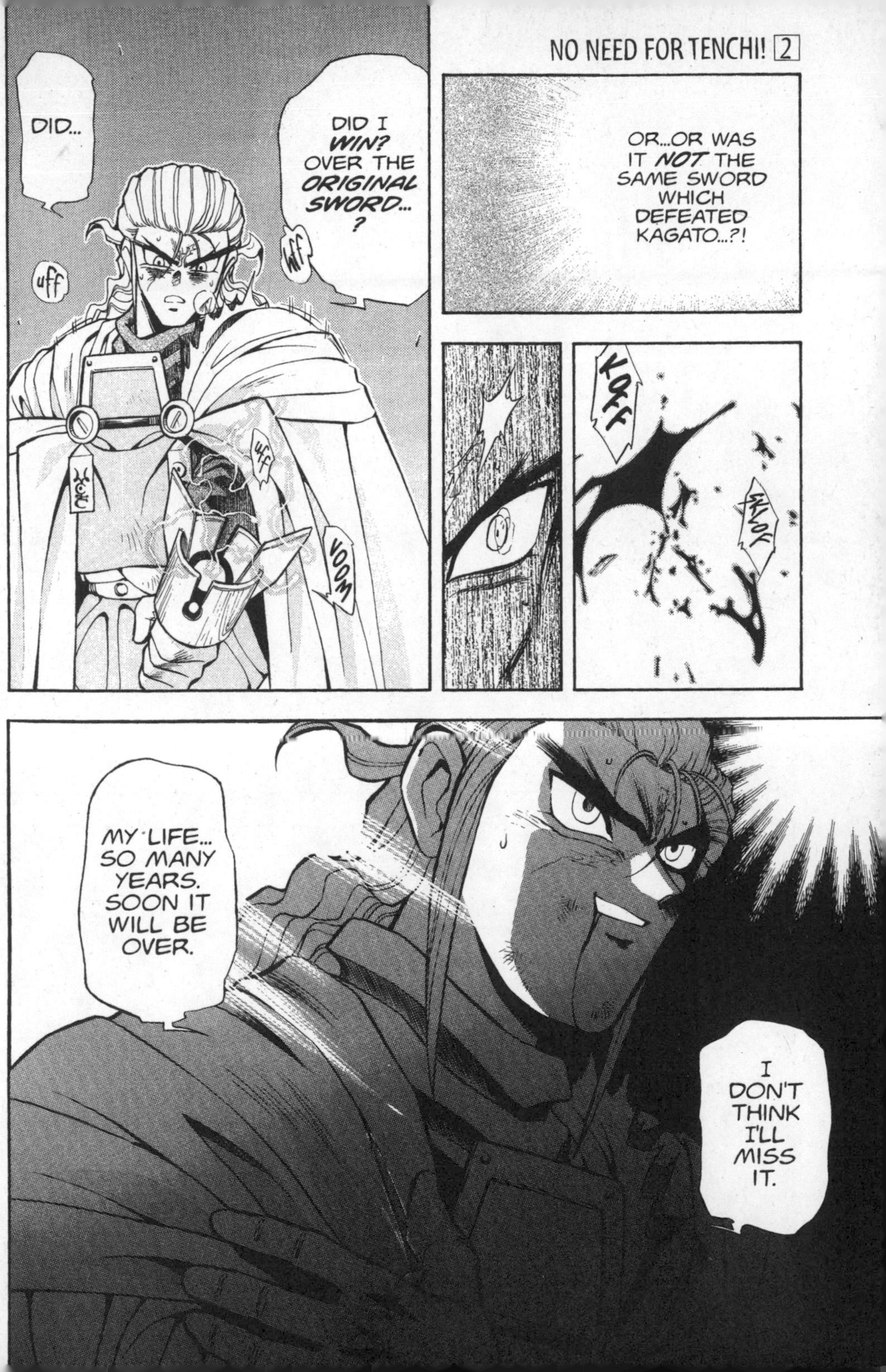
DID...
DID I *WIN?* OVER THE *ORIGINAL SWORD...* ?
uff
uff
uff
VOOM
OR...OR WAS IT *NOT* THE SAME SWORD WHICH DEFEATED KAGATO...?!
KOFF
SKLOK
MY LIFE... SO MANY YEARS. SOON IT WILL BE OVER.
I DON'T THINK I'LL MISS IT.

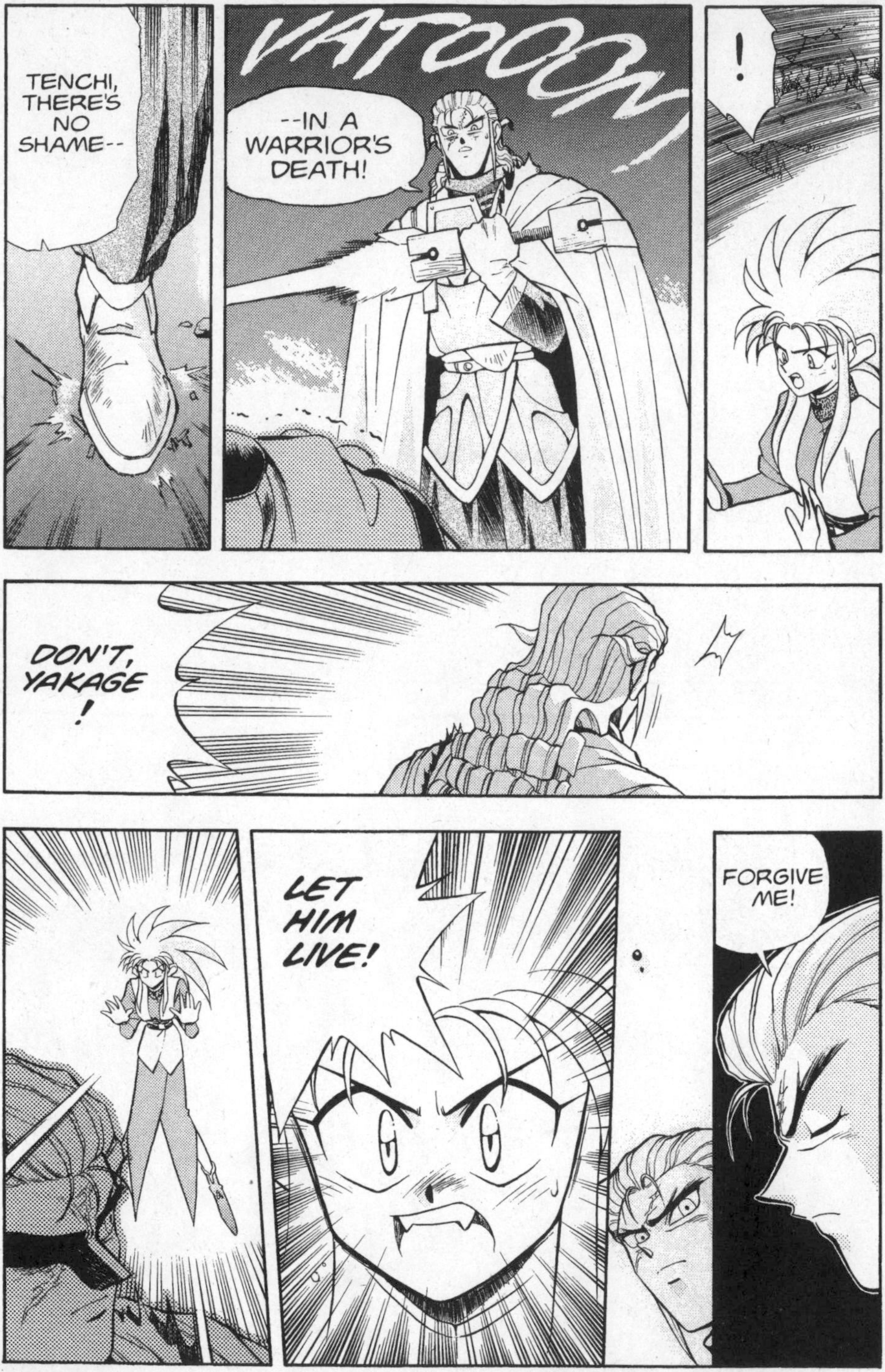
TENCHI, THERE'S NO SHAME--
VATOOON
--IN A WARRIOR'S DEATH!
!
DON'T, YAKAGE!
LET HIM LIVE!
FORGIVE ME!

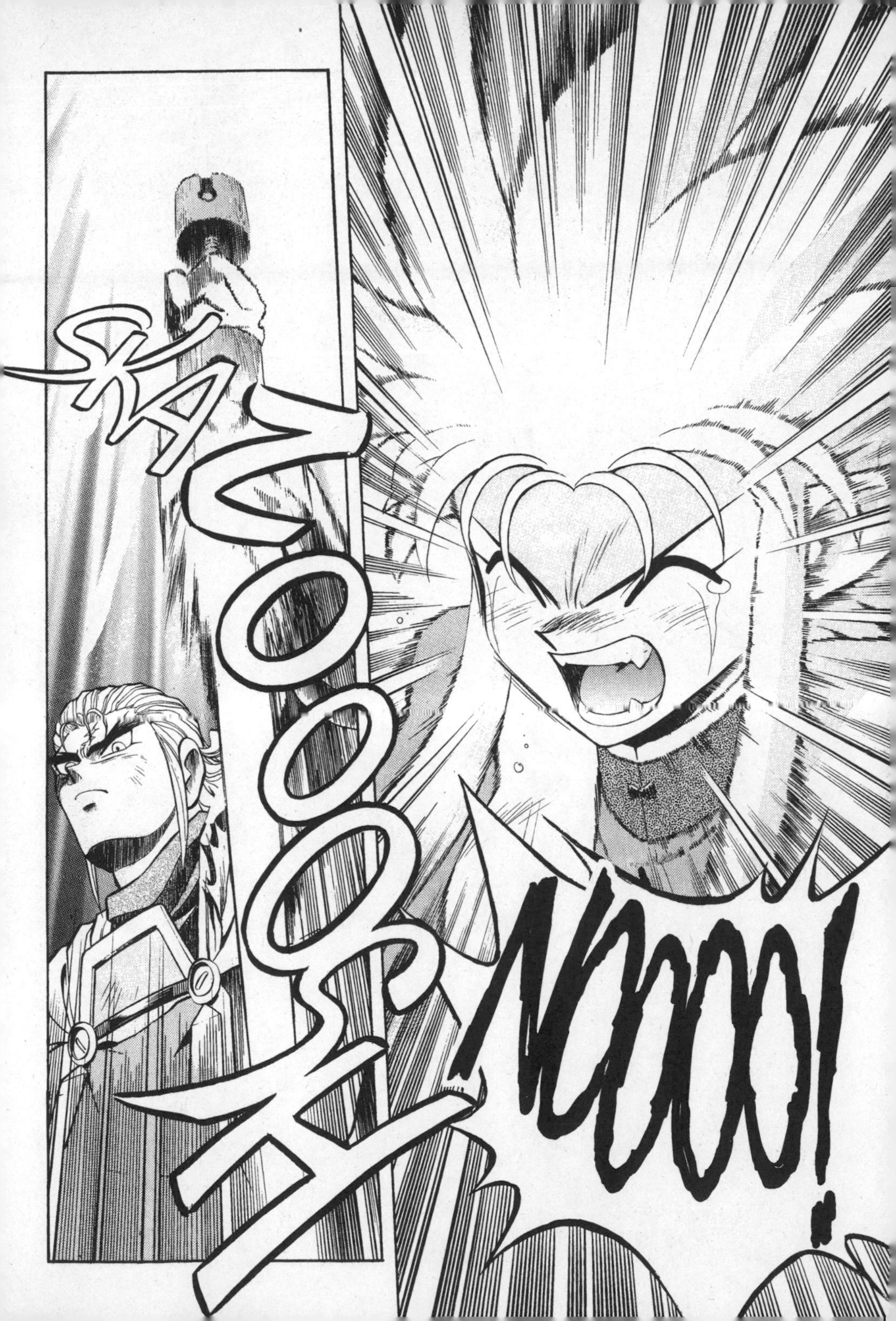
SKAVOOOOSH
NOOOO!

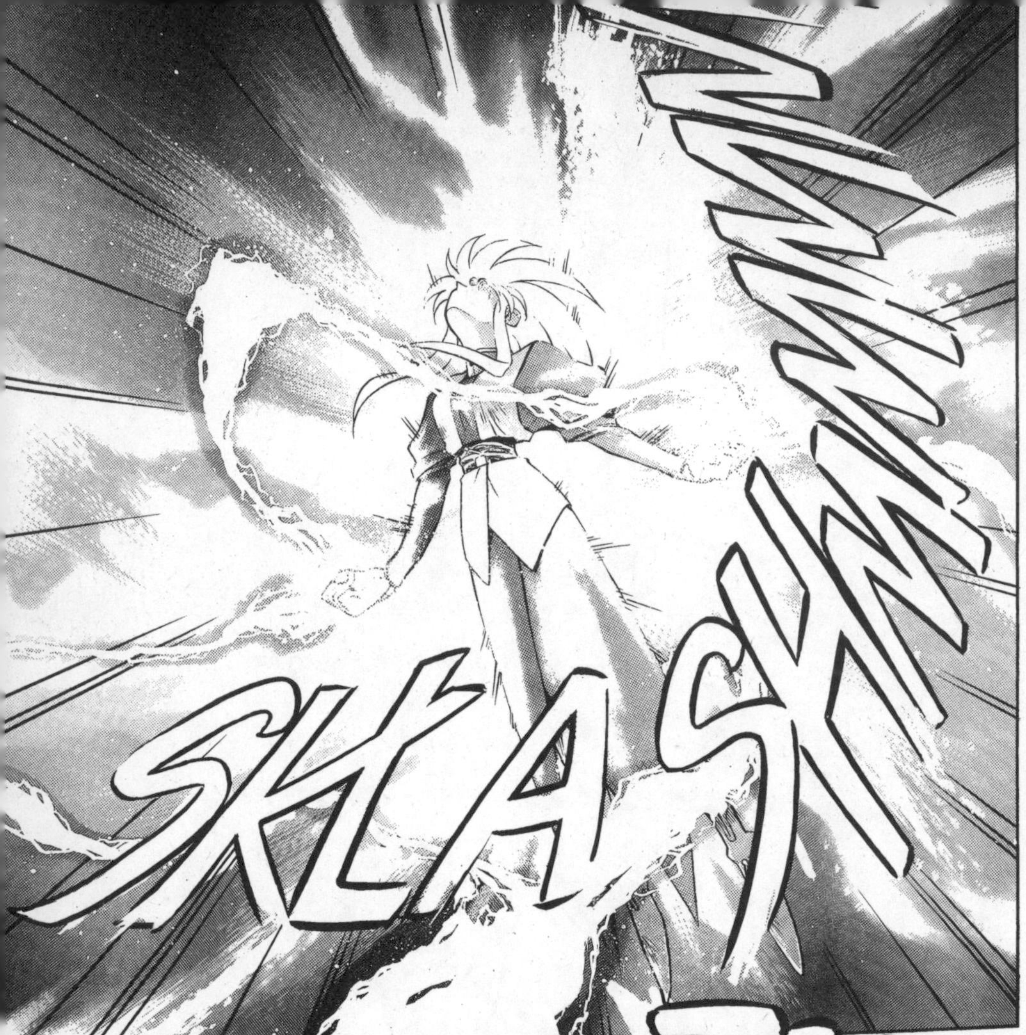
SKLASH

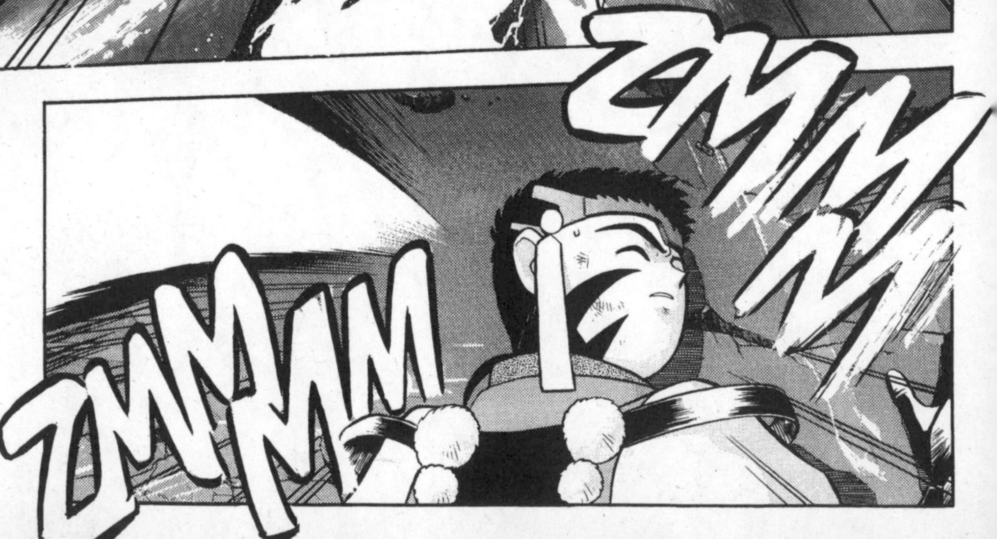
ZMMMM
ZMMMMM

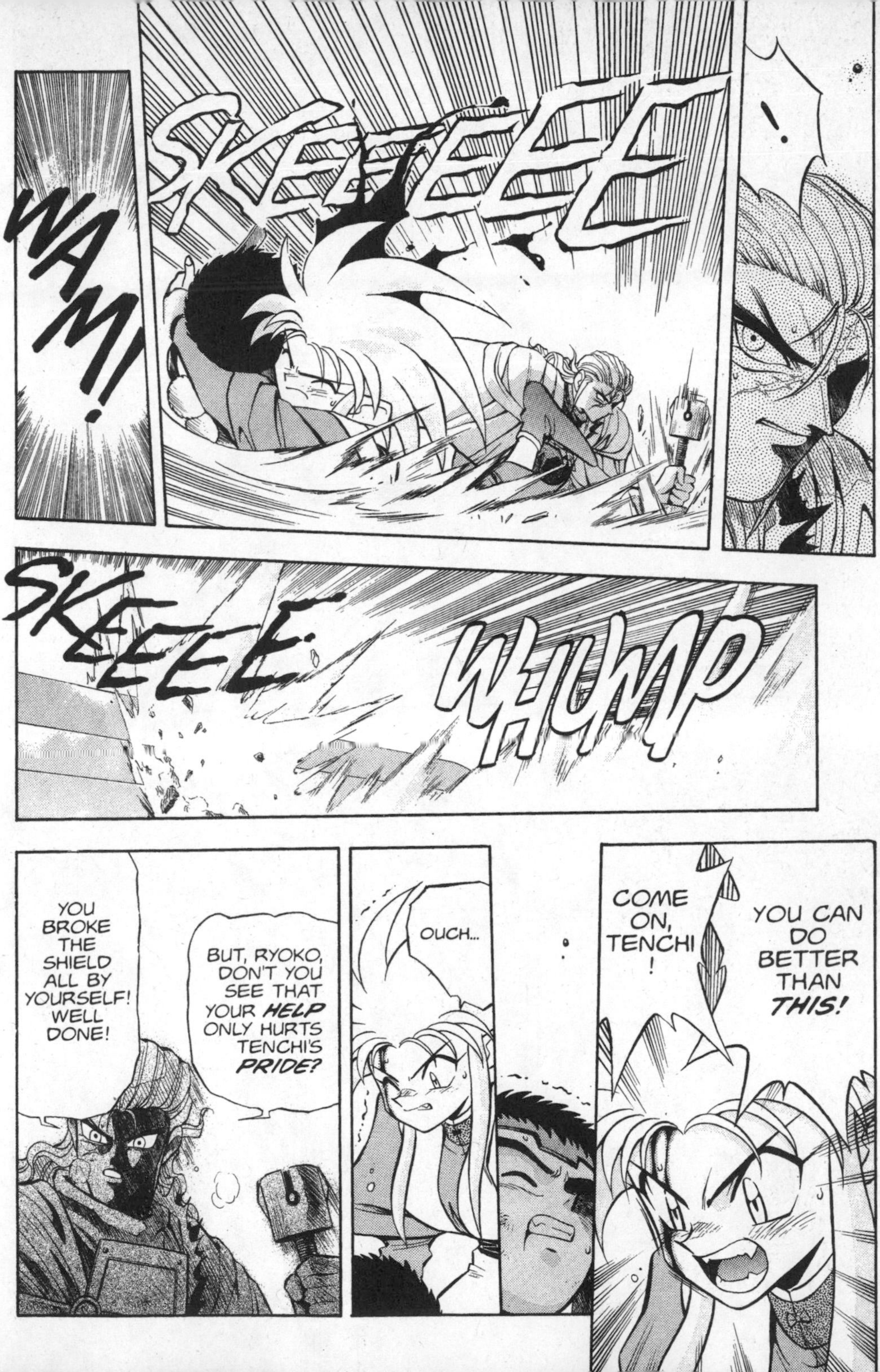
WAM!!
SKEEEEE
!
SKEEEE
WHUMP
YOU BROKE THE SHIELD ALL BY YOURSELF! WELL DONE!
BUT, RYOKO, DON'T YOU SEE THAT YOUR *HELP* ONLY HURTS TENCHI'S *PRIDE?*
OUCH...
COME ON, TENCHI!
YOU CAN DO BETTER THAN *THIS!*

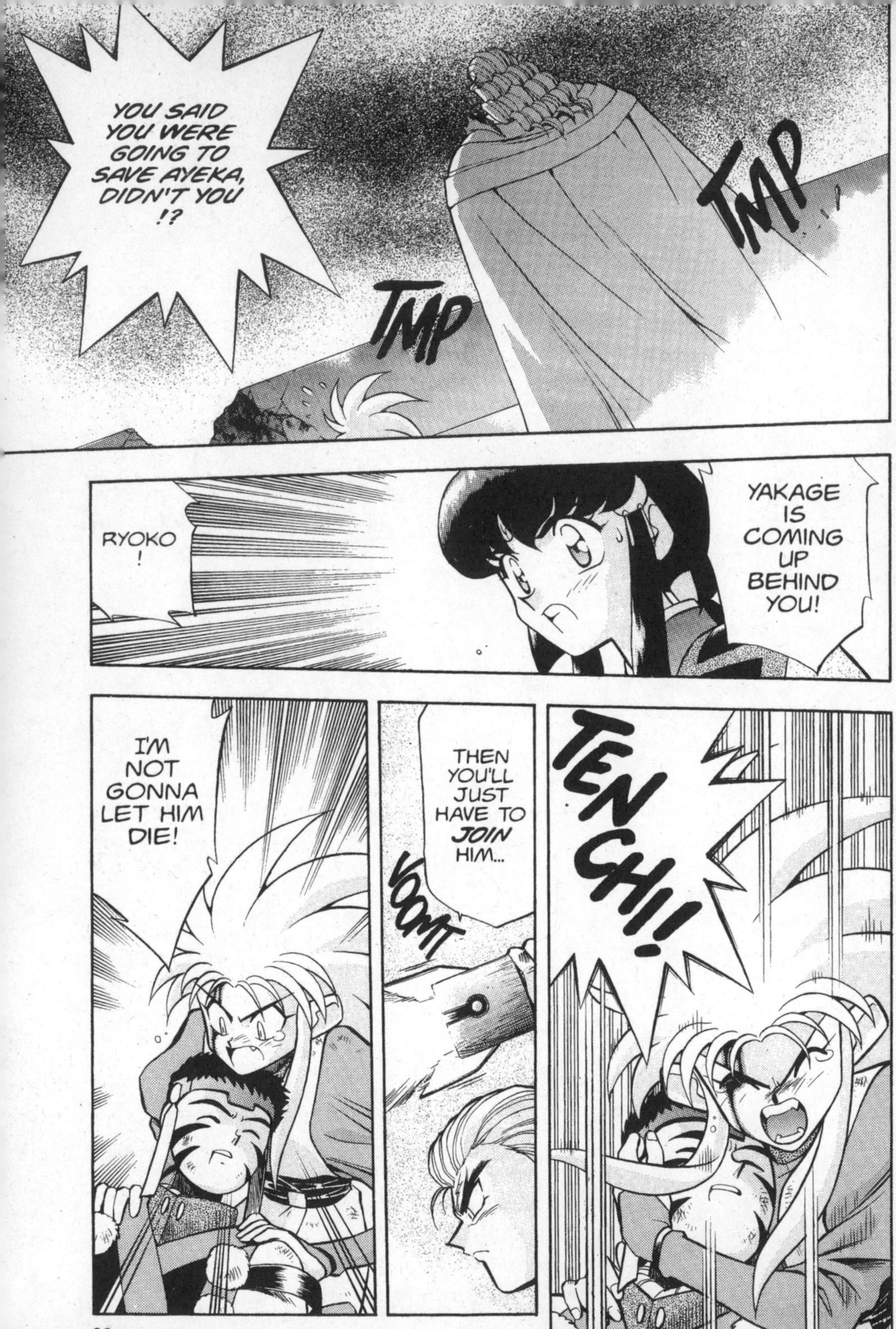
YOU SAID YOU WERE GOING TO SAVE AYEKA, DIDN'T YOU !?
TMP
TMP
RYOKO!
YAKAGE IS COMING UP BEHIND YOU!
I'M NOT GONNA LET HIM DIE!
THEN YOU'LL JUST HAVE TO *JOIN* HIM...
VOOMT
TENCHI!!

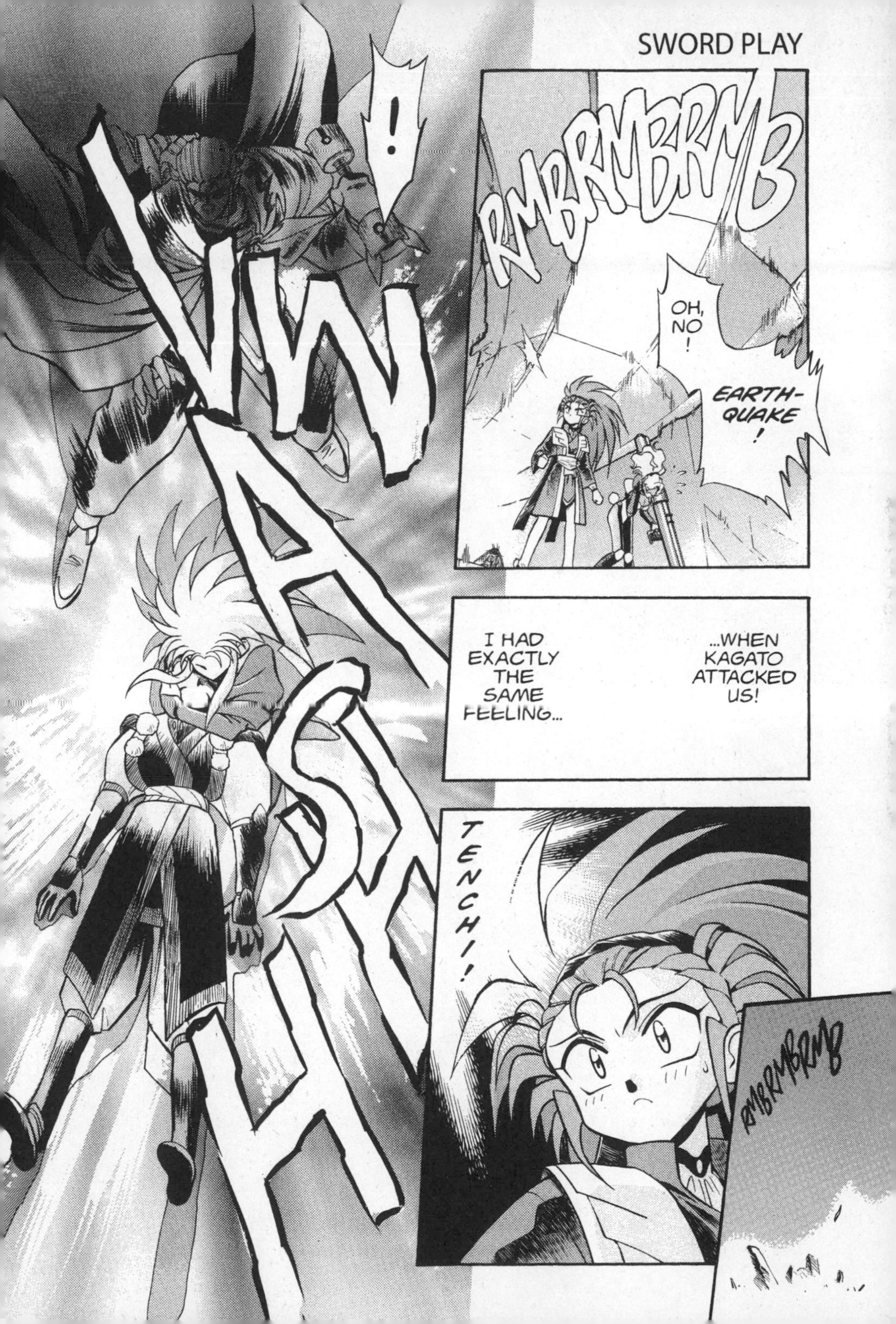
!
VWASH
RMBRMBRMB
OH, NO!
EARTH-QUAKE!
I HAD EXACTLY THE SAME FEELING...
...WHEN KAGATO ATTACKED US!
TENCHI!
RMBRMBRMB

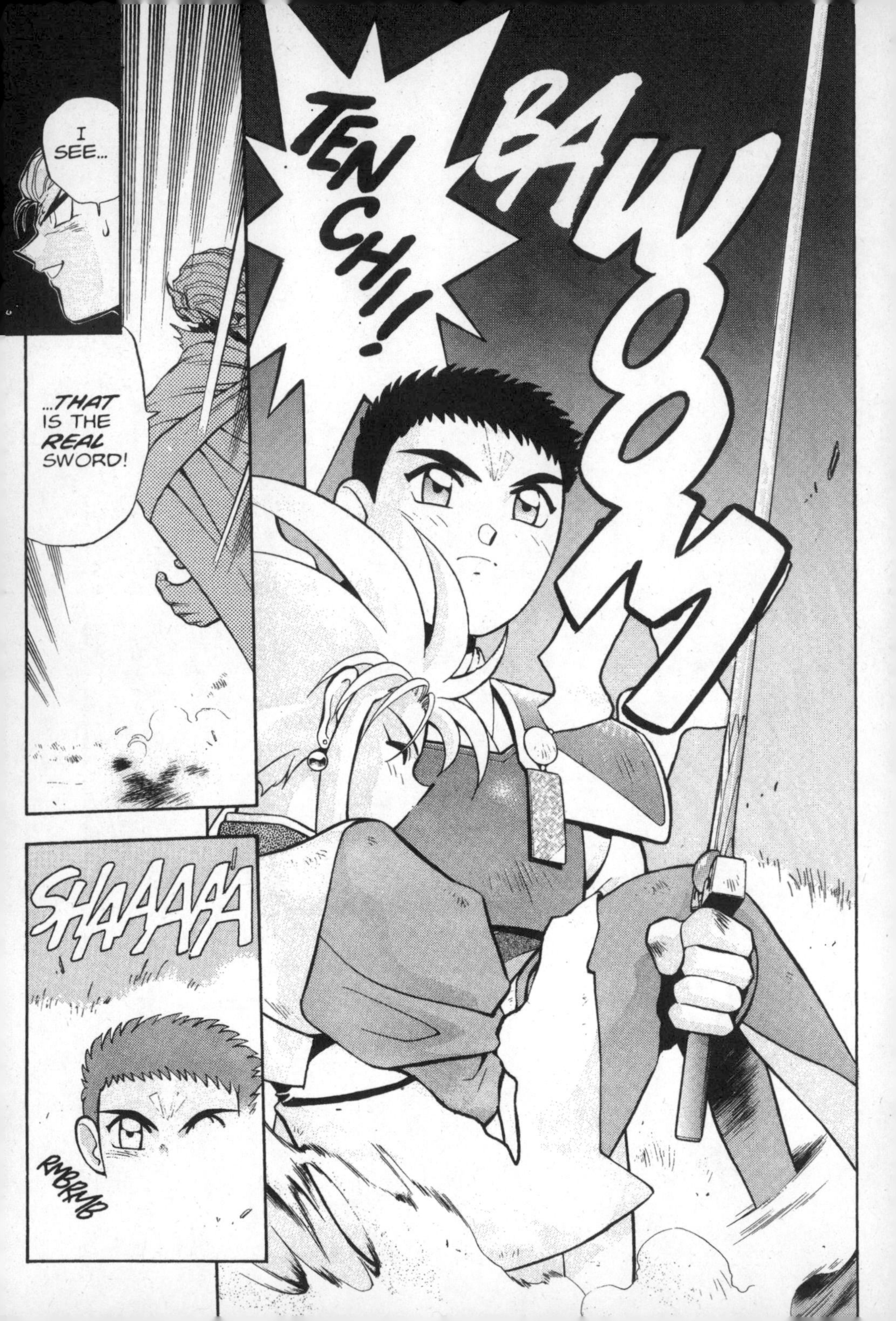
I SEE...
...THAT IS THE REAL SWORD!
BAWOOM
TENCHI!!
SHAAAAA
RMBRMB

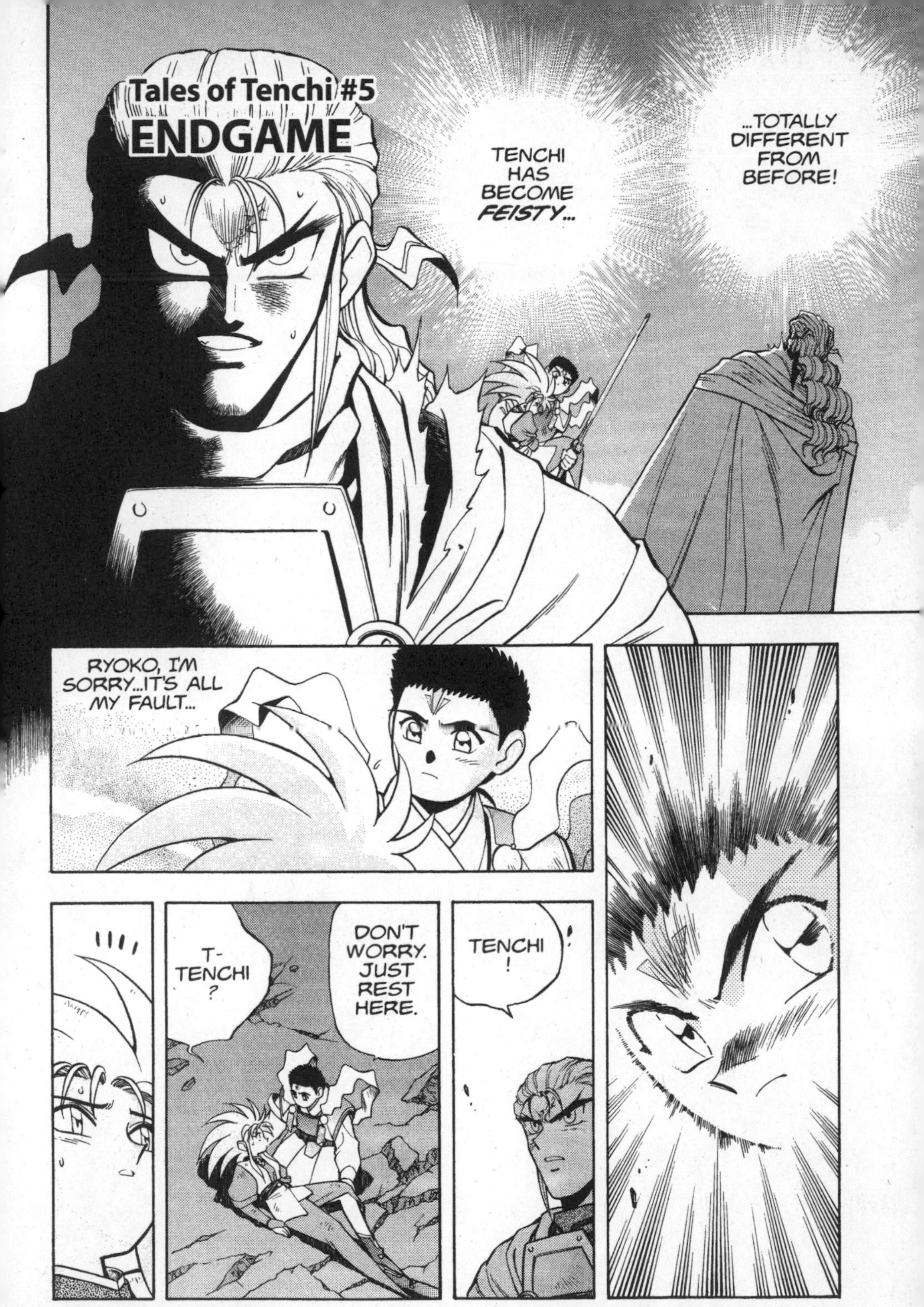
Tales of Tenchi #5
ENDGAME
TENCHI HAS BECOME *FEISTY*...
...TOTALLY DIFFERENT FROM BEFORE!
RYOKO, I'M SORRY...IT'S ALL MY FAULT...
!!!
T- TENCHI ?
DON'T WORRY. JUST REST HERE.
TENCHI !

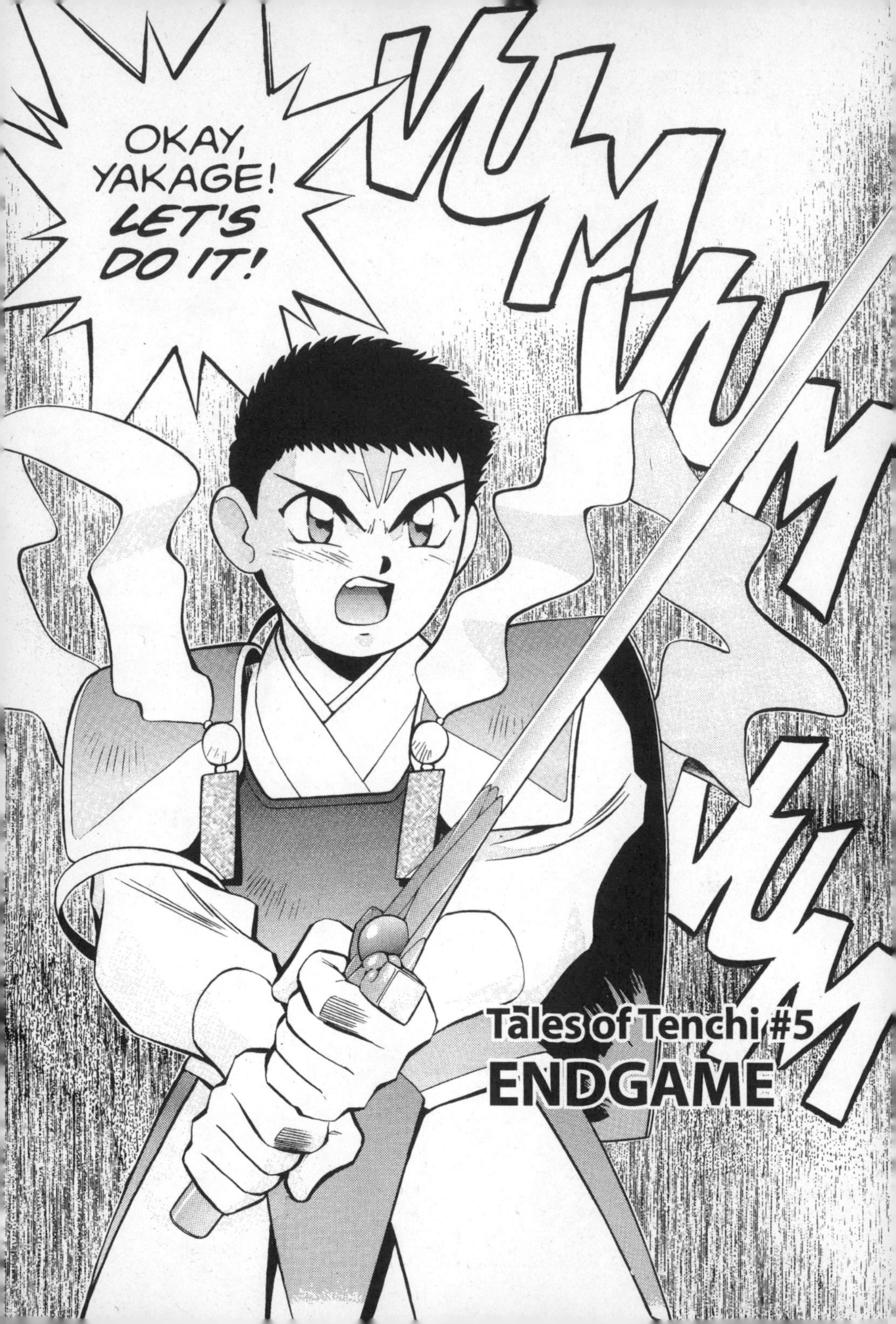
OKAY, YAKAGE! LET'S DO IT!
VUMMMMM
Tales of Tenchi #5
ENDGAME

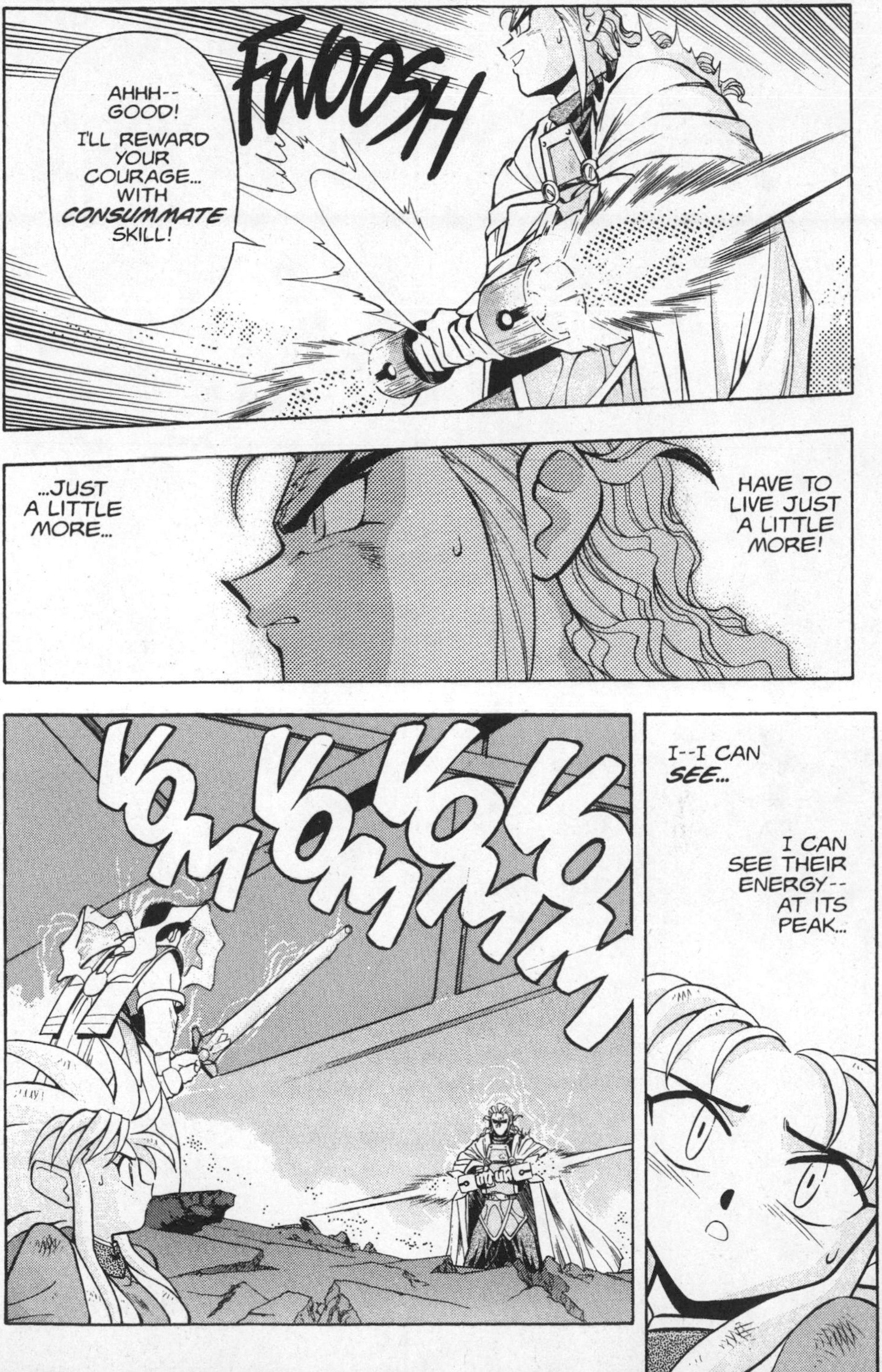
AHHH-- GOOD! I'LL REWARD YOUR COURAGE... WITH *CONSUMMATE* SKILL!
FWOOSH
...JUST A LITTLE MORE...
HAVE TO LIVE JUST A LITTLE MORE!
VOM VOM VOMMMM
I--I CAN *SEE*...
I CAN SEE THEIR ENERGY-- AT ITS PEAK...

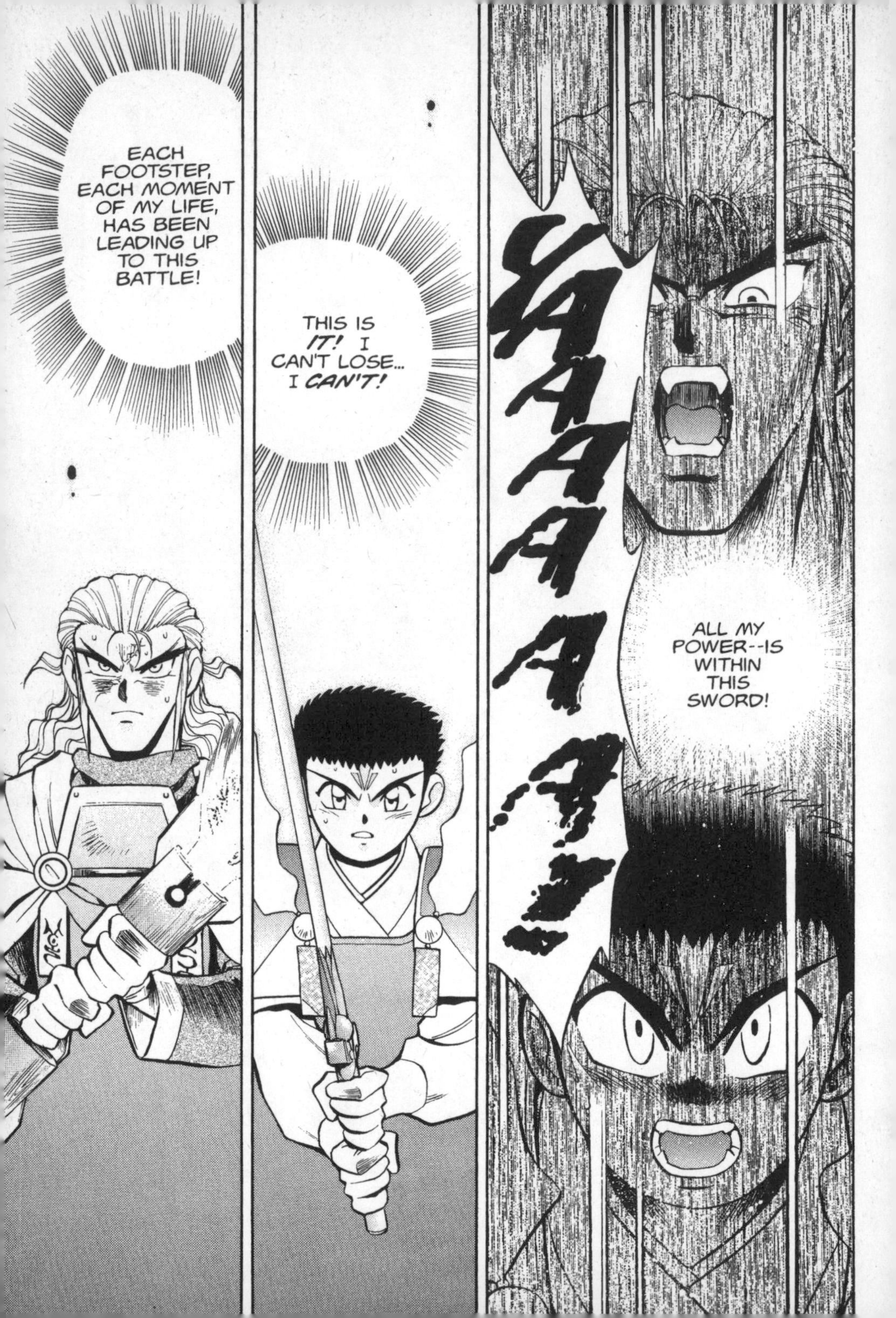
EACH FOOTSTEP, EACH MOMENT OF MY LIFE, HAS BEEN LEADING UP TO THIS BATTLE!
THIS IS *IT!* I CAN'T LOSE... I *CAN'T!*
YAAAAAA!!
ALL MY POWER--IS WITHIN THIS SWORD!

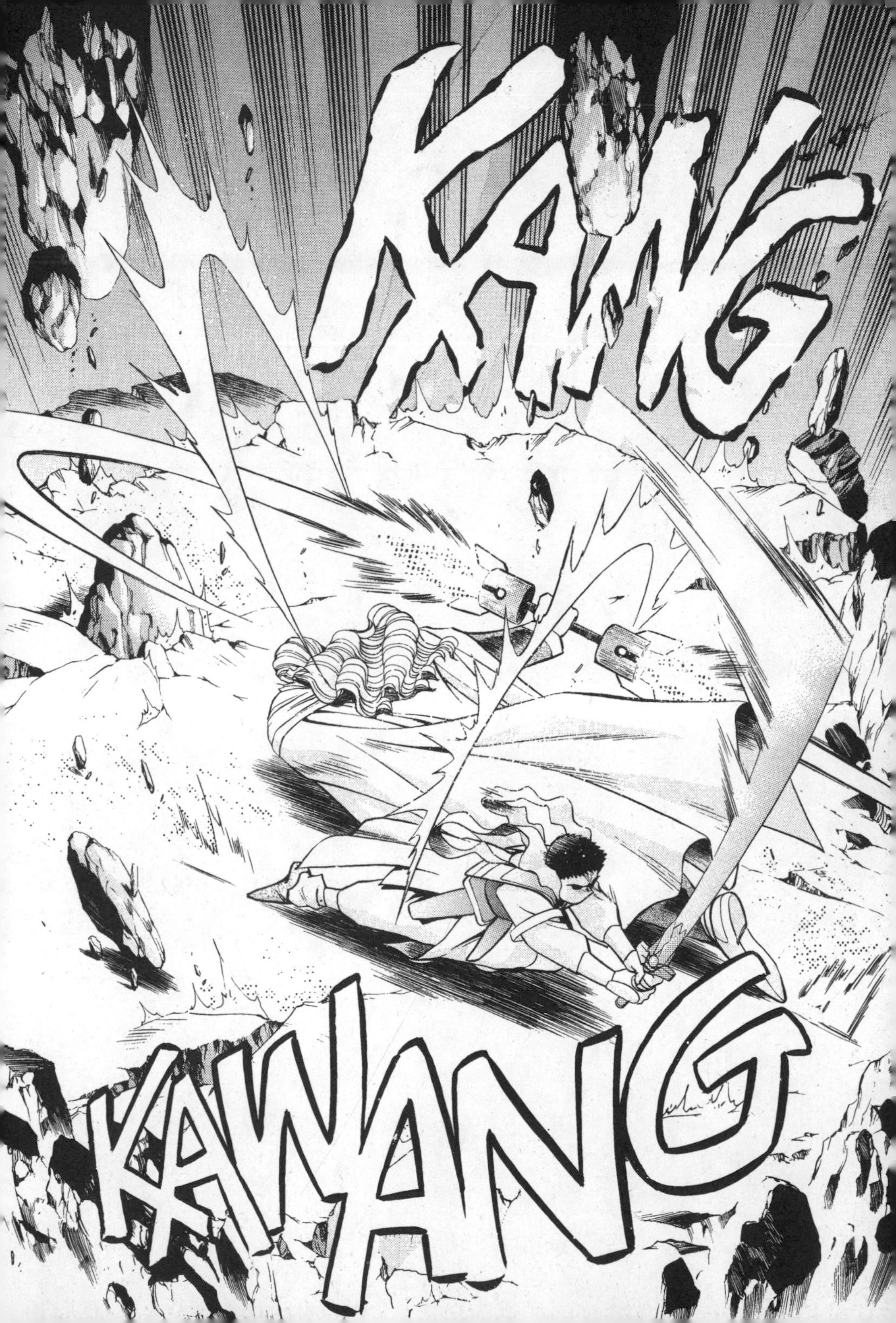
KANG!
KAWANG

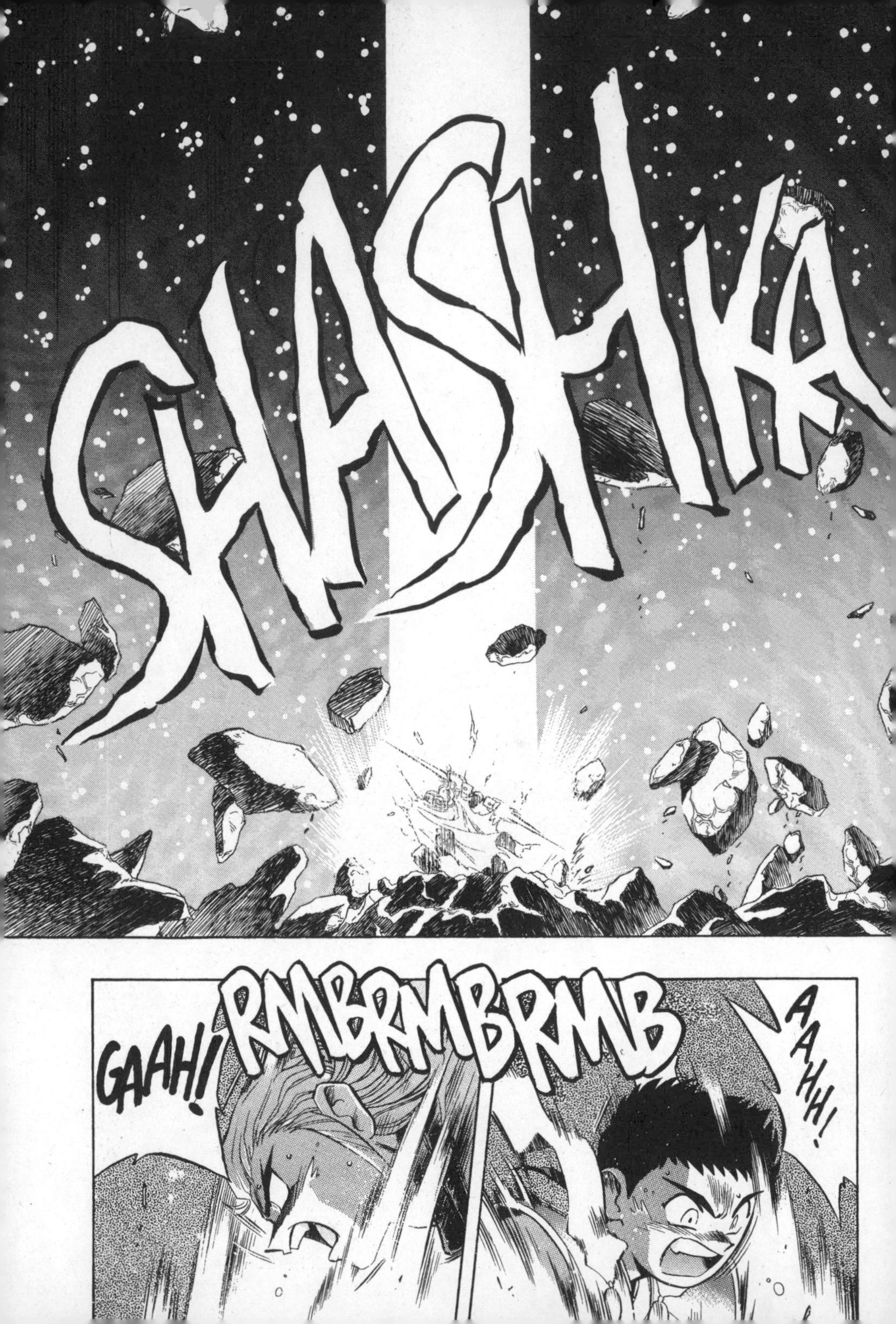
SHASHKA
GAAH!
RMBRMBRMB
AAHH!

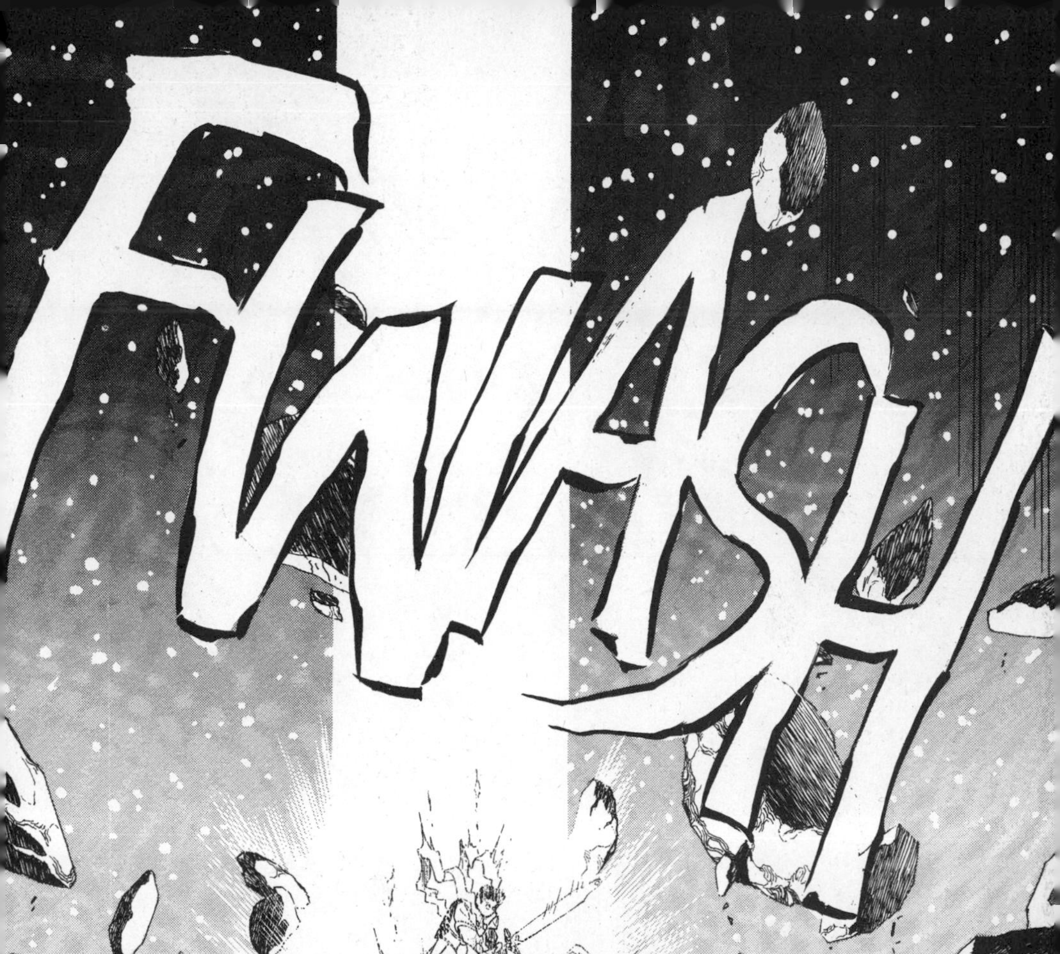
FWASH
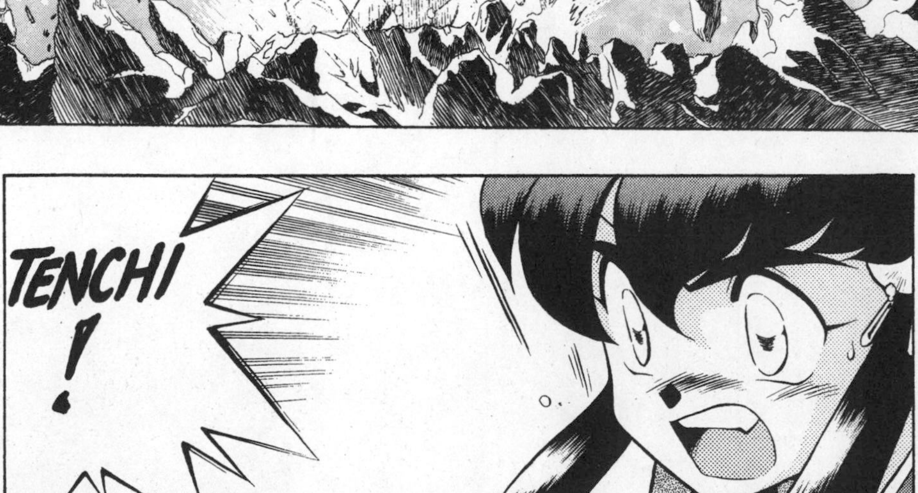
TENCHI!

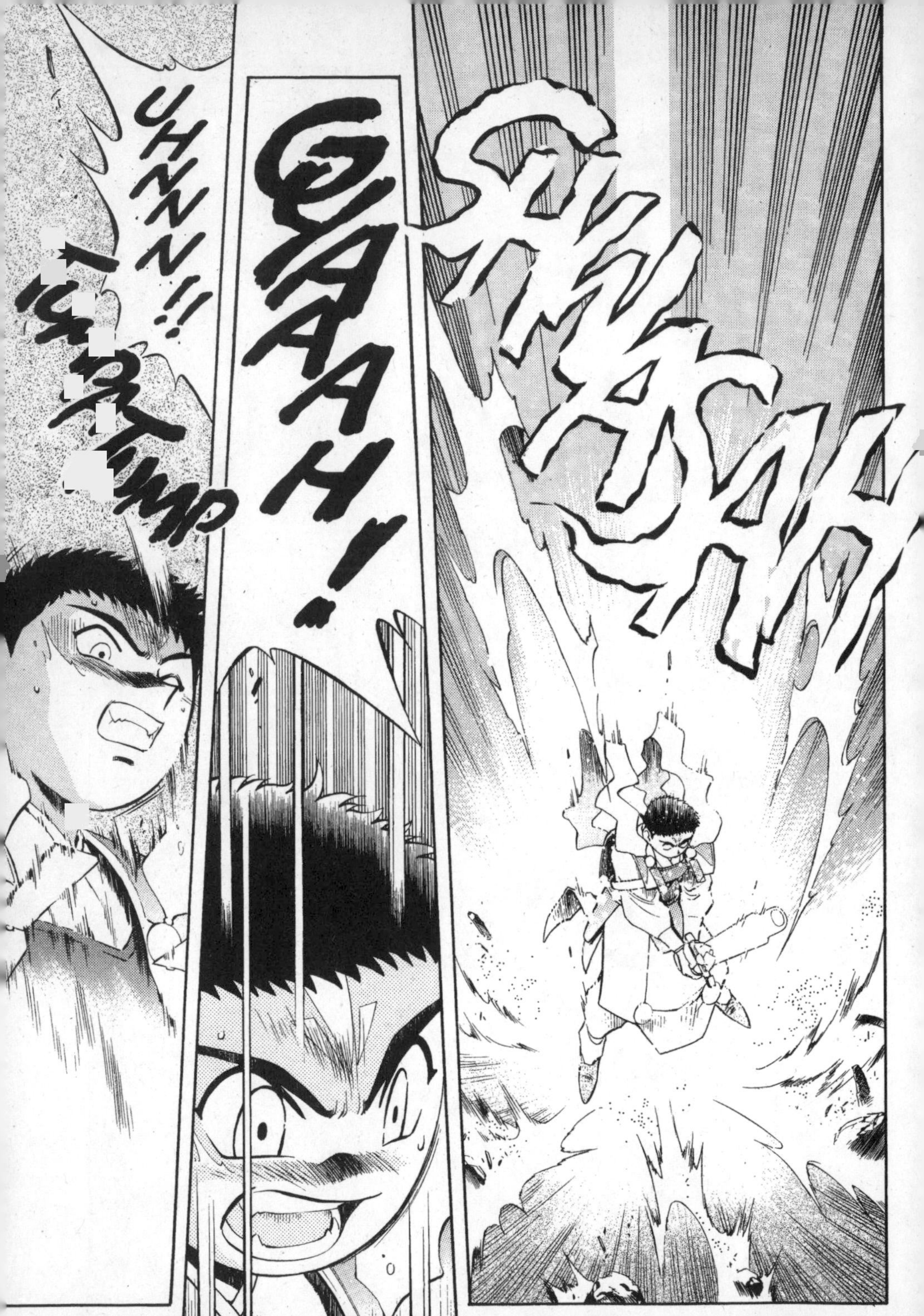
UHNNN!!
GAAAH!

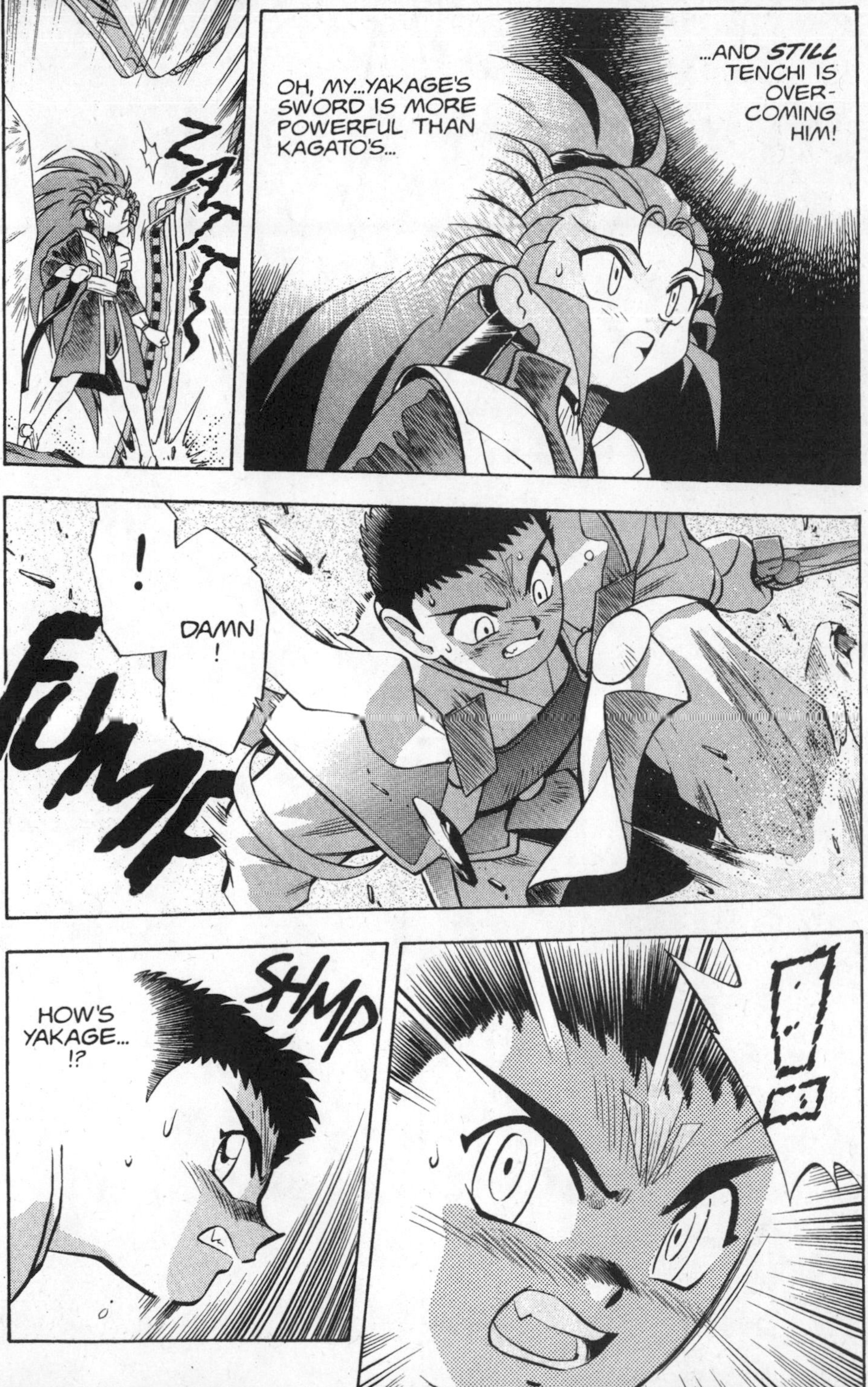
ZATT
OH, MY...YAKAGE'S SWORD IS MORE POWERFUL THAN KAGATO'S...
...AND STILL TENCHI IS OVER-COMING HIM!
!
DAMN!
FUMP
HOW'S YAKAGE...!?
SHMP
!!

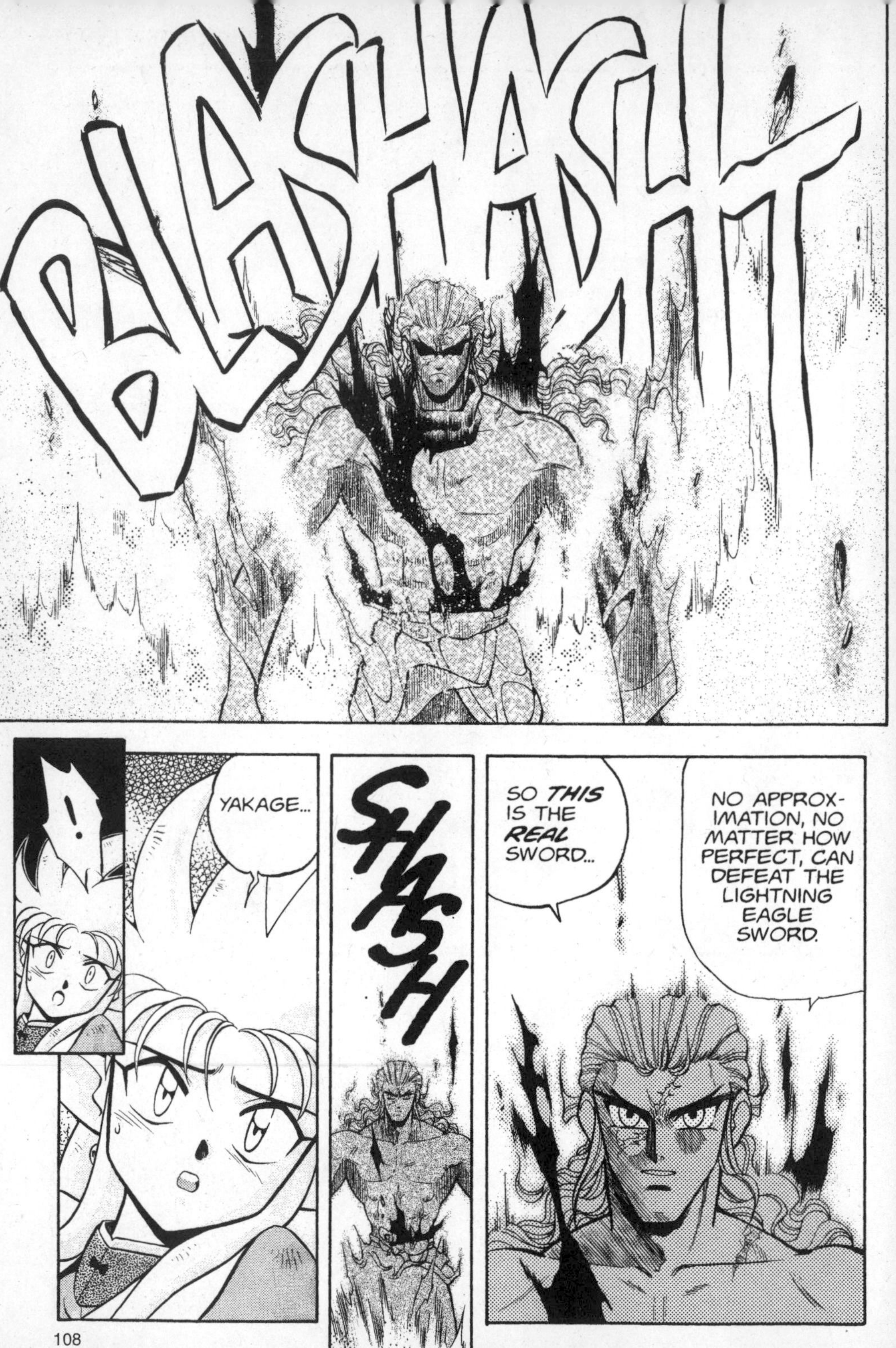
!
YAKAGE...
SHASH
SO ***THIS*** IS THE ***REAL*** SWORD...
NO APPROXIMATION, NO MATTER HOW PERFECT, CAN DEFEAT THE LIGHTNING EAGLE SWORD.

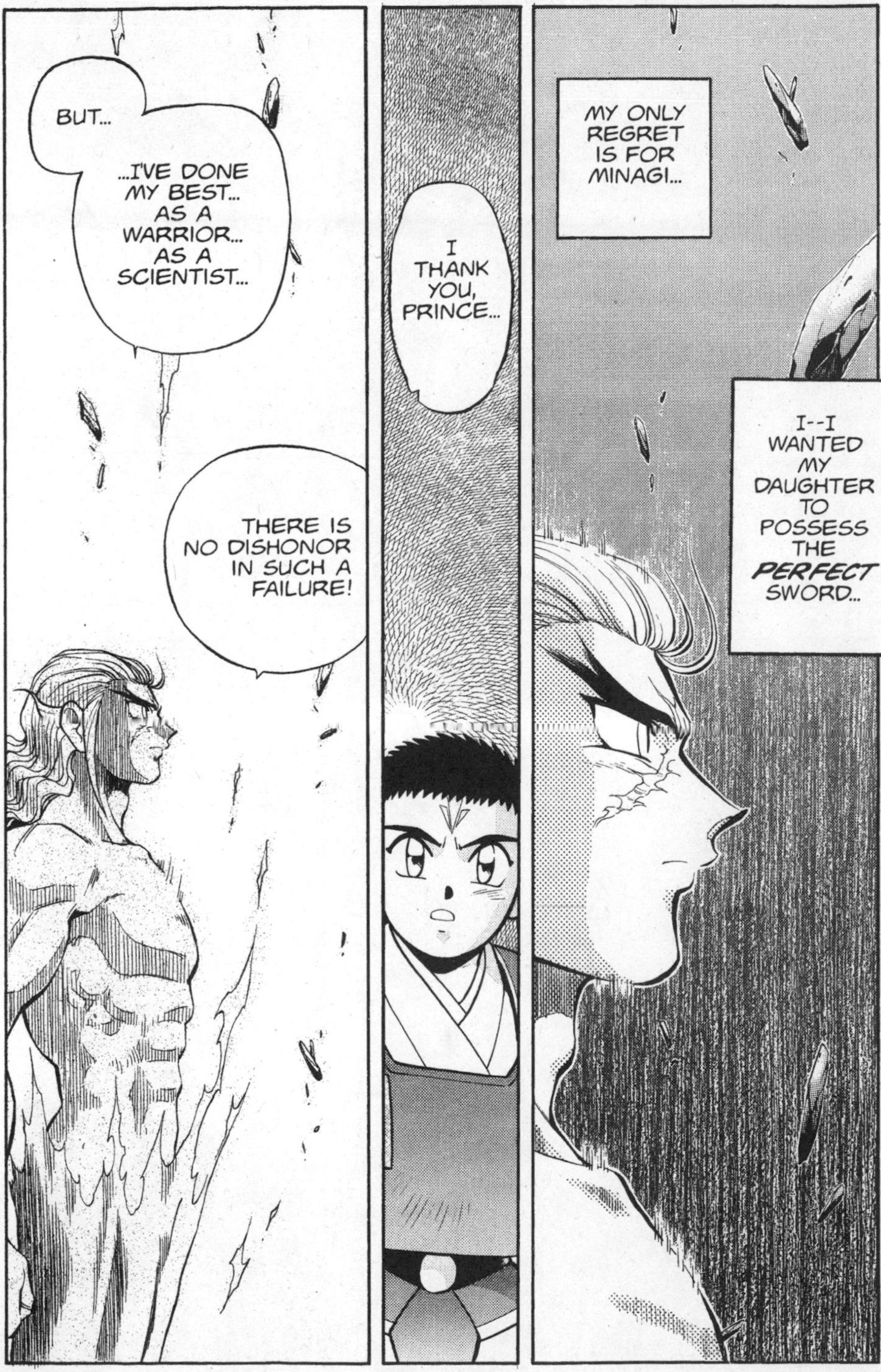
BUT...
...I'VE DONE MY BEST... AS A WARRIOR... AS A SCIENTIST...
THERE IS NO DISHONOR IN SUCH A FAILURE!
I THANK YOU, PRINCE...
MY ONLY REGRET IS FOR MINAGI...
I--I WANTED MY DAUGHTER TO POSSESS THE PERFECT SWORD...

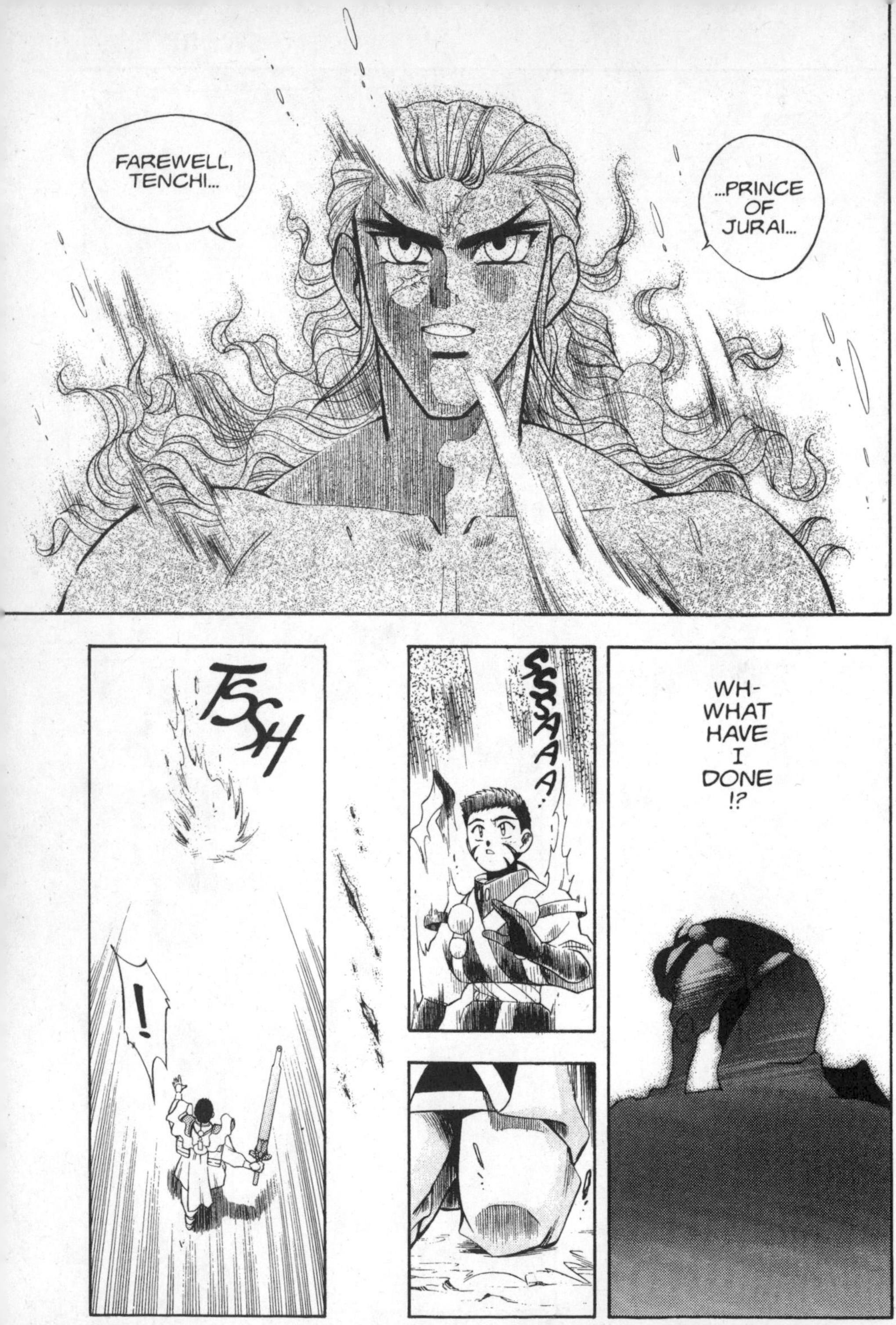
FAREWELL, TENCHI...
...PRINCE OF JURAI...
TSSH
!
SSSHAAA...
WH- WHAT HAVE I DONE !?

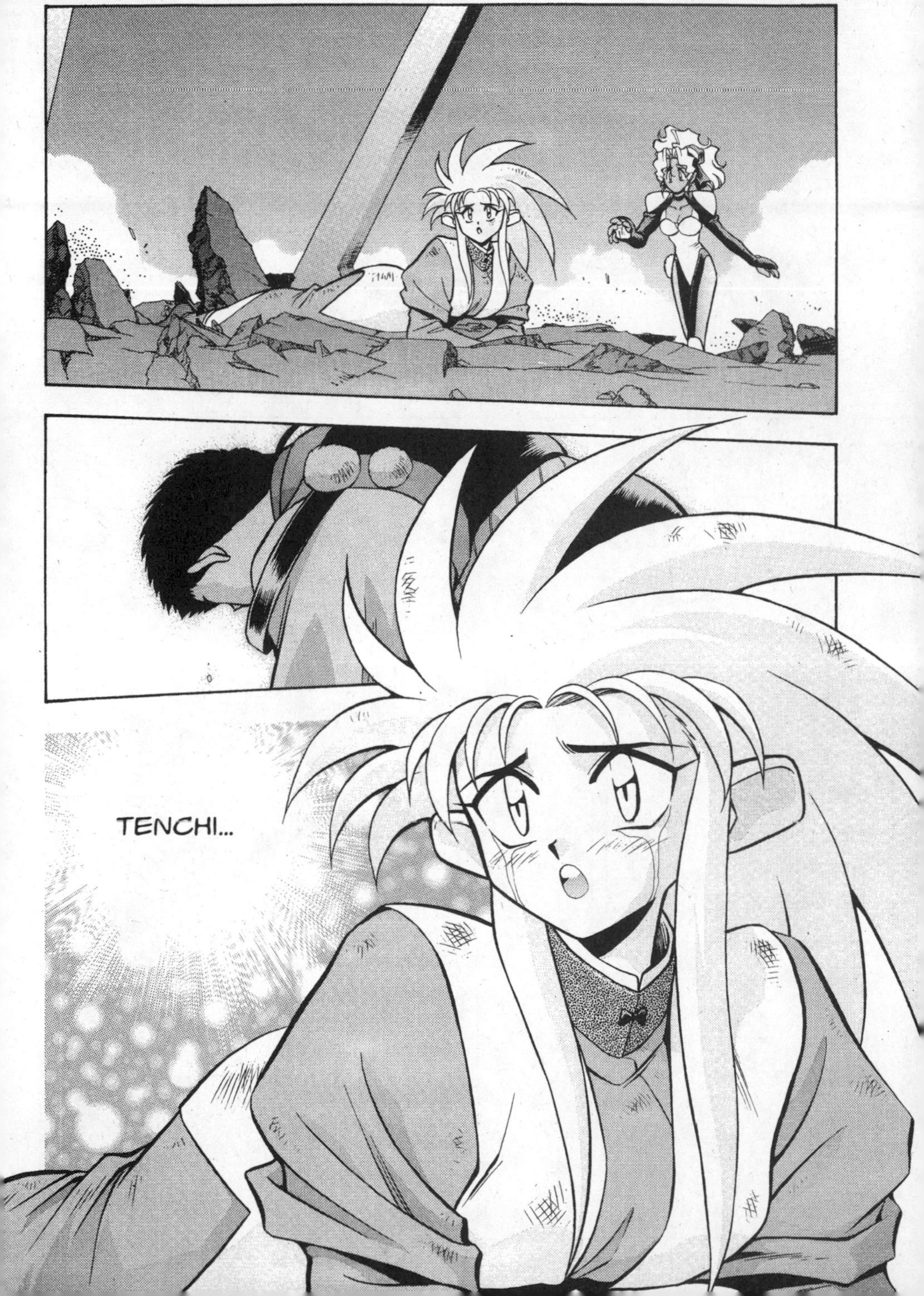
TENCHI...

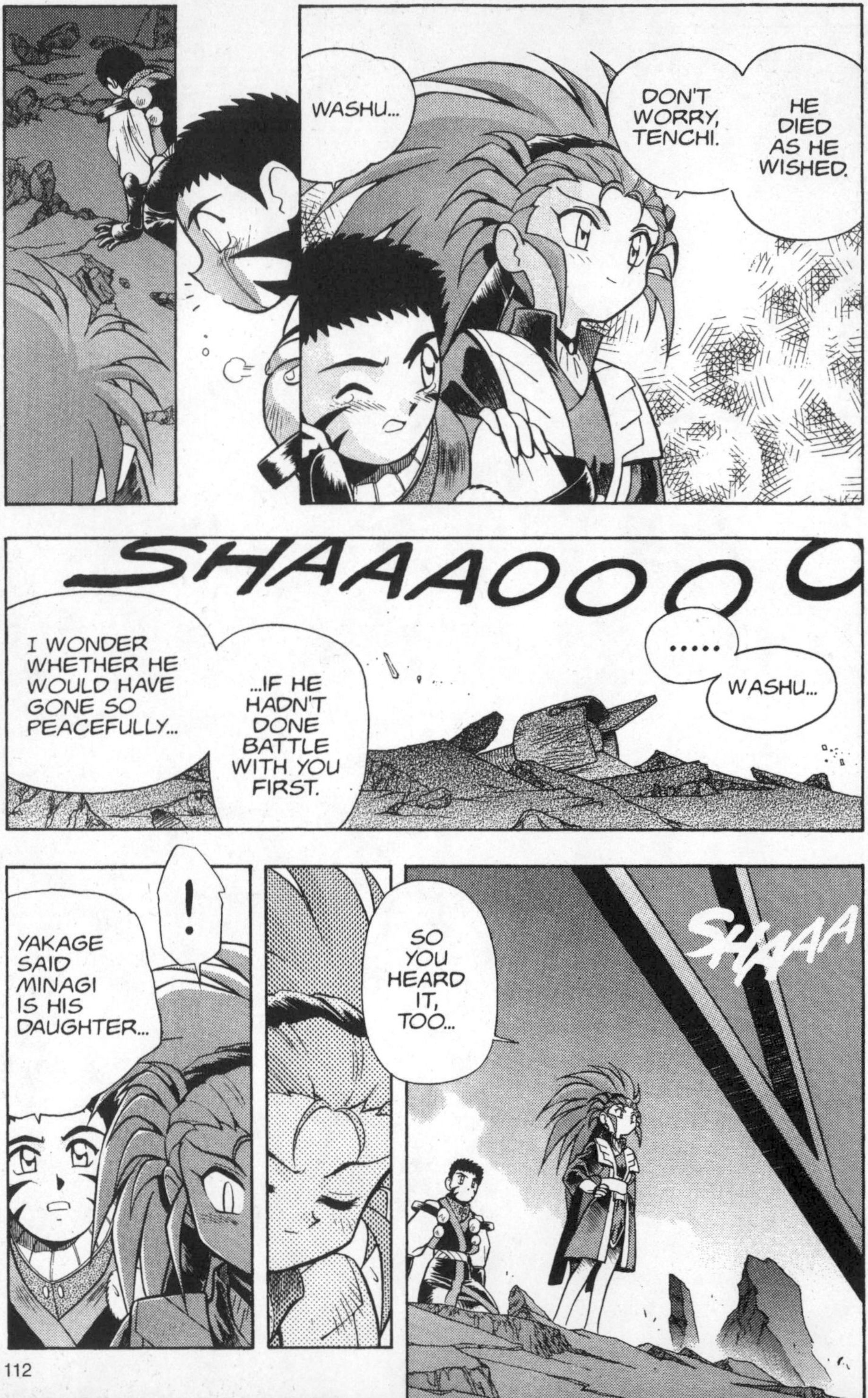
WASHU...
DON'T WORRY, TENCHI.
HE DIED AS HE WISHED.
SHAAAOOOO
I WONDER WHETHER HE WOULD HAVE GONE SO PEACEFULLY...
...IF HE HADN'T DONE BATTLE WITH YOU FIRST.
.....
WASHU...
YAKAGE SAID MINAGI IS HIS DAUGHTER...
!
SO YOU HEARD IT, TOO...
SHAAA

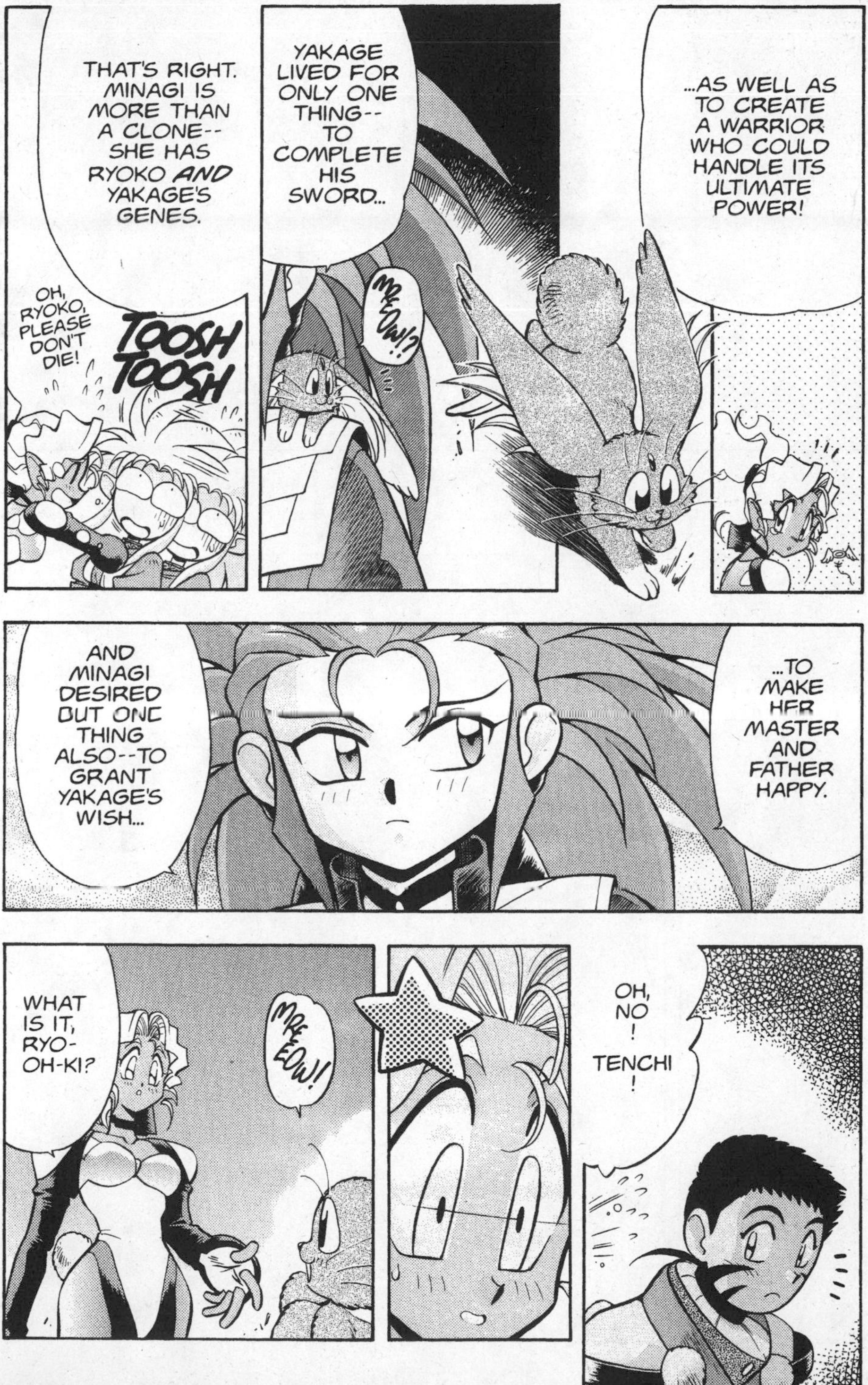
THAT'S RIGHT. MINAGI IS MORE THAN A CLONE-- SHE HAS RYOKO *AND* YAKAGE'S GENES.
OH, RYOKO, PLEASE DON'T DIE!
TOOSH TOOSH
YAKAGE LIVED FOR ONLY ONE THING-- TO COMPLETE HIS SWORD...
MREOW!?
...AS WELL AS TO CREATE A WARRIOR WHO COULD HANDLE ITS ULTIMATE POWER!
AND MINAGI DESIRED BUT ONE THING ALSO--TO GRANT YAKAGE'S WISH...
...TO MAKE HER MASTER AND FATHER HAPPY.
WHAT IS IT, RYO-OH-KI?
MREEOW!!
OH, NO! TENCHI!

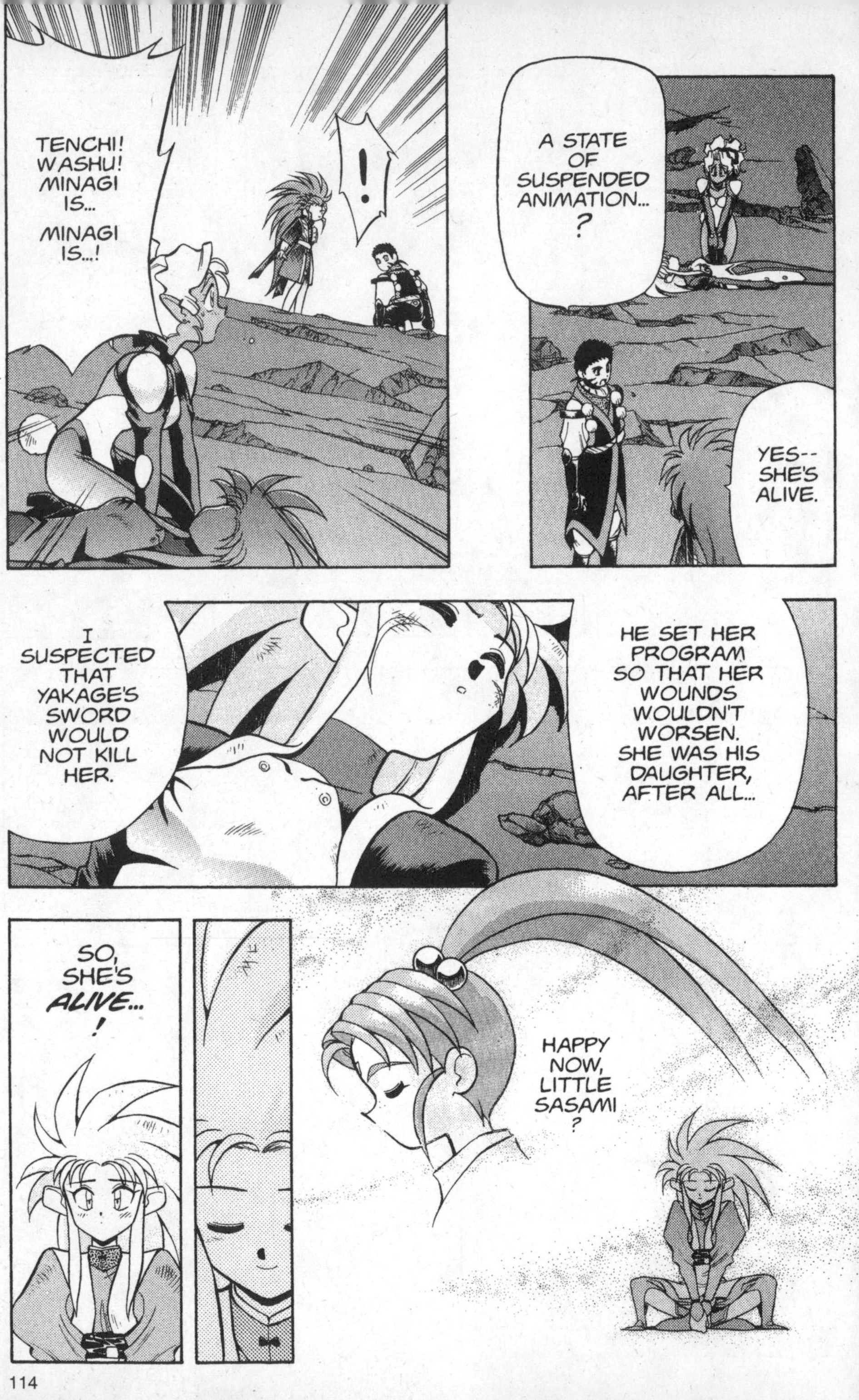
TENCHI! WASHU! MINAGI IS...
MINAGI IS...!
!
A STATE OF SUSPENDED ANIMATION...?
YES-- SHE'S ALIVE.
I SUSPECTED THAT YAKAGE'S SWORD WOULD NOT KILL HER.
HE SET HER PROGRAM SO THAT HER WOUNDS WOULDN'T WORSEN. SHE WAS HIS DAUGHTER, AFTER ALL...
SO, SHE'S *ALIVE*...!
HAPPY NOW, LITTLE SASAMI?

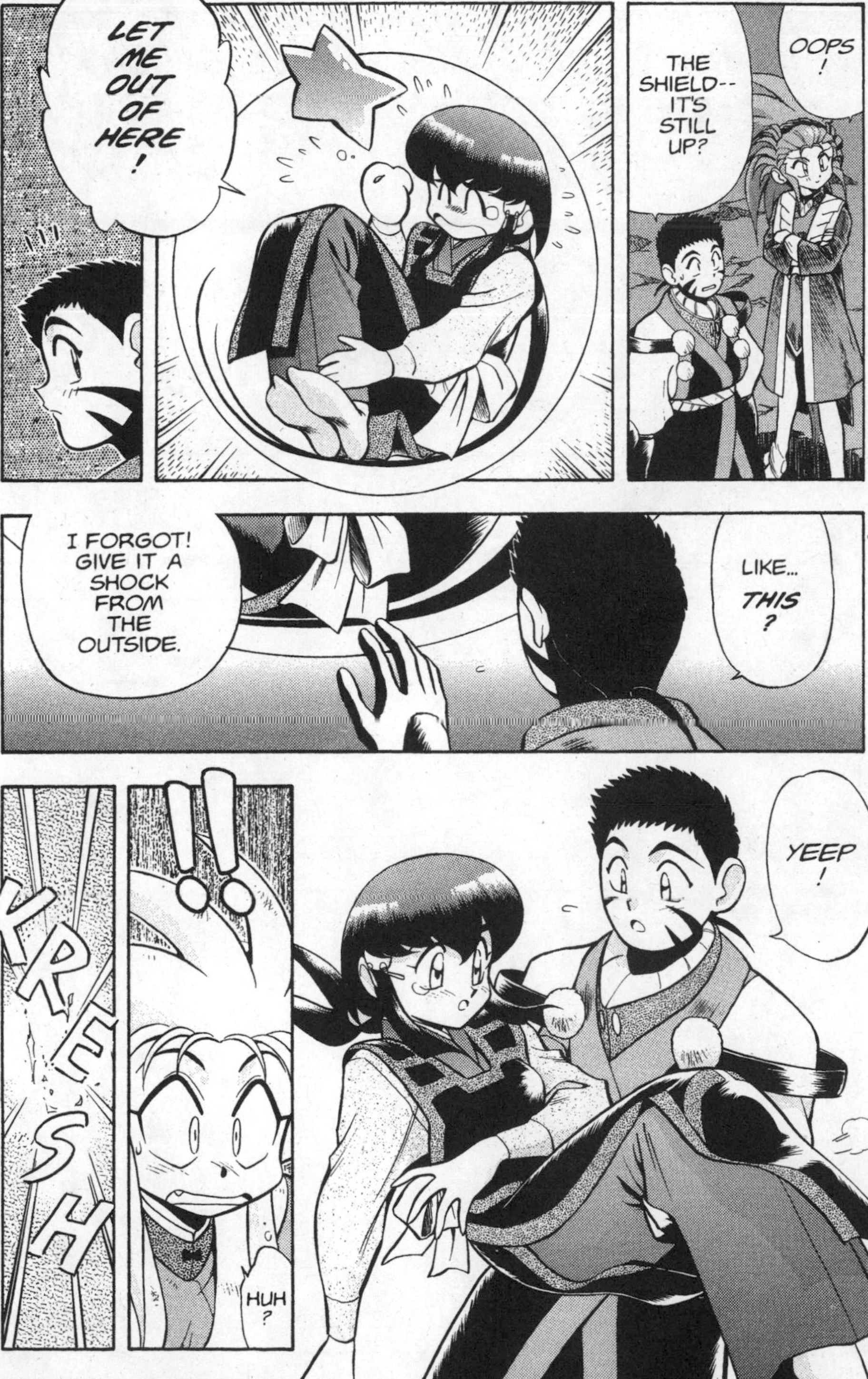
LET ME OUT OF HERE!
OOPS!
THE SHIELD-- IT'S STILL UP?
I FORGOT! GIVE IT A SHOCK FROM THE OUTSIDE.
LIKE... THIS?
KRESH
!!
HUH?
YEEP!

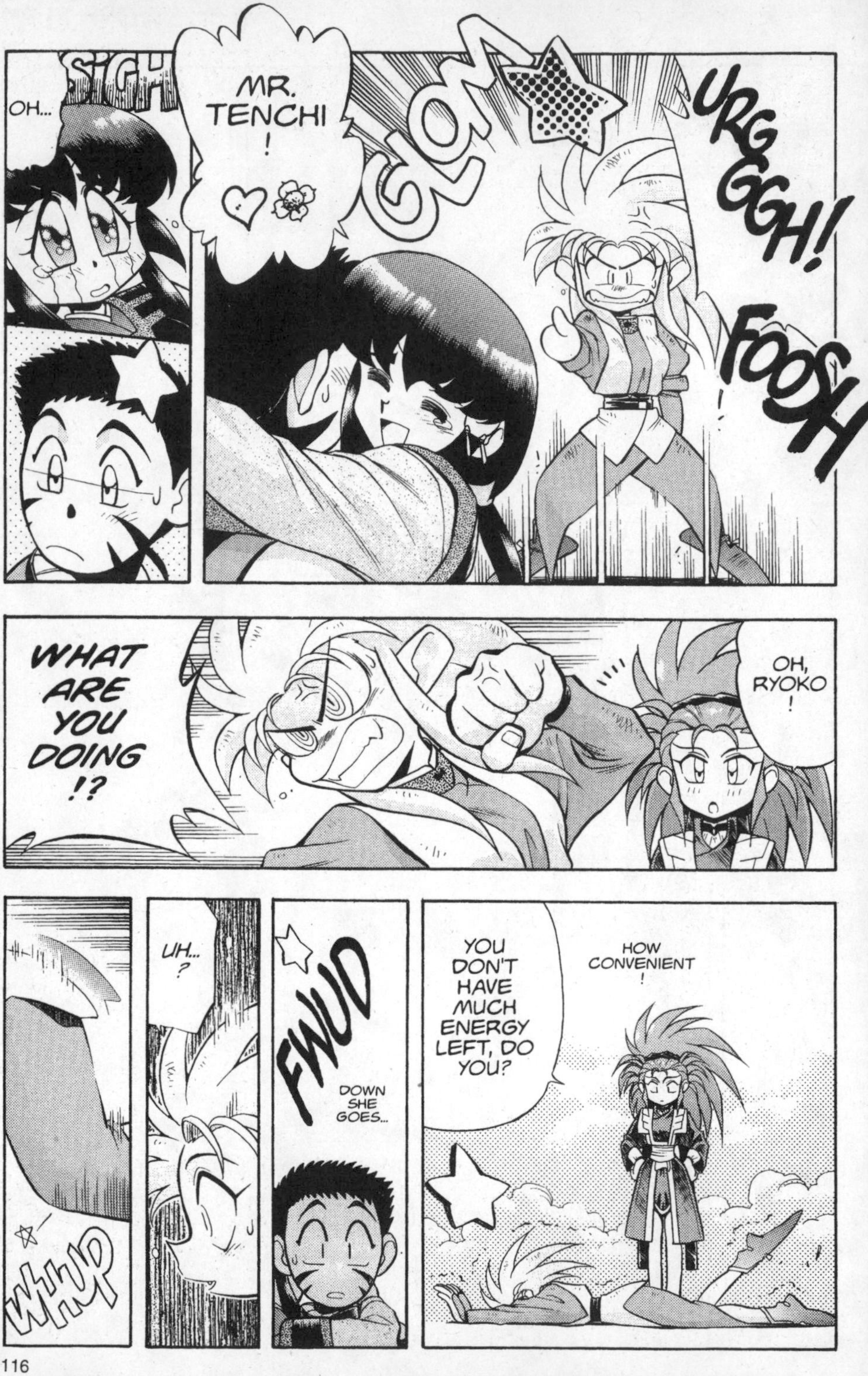
SIGH
OH...
MR. TENCHI !
GLOMP
URGGGH!
FOOSH
WHAT ARE YOU DOING !?
OH, RYOKO !
WHUP
UH... ?
FWUD
DOWN SHE GOES...
YOU DON'T HAVE MUCH ENERGY LEFT, DO YOU?
HOW CONVENIENT !

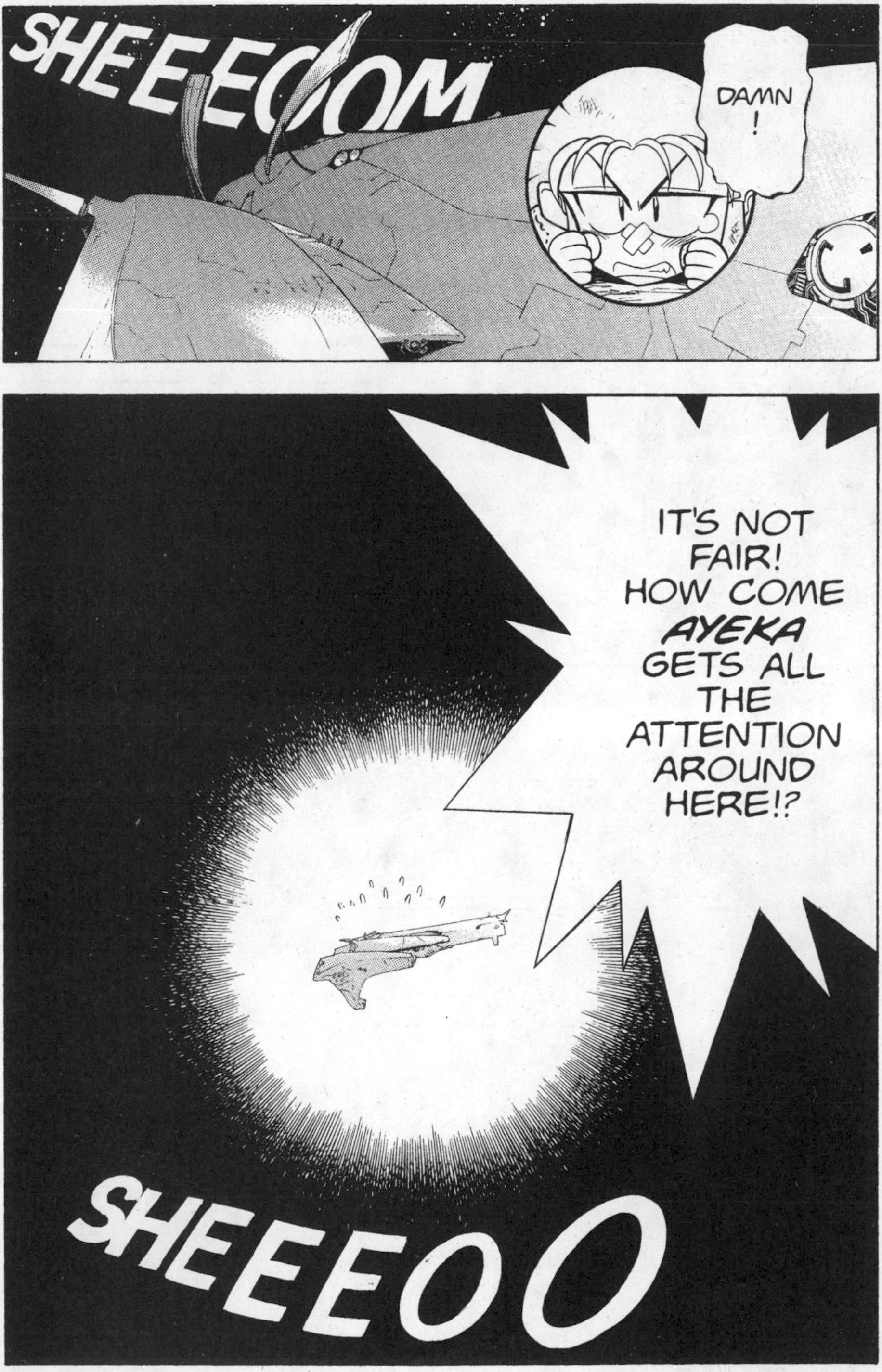
SHEEEOOM
DAMN!
IT'S NOT FAIR! HOW COME AYEKA GETS ALL THE ATTENTION AROUND HERE!?
SHEEEOO

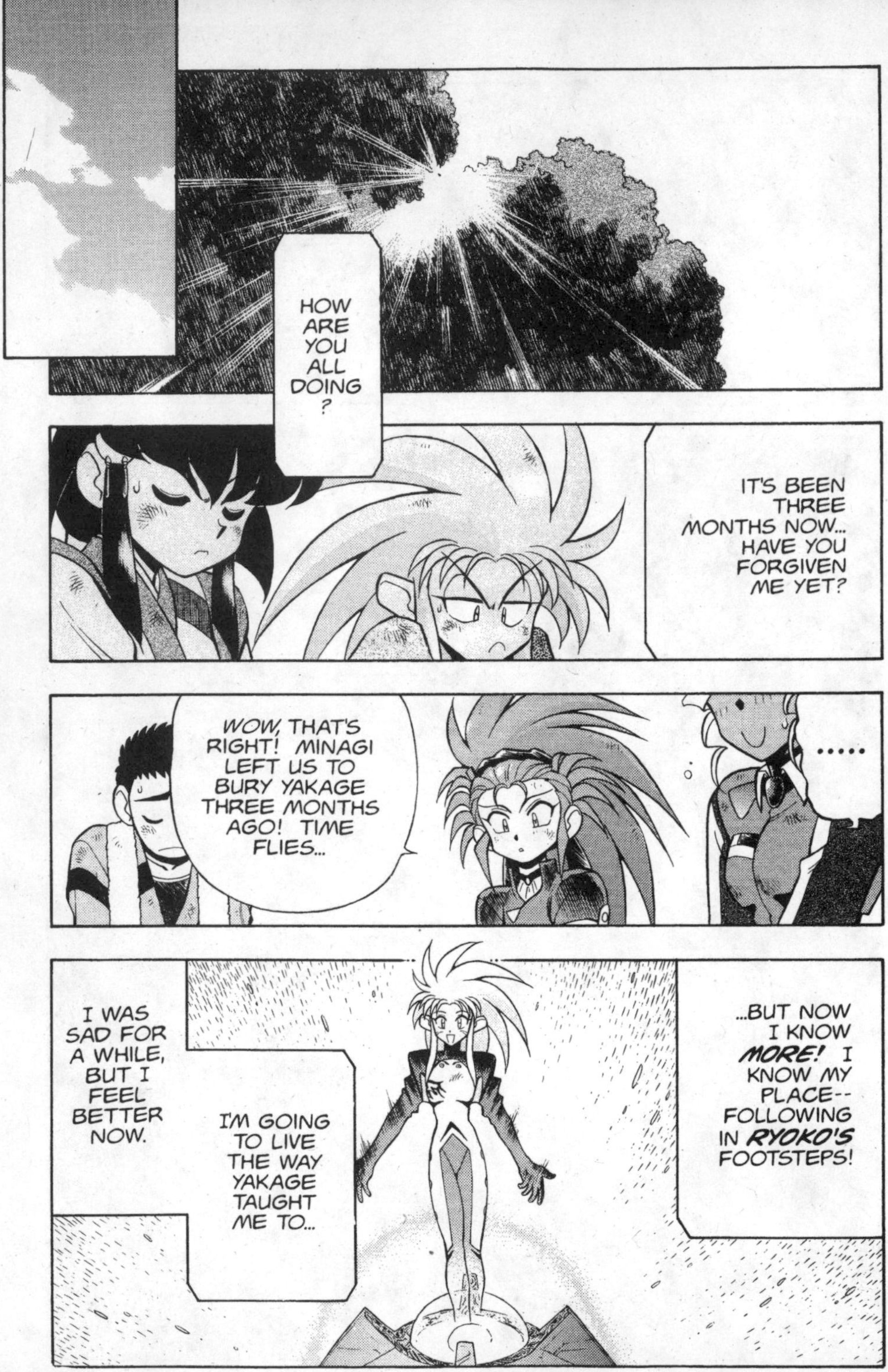
HOW ARE YOU ALL DOING?
IT'S BEEN THREE MONTHS NOW... HAVE YOU FORGIVEN ME YET?
WOW, THAT'S RIGHT! MINAGI LEFT US TO BURY YAKAGE THREE MONTHS AGO! TIME FLIES...
.....
I WAS SAD FOR A WHILE, BUT I FEEL BETTER NOW.
I'M GOING TO LIVE THE WAY YAKAGE TAUGHT ME TO...
...BUT NOW I KNOW MORE! I KNOW MY PLACE--FOLLOWING IN RYOKO'S FOOTSTEPS!

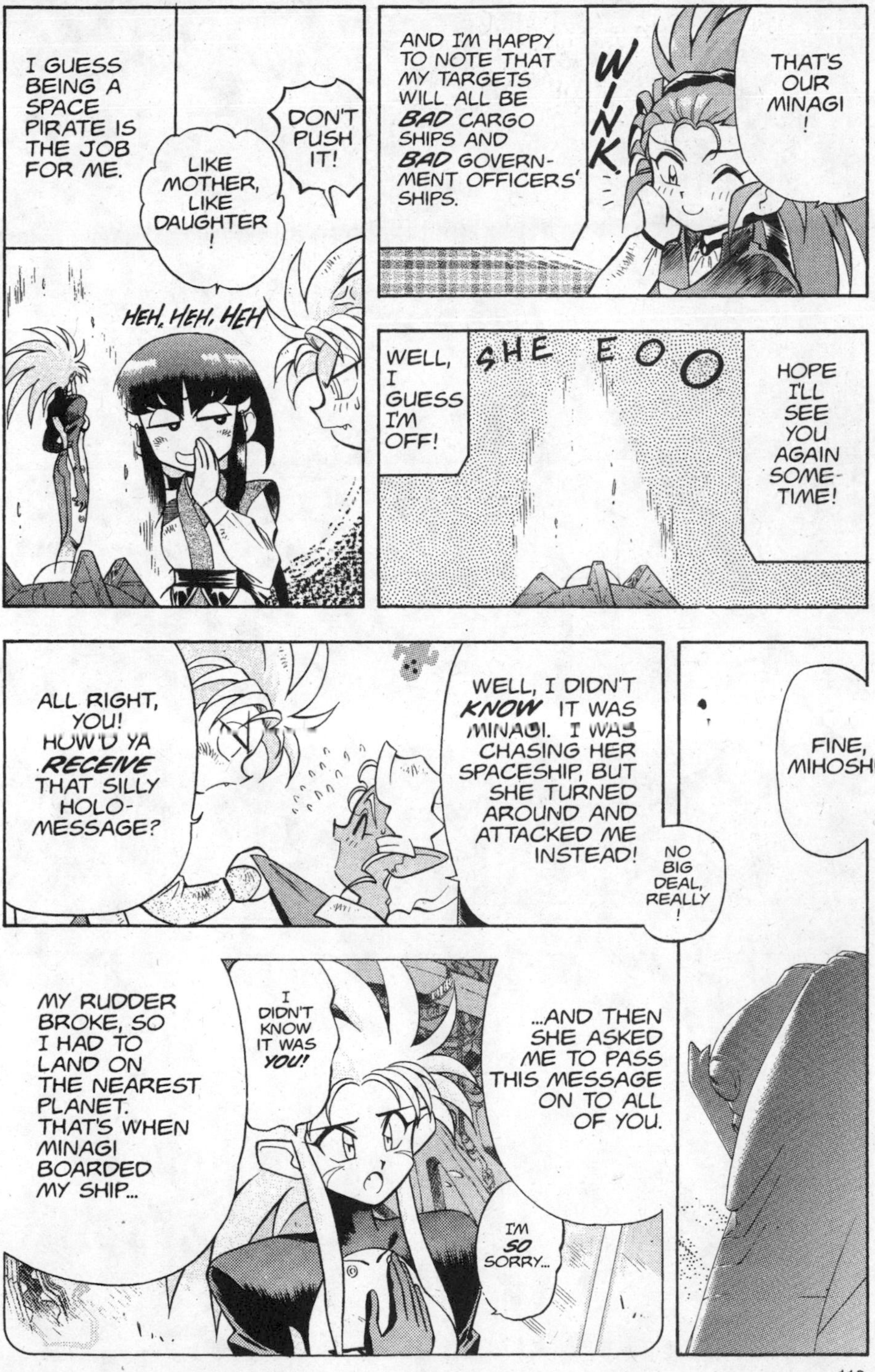
I GUESS BEING A SPACE PIRATE IS THE JOB FOR ME.
DON'T PUSH IT!
LIKE MOTHER, LIKE DAUGHTER!
HEH, HEH, HEH
AND I'M HAPPY TO NOTE THAT MY TARGETS WILL ALL BE BAD CARGO SHIPS AND BAD GOVERNMENT OFFICERS' SHIPS.
WINK
THAT'S OUR MINAGI!
WELL, I GUESS I'M OFF!
SHE EOO
HOPE I'LL SEE YOU AGAIN SOMETIME!
ALL RIGHT, YOU! HOW'D YA RECEIVE THAT SILLY HOLO-MESSAGE?
WELL, I DIDN'T KNOW IT WAS MINAGI. I WAS CHASING HER SPACESHIP, BUT SHE TURNED AROUND AND ATTACKED ME INSTEAD!
NO BIG DEAL, REALLY!
FINE, MIHOSHI...
MY RUDDER BROKE, SO I HAD TO LAND ON THE NEAREST PLANET. THAT'S WHEN MINAGI BOARDED MY SHIP...
I DIDN'T KNOW IT WAS YOU!
...AND THEN SHE ASKED ME TO PASS THIS MESSAGE ON TO ALL OF YOU.
I'M SO SORRY...

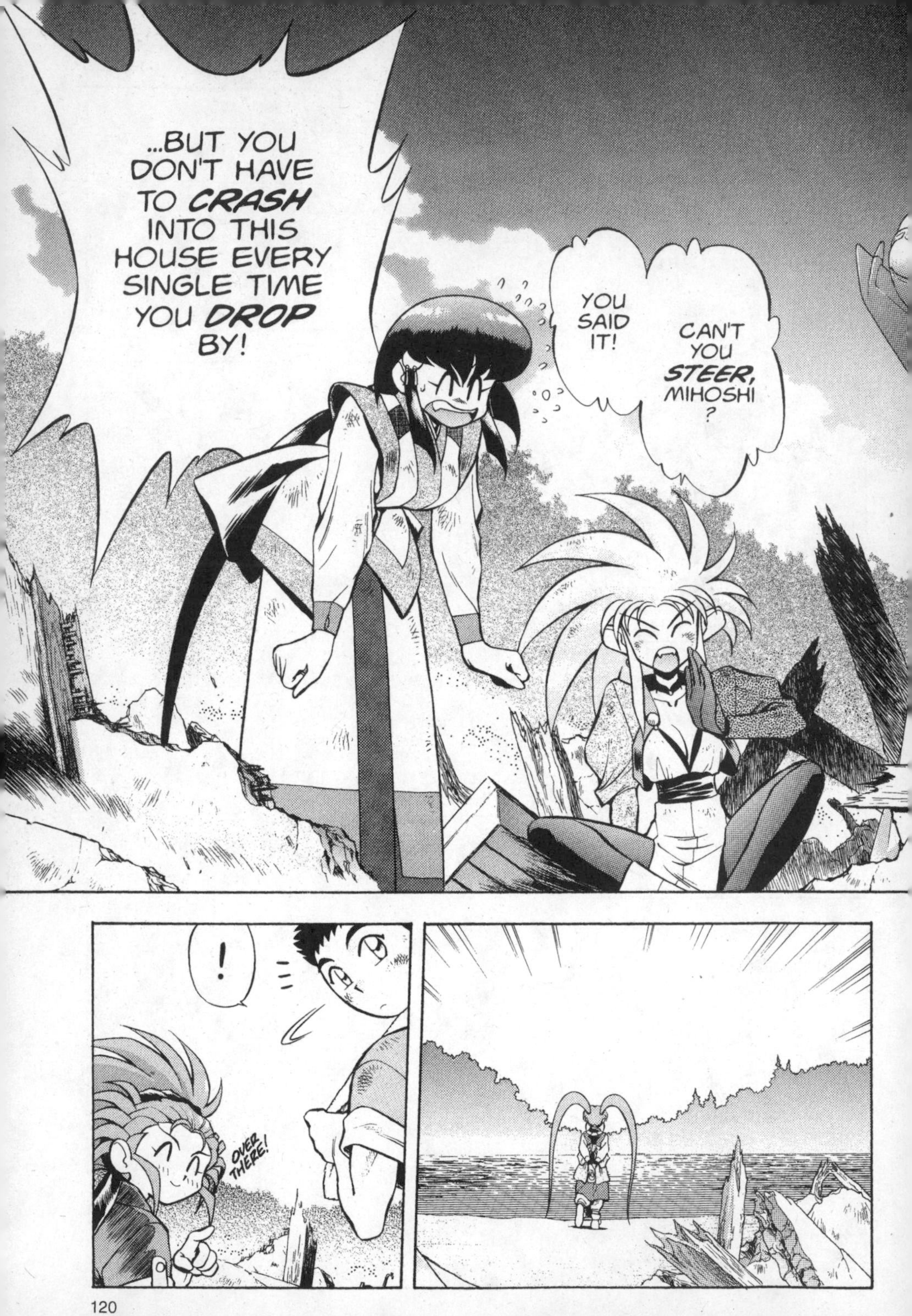
...BUT YOU DON'T HAVE TO CRASH INTO THIS HOUSE EVERY SINGLE TIME YOU DROP BY!
YOU SAID IT!
CAN'T YOU STEER, MIHOSHI?
!
OVER THERE!

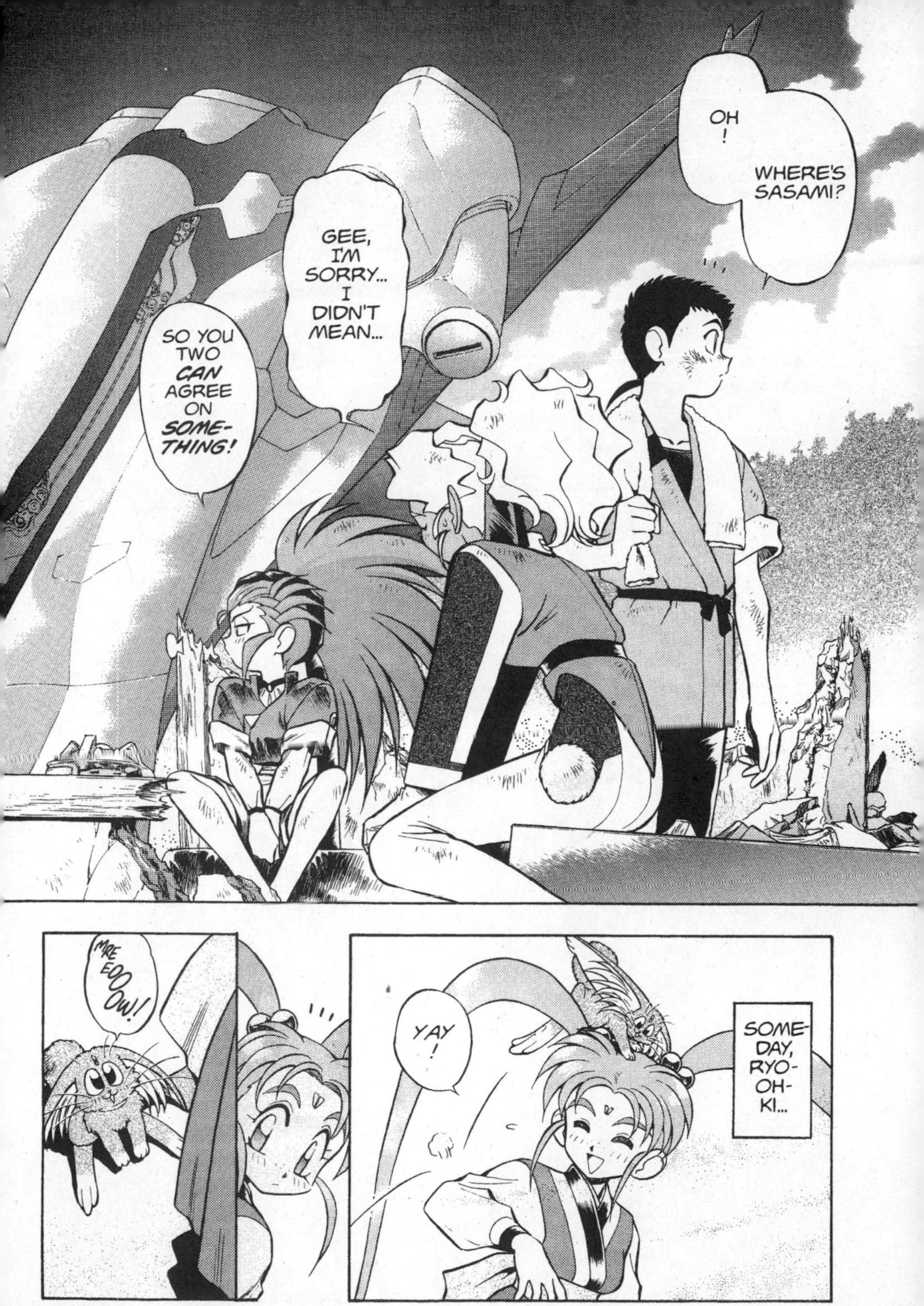
SO YOU TWO CAN AGREE ON SOME-THING!
GEE, I'M SORRY... I DIDN'T MEAN...
OH! WHERE'S SASAMI?
MREOOOOW!
YAY!
SOME-DAY, RYO-OH-KI...

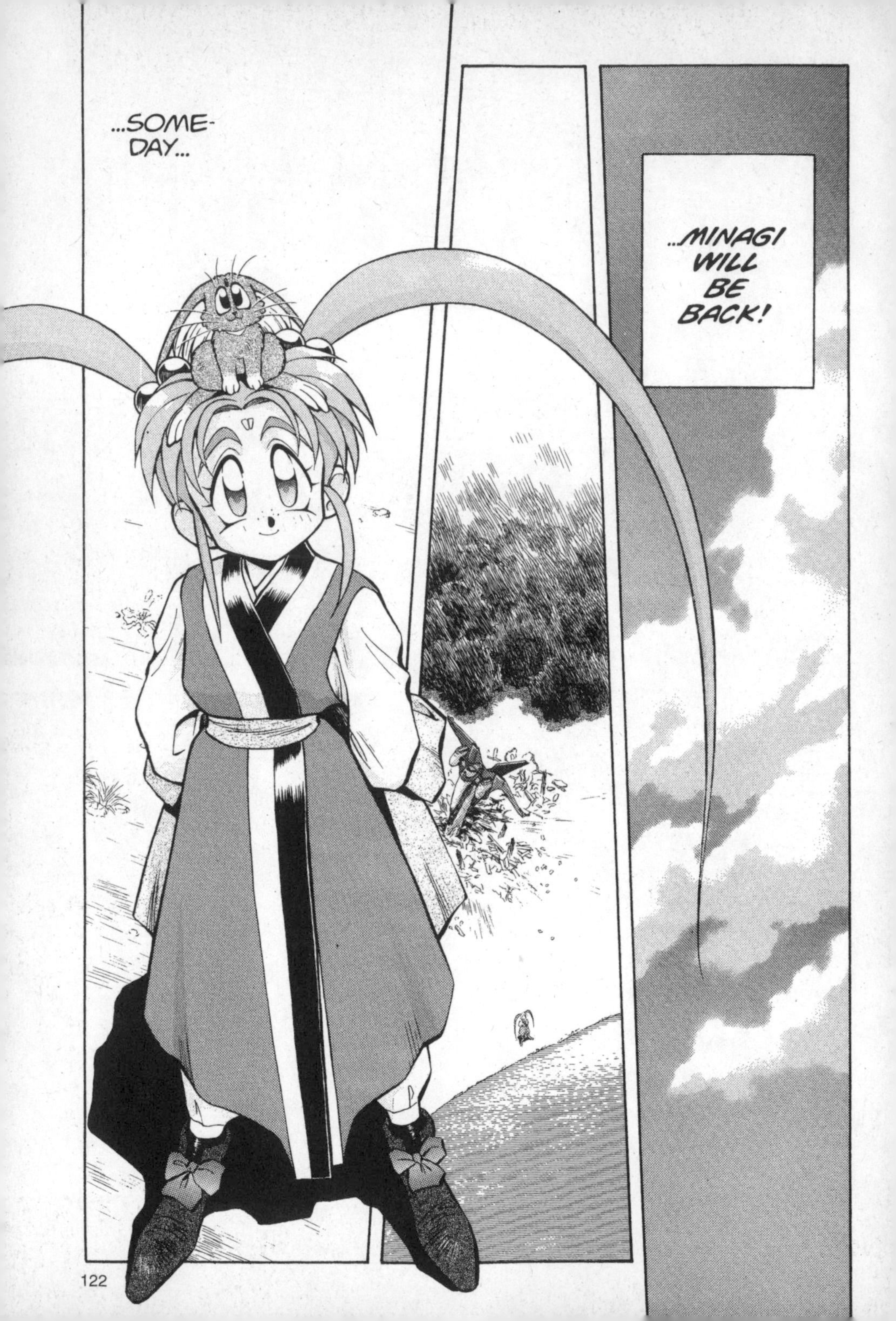
...SOME-
DAY...
...MINAGI
WILL
BE
BACK!

Tales of Tenchi #6

CATCHING COLDS

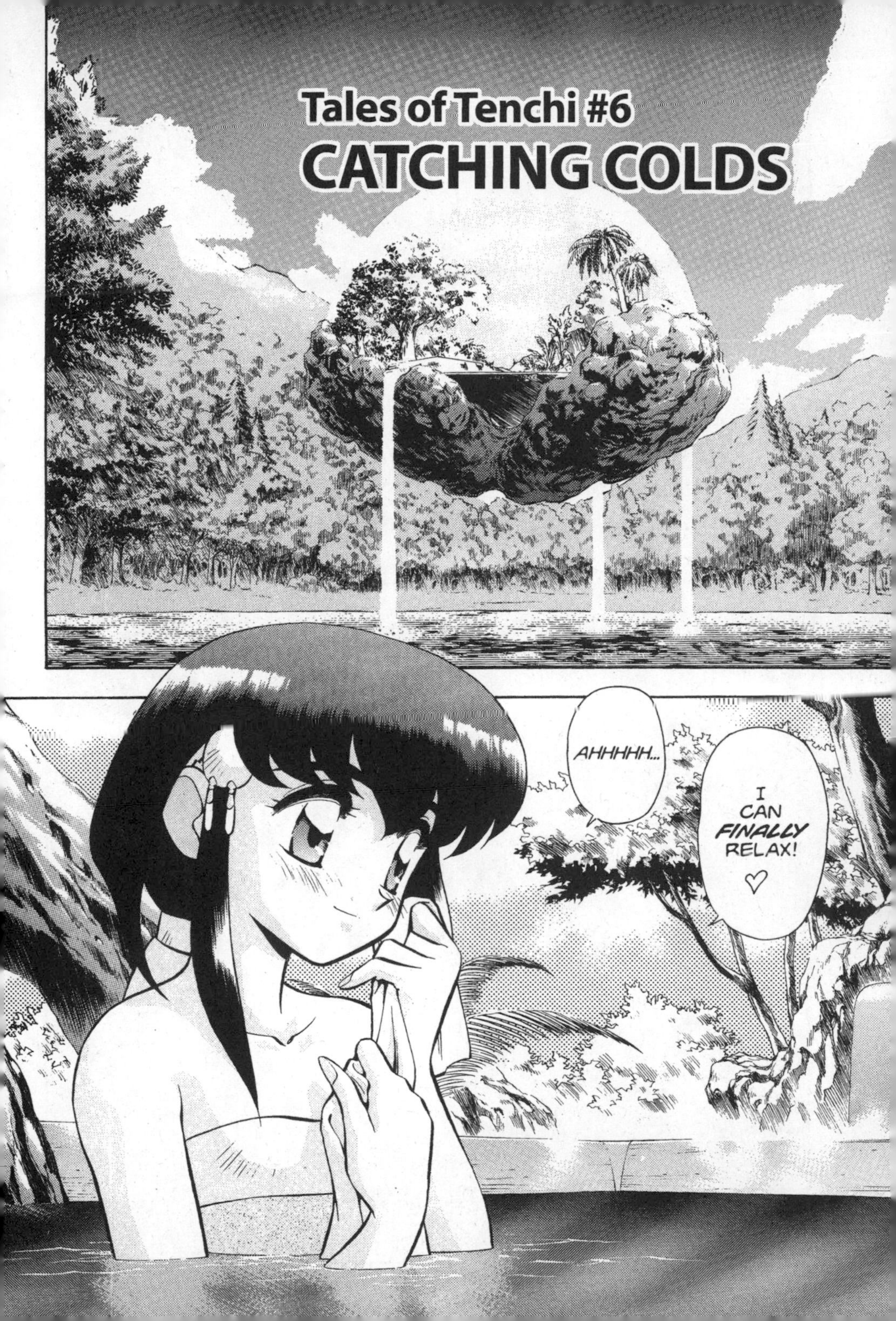
AHHHHH...
I CAN FINALLY RELAX! ♡

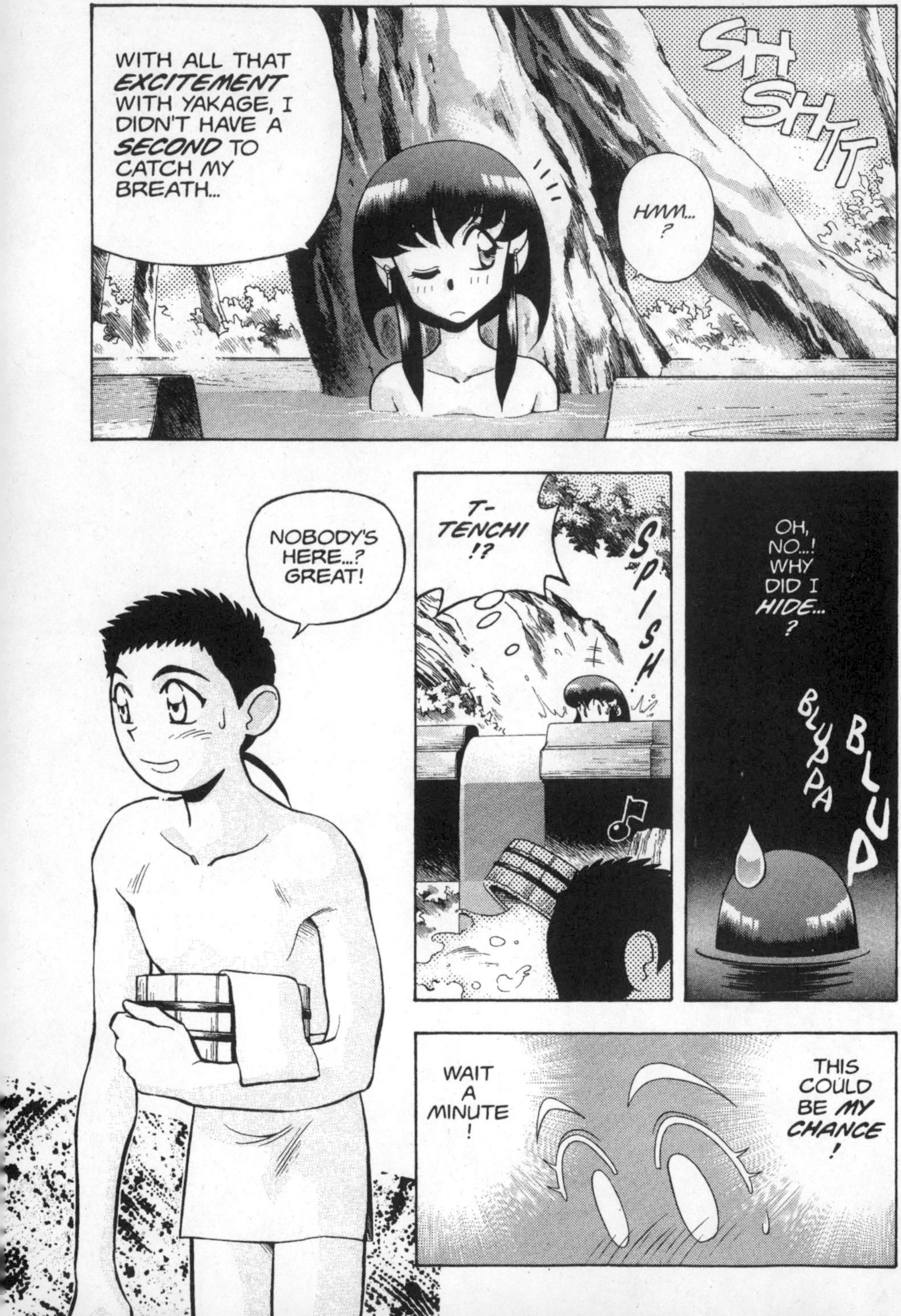
WITH ALL THAT *EXCITEMENT* WITH YAKAGE, I DIDN'T HAVE A *SECOND* TO CATCH MY BREATH...
SH SHTT
HMM... ?
NOBODY'S HERE...? GREAT!
T-TENCHI!?
SPISH!
OH, NO...! WHY DID I *HIDE*...?
BLUPPA
BLUD
WAIT A MINUTE!
THIS COULD BE *MY CHANCE*!

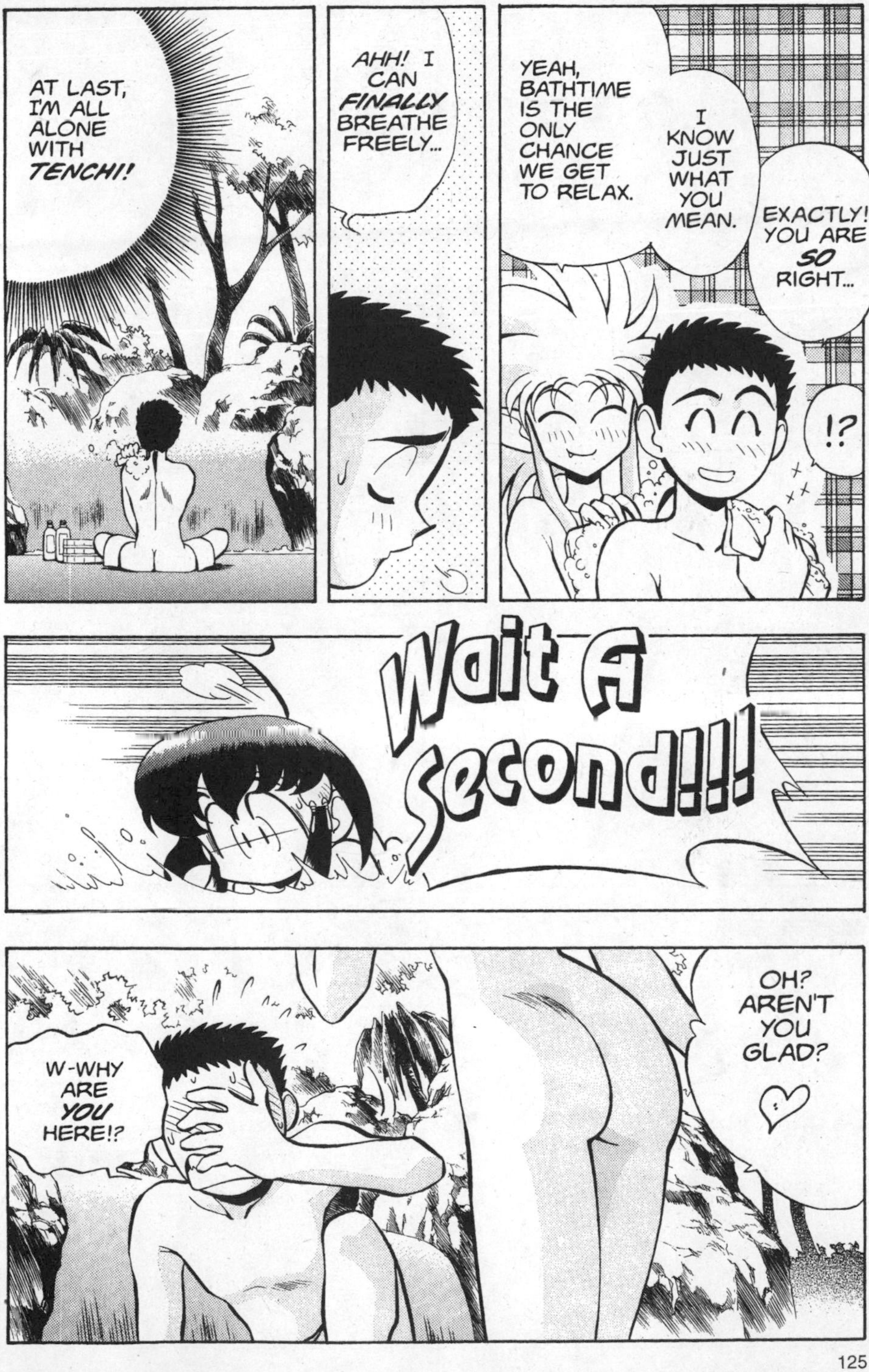
AT LAST, I'M ALL ALONE WITH *TENCHI!*
AHH! I CAN *FINALLY* BREATHE FREELY...
YEAH, BATHTIME IS THE ONLY CHANCE WE GET TO RELAX.
I KNOW JUST WHAT YOU MEAN.
EXACTLY! YOU ARE *SO* RIGHT...
!?
Wait A second!!!
W-WHY ARE *YOU* HERE!?
OH? AREN'T YOU GLAD?

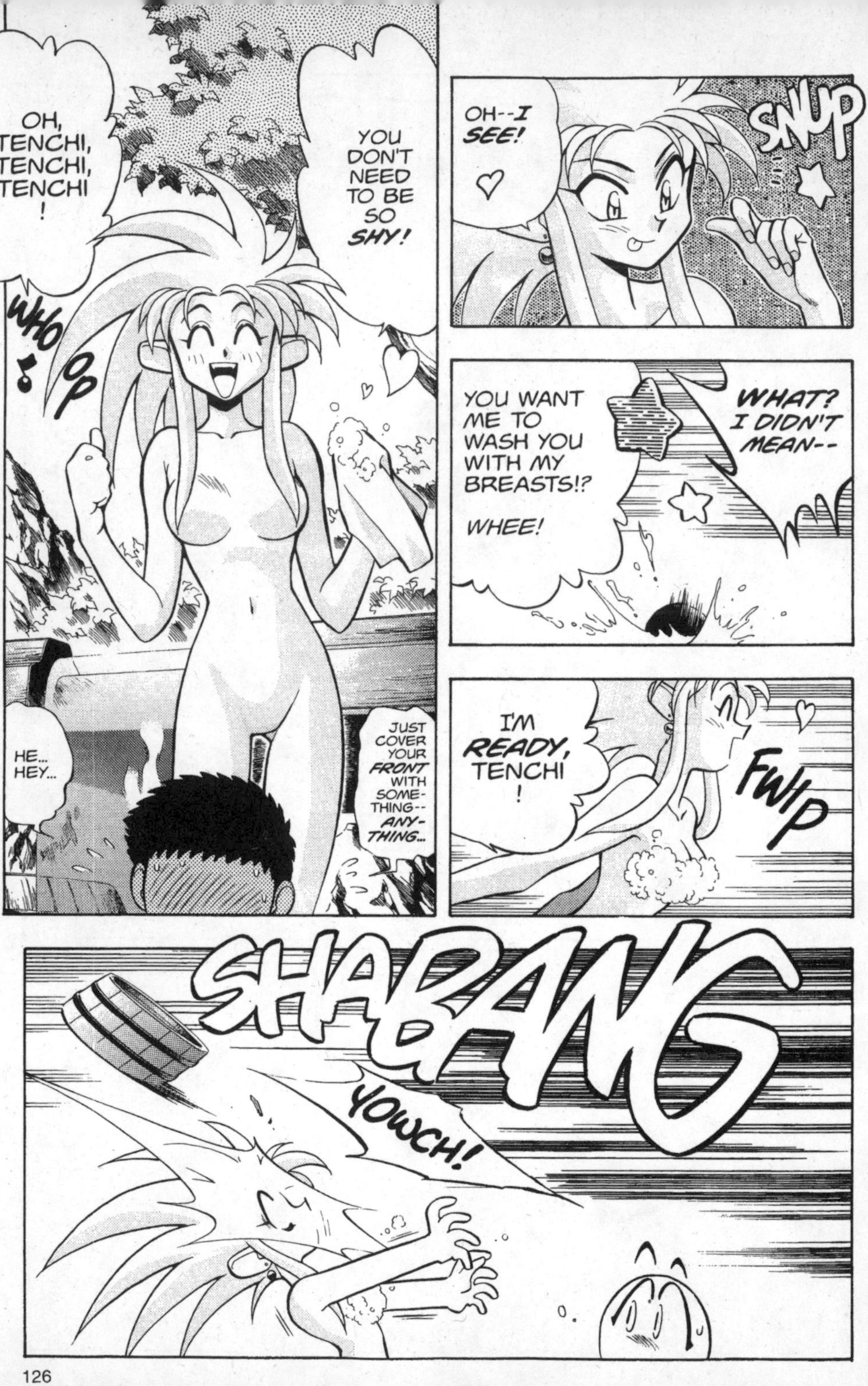
OH, TENCHI, TENCHI, TENCHI!
YOU DON'T NEED TO BE SO SHY!
WHOOP
HE... HEY...
JUST COVER YOUR FRONT WITH SOMETHING-- ANYTHING...
OH--I SEE!
SNUP
YOU WANT ME TO WASH YOU WITH MY BREASTS!?
WHEE!
WHAT? I DIDN'T MEAN--
I'M READY, TENCHI!
FWIP
SHABANG
YOWCH!

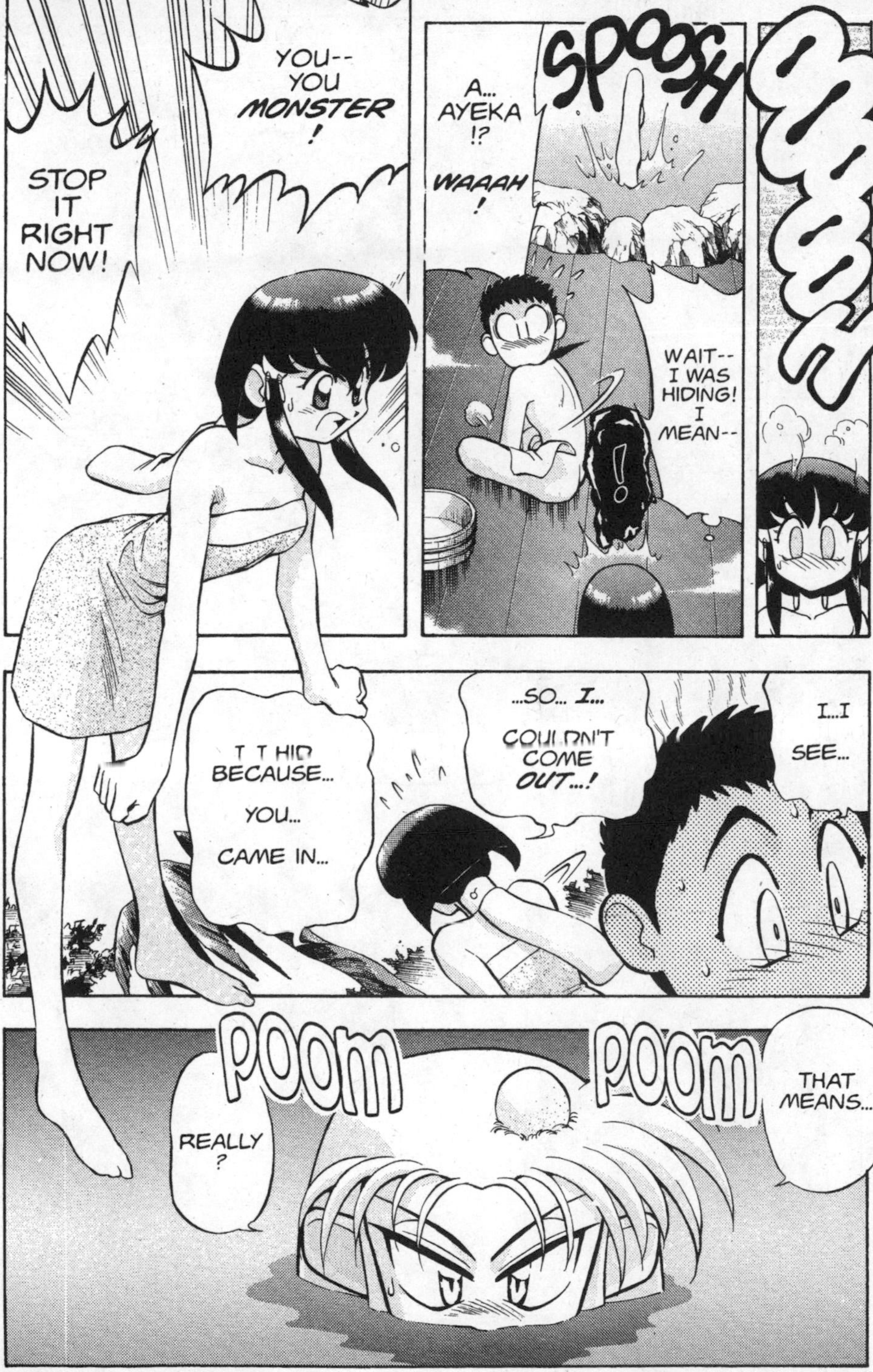

YOU-- YOU MONSTER!
STOP IT RIGHT NOW!
SPOOSH
A... AYEKA!?
WAAAH!
WAIT-- I WAS HIDING! I MEAN--
I... I HID BECAUSE... YOU... CAME IN...
...SO... I... COULDN'T COME OUT...!
I...I SEE...
POOM
POOM
REALLY?
THAT MEANS...

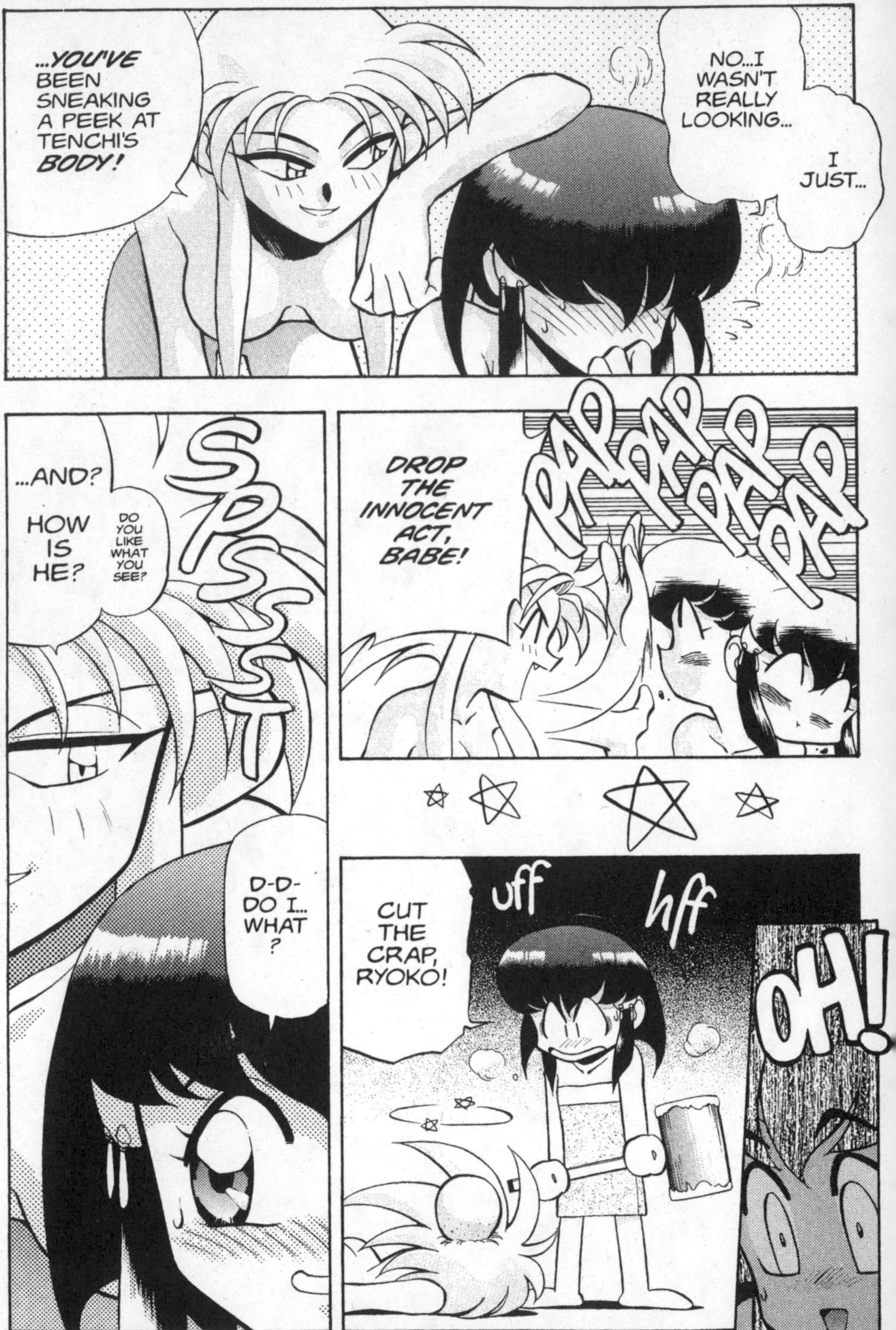
...YOU'VE BEEN SNEAKING A PEEK AT TENCHI'S BODY!
NO...I WASN'T REALLY LOOKING...
I JUST...
...AND?
HOW IS HE?
DO YOU LIKE WHAT YOU SEE?
SPSSST
D-D-DO I... WHAT?
DROP THE INNOCENT ACT, BABE!
PAP PAP PAP PAP PAP PAP
uff
hff
CUT THE CRAP, RYOKO!
OH!

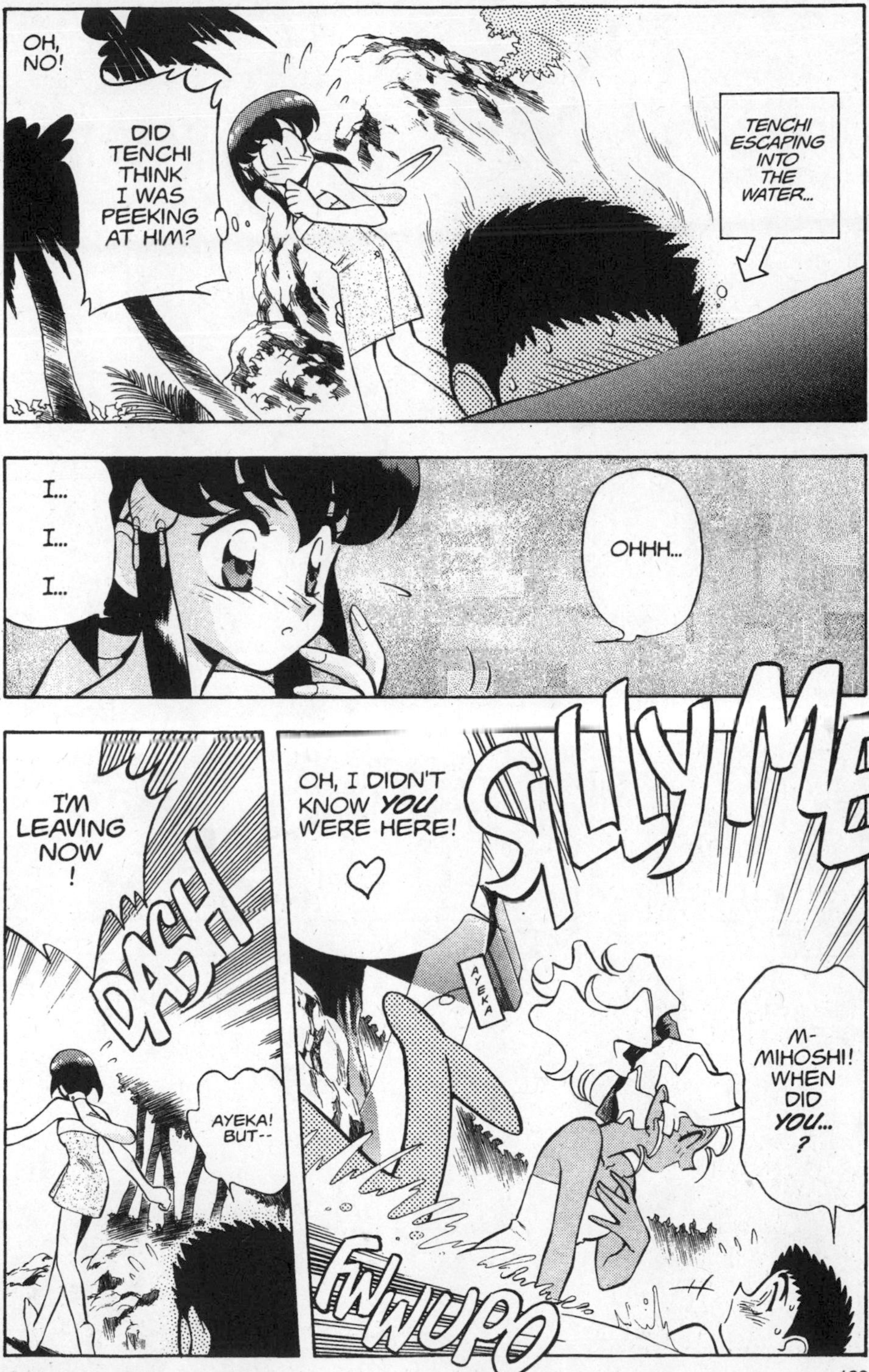
OH, NO!
DID TENCHI THINK I WAS PEEKING AT HIM?
TENCHI ESCAPING INTO THE WATER...
I... I... I...
OHHH...
I'M LEAVING NOW !
DASH
AYEKA! BUT--
OH, I DIDN'T KNOW *YOU* WERE HERE!
SILLY ME!
AYEKA
M-MIHOSHI! WHEN DID *YOU*... ?
FWWUPO

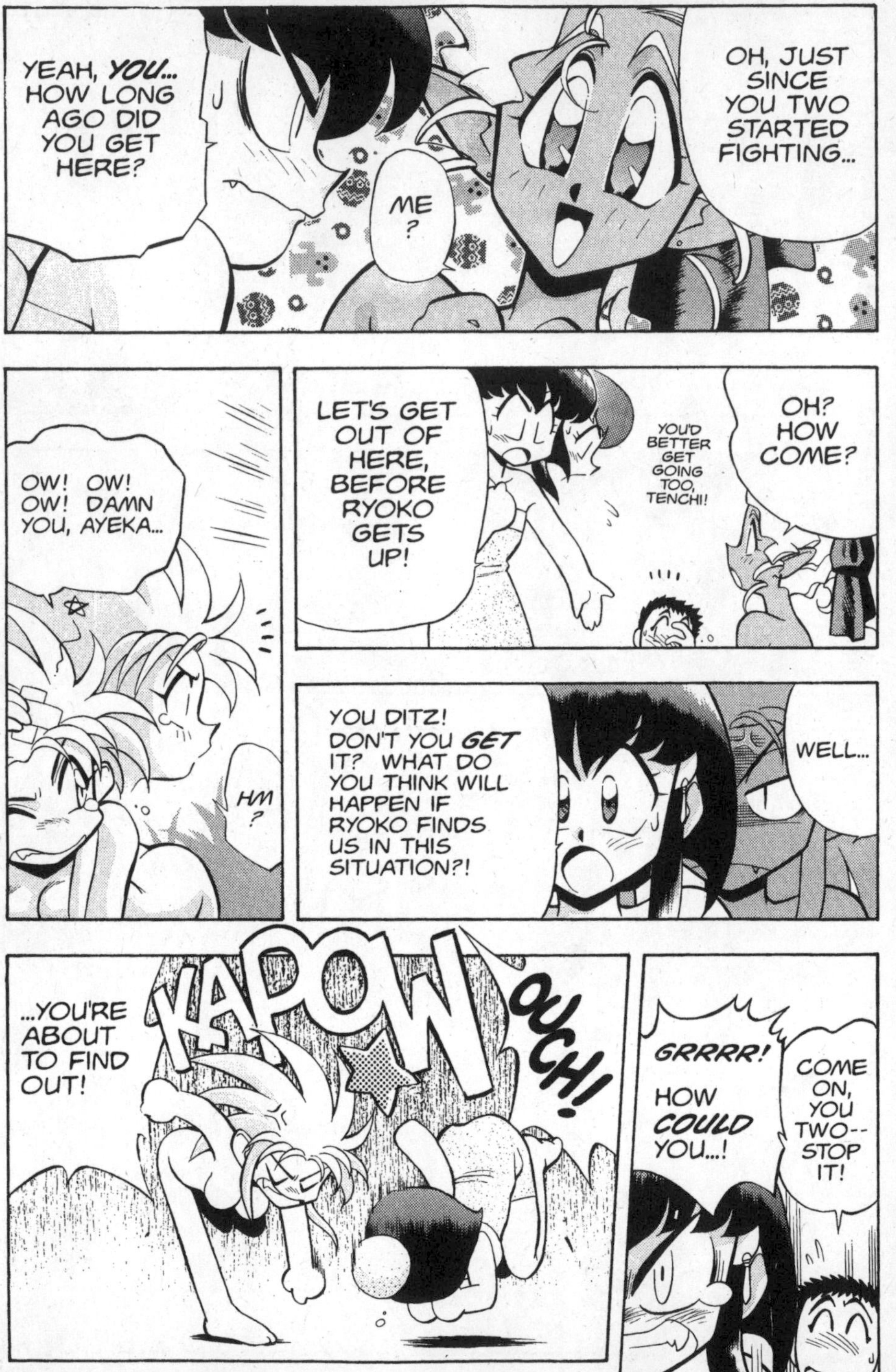
YEAH, *YOU*... HOW LONG AGO DID YOU GET HERE?
ME ?
OH, JUST SINCE YOU TWO STARTED FIGHTING...
OW! OW! OW! DAMN YOU, AYEKA...
HM ?
LET'S GET OUT OF HERE, BEFORE RYOKO GETS UP!
YOU'D BETTER GET GOING TOO, TENCHI!
OH? HOW COME?
YOU DITZ! DON'T YOU *GET* IT? WHAT DO YOU THINK WILL HAPPEN IF RYOKO FINDS US IN THIS SITUATION?!
WELL...
...YOU'RE ABOUT TO FIND OUT!
KAPOW
OUCH!
GRRRR!
HOW *COULD* YOU...!
COME ON, YOU TWO-- STOP IT!

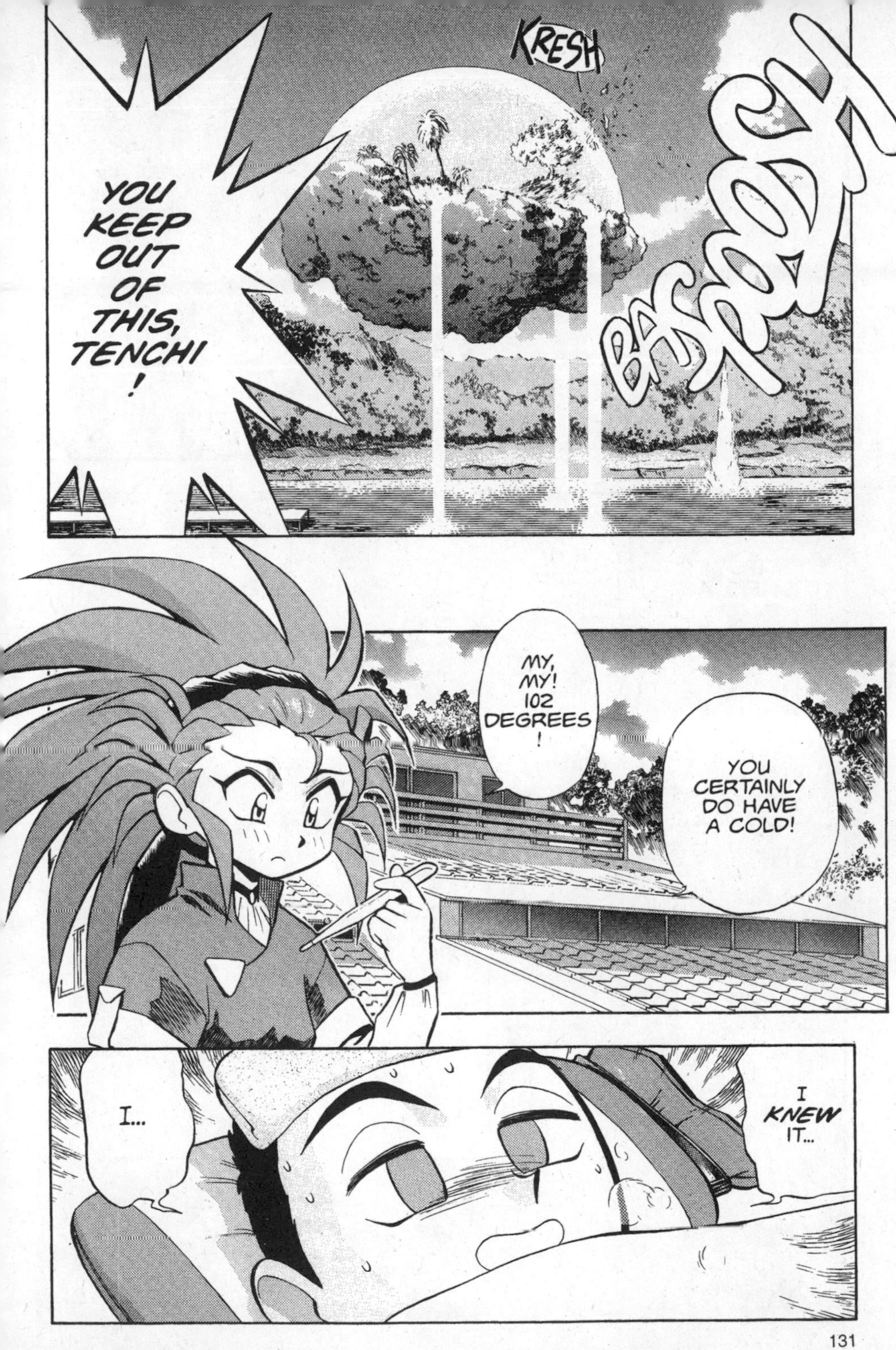

KRESH
YOU KEEP OUT OF THIS, TENCHI!
MY, MY! 102 DEGREES!
YOU CERTAINLY DO HAVE A COLD!
I...
I KNEW IT...

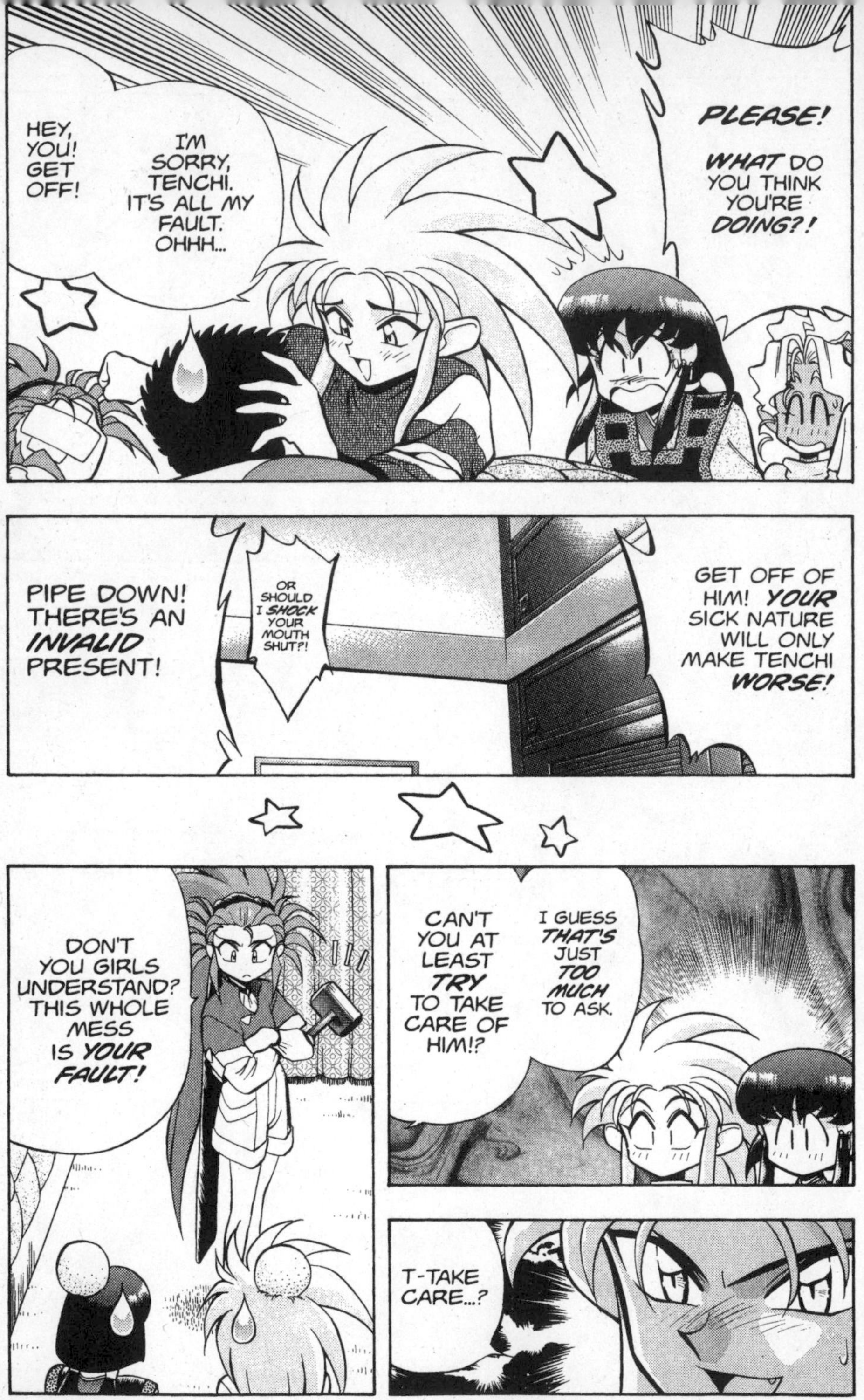
HEY, YOU! GET OFF!
I'M SORRY, TENCHI. IT'S ALL MY FAULT. OHHH...
PLEASE! WHAT DO YOU THINK YOU'RE DOING?!
PIPE DOWN! THERE'S AN INVALID PRESENT!
OR SHOULD I SHOCK YOUR MOUTH SHUT?!
GET OFF OF HIM! YOUR SICK NATURE WILL ONLY MAKE TENCHI WORSE!
DON'T YOU GIRLS UNDERSTAND? THIS WHOLE MESS IS YOUR FAULT!
CAN'T YOU AT LEAST TRY TO TAKE CARE OF HIM!?
I GUESS THAT'S JUST TOO MUCH TO ASK.
T-TAKE CARE...?

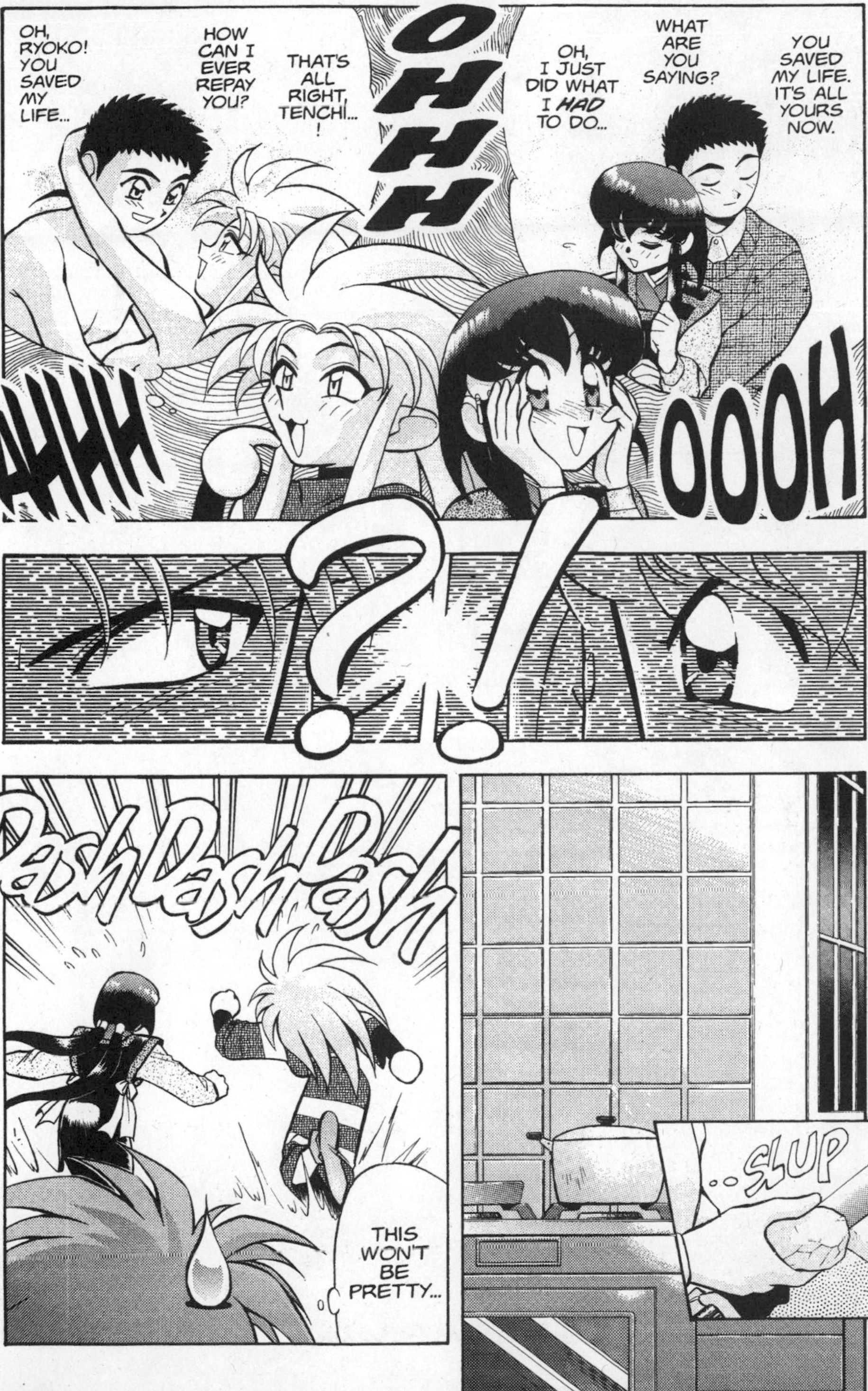
OH, RYOKO! YOU SAVED MY LIFE...
HOW CAN I EVER REPAY YOU?
THAT'S ALL RIGHT, TENCHI...!
OHHH
OH, I JUST DID WHAT I HAD TO DO...
WHAT ARE YOU SAYING?
YOU SAVED MY LIFE. IT'S ALL YOURS NOW.
AHHH
OOOH
?!
DashDashDash
THIS WON'T BE PRETTY...
..SLUP

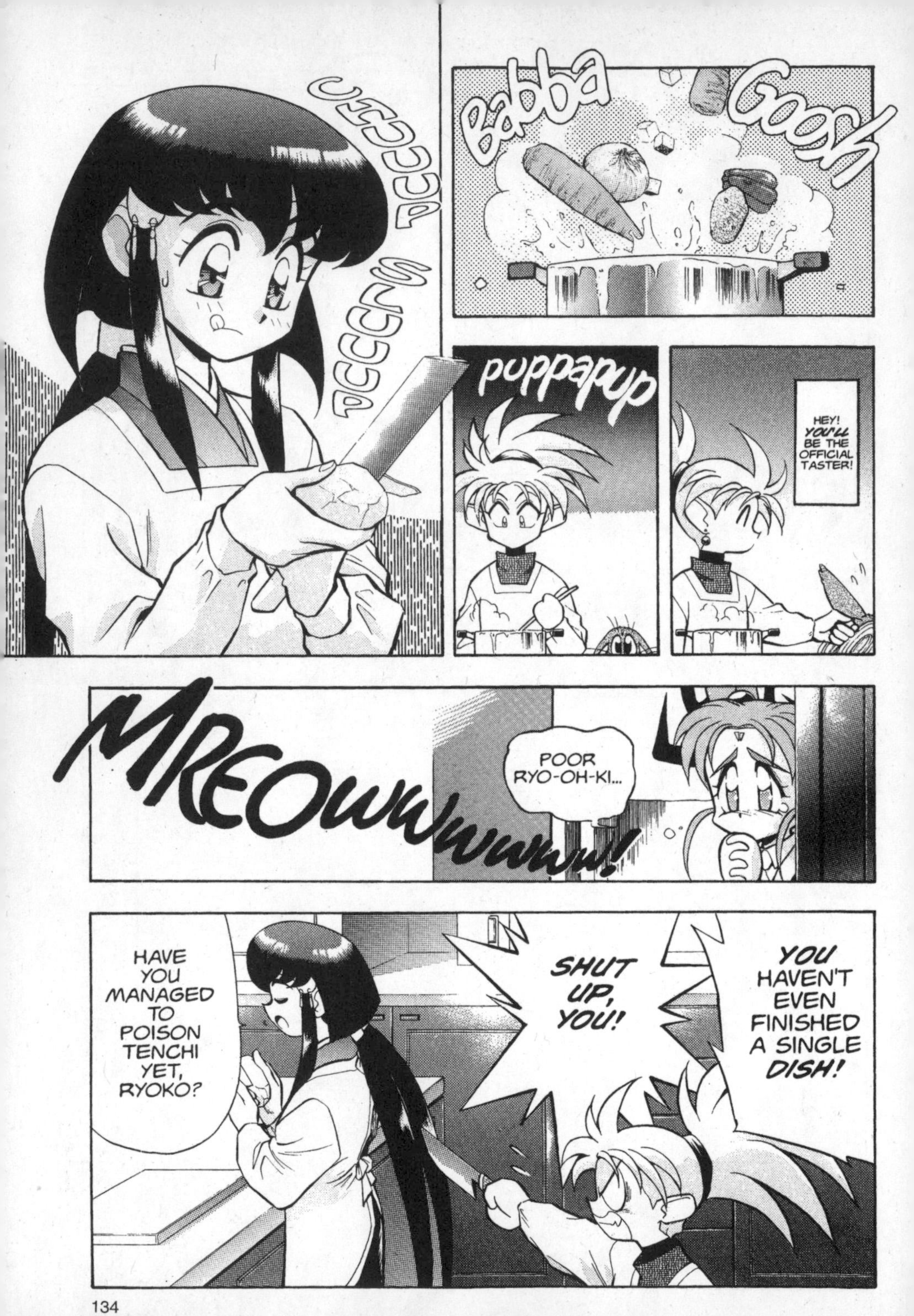

Babba Goosh
puppapup
HEY! YOU'LL BE THE OFFICIAL TASTER!
MREOWWwwwww!
POOR RYO-OH-KI...
HAVE YOU MANAGED TO POISON TENCHI YET, RYOKO?
SHUT UP, YOU!
YOU HAVEN'T EVEN FINISHED A SINGLE DISH!

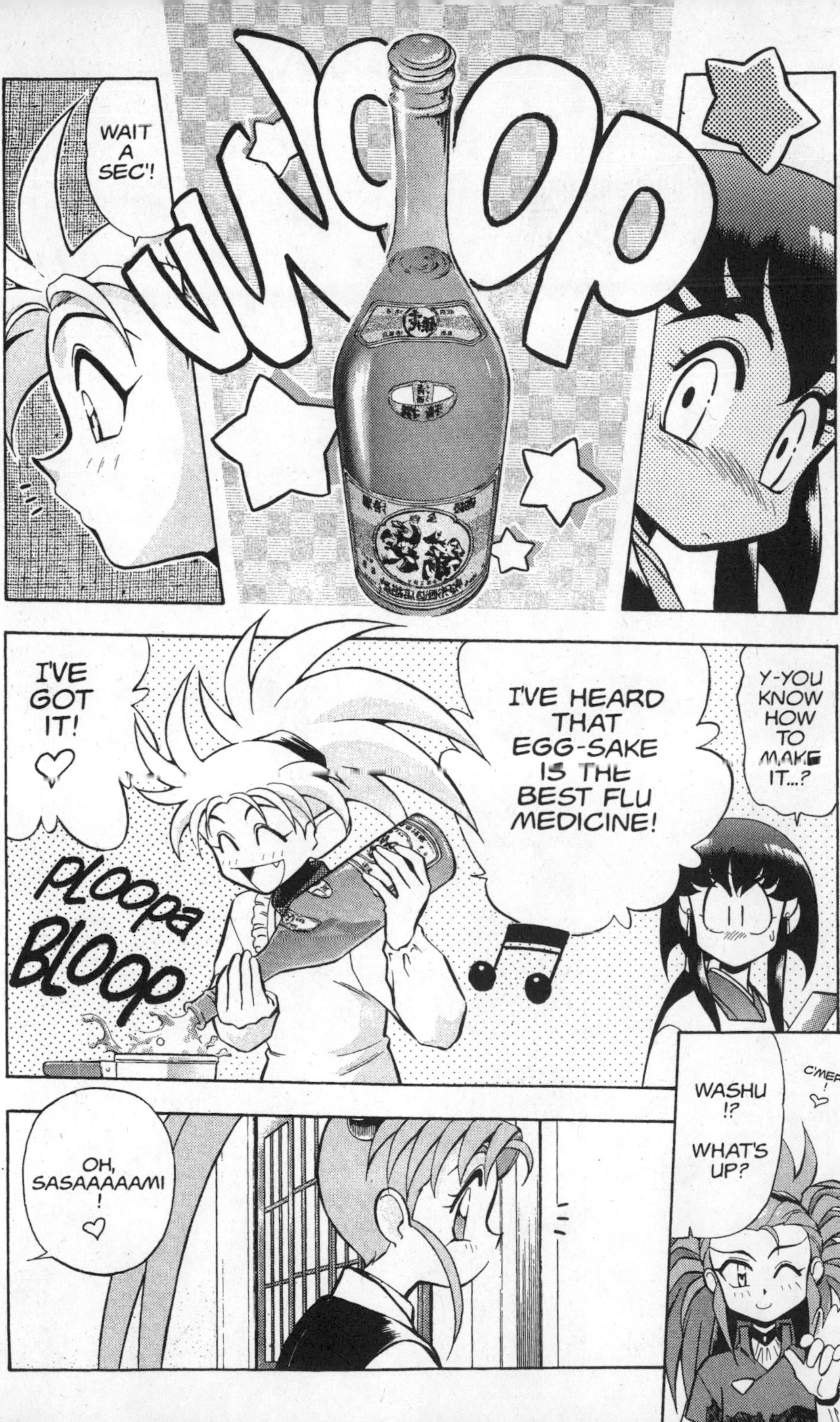
WAIT A SEC'!
WHOOP
I'VE GOT IT! ♡
I'VE HEARD THAT EGG-SAKE IS THE BEST FLU MEDICINE!
Y-YOU KNOW HOW TO MAKE IT...?
PLOOPA BLOOP
OH, SASAAAAAMI! ♡
WASHU!? WHAT'S UP?
C'MERE! ♡

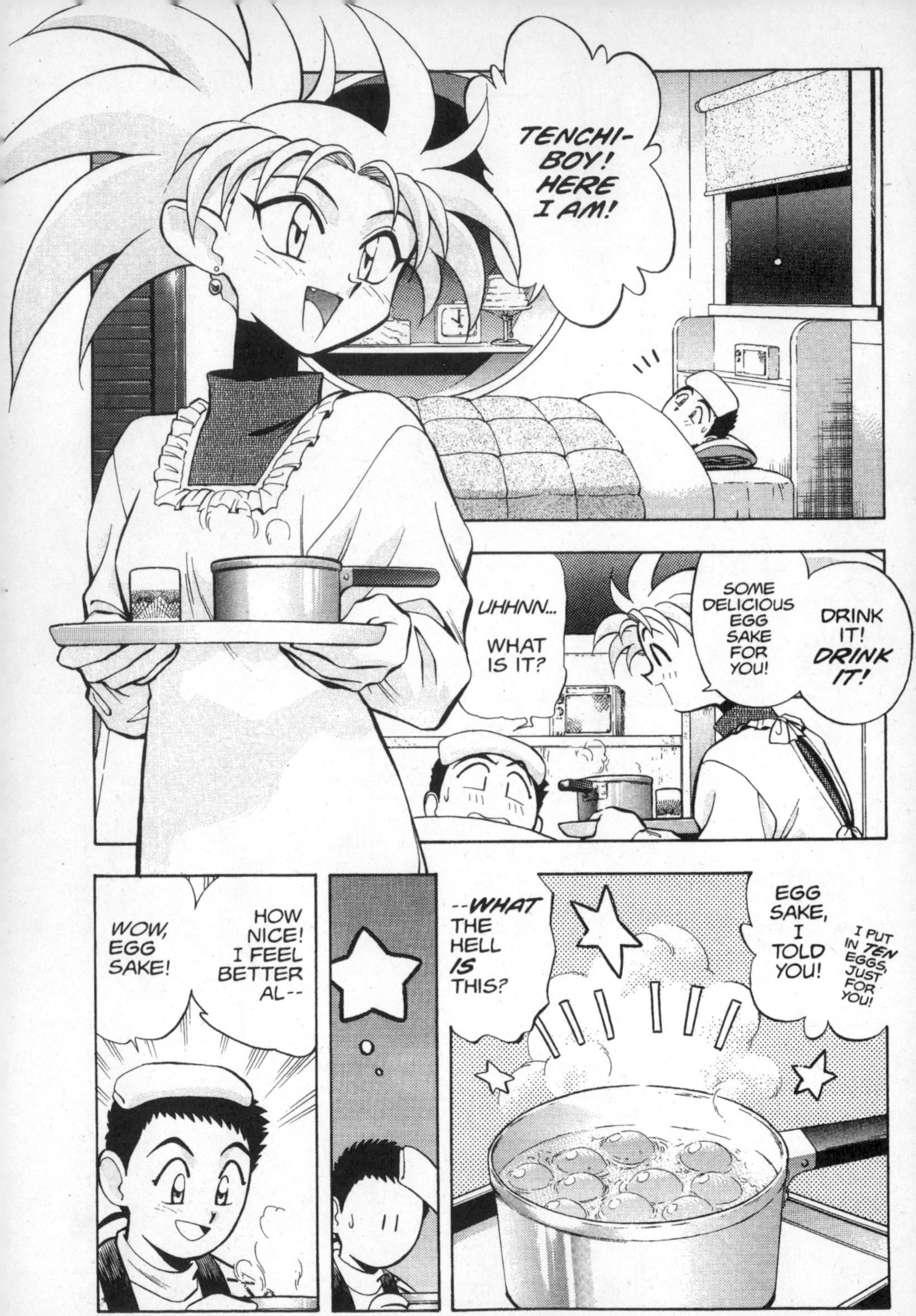
TENCHI-BOY! HERE I AM!
UHHNN... WHAT IS IT?
SOME DELICIOUS EGG SAKE FOR YOU!
DRINK IT! DRINK IT!
WOW, EGG SAKE!
HOW NICE! I FEEL BETTER AL--
--WHAT THE HELL IS THIS?
EGG SAKE, I TOLD YOU!
I PUT IN TEN EGGS, JUST FOR YOU!

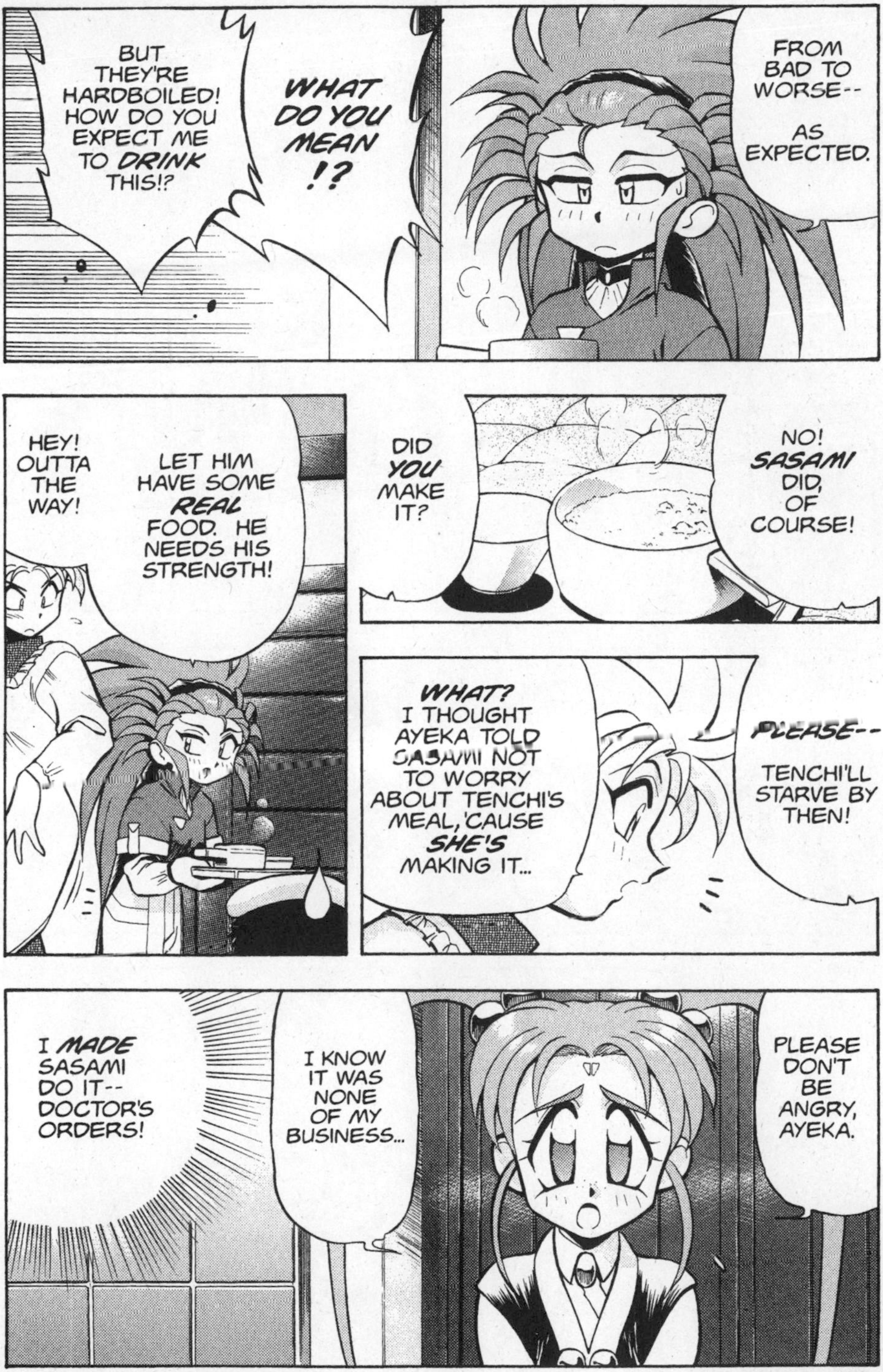
BUT THEY'RE HARDBOILED! HOW DO YOU EXPECT ME TO DRINK THIS!?
WHAT DO YOU MEAN !?
FROM BAD TO WORSE--
AS EXPECTED.
HEY! OUTTA THE WAY!
LET HIM HAVE SOME REAL FOOD. HE NEEDS HIS STRENGTH!
DID YOU MAKE IT?
NO! SASAMI DID, OF COURSE!
WHAT? I THOUGHT AYEKA TOLD SASAMI NOT TO WORRY ABOUT TENCHI'S MEAL, 'CAUSE SHE'S MAKING IT...
PLEASE--
TENCHI'LL STARVE BY THEN!
I MADE SASAMI DO IT-- DOCTOR'S ORDERS!
I KNOW IT WAS NONE OF MY BUSINESS...
PLEASE DON'T BE ANGRY, AYEKA.

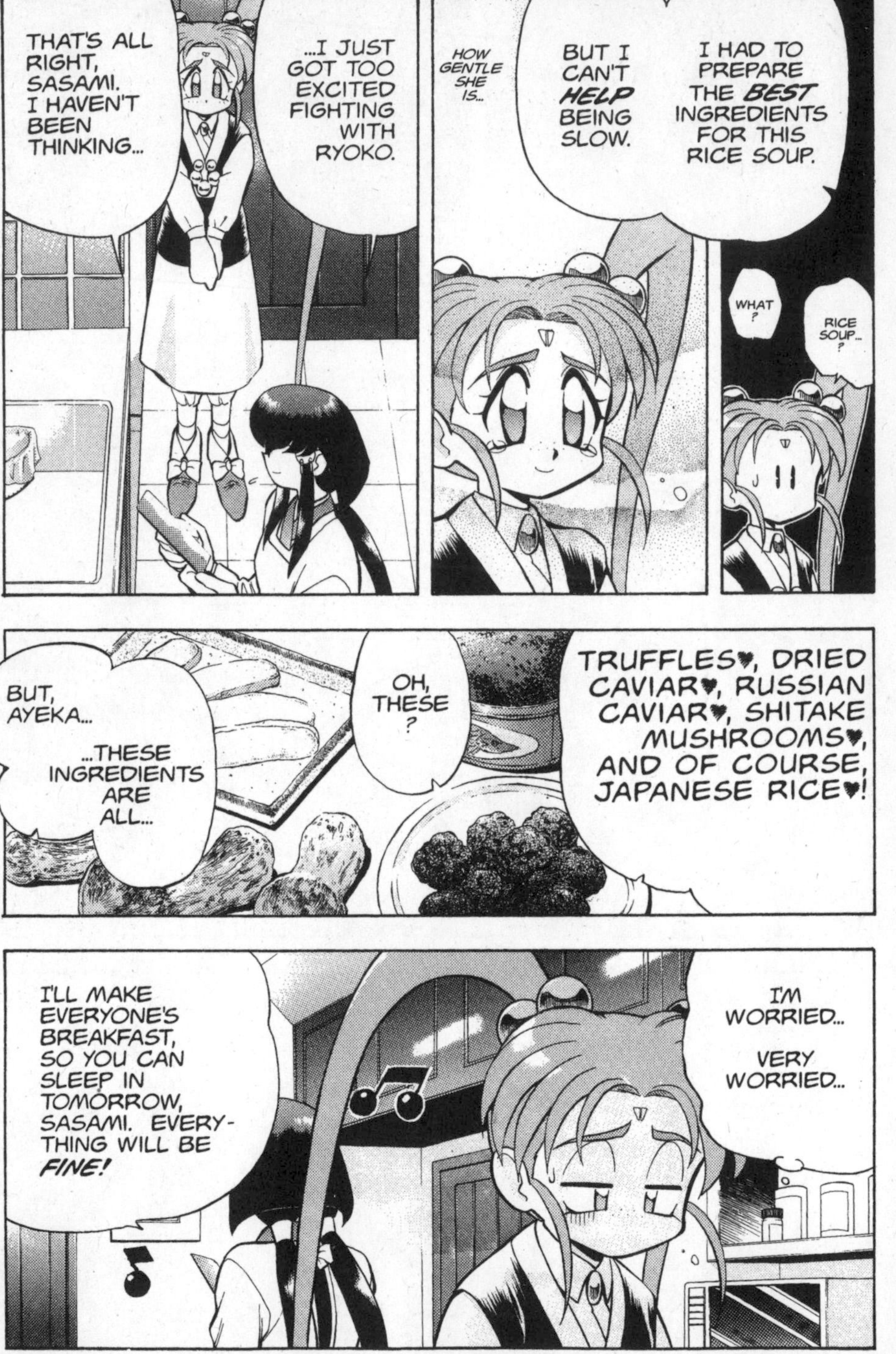
THAT'S ALL RIGHT, SASAMI. I HAVEN'T BEEN THINKING...
...I JUST GOT TOO EXCITED FIGHTING WITH RYOKO.
HOW GENTLE SHE IS...
BUT I CAN'T HELP BEING SLOW.
I HAD TO PREPARE THE BEST INGREDIENTS FOR THIS RICE SOUP.
WHAT?
RICE SOUP...?
BUT, AYEKA...
...THESE INGREDIENTS ARE ALL...
OH, THESE?
TRUFFLES♥, DRIED CAVIAR♥, RUSSIAN CAVIAR♥, SHITAKE MUSHROOMS♥, AND OF COURSE, JAPANESE RICE♥!
I'LL MAKE EVERYONE'S BREAKFAST, SO YOU CAN SLEEP IN TOMORROW, SASAMI. EVERY-THING WILL BE FINE!
I'M WORRIED...
VERY WORRIED...

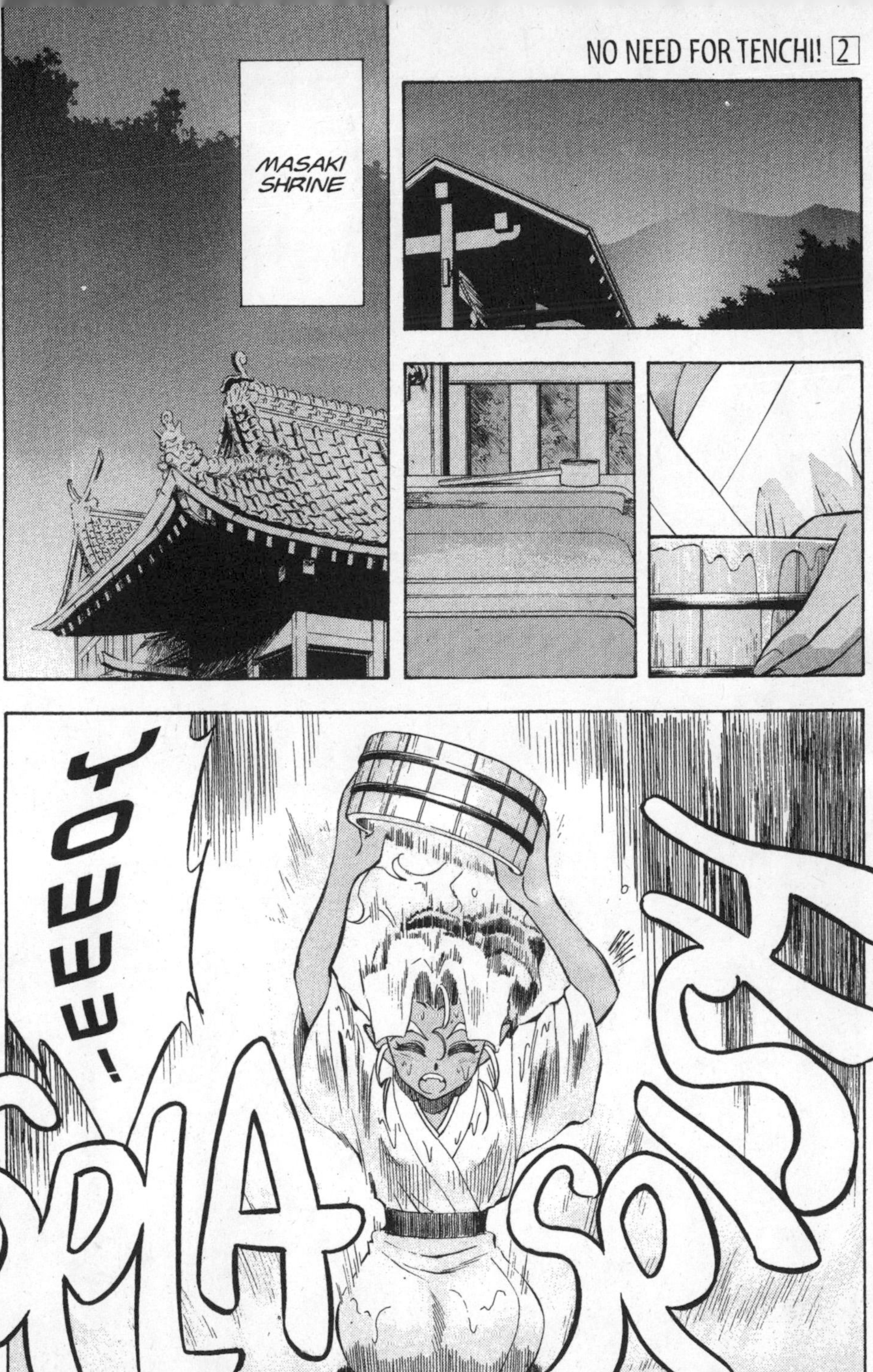
MASAKI SHRINE
YOWWEEE-!
SPLA
SPLASH

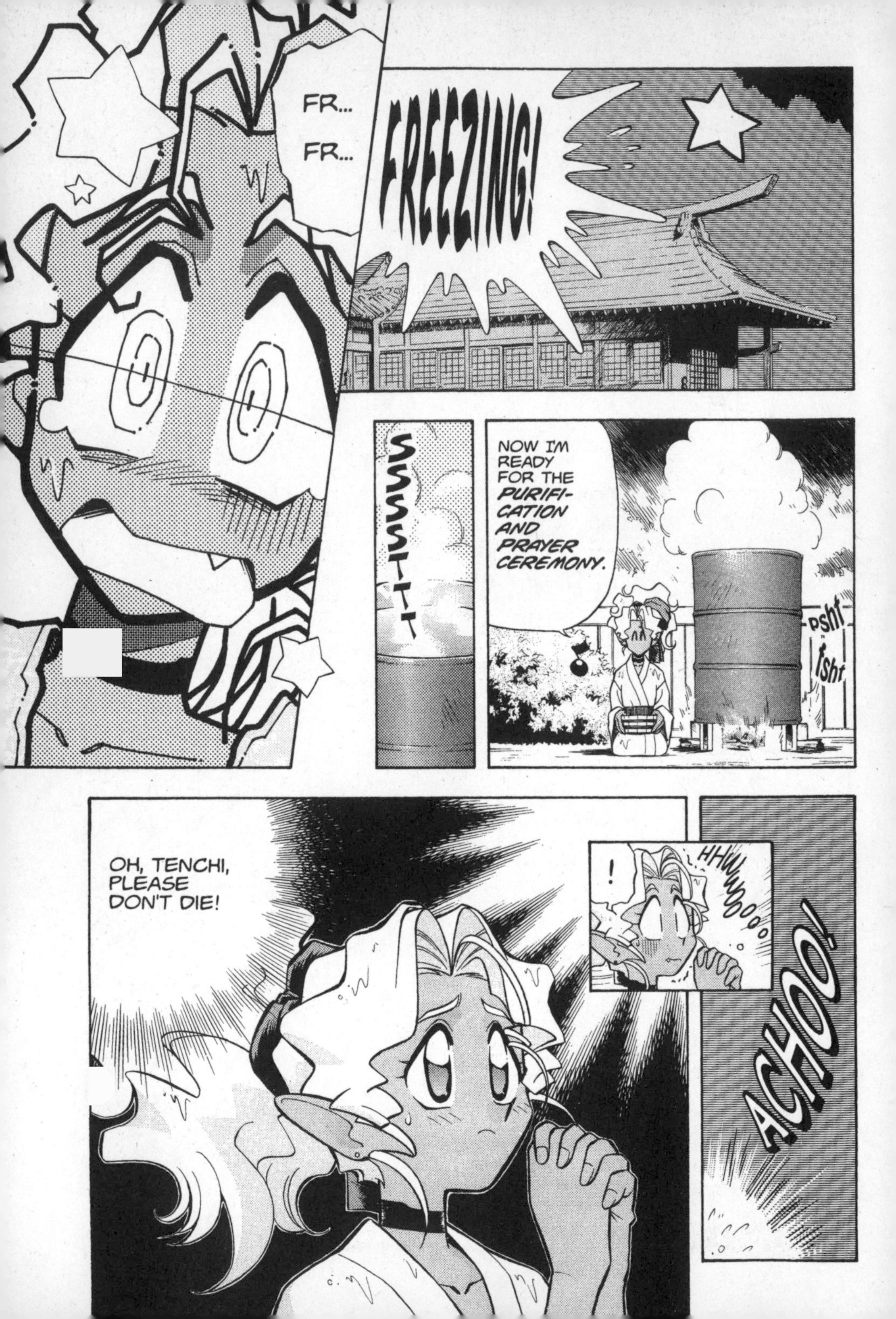
FR...
FR...
FREEZING!
SSSSTTTT
NOW I'M READY FOR THE *PURIFICATION AND PRAYER CEREMONY.*
psht
fsht
OH, TENCHI, PLEASE DON'T DIE!
!
HHWoooooo
ACHOO!

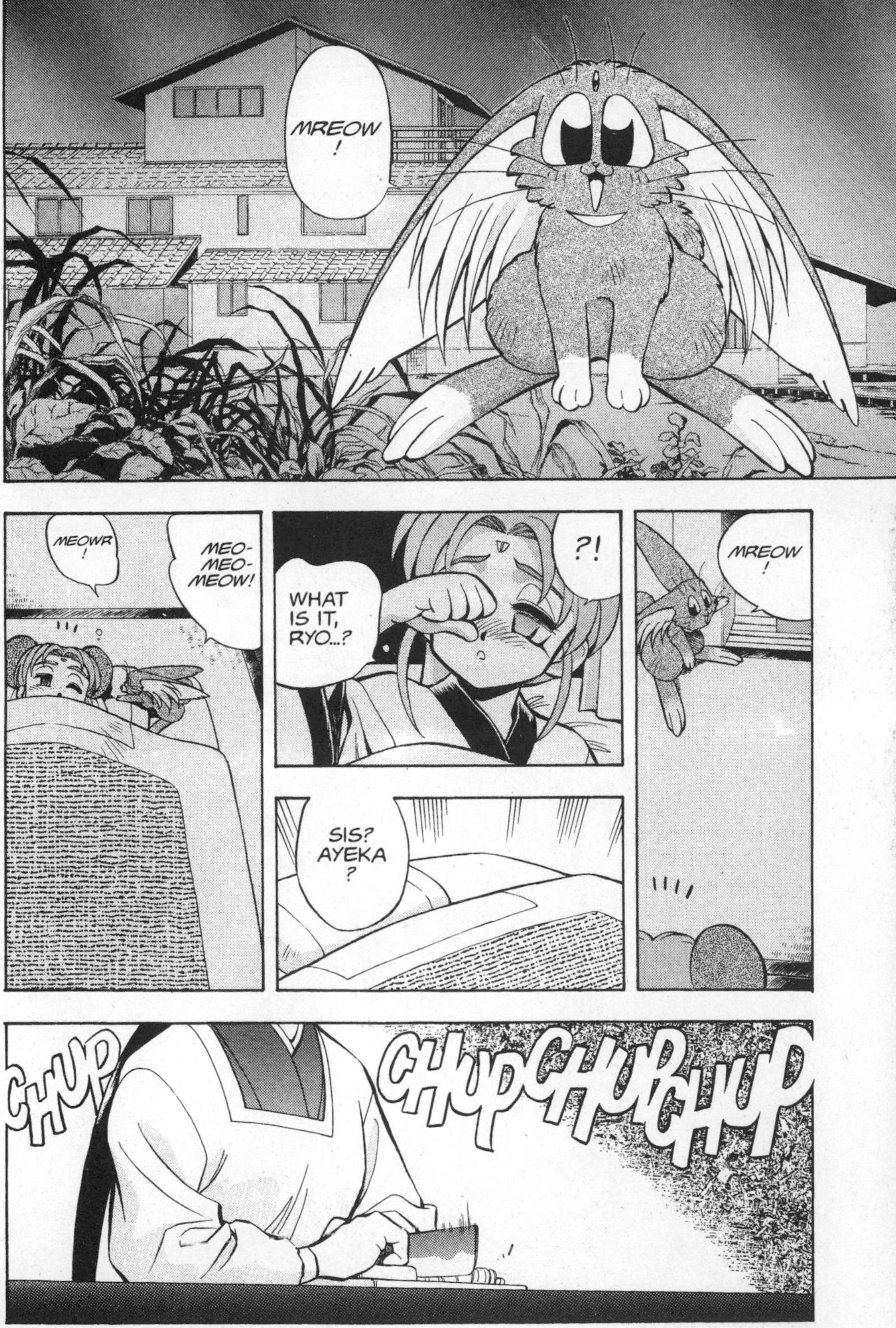
MREOW !
MEOWR !
MEO-MEO-MEOW!
WHAT IS IT, RYO...?
?!
SIS? AYEKA ?
MREOW !
CHUP
CHUPCHUPCHUP

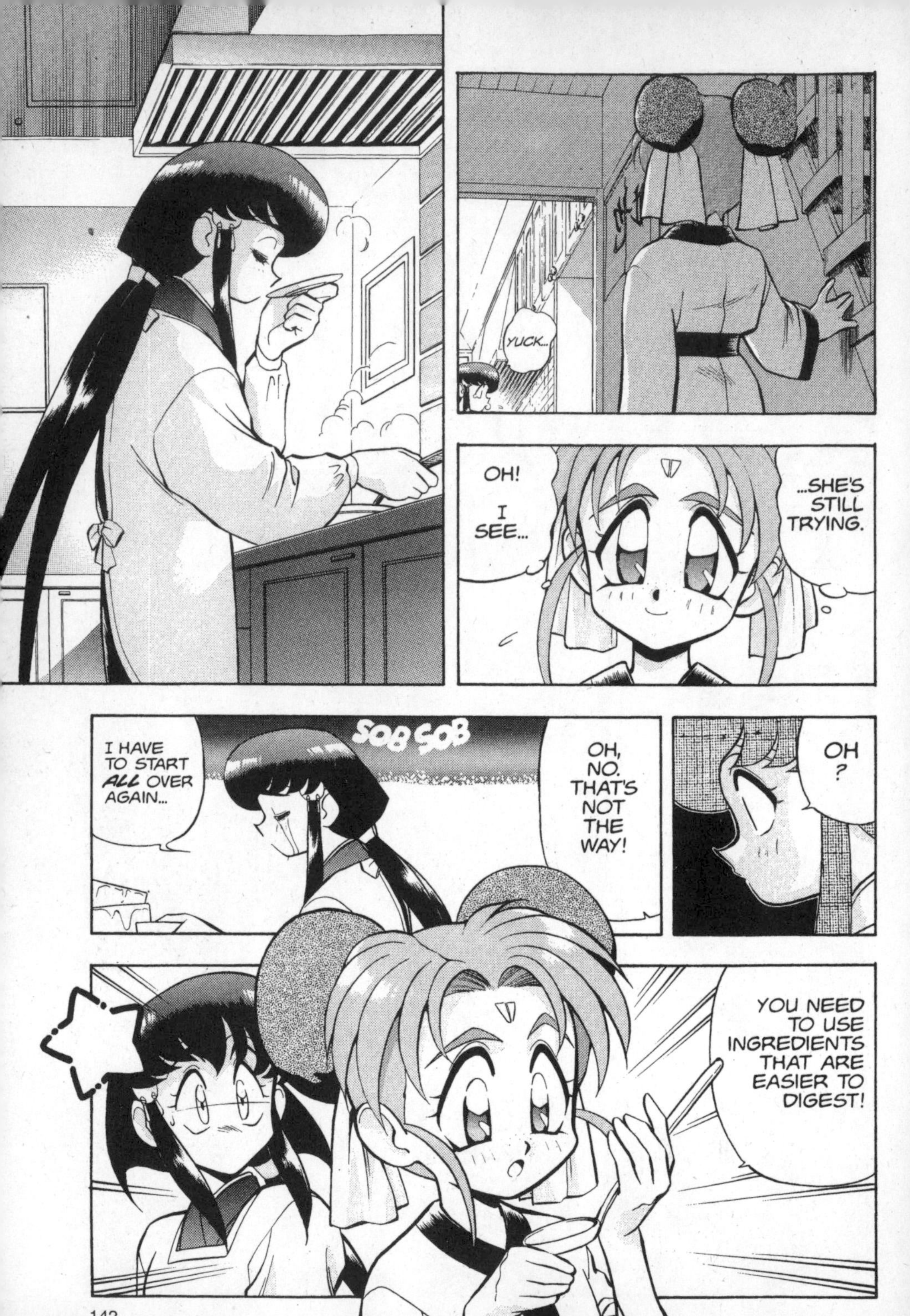
YUCK...
OH! I SEE...
...SHE'S STILL TRYING.
I HAVE TO START ALL OVER AGAIN...
SOB SOB
OH, NO. THAT'S NOT THE WAY!
OH ?
YOU NEED TO USE INGREDIENTS THAT ARE EASIER TO DIGEST!

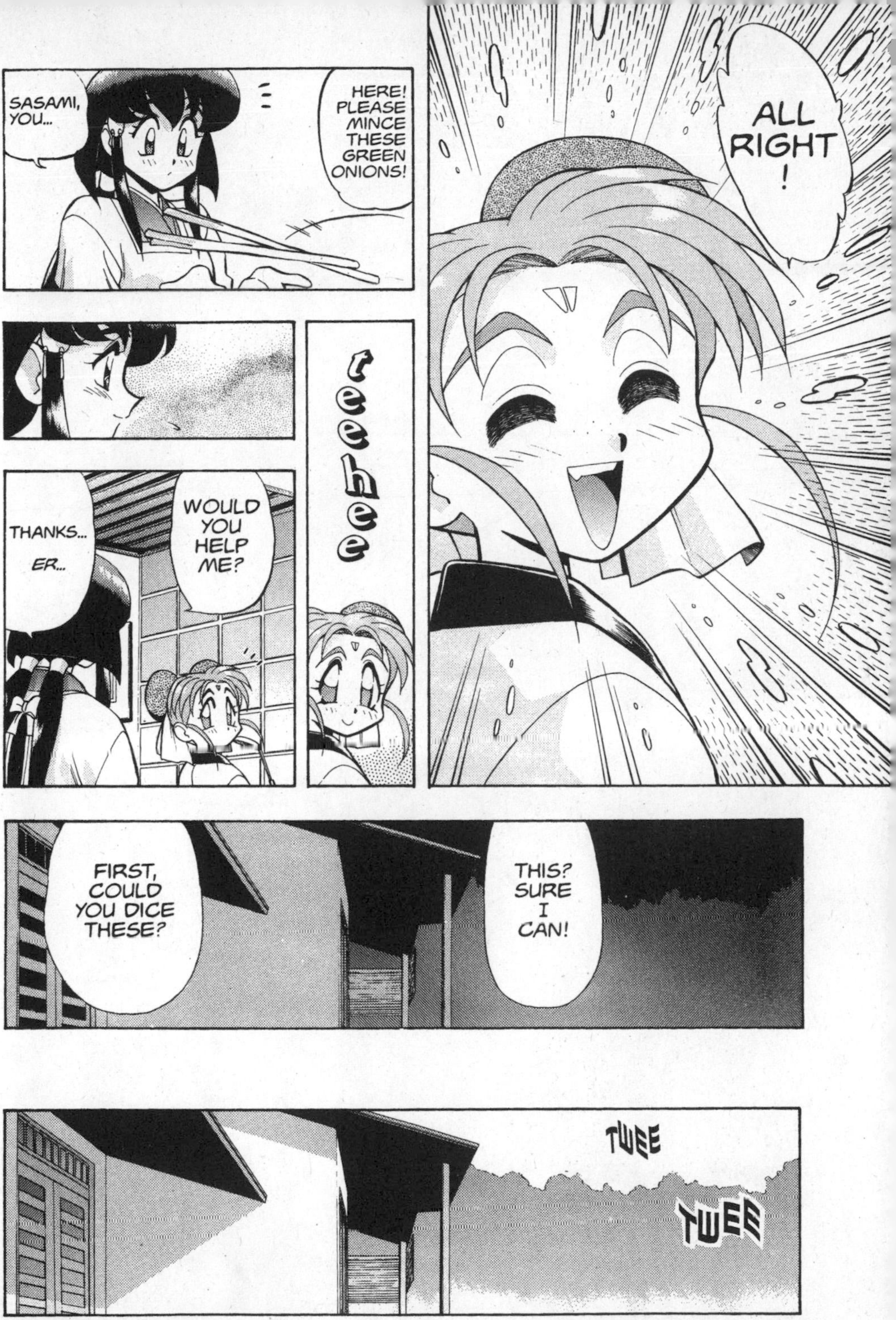

SASAMI, YOU...
HERE! PLEASE MINCE THESE GREEN ONIONS!
THANKS... ER...
WOULD YOU HELP ME?
teehee
ALL RIGHT!
FIRST, COULD YOU DICE THESE?
THIS? SURE I CAN!
TWEE
TWEE

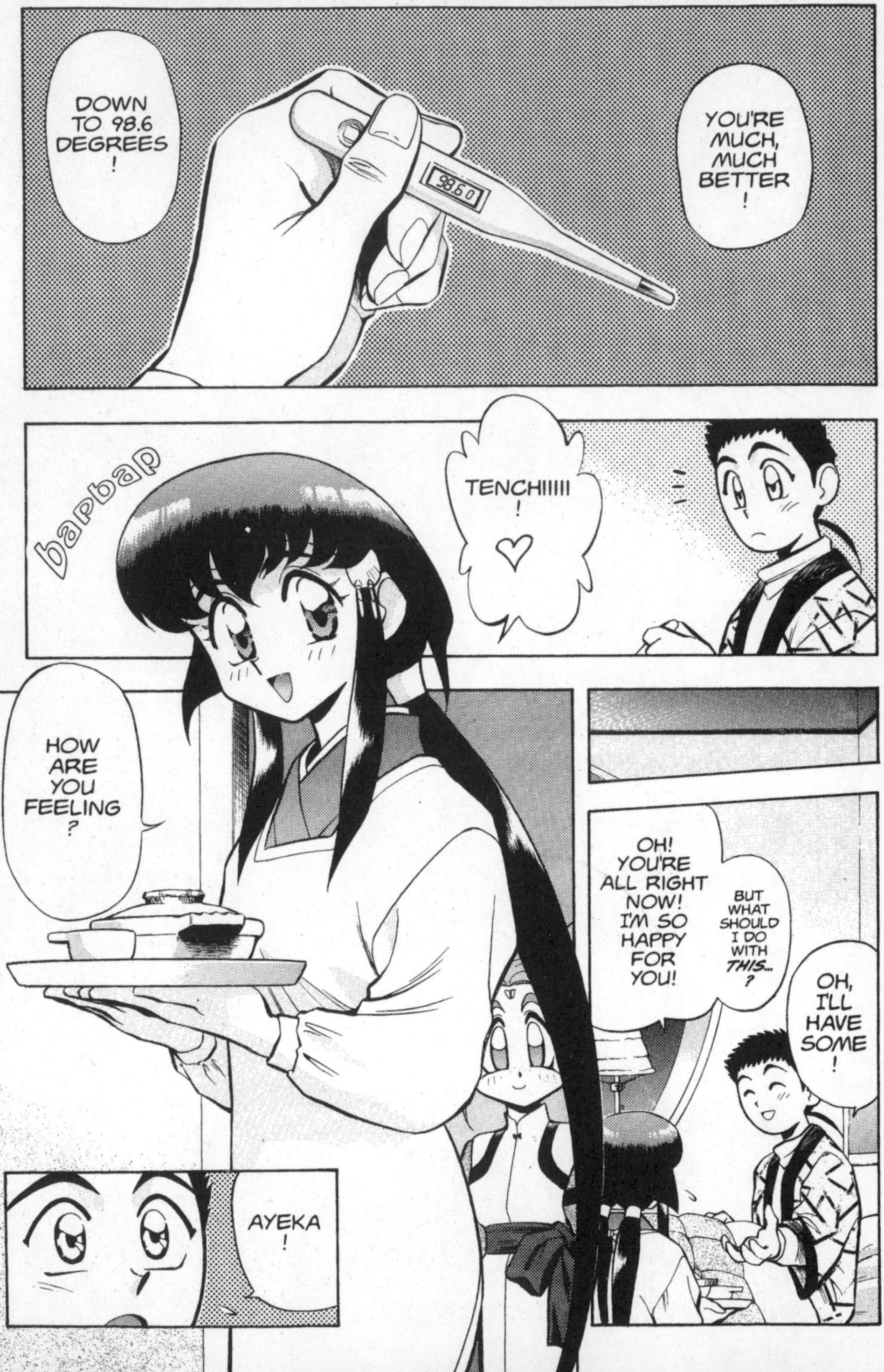
DOWN TO 98.6 DEGREES!
98.6
YOU'RE MUCH, MUCH BETTER!
bapbap
TENCHIIIIII!
HOW ARE YOU FEELING?
OH! YOU'RE ALL RIGHT NOW! I'M SO HAPPY FOR YOU!
BUT WHAT SHOULD I DO WITH THIS...?
OH, I'LL HAVE SOME!
AYEKA!

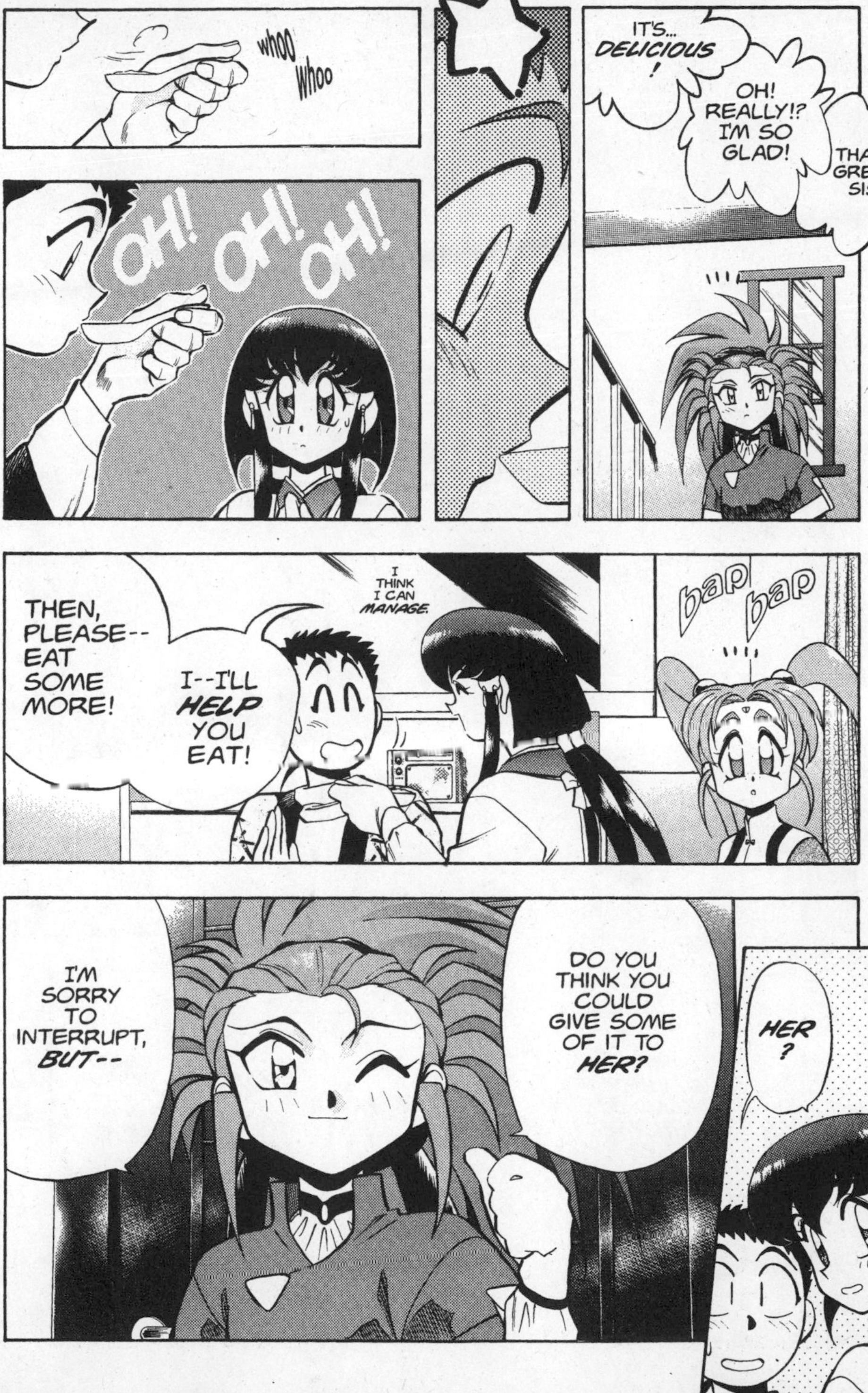
whoo
whoo
OH!
OH!
OH!
IT'S... *DELICIOUS*!
OH! REALLY!? I'M SO GLAD!
THAT'S GREAT, SIS!
THEN, PLEASE-- EAT SOME MORE!
I--I'LL *HELP* YOU EAT!
I THINK I CAN *MANAGE*.
bap
bap
I'M SORRY TO INTERRUPT, *BUT--*
DO YOU THINK YOU COULD GIVE SOME OF IT TO *HER?*
HER?

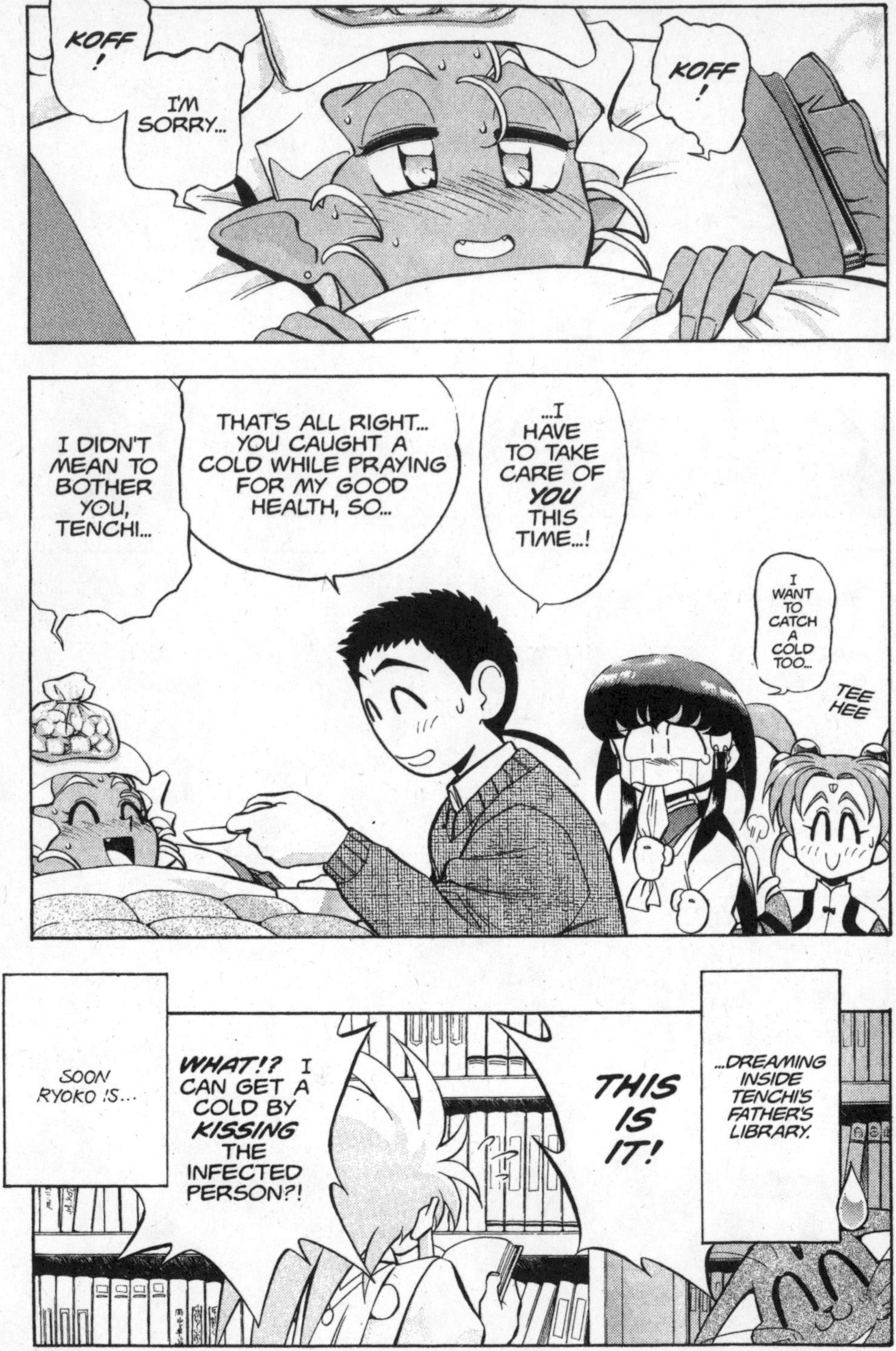
KOFF!
I'M SORRY...
KOFF!
I DIDN'T MEAN TO BOTHER YOU, TENCHI...
THAT'S ALL RIGHT... YOU CAUGHT A COLD WHILE PRAYING FOR MY GOOD HEALTH, SO...
...I HAVE TO TAKE CARE OF YOU THIS TIME...!
I WANT TO CATCH A COLD TOO...
TEE HEE
SOON RYOKO IS...
WHAT!? I CAN GET A COLD BY KISSING THE INFECTED PERSON?!
THIS IS IT!
...DREAMING INSIDE TENCHI'S FATHER'S LIBRARY.

Tales of Tenchi #7

DRIVING LESSONS

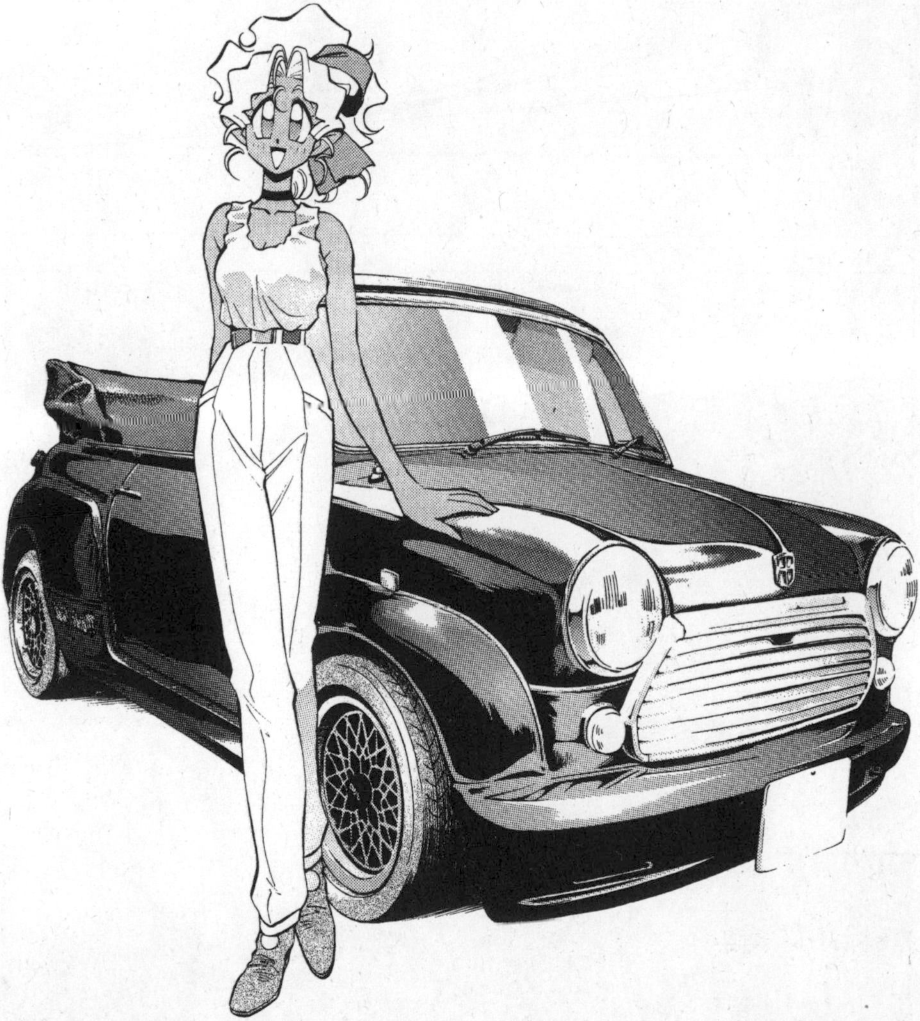

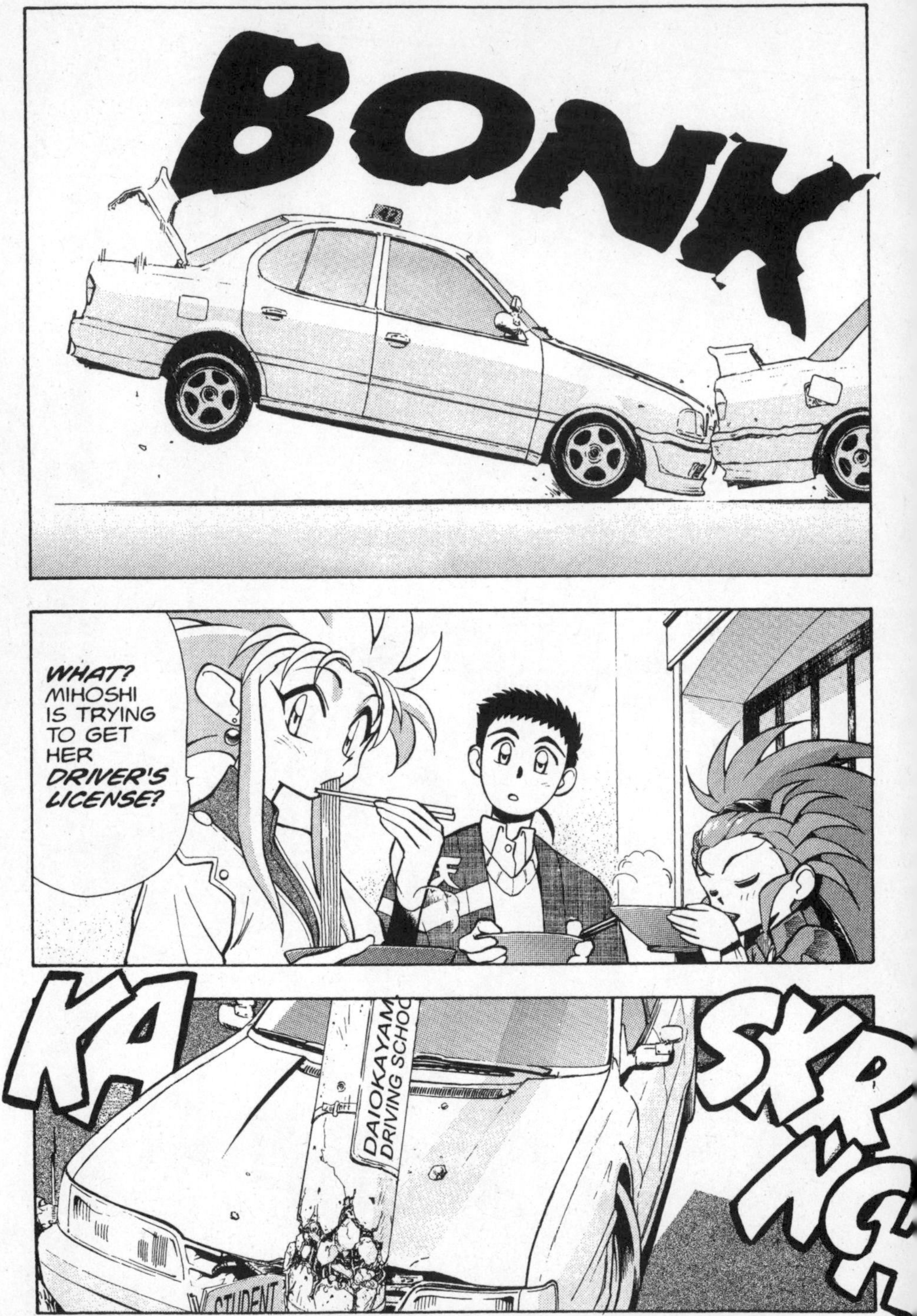
BONK
WHAT? MIHOSHI IS TRYING TO GET HER DRIVER'S LICENSE?
KA
DAIOKAYAM
DRIVING SCHOO
STUDENT

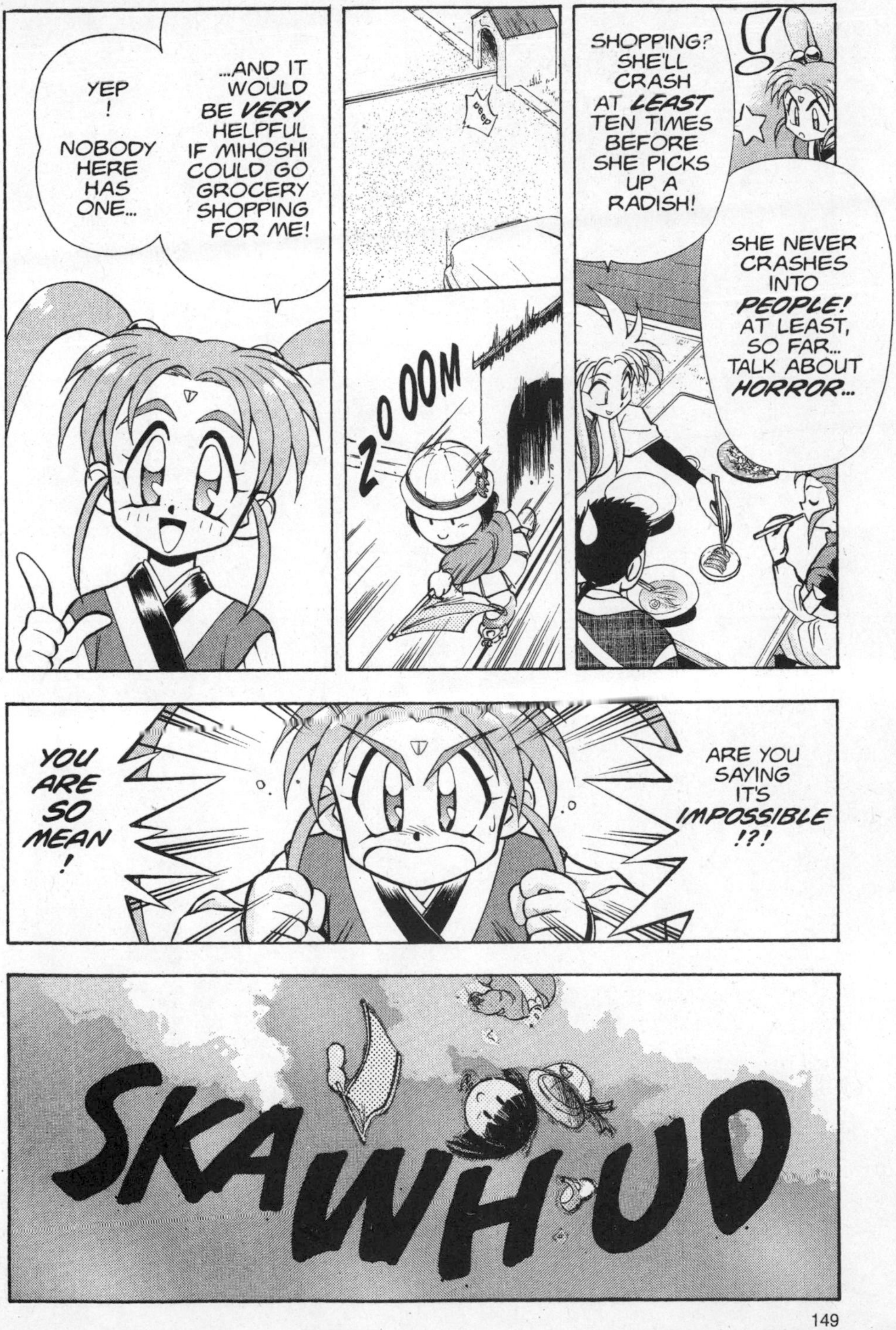
YEP! NOBODY HERE HAS ONE...
...AND IT WOULD BE *VERY* HELPFUL IF MIHOSHI COULD GO GROCERY SHOPPING FOR ME!
beep
ZOOOM
SHOPPING? SHE'LL CRASH AT *LEAST* TEN TIMES BEFORE SHE PICKS UP A RADISH!
SHE NEVER CRASHES INTO *PEOPLE!* AT LEAST, SO FAR... TALK ABOUT *HORROR...*
YOU ARE SO MEAN!
ARE YOU SAYING IT'S *IMPOSSIBLE!?!*
SKAWHUD

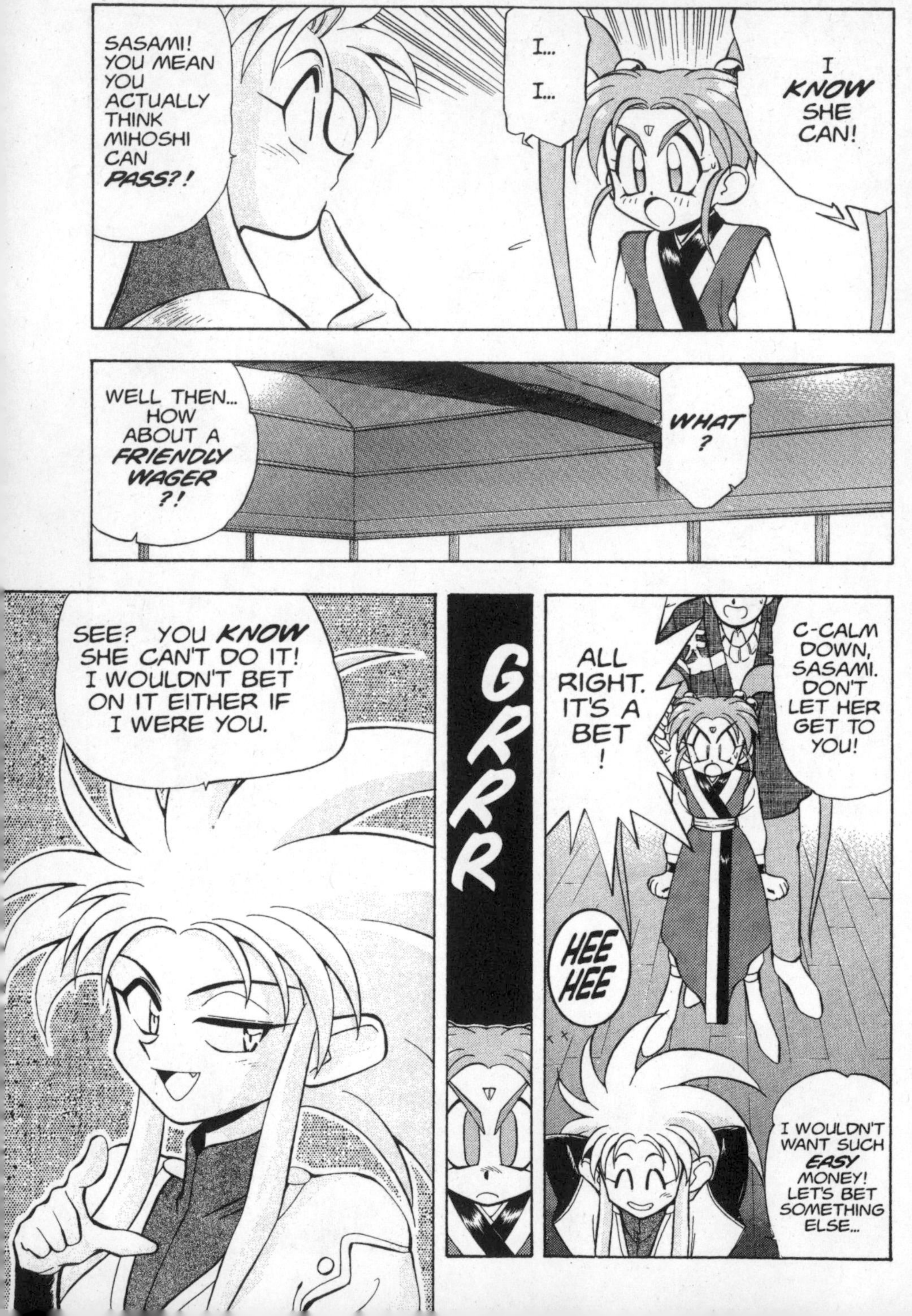
SASAMI! YOU MEAN YOU ACTUALLY THINK MIHOSHI CAN PASS?!
I... I...
I KNOW SHE CAN!
WELL THEN... HOW ABOUT A FRIENDLY WAGER?!
WHAT?
SEE? YOU KNOW SHE CAN'T DO IT! I WOULDN'T BET ON IT EITHER IF I WERE YOU.
GRRR
ALL RIGHT. IT'S A BET!
C-CALM DOWN, SASAMI. DON'T LET HER GET TO YOU!
HEE HEE
I WOULDN'T WANT SUCH EASY MONEY! LET'S BET SOMETHING ELSE...

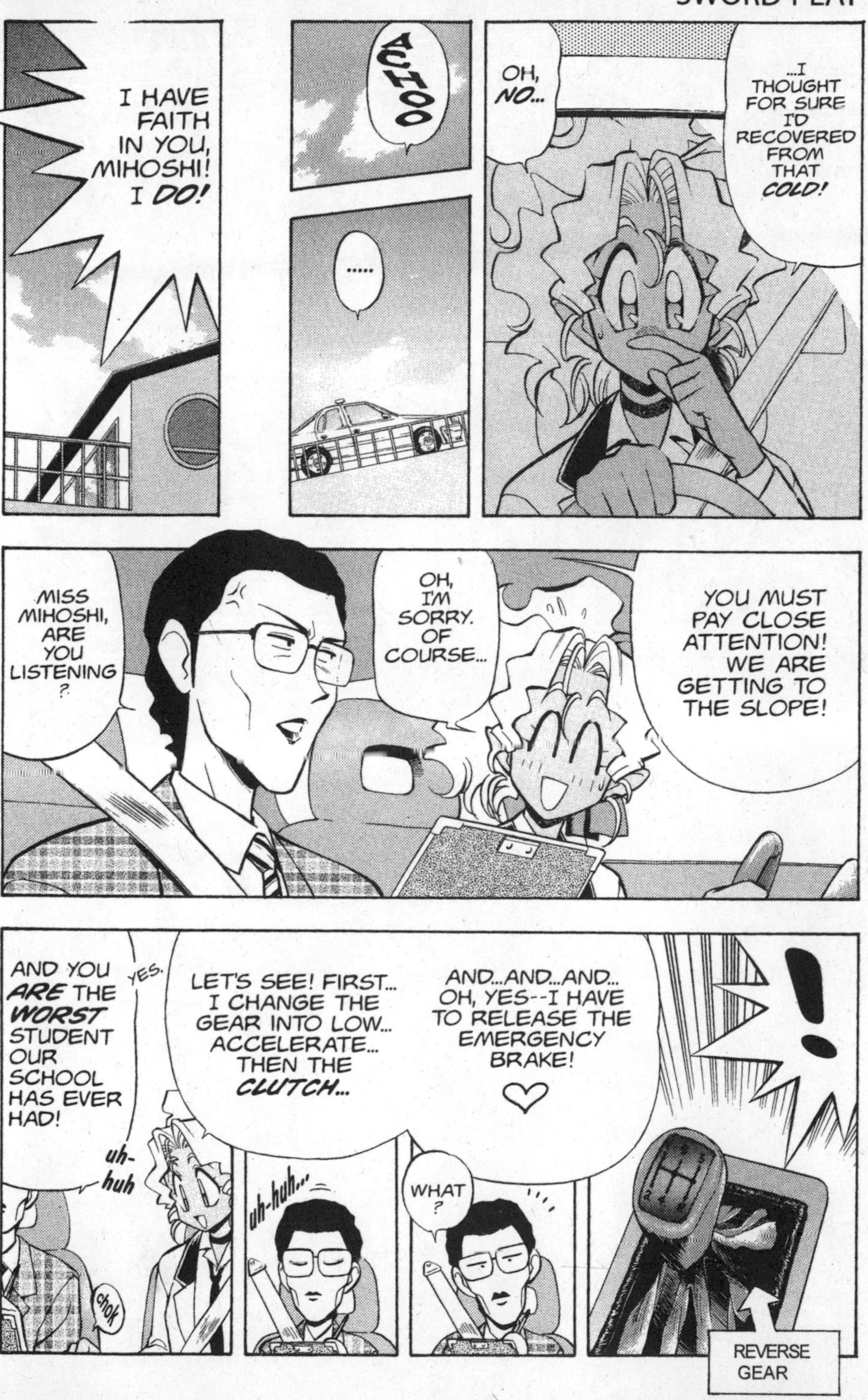
I HAVE FAITH IN YOU, MIHOSHI! I DO!
ACHOO
......
OH, NO...
...I THOUGHT FOR SURE I'D RECOVERED FROM THAT COLD!
MISS MIHOSHI, ARE YOU LISTENING?
OH, I'M SORRY. OF COURSE...
YOU MUST PAY CLOSE ATTENTION! WE ARE GETTING TO THE SLOPE!
AND YOU ARE THE WORST STUDENT OUR SCHOOL HAS EVER HAD!
YES.
uh-huh
chok
LET'S SEE! FIRST... I CHANGE THE GEAR INTO LOW... ACCELERATE... THEN THE CLUTCH...
uh-huh...
AND...AND...AND... OH, YES--I HAVE TO RELEASE THE EMERGENCY BRAKE!
WHAT?
!
REVERSE GEAR

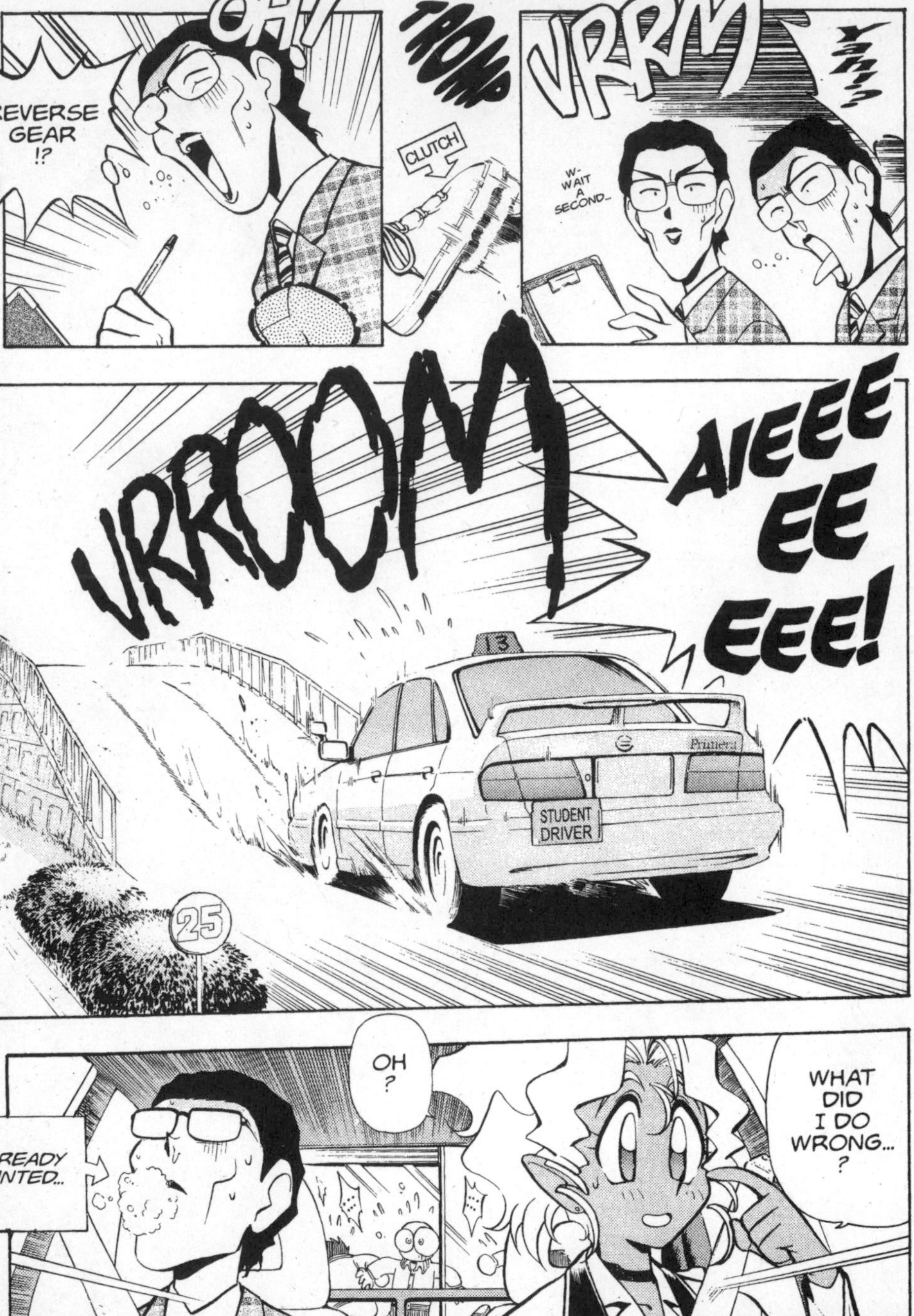
OH!
REVERSE GEAR !?
THOMP
CLUTCH
VRRM
W-WAIT A SECOND...
VRROOM
AIEEE EE EEE!
13
STUDENT DRIVER
25
ALREADY FAINTED...
OH ?
WHAT DID I DO WRONG... ?

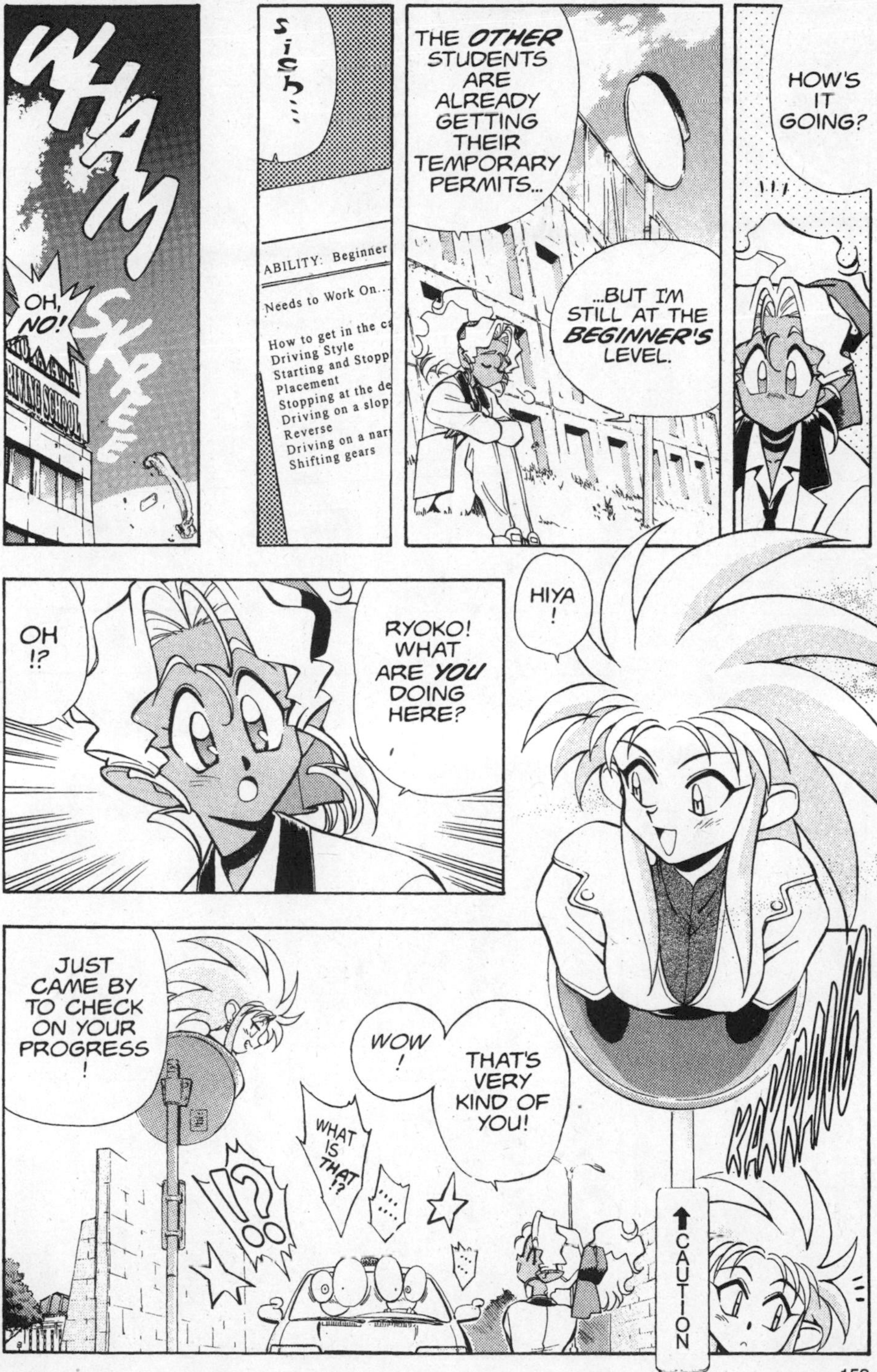
WHAM
OH, NO!
RIVING SCHOOL
ABILITY: Beginner
Needs to Work On...
How to get in the ca
Driving Style
Starting and Stopp
Placement
Stopping at the de
Driving on a slop
Reverse
Driving on a nar
Shifting gears
THE OTHER STUDENTS ARE ALREADY GETTING THEIR TEMPORARY PERMITS...
...BUT I'M STILL AT THE BEGINNER'S LEVEL.
HOW'S IT GOING?
OH !?
RYOKO! WHAT ARE YOU DOING HERE?
HIYA !
JUST CAME BY TO CHECK ON YOUR PROGRESS !
WOW !
THAT'S VERY KIND OF YOU!
WHAT IS THAT !?
CAUTION

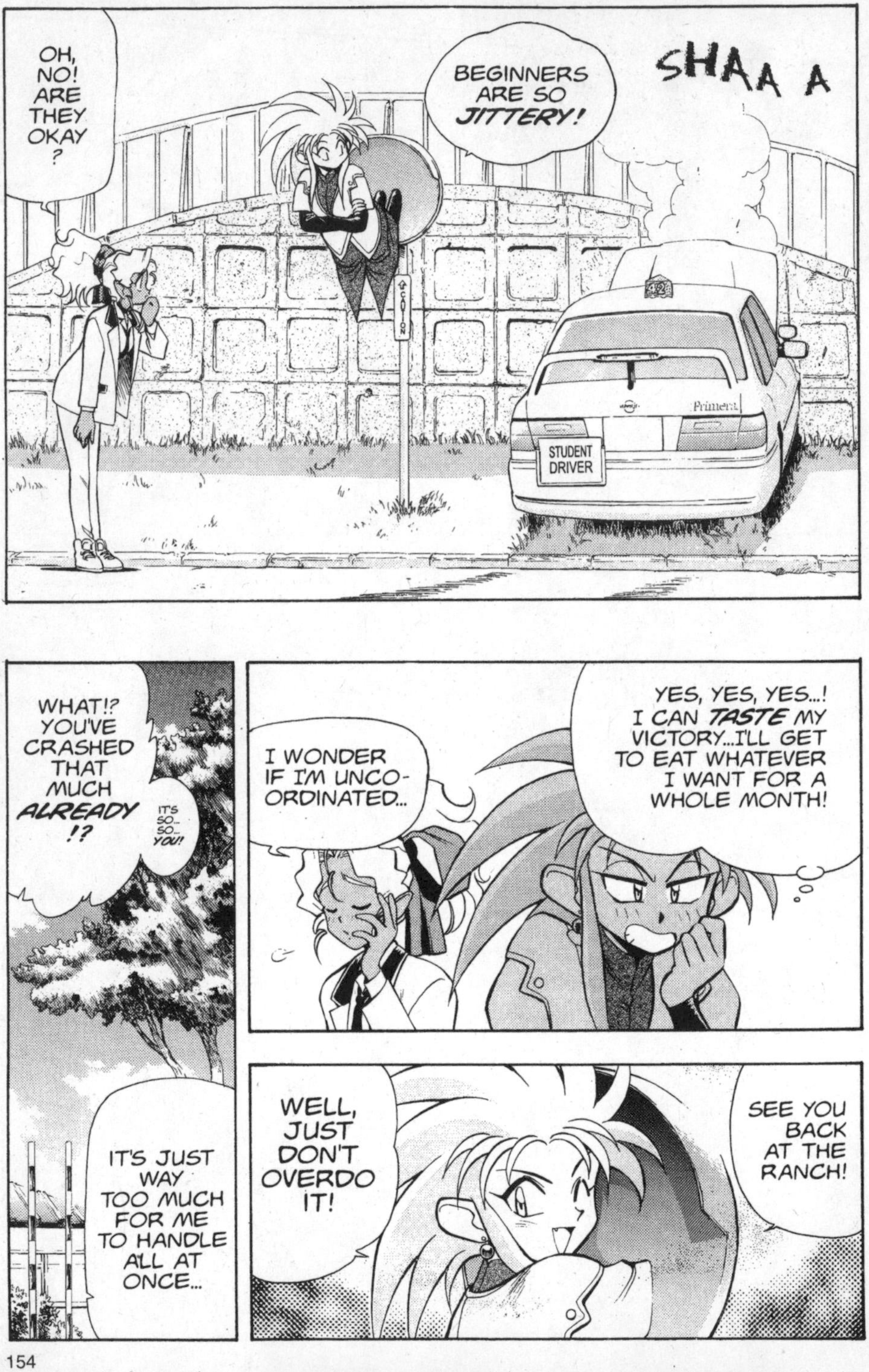
OH, NO! ARE THEY OKAY?
BEGINNERS ARE SO *JITTERY!*
SHAA A
CAUTION
Primera
STUDENT DRIVER
WHAT!? YOU'VE CRASHED THAT MUCH *ALREADY!?*
IT'S SO... SO... *YOU!*
IT'S JUST WAY TOO MUCH FOR ME TO HANDLE ALL AT ONCE...
I WONDER IF I'M UNCO-ORDINATED...
YES, YES, YES...! I CAN *TASTE* MY VICTORY...I'LL GET TO EAT WHATEVER I WANT FOR A WHOLE MONTH!
WELL, JUST DON'T OVERDO IT!
SEE YOU BACK AT THE RANCH!

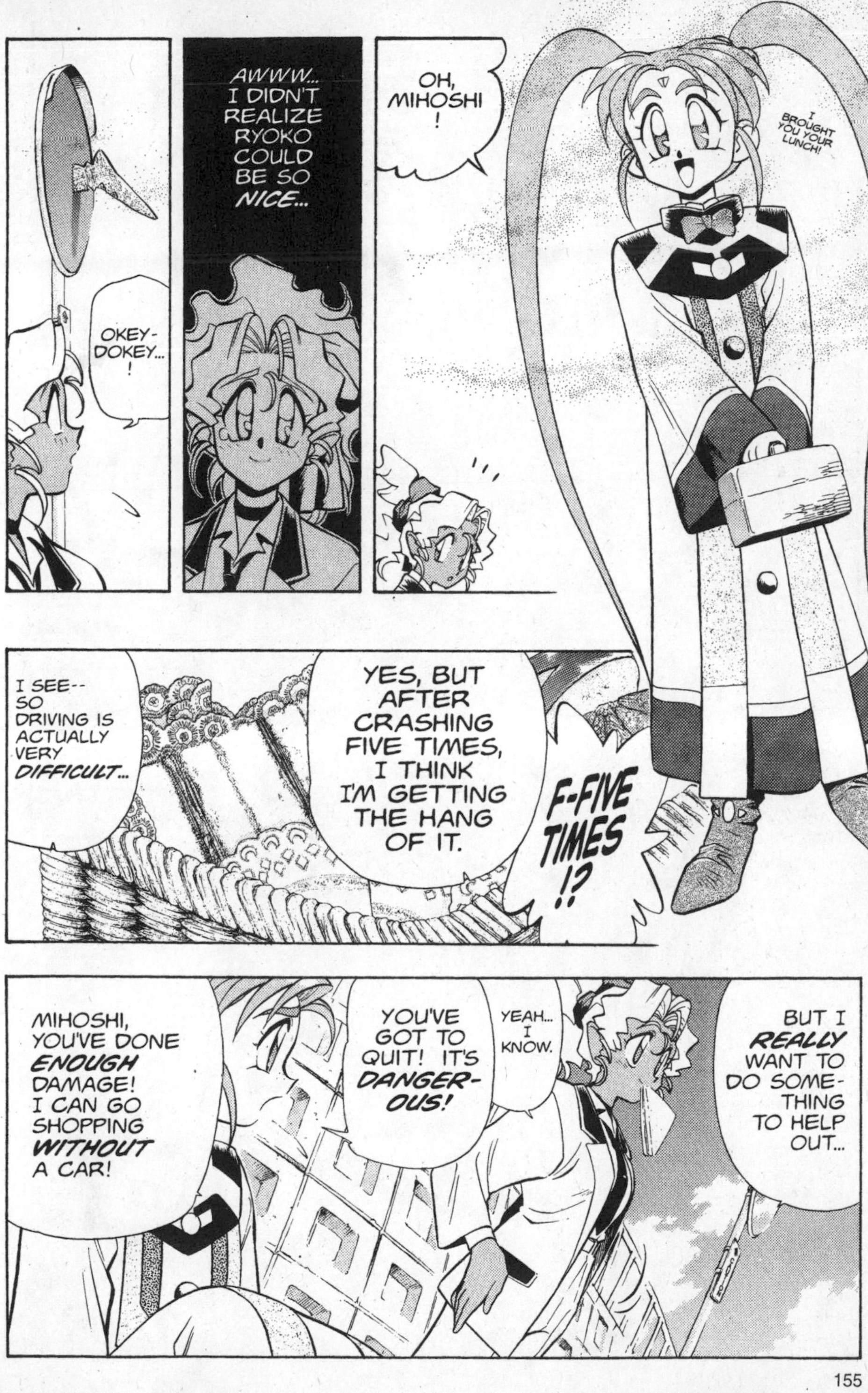
OKEY-DOKEY...!
AWWW... I DIDN'T REALIZE RYOKO COULD BE SO NICE...
OH, MIHOSHI!
I BROUGHT YOU YOUR LUNCH!
I SEE-- SO DRIVING IS ACTUALLY VERY DIFFICULT...
YES, BUT AFTER CRASHING FIVE TIMES, I THINK I'M GETTING THE HANG OF IT.
F-FIVE TIMES!?
MIHOSHI, YOU'VE DONE ENOUGH DAMAGE! I CAN GO SHOPPING WITHOUT A CAR!
YOU'VE GOT TO QUIT! IT'S DANGEROUS!
YEAH... I KNOW.
BUT I REALLY WANT TO DO SOMETHING TO HELP OUT...

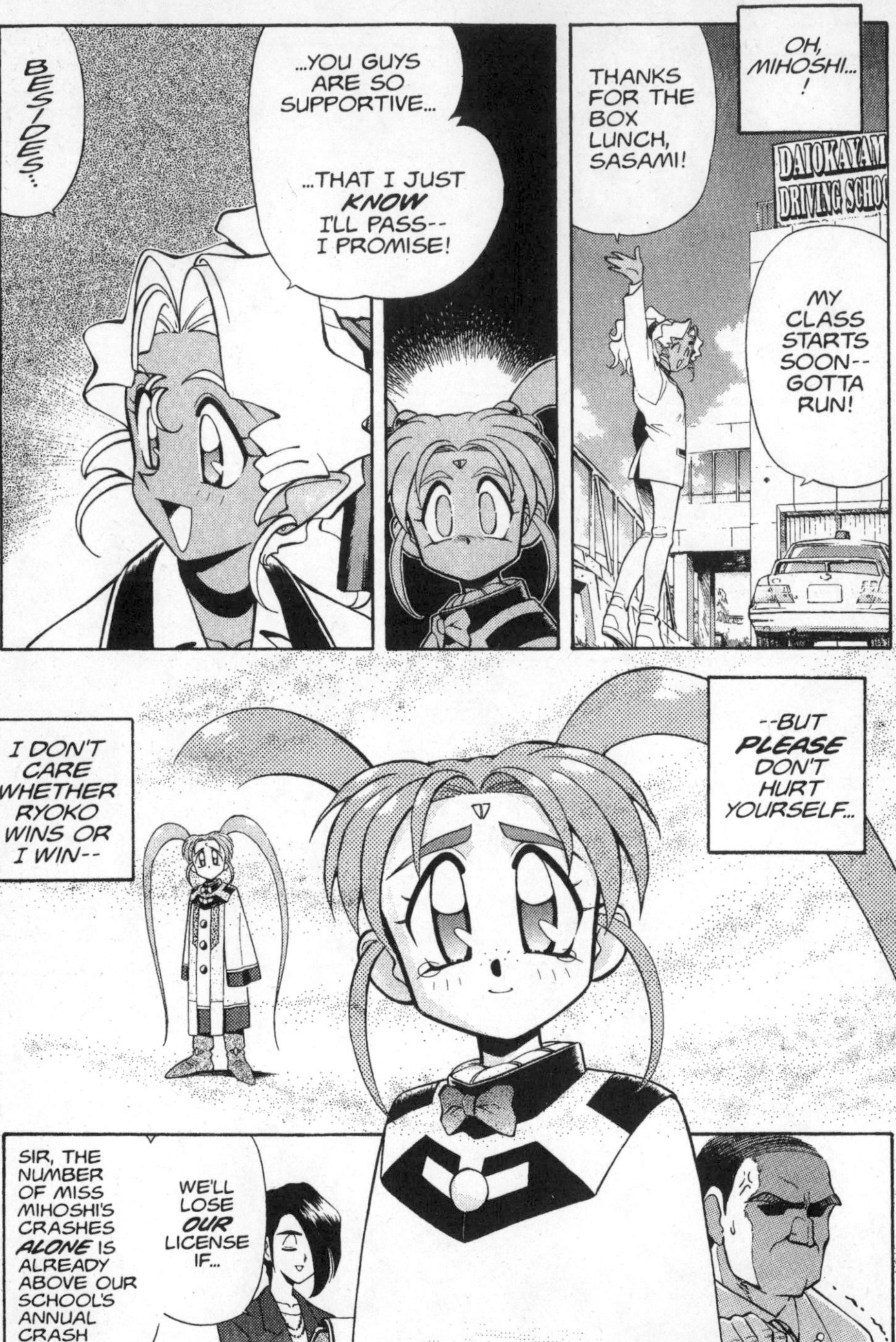
BESIDES...
...YOU GUYS ARE SO SUPPORTIVE...
...THAT I JUST *KNOW* I'LL PASS-- I PROMISE!
THANKS FOR THE BOX LUNCH, SASAMI!
OH, MIHOSHI... !
DAIOKAYAM
DRIVING SCHOO
MY CLASS STARTS SOON-- GOTTA RUN!
I DON'T CARE WHETHER RYOKO WINS OR I WIN--
--BUT **PLEASE** DON'T HURT YOURSELF...
SIR, THE NUMBER OF MISS MIHOSHI'S CRASHES **ALONE** IS ALREADY ABOVE OUR SCHOOL'S ANNUAL CRASH LIMITS.
WE'LL LOSE **OUR** LICENSE IF...

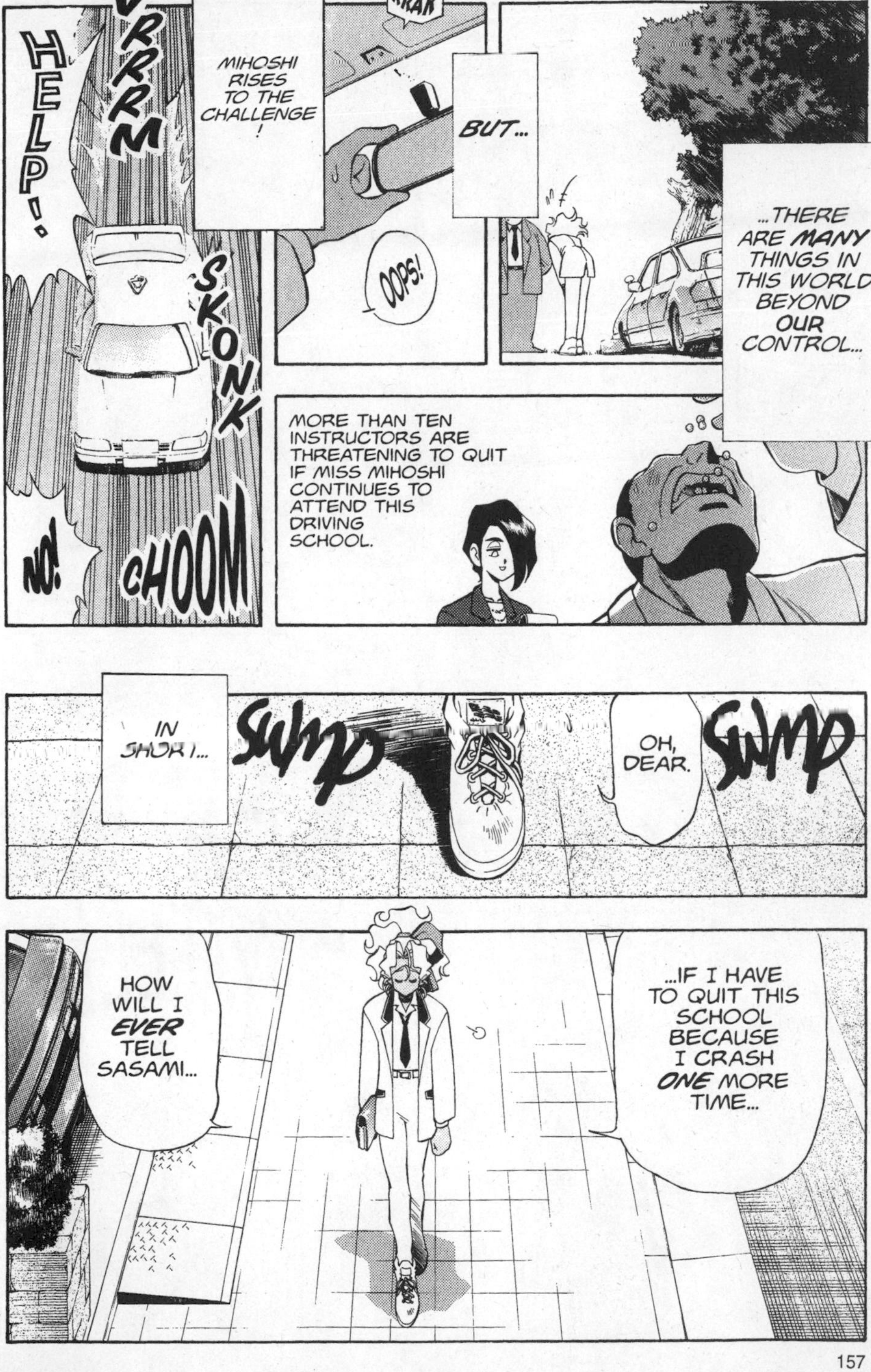
VRRRM
HELP!
SKONK
NO!
CHOOM
MIHOSHI RISES TO THE CHALLENGE!
KRAK
BUT...
OOPS!
...THERE ARE MANY THINGS IN THIS WORLD BEYOND OUR CONTROL...
MORE THAN TEN INSTRUCTORS ARE THREATENING TO QUIT IF MISS MIHOSHI CONTINUES TO ATTEND THIS DRIVING SCHOOL.
IN SHORT...
SWMP
OH, DEAR.
SWMP
HOW WILL I EVER TELL SASAMI...
...IF I HAVE TO QUIT THIS SCHOOL BECAUSE I CRASH ONE MORE TIME...

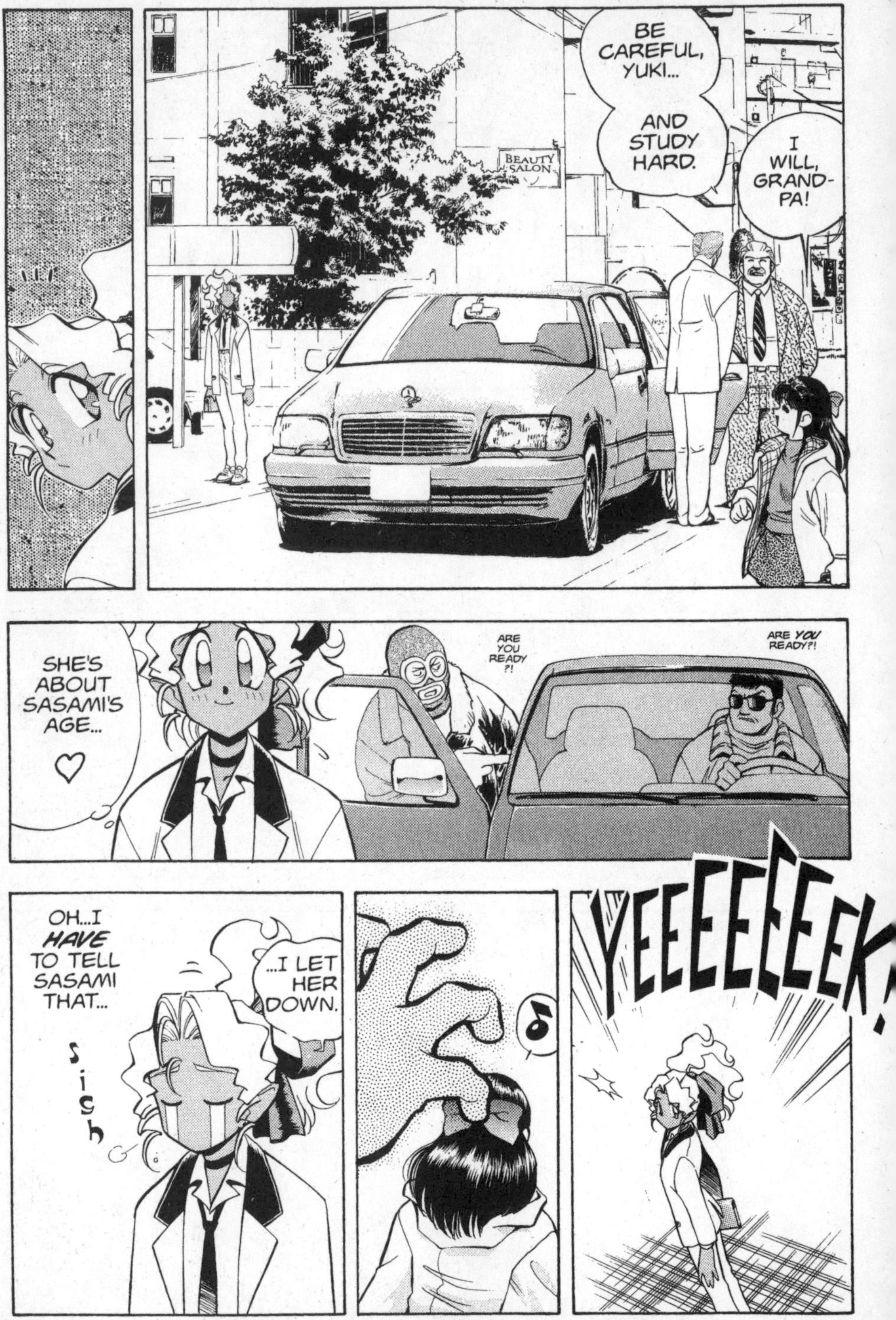
BE CAREFUL, YUKI...
AND STUDY HARD.
I WILL, GRAND-PA!
BEAUTY SALON
SHE'S ABOUT SASAMI'S AGE...
ARE YOU READY ?!
ARE YOU READY?!
OH...I HAVE TO TELL SASAMI THAT...
...I LET HER DOWN.
sigh
YEEEEEEK!

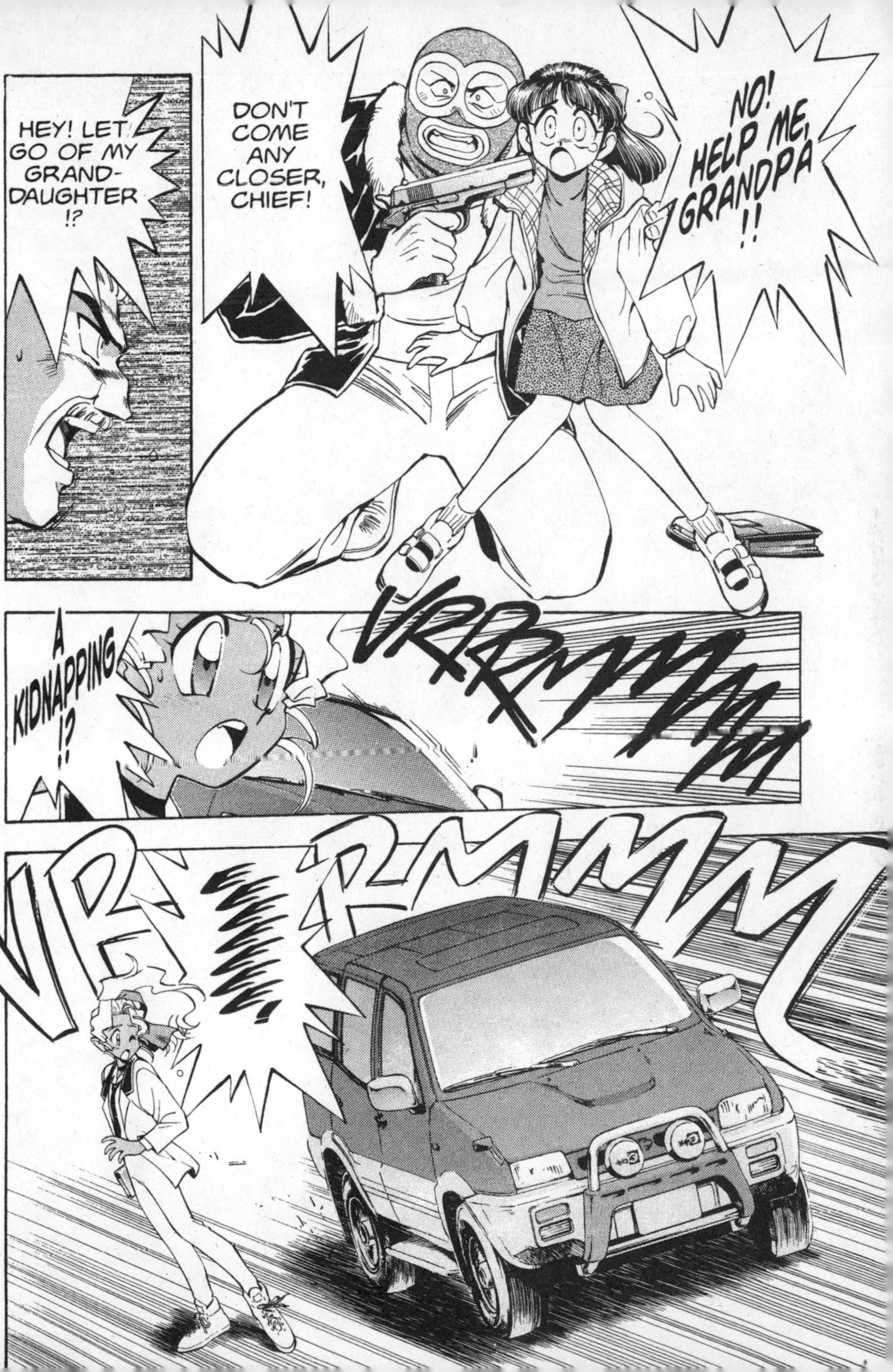
HEY! LET GO OF MY GRAND-DAUGHTER !?
DON'T COME ANY CLOSER, CHIEF!
NO! HELP ME, GRANDPA !!
A KIDNAPPING !?
VRRMMMMM
VRRMMMM

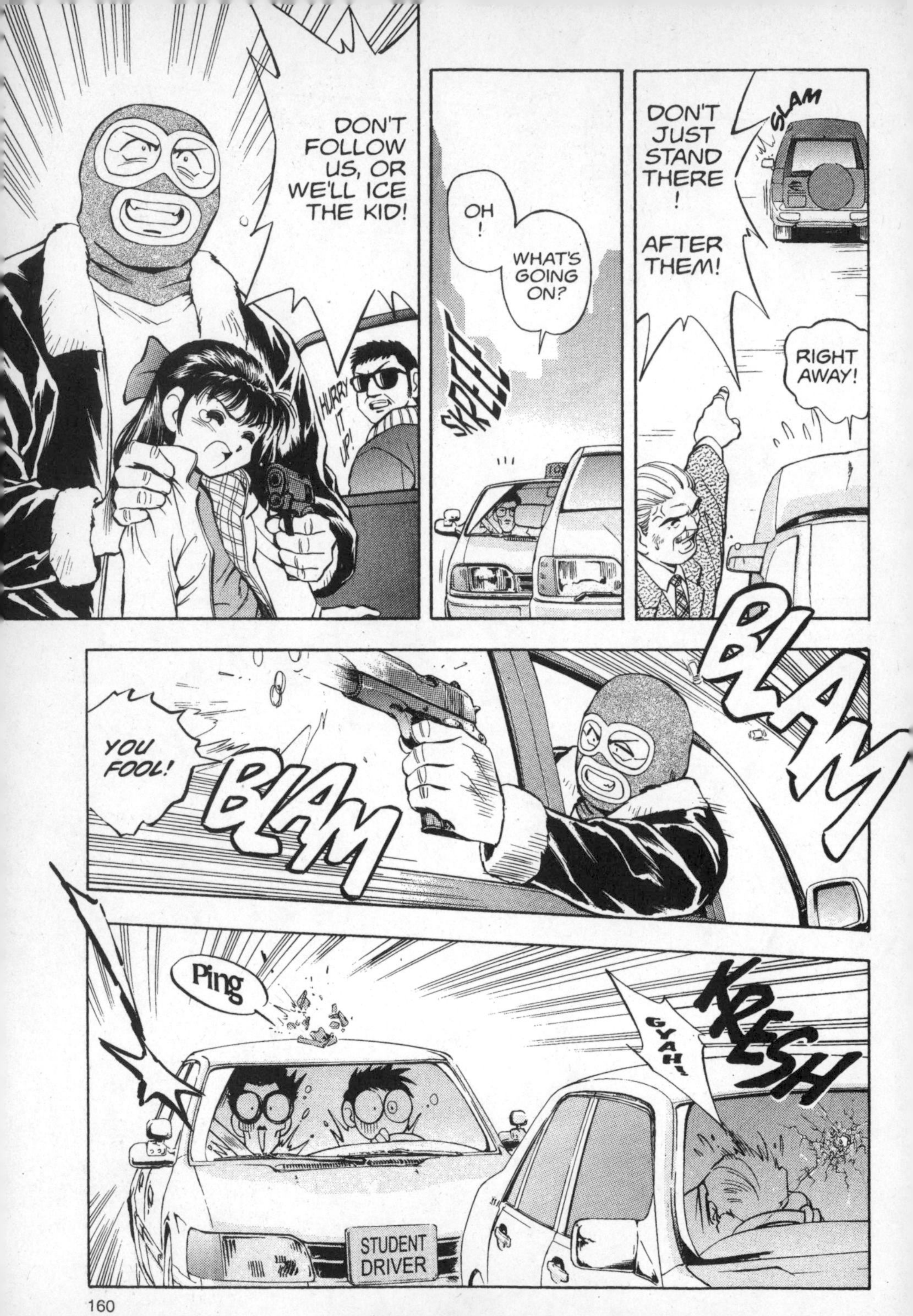
DON'T FOLLOW US, OR WE'LL ICE THE KID!
HURRY IT UP!
OH!
WHAT'S GOING ON?
SKREEE
DON'T JUST STAND THERE!
AFTER THEM!
SLAM
RIGHT AWAY!
YOU FOOL!
BLAM
BLAM
Ping
GYAH!
KRESH
STUDENT DRIVER

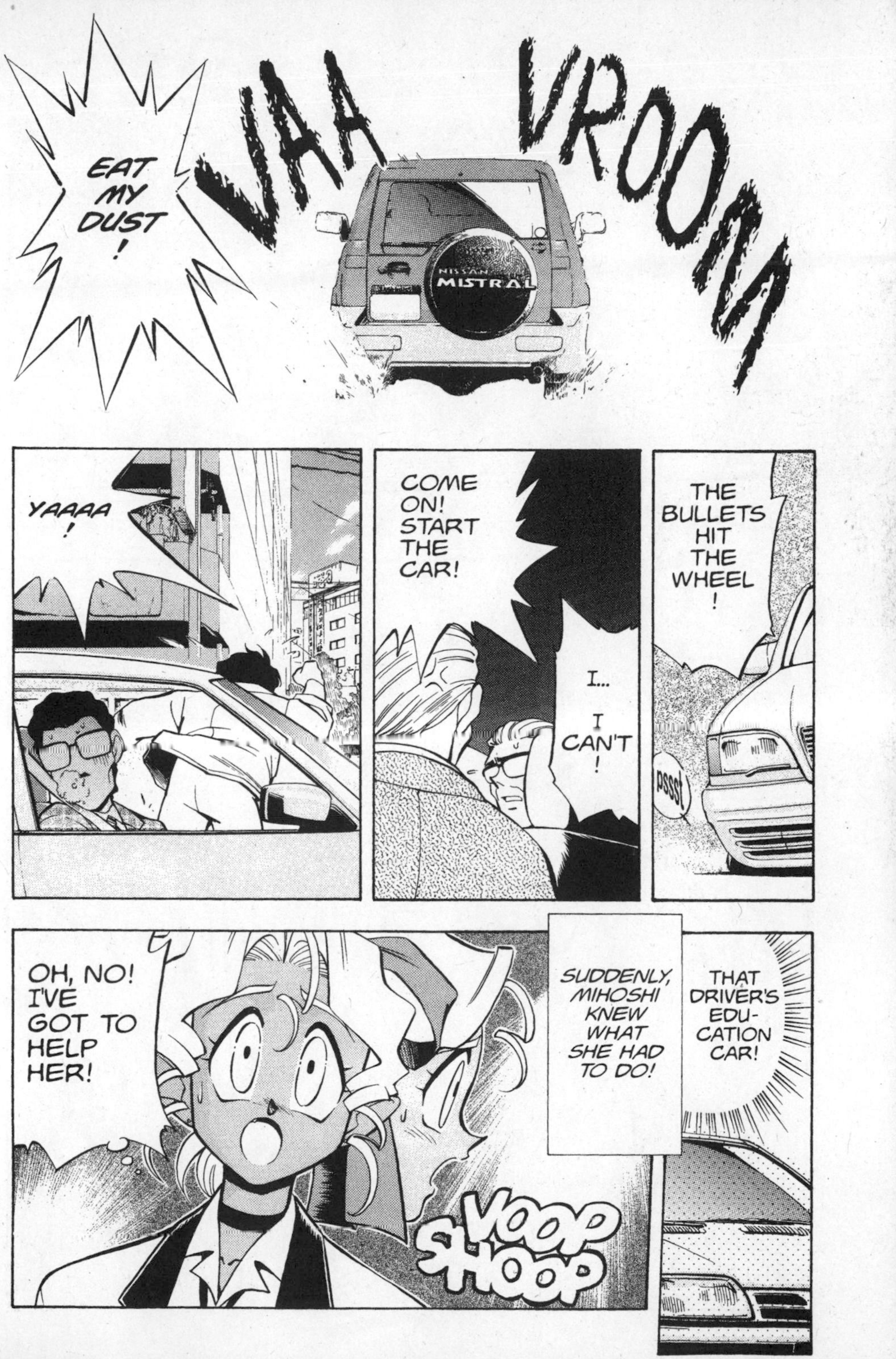
EAT MY DUST!
JAA VROOM
NISSAN MISTRAL
YAAAA!
COME ON! START THE CAR!
I... I CAN'T!
THE BULLETS HIT THE WHEEL!
pssst
OH, NO! I'VE GOT TO HELP HER!
SUDDENLY, MIHOSHI KNEW WHAT SHE HAD TO DO!
THAT DRIVER'S EDU-CATION CAR!
VOOP SHOOP

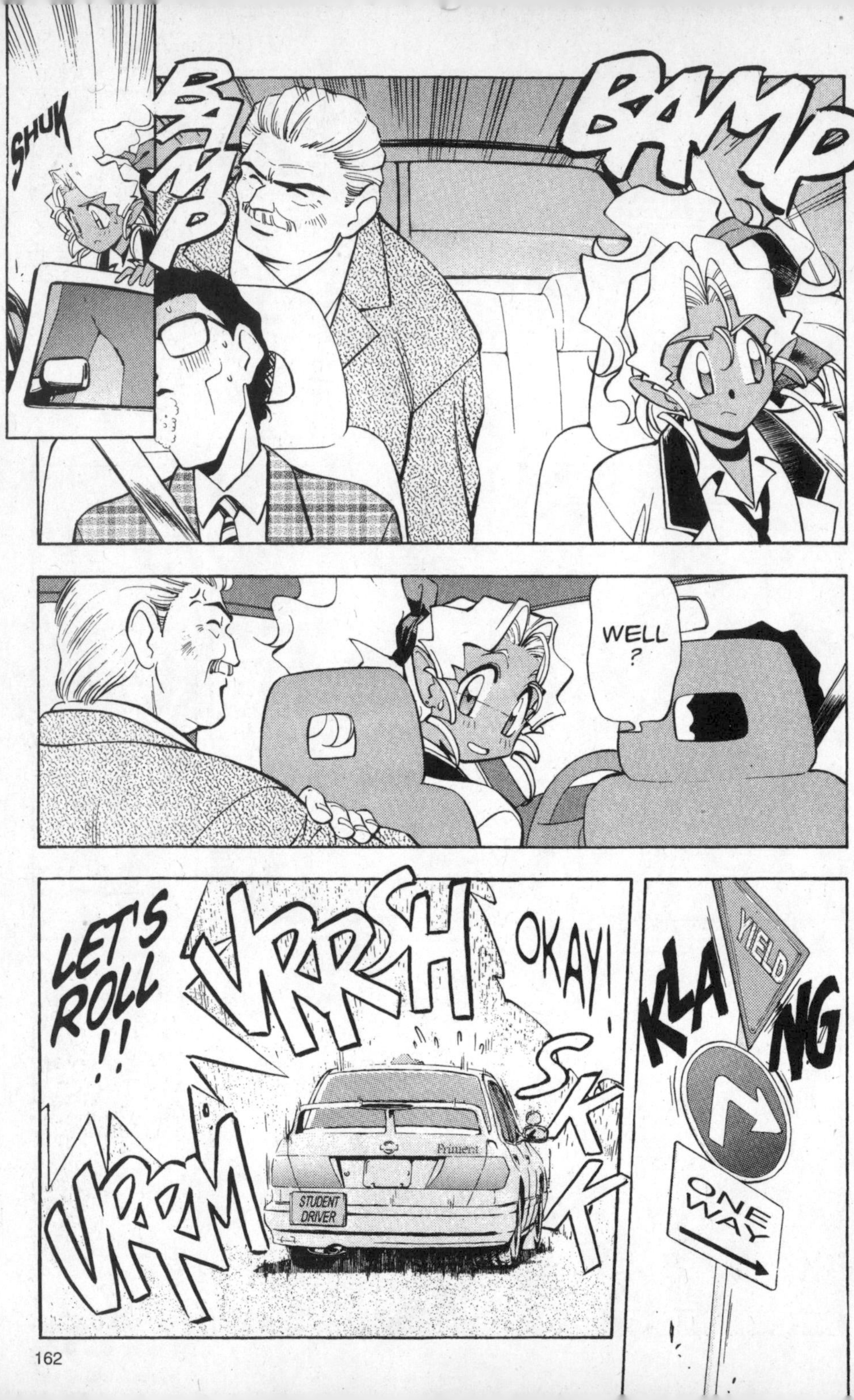
SHUK
BAMP
BAMP
WELL?
LET'S ROLL!!
VRRSH
OKAY!
VRRM
STUDENT DRIVER
SKK
KLANG
YIELD
ONE WAY

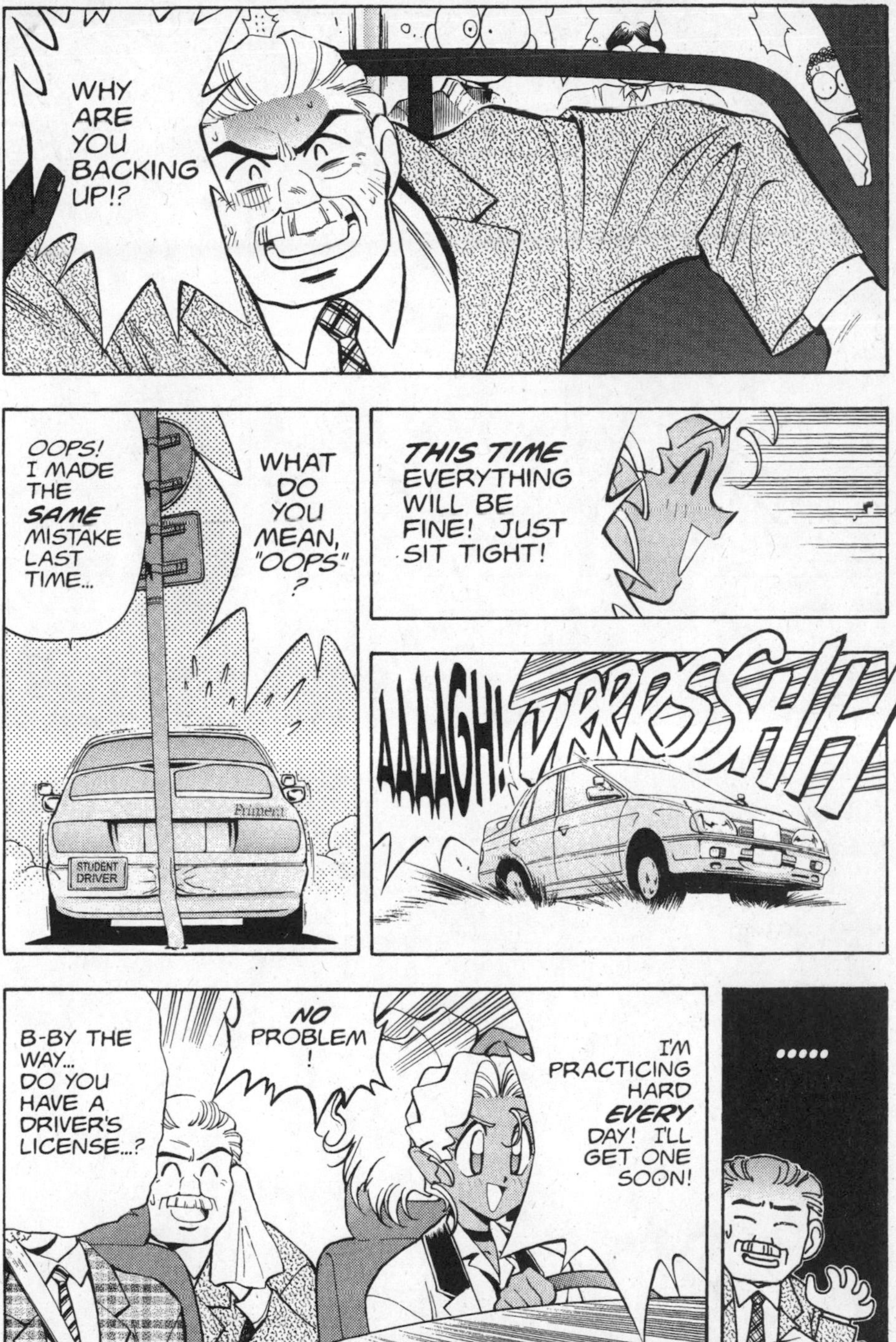
WHY ARE YOU BACKING UP!?
OOPS! I MADE THE SAME MISTAKE LAST TIME...
WHAT DO YOU MEAN, "OOPS"?
STUDENT DRIVER
THIS TIME EVERYTHING WILL BE FINE! JUST SIT TIGHT!
AAAAGH!
VRRRSSHH!
B-BY THE WAY... DO YOU HAVE A DRIVER'S LICENSE...?
NO PROBLEM!
I'M PRACTICING HARD EVERY DAY! I'LL GET ONE SOON!
.....

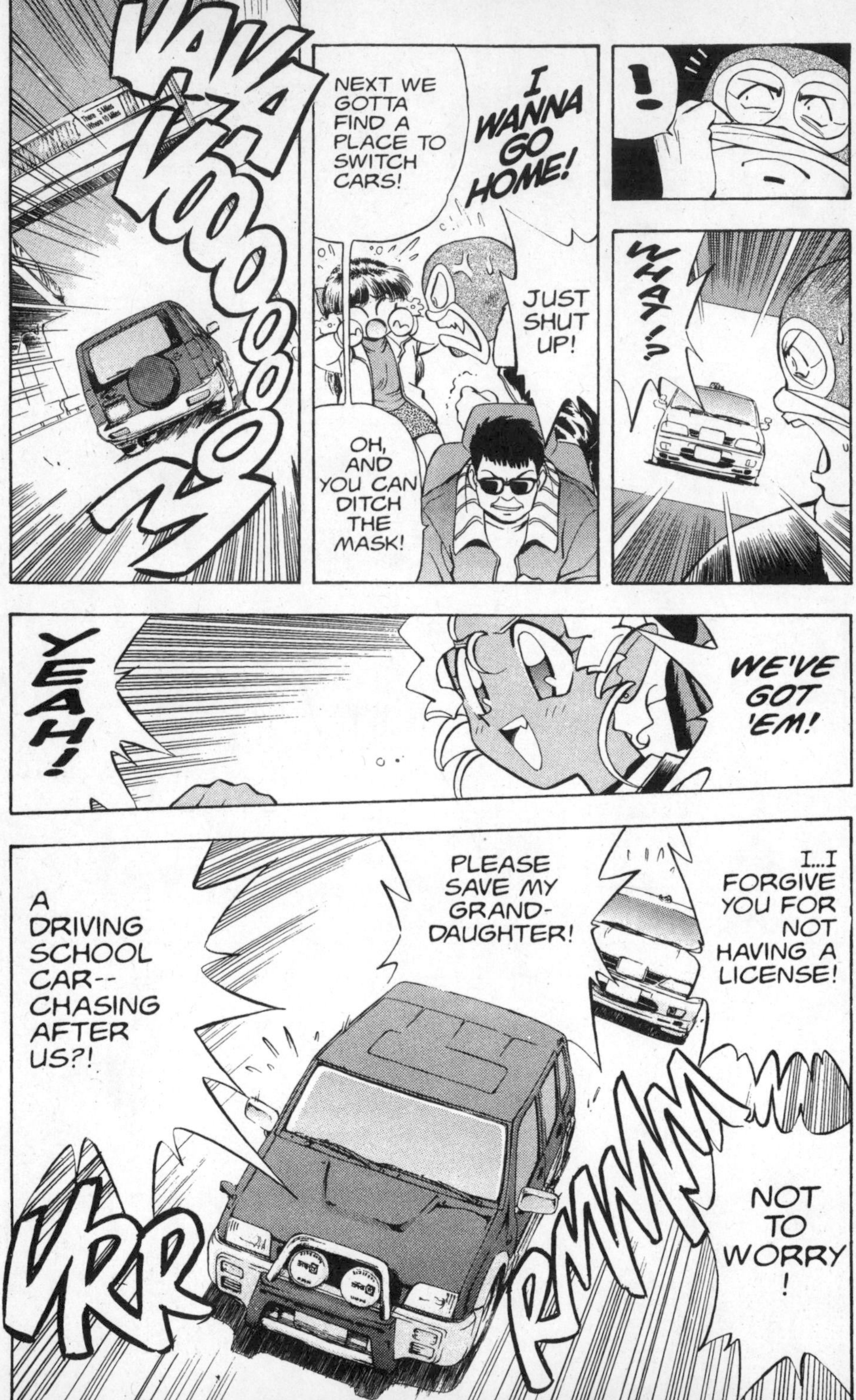
VAVAVAVOOOOOOOM
NEXT WE GOTTA FIND A PLACE TO SWITCH CARS!
I WANNA GO HOME!
JUST SHUT UP!
OH, AND YOU CAN DITCH THE MASK!
!
WHAT!?
YEAH!
WE'VE GOT 'EM!
A DRIVING SCHOOL CAR--CHASING AFTER US?!
PLEASE SAVE MY GRAND-DAUGHTER!
I...I FORGIVE YOU FOR NOT HAVING A LICENSE!
VRR
RMMMMMM
NOT TO WORRY!

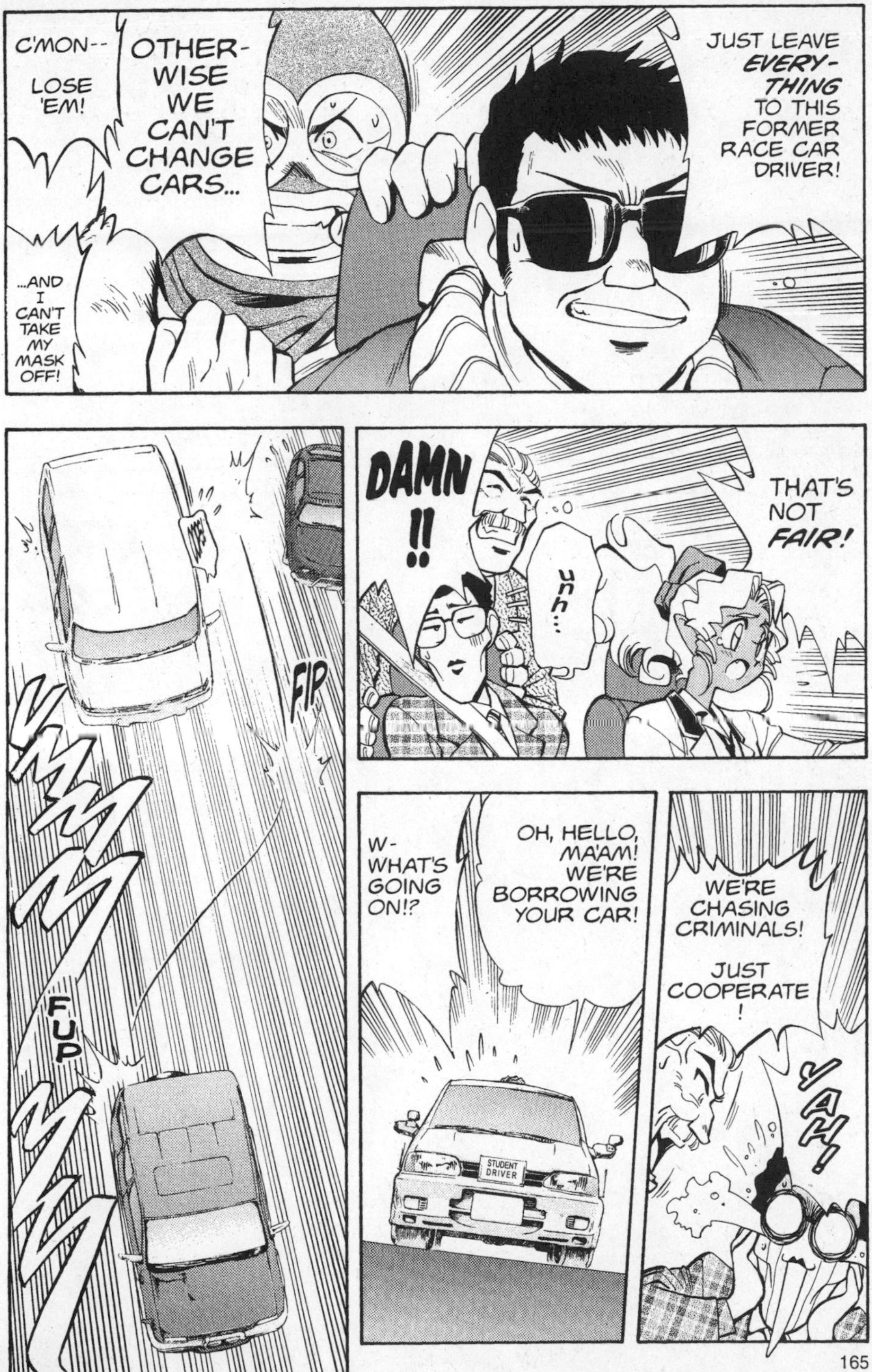
C'MON--
LOSE 'EM!
OTHER-WISE WE CAN'T CHANGE CARS...
...AND I CAN'T TAKE MY MASK OFF!
JUST LEAVE EVERYTHING TO THIS FORMER RACE CAR DRIVER!
FIP
FUP
DAMN!!
unh...
THAT'S NOT FAIR!
W-WHAT'S GOING ON!?
OH, HELLO, MA'AM! WE'RE BORROWING YOUR CAR!
STUDENT DRIVER
WE'RE CHASING CRIMINALS!
JUST COOPERATE!
YAH!

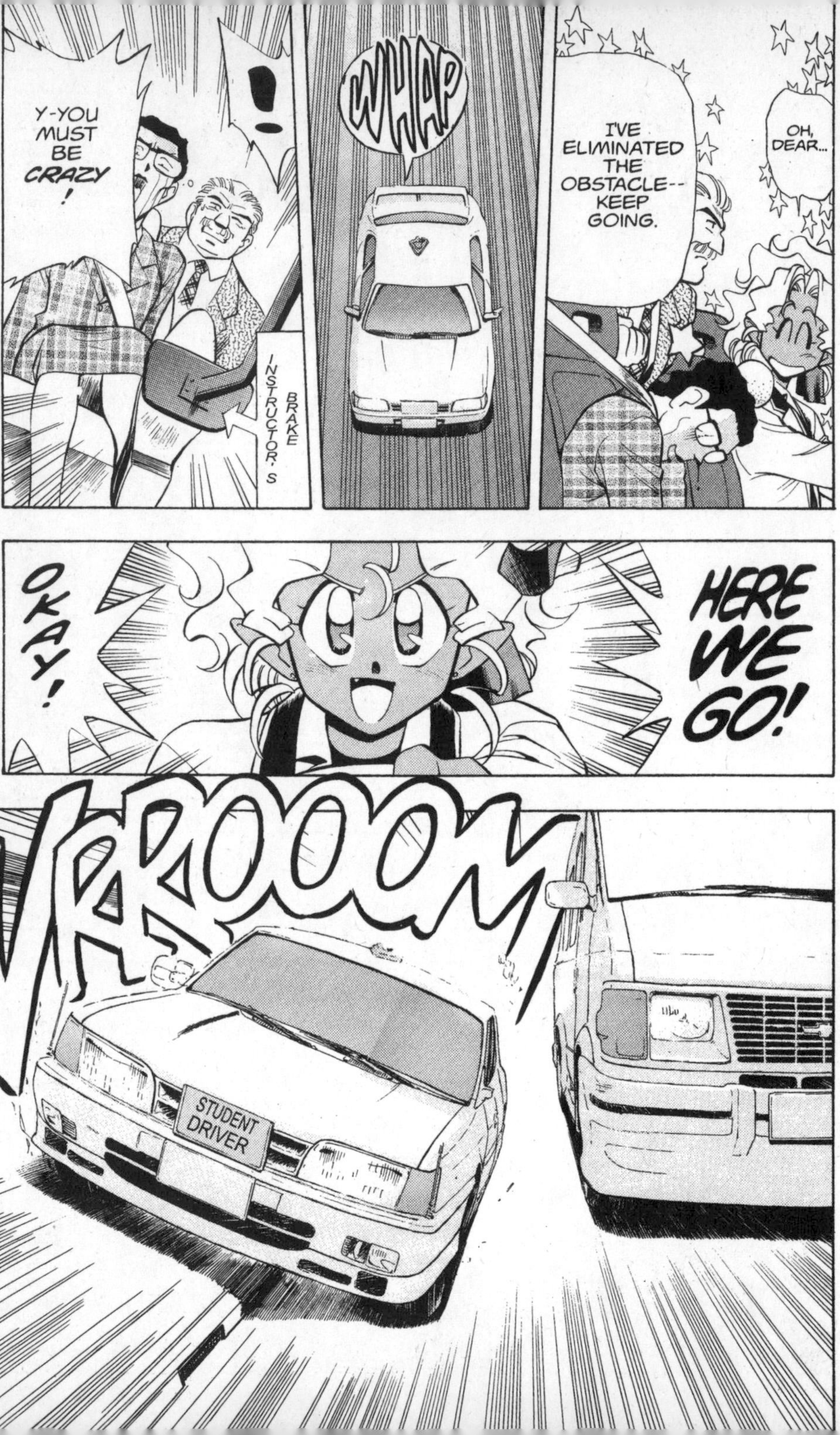
Y-YOU MUST BE CRAZY!
!
INSTRUCTOR'S BRAKE
WHAP
I'VE ELIMINATED THE OBSTACLE-- KEEP GOING.
OH, DEAR...
OKAY!
HERE WE GO!
VRROOOM
STUDENT DRIVER

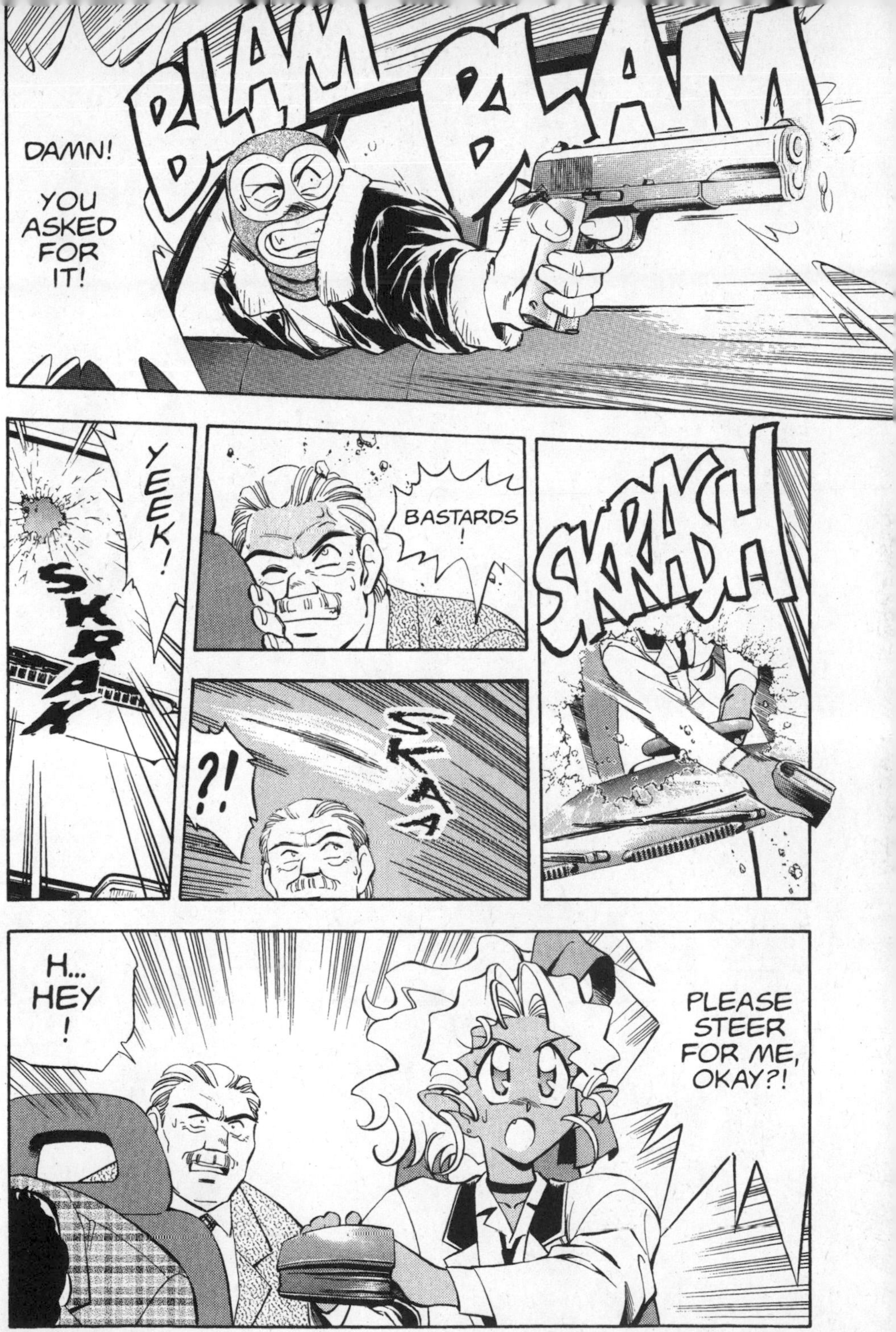
BLAM
BLAM!
DAMN!
YOU ASKED FOR IT!
YEEK!
SKRAAK
BASTARDS!
?!
SKAA
SKRACH
H... HEY!
PLEASE STEER FOR ME, OKAY?!

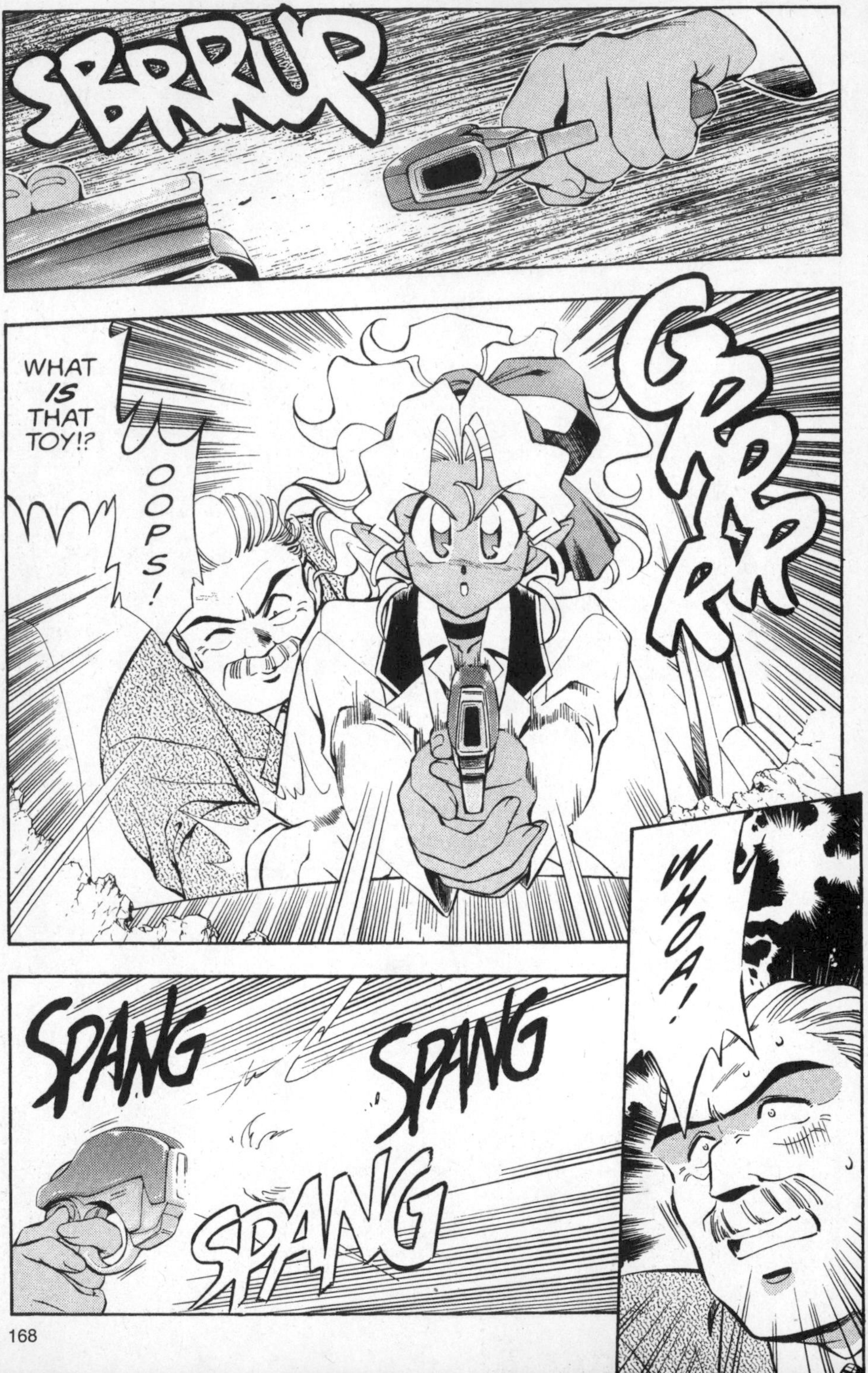
SBRRUP
WHAT *IS* THAT TOY!?
OOPS!
GRRRRR
SPANG
SPANG
SPANG
WHOA!

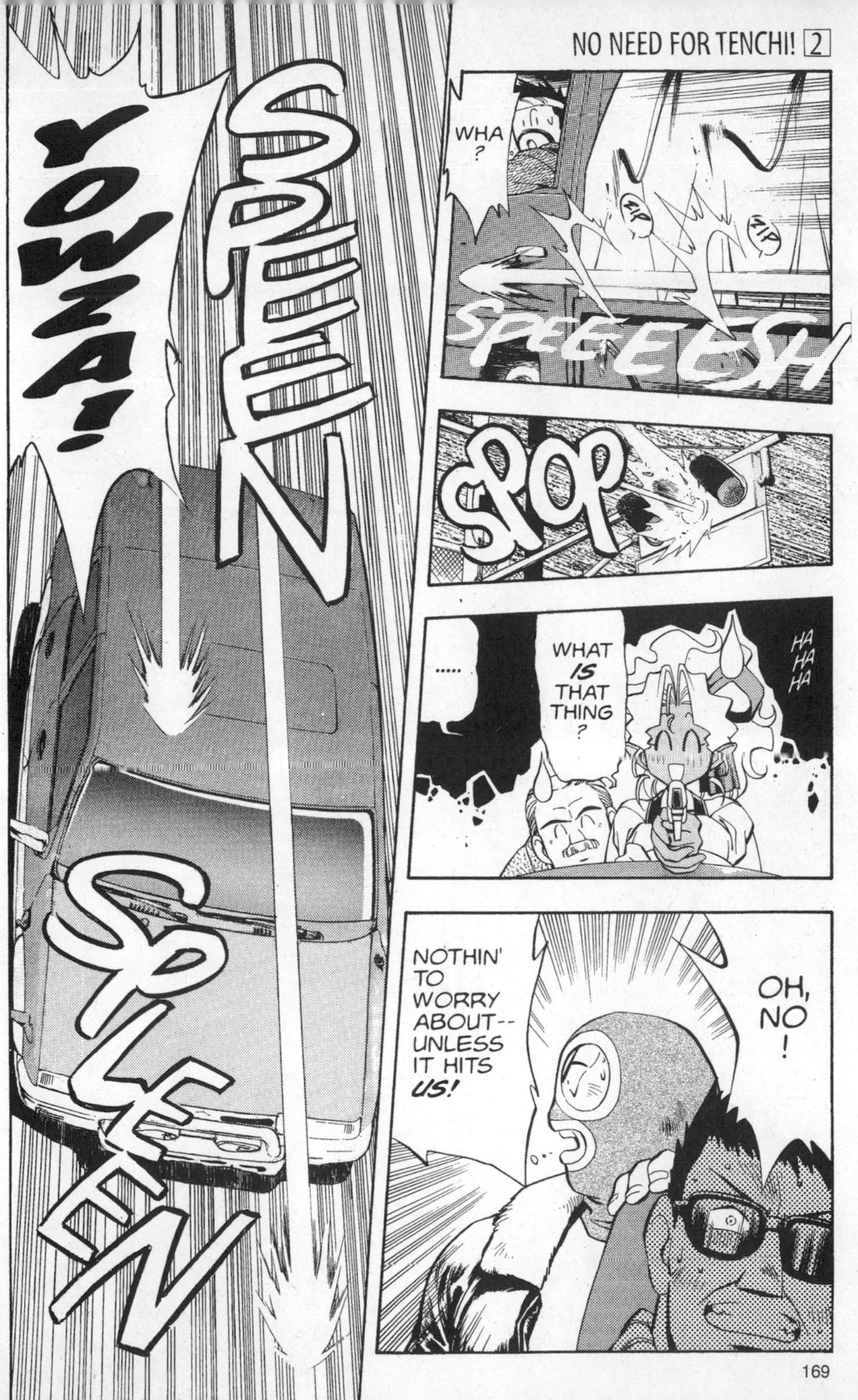
SPEEEN
YOWZA!
SPLEEEN
WHA?
ZIP
ZIP
SPEEESH
SPOP
.....
WHAT IS THAT THING?
HA HA HA
NOTHIN' TO WORRY ABOUT-- UNLESS IT HITS US!
OH, NO!

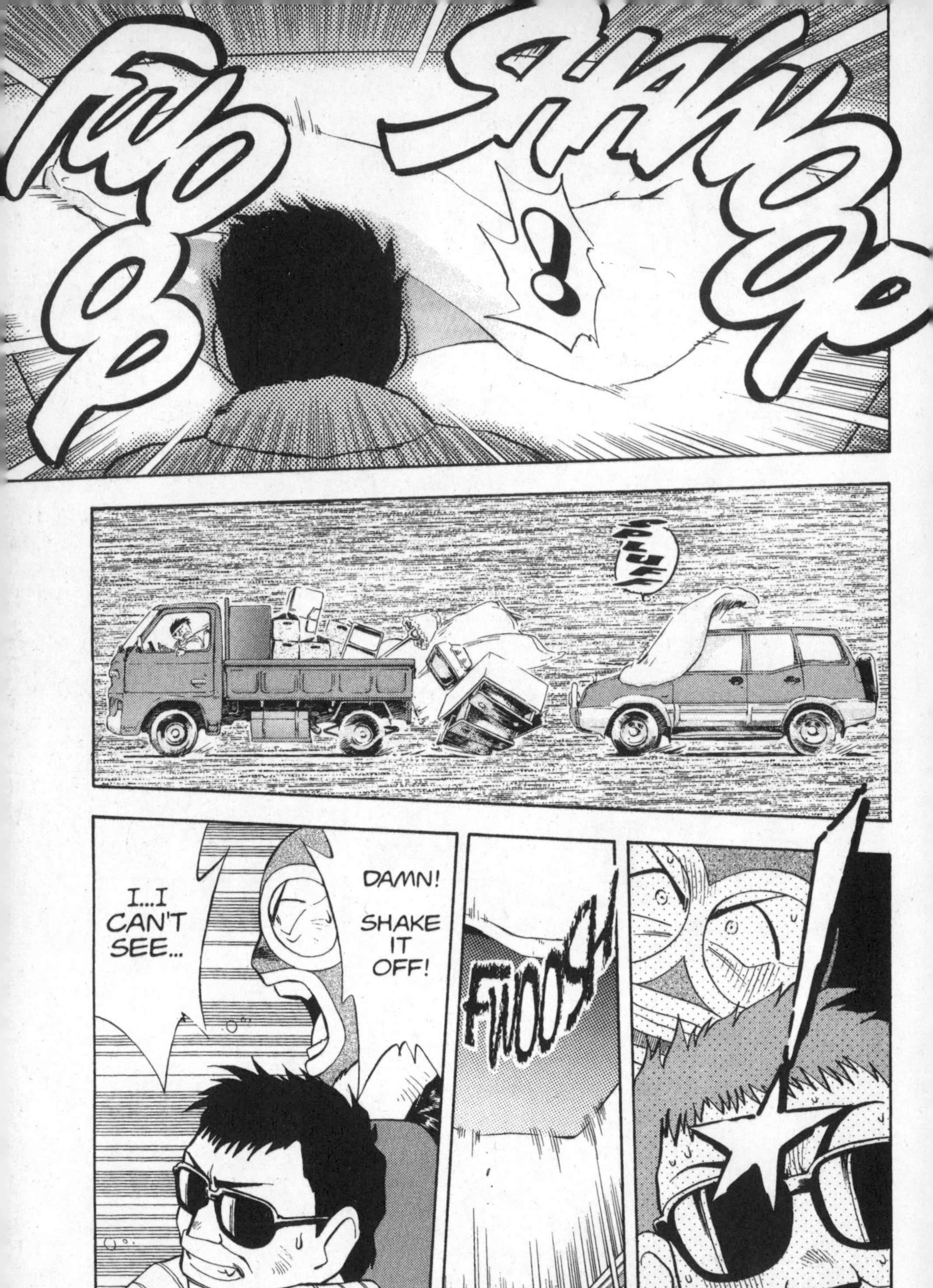
!
SPLUFF
I...I CAN'T SEE...
DAMN! SHAKE IT OFF!
FWOOSH

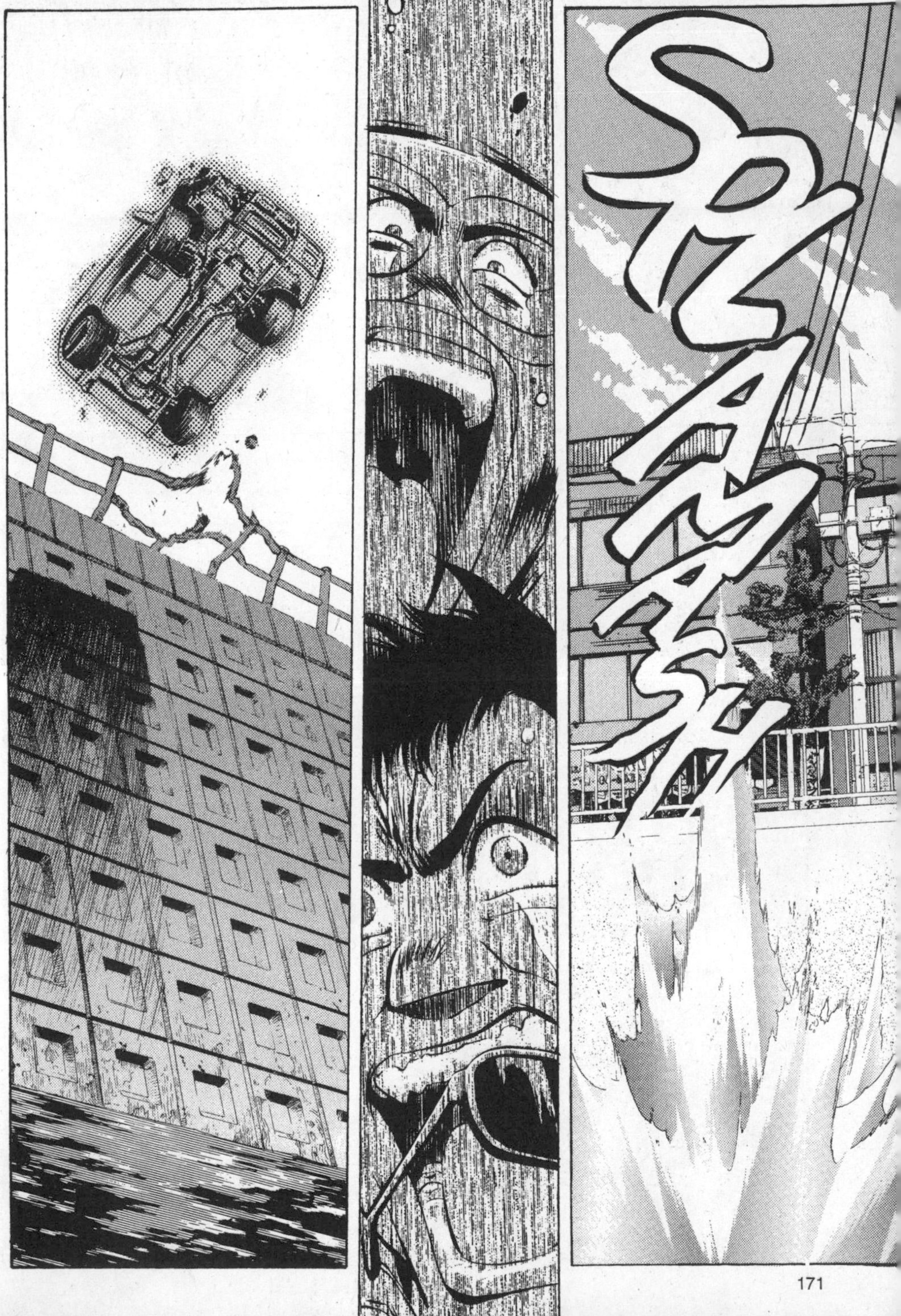
SPLAASH

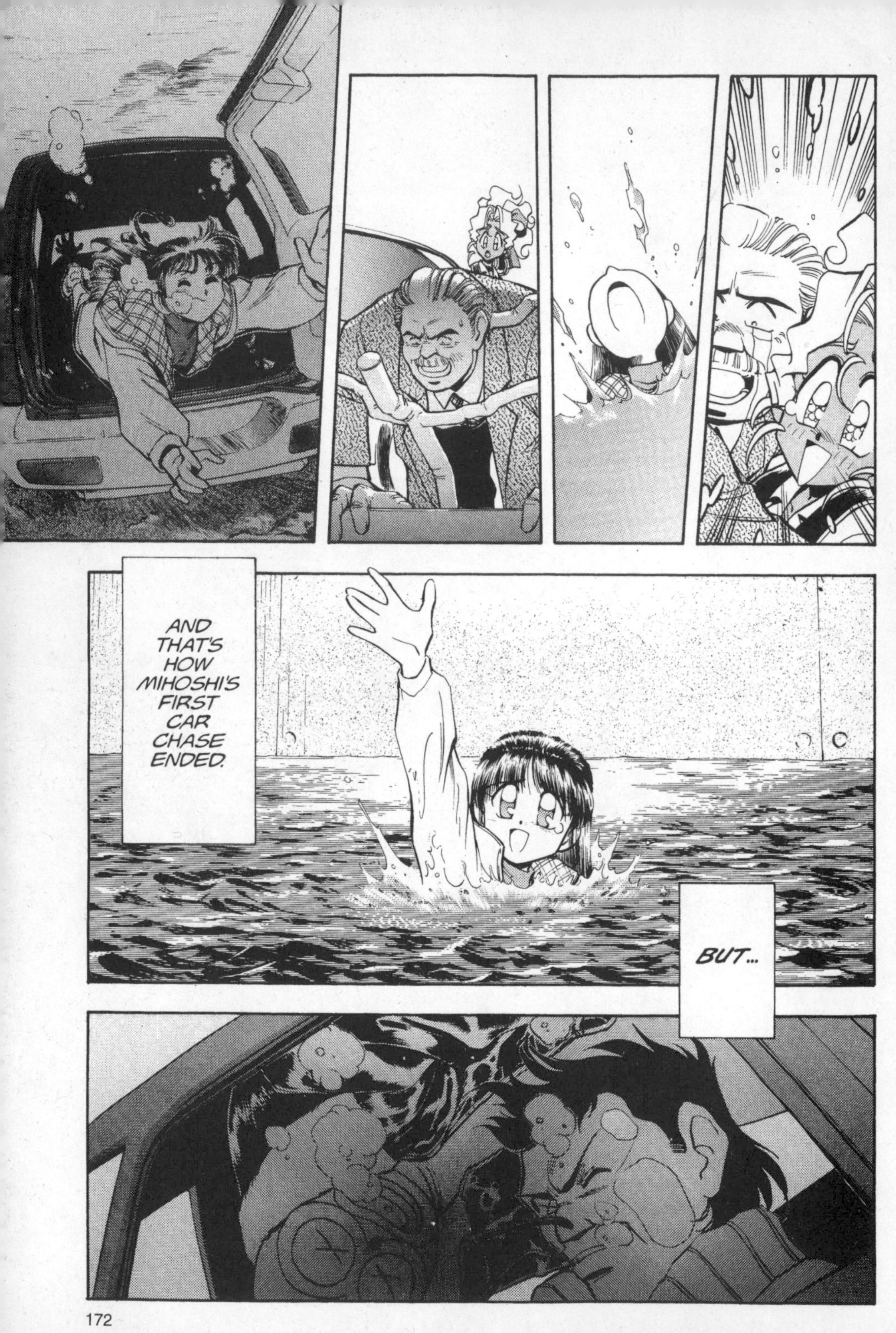
AND THAT'S HOW MIHOSHI'S FIRST CAR CHASE ENDED.
BUT...

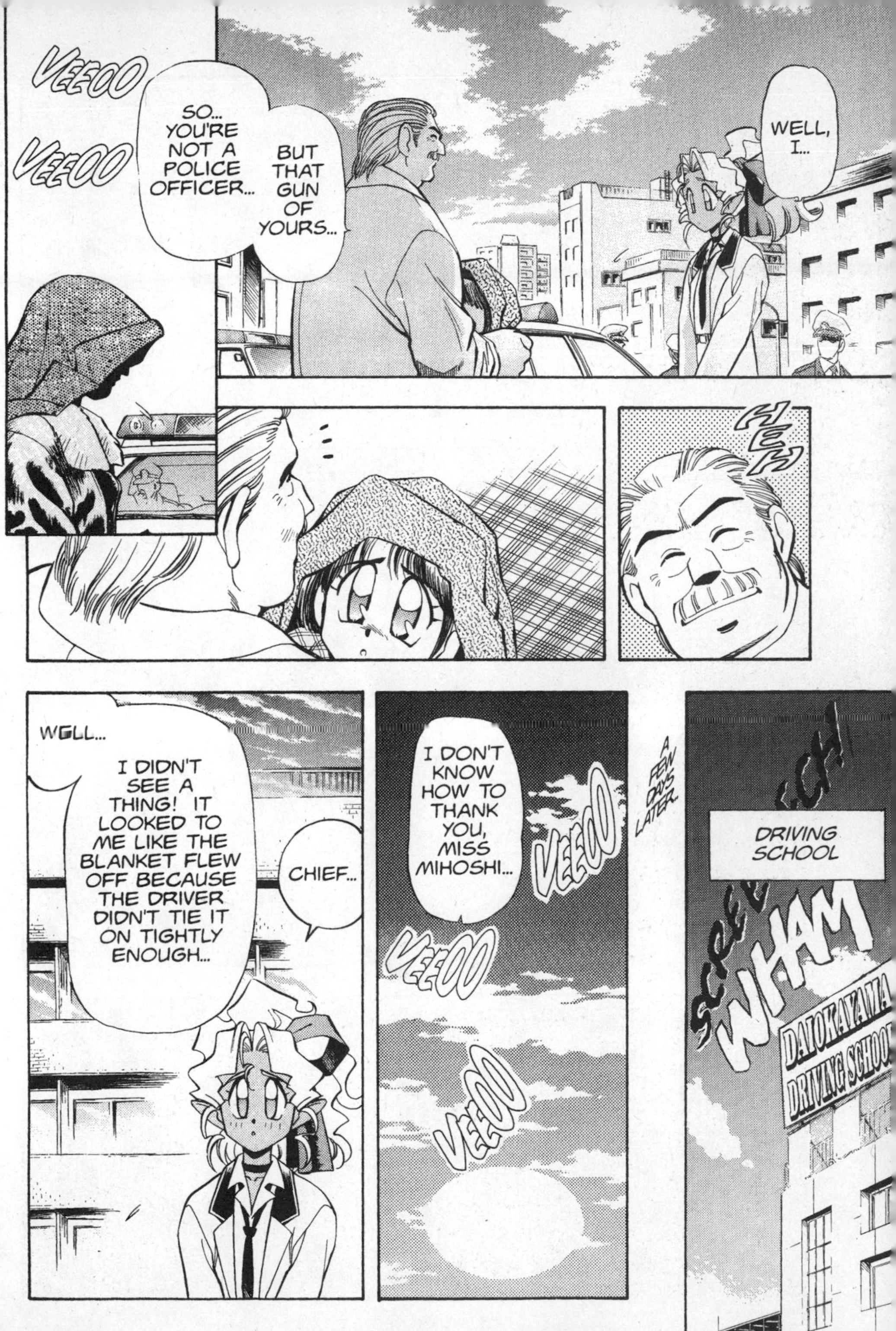
VEEOO
VEEOO
SO... YOU'RE NOT A POLICE OFFICER...
BUT THAT GUN OF YOURS...
WELL, I...
HEH
WELL...
I DIDN'T SEE A THING! IT LOOKED TO ME LIKE THE BLANKET FLEW OFF BECAUSE THE DRIVER DIDN'T TIE IT ON TIGHTLY ENOUGH...
CHIEF...
I DON'T KNOW HOW TO THANK YOU, MISS MIHOSHI...
VEEOO
VEEOO
VEEOO
A FEW DAYS LATER.
DRIVING SCHOOL
WHAM
DAIOKAYAMA DRIVING SCHOOL

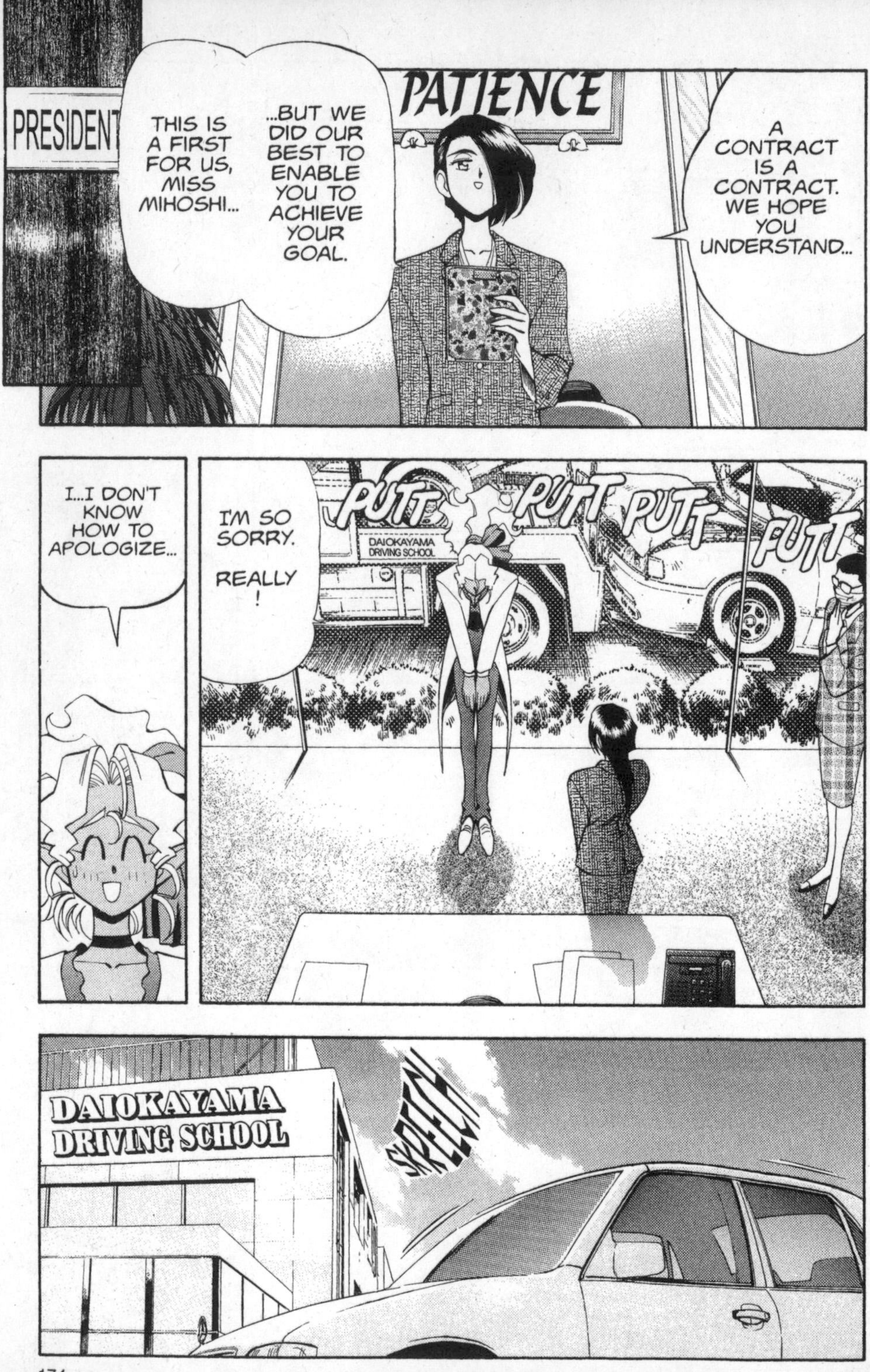
PRESIDENT
THIS IS A FIRST FOR US, MISS MIHOSHI...
...BUT WE DID OUR BEST TO ENABLE YOU TO ACHIEVE YOUR GOAL.
PATIENCE
A CONTRACT IS A CONTRACT. WE HOPE YOU UNDERSTAND...
I...I DON'T KNOW HOW TO APOLOGIZE...
I'M SO SORRY.
REALLY!
PUTT PUTT PUTT PUTT
DAIOKAYAMA DRIVING SCHOOL
DAIOKAYAMA DRIVING SCHOOL
SKREECH

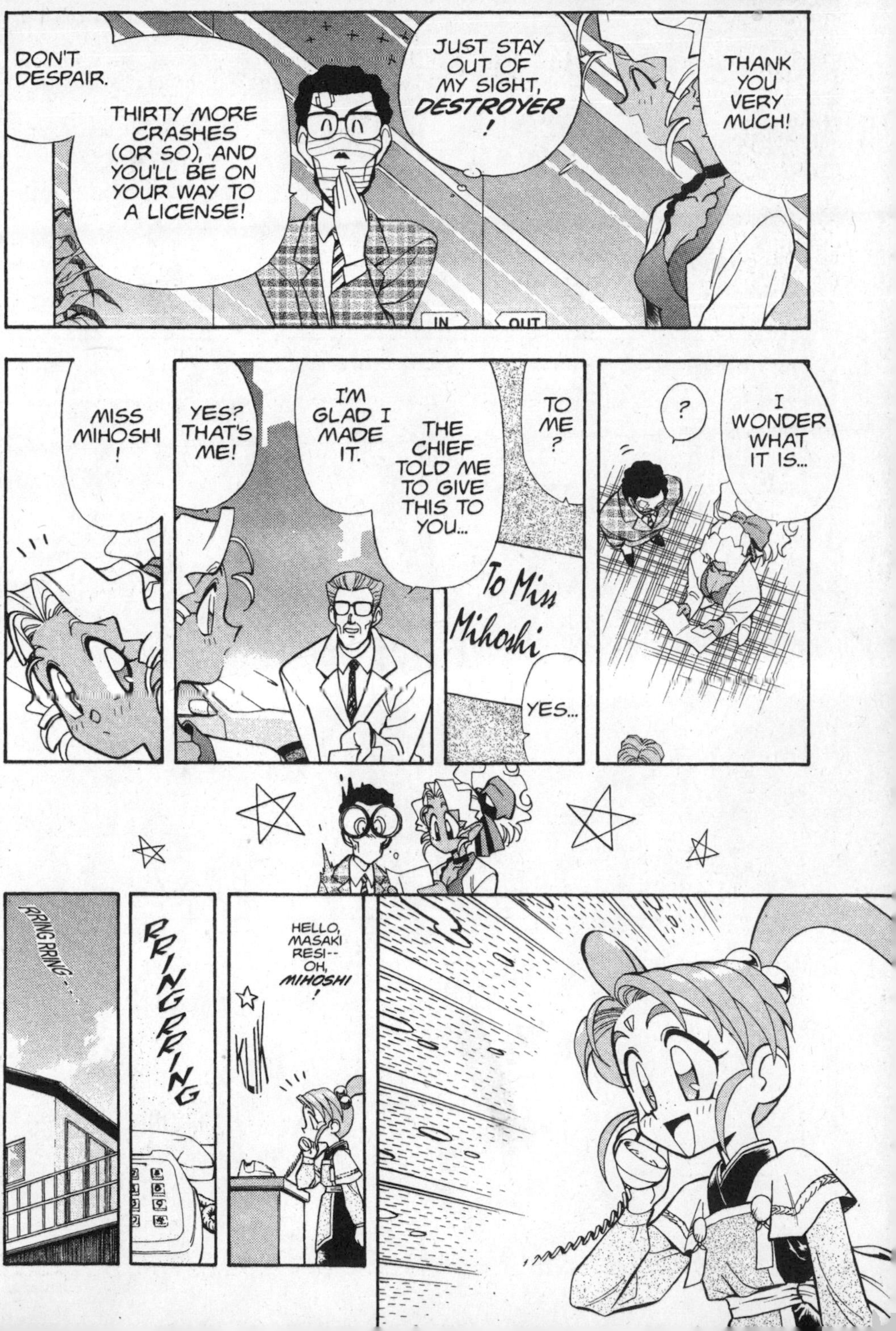
DON'T DESPAIR.
THIRTY MORE CRASHES (OR SO), AND YOU'LL BE ON YOUR WAY TO A LICENSE!
JUST STAY OUT OF MY SIGHT, DESTROYER!
THANK YOU VERY MUCH!
IN
OUT
MISS MIHOSHI!
YES? THAT'S ME!
I'M GLAD I MADE IT.
THE CHIEF TOLD ME TO GIVE THIS TO YOU...
TO ME?
To Miss Mihoshi
YES...
?
I WONDER WHAT IT IS...
RRING RRING...
RRING RRING
KLIK
HELLO, MASAKI RESI-- OH, MIHOSHI!

"DEAR MISS MIHOSHI, THANK YOU AGAIN FOR ALL YOUR HELP."

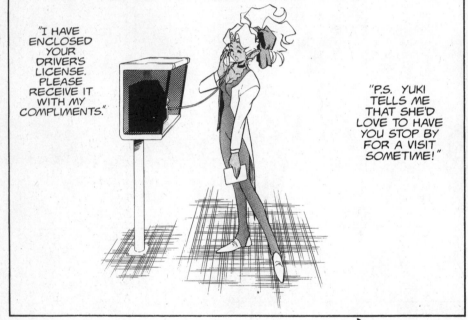

"I HAVE ENCLOSED YOUR DRIVER'S LICENSE. PLEASE RECEIVE IT WITH MY COMPLIMENTS."

"P.S. YUKI TELLS ME THAT SHE'D LOVE TO HAVE YOU STOP BY FOR A VISIT SOMETIME!"

THE POOR DRIVING TEACHER...

WHAT IS SHE DOING? IT'S *ANNOYING*. PLEASE GET RID OF HER!

YES, SIR.

...INSTANTLY TURNED TO STONE.

SHAAAA

AAAGH!

AND RYOKO?

SHE HAS TO WASH ALL THE DISHES FOR A WHOLE MONTH!

TO BE CONTINUED...